California
SAXON MATH™
Intermediate 5

Student Edition
Volume 2

Stephen Hake

A Harcourt Achieve Imprint

www.SaxonPublishers.com
1-800-284-7019

ACKNOWLEDGEMENTS

This book was made possible by the significant contributions of many individuals and the dedicated efforts of talented teams at Harcourt Achieve.

Special thanks to Chris Braun for conscientious work on Power Up exercises, Problem Solving scripts, and student assessments. The long hours and technical assistance of John and James Hake were invaluable in meeting publishing deadlines. As always, the patience and support of Mary is most appreciated.

– Stephen Hake

Staff Credits

Editorial: Joel Riemer, Paula Zamarra, Hirva Raj, Smith Richardson, Pamela Cox, Michael Ota, Stephanie Rieper, Ann Sissac, Gayle Lowery, Robin Adams, David Baceski, Brooke Butner, Cecilia Colome, James Daniels, Leslie Bateman, Chad Barrett, Heather Jernt

Design: Alison Klassen, Joan Cunningham, Alan Klemp, Julie Hubbard, Lorelei Supapo, Andy Hendrix, Rhonda Holcomb

Production: Mychael Ferris-Pacheco, Jennifer Cohorn, Greg Gaspard, Donna Brawley, John-Paxton Gremillion

Manufacturing: Cathy Voltaggio, Kathleen Stewart

Marketing: Marilyn Trow, Kimberly Sadler

E-Learning: Layne Hedrick

ISBN 13:   978-1-6003-2954-8 (California Student Edition Set)
ISBN 10:   1-6003-2954-3 (California Student Edition Set)

ISBN 13:   978-1-6027-7022-5 (California Student Edition, Vol. 2)
ISBN 10:   1-6027-7022-0 (California Student Edition, Vol. 2)

ABOUT THE AUTHOR

Stephen Hake has authored six books in the **Saxon Math** series. He writes from 17 years of classroom experience as a teacher in grades 5 through 12 and as a math specialist in El Monte, California. As a math coach, his students won honors and recognition in local, regional, and statewide competitions.

Stephen has been writing math curriculum since 1975 and for Saxon since 1985. He has also authored several math contests including Los Angeles County's first Math Field Day contest. Stephen contributed to the 1999 National Academy of Science publication on the Nature and Teaching of Algebra in the Middle Grades.

Stephen is a member of the National Council of Teachers of Mathematics and the California Mathematics Council. He earned his BA from United States International University and his MA from Chapman College.

CONTENTS OVERVIEW

TABLE OF CONTENTS

Integrated and Distributed Units of Instruction

California Strands Key:
NS = Number Sense
AF = Algebra and Functions
MG = Measurement and Geometry
SDAP = Statistics, Data Analysis, and Probability
MR = Mathematical Reasoning

TABLE OF CONTENTS

Section 3 *Lessons 21–30, Investigation 3*

California Strands Key:
NS = Number Sense
AF = Algebra and Functions
MG = Measurement and Geometry

SDAP = Statistics, Data Analysis, and Probability
MR = Mathematical Reasoning

TABLE OF CONTENTS

Section 5 — *Lessons 41–50, Investigation 5*

California Strands Key:
NS = Number Sense
AF = Algebra and Functions
MG = Measurement and Geometry
SDAP = Statistics, Data Analysis, and Probability
MR = Mathematical Reasoning

TABLE OF CONTENTS

Section 7 *Lessons 61–70, Investigation 7*

California Strands Key:
NS = Number Sense
AF = Algebra and Functions
MG = Measurement and Geometry
SDAP = Statistics, Data Analysis, and Probability
MR = Mathematical Reasoning

TABLE OF CONTENTS

Section 9 *Lessons 81–90, Investigation 9*

California Strands Key:
NS = Number Sense
AF = Algebra and Functions
MG = Measurement and Geometry
SDAP = Statistics, Data Analysis, and Probability
MR = Mathematical Reasoning

TABLE OF CONTENTS

Section 11 *Lessons 101–110, Investigation 11*

California Strands Key:
NS = Number Sense
AF = Algebra and Functions
MG = Measurement and Geometry
SDAP = Statistics, Data Analysis, and Probability
MR = Mathematical Reasoning

TABLE OF CONTENTS

Dear Student,

We study mathematics because it plays a very important role in our lives. Our school schedule, our trip to the store, the preparation of our meals, and many of the games we play involve mathematics. The word problems in this book are often drawn from everyday experiences.

When you become an adult, mathematics will become even more important. In fact, your future may depend on the mathematics you are learning now. This book will help you to learn mathematics and to learn it well. As you complete each lesson, you will see that similar problems are presented again and again. *Solving each problem day after day is the secret to success.*

Your book includes daily lessons and investigations. Each lesson has three parts.

1. The first part is a Power Up that includes practice of basic facts and mental math. These exercises improve your speed, accuracy, and ability to do math *in your head.* The Power Up also includes a problem-solving exercise to help you learn the strategies for solving complicated problems.

2. The second part of the lesson is the New Concept. This section introduces a new mathematical concept and presents examples that use the concept. The Lesson Practice provides a chance for you to solve problems using the new concept. The problems are lettered a, b, c, and so on.

3. The final part of the lesson is the Written Practice. This section reviews previously taught concepts and prepares you for concepts that will be taught in later lessons. Solving these problems will help you practice your skills and remember concepts you have learned.

Investigations are variations of the daily lesson. The investigations in this book often involve activities that fill an entire class period. Investigations contain their own set of questions but do not include Lesson Practice or Written Practice.

Remember to solve every problem in each Lesson Practice, Written Practice, and Investigation. Do your best work, and you will experience success and true learning that will stay with you and serve you well in the future.

Temple City, California

HOW TO USE YOUR TEXTBOOK

Saxon Math Intermediate 5 is unlike any math book you have used! It doesn't have colorful photos to distract you from learning. The Saxon approach lets you see the beauty and structure within math itself. You will understand more mathematics, become more confident in doing math, and will be well prepared when you take high school math classes.

Power Yourself Up

Start off each lesson by practicing your basic skills and concepts, mental math, and problem solving. Make your math brain stronger by exercising it every day. Soon you'll know these facts by memory!

Learn Something New!

Each day brings you a new concept, but you'll only have to learn a small part of it now. You'll be building on this concept throughout the year so that you understand and remember it by test time.

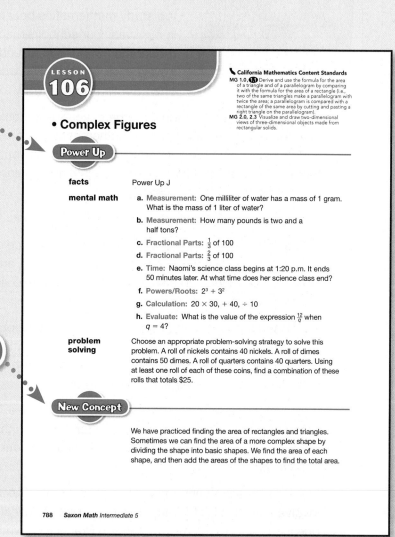

LESSON 106

California Mathematics Content Standards
MG 1.0, **1.1** Derive and use the formula for the area of a triangle and of a parallelogram by comparing it with the formula for the area of a rectangle (i.e., two of the same triangles make a parallelogram with twice the area; a parallelogram is compared with a rectangle of the same area by cutting and pasting a right triangle on the parallelogram).
MG 2.0, 2.3 Visualize and draw two-dimensional views of three-dimensional objects made from rectangular solids.

• Complex Figures

Power Up

facts   Power Up J

mental math
- **a. Measurement:** One milliliter of water has a mass of 1 gram. What is the mass of 1 liter of water?
- **b. Measurement:** How many pounds is two and a half tons?
- **c. Fractional Parts:** $\frac{1}{3}$ of 100
- **d. Fractional Parts:** $\frac{2}{3}$ of 100
- **e. Time:** Naomi's science class begins at 1:20 p.m. It ends 50 minutes later. At what time does her science class end?
- **f. Powers/Roots:** $2^3 + 3^2$
- **g. Calculation:** $20 \times 30, + 40, \div 10$
- **h. Evaluate:** What is the value of the expression $\frac{12}{q}$ when $q = 4$?

problem solving   Choose an appropriate problem-solving strategy to solve this problem. A roll of nickels contains 40 nickels. A roll of dimes contains 50 dimes. A roll of quarters contains 40 quarters. Using at least one roll of each of these coins, find a combination of these rolls that totals $25.

New Concept

We have practiced finding the area of rectangles and triangles. Sometimes we can find the area of a more complex shape by dividing the shape into basic shapes. We find the area of each shape, and then add the areas of the shapes to find the total area.

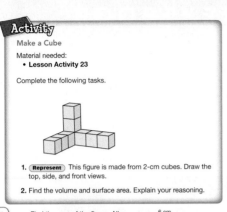

Activity

Make a Cube

Material needed:
• **Lesson Activity 23**

Complete the following tasks.

1. **Represent** This figure is made from 2-cm cubes. Draw the top, side, and front views.

2. Find the volume and surface area. Explain your reasoning.

Lesson Practice

a. Find the area of the figure. All angles are right angles.

6 cm
24 cm
8 cm
20 cm

b. A 4 in. by 4 in. square was cut from a 10 in. by 12 in. sheet of construction paper. What is the area of the hexagon that remains?

4 in.
4 in.
10 in.
12 in.

c. Find the perimeter and the area of this figure. Then find the m∠x.

A   B
x
5 yd
53°
3 yd   C
8 yd
4 yd
E   6 yd   D

Lesson

Get Active!

Dig into math with a hands-on activity. Explore a math concept with your friends as you work together and use manipulatives to see new connections in mathematics.

Check It Out!

The Lesson Practice lets you check to see if you understand today's new concept.

---

d. **Model** This figure is made from one-centimeter cubes. Draw the top, front, and right side views of the figure. Then find its volume and surface area.

Written Practice   *Distributed and Integrated*

1. **Estimate** A small car weighs about one ton. Many large elephants weigh four times that much. About how many pounds would a large elephant weigh?
(64)

2. **Estimate** The Arctic Ocean is almost completely covered with the polar ice cap, which averages about 10 feet thick. About how many inches thick is the polar ice cap?
(61)

3. What is the total cost of 10 movie tickets priced at $5.25 each?
(13, 100)

4. Which digit in 375.246 is in the hundredths place?
(55)

5. Use algebraic addition to simplify each expression:
(95)
 a. $(-0.8) - (-0.2)$ b. $\left(-\frac{1}{4}\right) + \left(-\frac{2}{4}\right)$
 c. $(1.3) + (-0.4)$ d. $\left(\frac{8}{9}\right) - \left(-\frac{2}{9}\right)$

6. Write 12.5 as a mixed number.
(58)

7. **Connect** Name the shaded portion of this square as a percent, as a decimal number, and as a reduced fraction.
(58)

8. Find each percent of a number by changing the percent to a fraction:
(102)
 a. 40% of $60   b. 90% of 300

Exercise Your Mind!

When you work the Written Practice exercises, you will review both today's new concept and also math you learned in earlier lessons. Each exercise will be on a different concept — you never know what you're going to get! It's like a mystery game — unpredictable and challenging.

As you review concepts from earlier in the book, you'll be asked to use higher-order thinking skills to show what you know and why the math works.

HOW TO USE YOUR TEXTBOOK

Become an Investigator!

Dive into math concepts and explore the depths of math connections in the Investigations.

Continue to develop your mathematical thinking through applications, activities, and extensions.

INVESTIGATION 3

California Mathematics Content Standards
MG 2.0, **2.1** Measure, identify, and draw angles, perpendicular and parallel lines, rectangles, and triangles by using appropriate tools (e.g., straightedge, ruler, compass, protractor, drawing software).
MR 3.0, 3.3 Develop generalizations of the results obtained and apply them in other circumstances.

Focus on

Measuring Angles

One way to measure an angle is with **degrees**. Here we show four angles and their measures in degrees. (Read 30° as "thirty degrees".)

acute angles   right angle

Note that right angles measure 90° and that acute angles measure less than 90°. Obtuse angles measure more than 90° and less than a straight angle, which measures 180°.

right angle   obtuse angles   straight angle

A full circle contains 360°, as demonstrated in the following activity.

Activity 1

Angle Exercise

1. Beginning with your arms extended forward at 0°, raise one arm to form a 90° angle.

2. Beginning with your arms extended forward at 0°, raise one arm up, around, and halfway down to form a 180° angle.

3. Beginning with your arms extended forward at 0°, move one arm up through 90°, down through 180°, and continue around to 360°.

Investigation 3   211

California Mathematics Content Standards

AF 1.0, 1.2 Use a letter to represent an unknown number; write and evaluate simple algebraic expressions in one variable by substitution.
AF 1.0, 1.3 Know and use the distributive property in equations and expressions with variables.
SDAP 1.0, 1.1 Know the concepts of mean, median, and mode; compute and compare simple examples to show that they may differ.

• Units of Length

facts	Power Up F
equivalent fraction	The following fractions are all equal to $\frac{1}{2}$. Read them aloud: $\frac{1}{2}, \frac{2}{4}, \frac{3}{6}, \frac{4}{8}, \frac{5}{10}, \frac{6}{12}, \frac{7}{14}, \frac{8}{16}, \frac{9}{18}, \frac{10}{20}$
mental math	**a. Fractional Parts:** How much is half of 5? Half of 9? Half of 15?
	b. Number Sense: $100 \div 10$
	c. Number Sense: $100 \div 20$
	d. Number Sense: $1 - \frac{1}{3}$
	e. Number Sense: $1 - \frac{1}{4}$
	f. Percent: Ten percent of the 500 children were left-handed. How many children were left-handed?
	g. Probability: If a bag contains 1 blue marble and 2 red marbles, what is the probability of drawing the blue marble with one draw?
	h. Estimation: The skyscraper is 796 feet tall. The antenna on top of the skyscraper is 48 feet tall. Estimate the combined height by rounding each measurement to the nearest ten feet and then adding.
problem solving	Choose an appropriate problem-solving strategy to solve this problem. If an $8\frac{1}{2}$ in. × 11 in. sheet of notebook paper is folded from top to bottom, two congruent rectangles are formed. What are the dimensions (length and width) of each rectangle?

New Concept

Math Language

The Metric System of Measurement is the standard international measurement system. It is a base-ten system.

The following table lists some common units of length used in the metric system and in the U.S. Customary System. Some units of length used in the metric system are millimeters (mm), centimeters (cm), meters (m), and **kilometers** (km). Some units of length used in the U.S. Customary System are inches (in.), feet (ft), yards (yd), and miles (mi). The table also shows equivalences between units of length.

Units of Length

U.S. Customary System	Metric System
12 in. = 1 ft	10 mm = 1 cm
3 ft = 1 yd	1000 mm = 1 m
5280 ft = 1 mi	100 cm = 1 m
1760 yd = 1 mi	1000 m = 1 km
A meter is about 3 inches longer than a yard.	

Estimate A kilometer is about $\frac{3}{5}$ of a mile. Estimate the number of feet in a kilometer. Explain how you found your answer.

Example 1

The tallest player on the basketball team is 197 centimeters tall. About how many meters tall is the tallest player?

The chart shows that 100 centimeters equals 1 meter. The prefix *cent-* can help us remember this fact because there are 100 cents in 1 dollar. Since 197 centimeters is nearly 200 centimeters, the height of the basketball player is **about 2 meters.**

Example 2

Two yards is the same length as how many inches?

The equivalence table shows that 1 yard equals 3 feet and that each foot equals 12 inches.

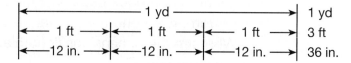

Thus, 1 yard equals 36 inches. Two yards is twice that amount, so two yards equals **72 inches.**

Example 3

Hina walks the same route each morning and each evening for exercise. She walks at an average speed of 4 miles per hour. What is the total distance Hina walks each day if she walks *k* hours in the morning and *h* hours in the evening?

We write an expression to represent the number of miles Hina walks each day.

The expression $4 \times h$ represents the number of miles
Hina walks in the morning.
The expression $4 \times k$ represents the number of miles
Hina walks in the evening.

We can apply the Distributive Property to find that the expression $4(h + k)$ can be used to represent the distance in miles Hina walks each day.

Evaluate What is the value of the expression when $h = 1$ hour and $k = \frac{1}{2}$ hour? Explain your reasoning.

Example 4

During physical education, students performed a jump-and-reach activity to measure their vertical leaping ability. Class results are indicated on the line plot below. Each X indicates the vertical leap in inches of one student.

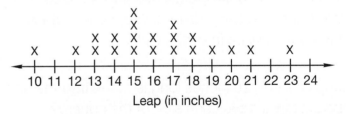

Jump-and-Reach Results

Leap (in inches)

What is the mode, median, and range of this data?

From the line plot, we find that 15 inches was the vertical leap recorded most frequently, so the mode is **15 inches.**

There are 21 measures shown, so the median is the eleventh measure. Counting up or down we find the eleventh measure is 16, so the median is **16 inches.**

The range is the difference between the least and greatest measures.

23 in. − 10 in. = 13 in.

We find the range is **13 inches.**

a. How many yards are in one fourth of a mile?

b. Fifty millimeters is how many centimeters?

c. Dewayne's height is 5 feet 1 inch. How many inches tall is he?

d. A 10K race is a 10-kilometer race. How many meters is 10 kilometers?

e. **Multiple Choice** The length of a pencil is best measured in

   A centimeters   **B** meters   **C** kilometers

f. **Multiple Choice** The height of a skyscraper is best measured in

   A inches   **B** feet   **C** miles

g. Latisha walks the same route each morning and each evening for exercise. She walks at an average speed of 3 miles per hour. What is the total distance Latisha walks each day if she walks for 1 hour in the morning and 1 hour in the evening?

Written Practice   *Distributed and Integrated*

1. **Analyze** The books are divided into 4 stacks with 15 books in each
(13, 37) stack. If the books are divided into 5 equal stacks instead of 4, how many books will be in each stack?

2. A loop of string 20 inches long is made into the shape of a
(33) square. How long is each side of the square?

3. Find the measure of the ∠B in the right triangle.
(31)

B

A ⌐ 40° C

4. **Represent** Write the mixed number $2\frac{3}{10}$ with words and as a decimal
(27, 53) number.

*5. In the triple long jump competition, Taniel jumped twelve and six
(55) hundredths meters. Use digits to write this decimal number.

*6. Miranda was surprised to see a sign in the restaurant that said tacos were
(57) 2 for .89¢. She knew the sign was written incorrectly. Show two ways to
write the sign correctly.

7. Use both a fraction and a decimal number to name the
(53) unshaded portion of this rectangle.

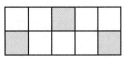

8. Find the length of this segment in centimeters and in
(32) millimeters.

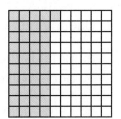

*9. Name the shaded part of this square as a fraction and as a
(26, 53) decimal number.

*10. Compare. You may use your fraction manipulatives to help you answer
(58) each question.

a. $0.5 + 0.25 \bigcirc 0.75$ **b.** $0.8 - 0.5 \bigcirc 0.4$ **c.** $\frac{7}{10} + \frac{2}{10} \bigcirc 0.8$

*11. (Connect) Use both a common fraction and a decimal number to name
(54) the point marked by the arrow.

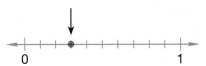

12. (List) Which factors of 12 are also factors of 20?
(16)

13. $\frac{12}{25} + \frac{12}{25}$
(28)

14. $3\frac{5}{8} - 1$
(30)

*15. Ernesto is remodeling his mother's kitchen. He plans to put 12-inch-
(59) square tiles in the rectangular kitchen. The kitchen measures 10 feet by
12 feet. What is the area of the kitchen floor?

16. $100 - (\$90 + \$9 + \$0.01)$
(7)

17. $\dfrac{7848}{9}$
(17)

18. $\dfrac{3640}{70}$
(42)

*19. One of the trees in Sherrod's backyard has a broken limb he wants
(60) to cut off. The limb is 5.9 meters from the ground. His ladder reaches
only 4.27 meters up the tree. How far above the top of the ladder is the
broken limb?

*20. $10 - \left(3 + 1\dfrac{1}{3}\right)$
(30, 51)

*21. $3\dfrac{1}{4} + \left(2 - 1\dfrac{1}{4}\right)$
(28, 51)

22. $24 \times 8 \times 50$
(18)

23. Write two fractions which equal $\dfrac{1}{2}$. Make 30 the denominator of the first
(15) fraction, and make 25 the numerator of the second fraction.

*24. Use the menu to answer parts **a–c.**
(Inv. 5)

    a. What is the total cost of one chicken salad and
one small drink?

    b. Leroy paid for 2 fruit salads with a $10 bill. How
much money should he get back?

    c. (**Estimate**) Mr. Howard bought one of every salad for
his family. About how much did he spend?

Menu	
Shrimp Salad	$6.50
Chicken Salad	$5.25
Fruit Salad	$3.00
Drinks:	
Regular	$0.80
Small	$0.50
Prices include sales tax.	

*25. a. (**Conclude**) What type of polygon is figure *ABCDEF*?
(21)

    b. If this polygon is regular and the perimeter is
12 inches, then how long is each side?

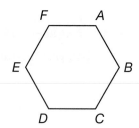

26. The numbers 1, 2, 3, 4, 5, 6, 7, 8, 9, 10, and 11 are written on separate
(45) cards. The cards are then turned over and mixed up, and one card is
selected.

    a. What is the probability that the number on the card is 7?

    b. What is the probability that the number on the card is odd?

*27. Multiple Choice The height of a garage door is best measured in
(61)
    A inches   **B** feet   **C** miles

*28. The front door of Seiko's house is 8 feet 2 inches tall. How many inches
(35, 61) tall is Seiko's door?

29. ✎ Explain Students in a 45-minute math class spent 8 minutes
(37) correcting homework and 18 minutes learning about a new concept.
The remainder of the time was spent doing homework. What length of
time did the students spend that day doing homework in class? Explain
how you found the answer.

*30. Multiple Choice Which of the following choices best describes your
(61) height?

    A between 1 and 2 meters

    B between 2 and 3 meters

    C more than 3 meters

    D less than 1 meter

California Mathematics Content Standards
NS 1.0, **1.5** Identify and represent on a number line
    decimals, fractions, mixed numbers, and positive
    and negative integers.
NS 2.0, **2.3** Solve simple problems, including
    ones arising in concrete situations, involving the
    addition and subtraction of fractions and mixed
    numbers (like and unlike denominators of 20 or
    less), and express answers in the simplest form.
MR 3.0, 3.3 Develop generalizations of the results
    obtained and apply them in other circumstances.

• Changing Improper Fractions to Whole or Mixed Numbers

Power Up

facts	Power Up G
equivalent fraction	The following fractions are equal to $\frac{1}{2}$: $\frac{1}{2}, \frac{2}{4}, \frac{3}{6}, \frac{4}{8}$. Read them aloud and continue the pattern to $\frac{10}{20}$.
mental math	**a. Fractional Parts:** One third of 7 is $2\frac{1}{3}$. How much is $\frac{1}{3}$ of 8? $\frac{1}{3}$ of 10?
	b. Number Sense: $1000 \div 2$
	c. Number Sense: $1000 \div 4$
	d. Number Sense: $1 - \frac{1}{5}$
	e. Number Sense: $1 - \frac{4}{5}$
	f. Percent: Of the 200 students, 25% had blue eyes. How many students had blue eyes?
	g. Measurement: Roger and Mickey have completed 50% of their 400-kilometer trip. How many kilometers have they traveled?
	h. Calculation: $100 \div 10, -2, \div 2, -2, \div 2$
problem solving	Choose an appropriate problem-solving strategy to solve this problem. Two figures are similar if they have the same shape. Draw a rectangle that is similar to this rectangle. Make the rectangle 2 inches long. How wide should you make the rectangle?

1 in.

$\frac{1}{2}$ in. ▭

New Concept

A fraction may be less than 1, equal to 1, or greater than 1.

For example, we can see from the following number line that $\frac{5}{4}$ is greater than 1 because $\frac{5}{4}$ is $\frac{1}{4}$ unit beyond 1.

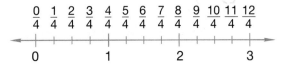

$\frac{0}{4}$ $\frac{1}{4}$ $\frac{2}{4}$ $\frac{3}{4}$ $\frac{4}{4}$ $\frac{5}{4}$ $\frac{6}{4}$ $\frac{7}{4}$ $\frac{8}{4}$ $\frac{9}{4}$ $\frac{10}{4}$ $\frac{11}{4}$ $\frac{12}{4}$

0   1   2   3

$1\frac{1}{4}$ is another way to write $\frac{5}{4}$.

A fraction that is less than 1 is called a **proper fraction.** A fraction that is equal to 1 or greater than 1 is called an **improper fraction.** An improper fraction has a numerator equal to or greater than its denominator.

Less than 1	Equal to 1	Greater than 1
$\frac{3}{4}$	$\frac{4}{4}$	$\frac{5}{4}$
Proper fraction	Improper fractions	

Every improper fraction can be changed either to a whole number or to a mixed number. Consider the fractions above. The fraction $\frac{4}{4}$ is equal to 1, and the fraction $\frac{5}{4}$ is equal to $\frac{4}{4} + \frac{1}{4}$, which is $1 + \frac{1}{4}$, or $1\frac{1}{4}$.

$$\frac{5}{4} = \frac{4}{4} + \frac{1}{4} = 1\frac{1}{4}$$

Example 1

Separate $\frac{8}{3}$ into fractions equal to 1 plus a proper fraction. Then write the result as a mixed number.

The denominator is 3, so we separate eight thirds into groups of three thirds. We make two whole groups and two thirds remain.

$$\frac{8}{3} = \frac{3}{3} + \frac{3}{3} + \frac{2}{3} = 2\frac{2}{3}$$

When the answer to an arithmetic problem is an improper fraction, we usually convert the answer to a whole number or a mixed number.

Example 2

The chef baked two casseroles. At the end of the day, $\frac{3}{5}$ of one casserole and $\frac{4}{5}$ of the other casserole remained. Altogether, how many casseroles remained?

We add and find that the sum is the improper fraction $\frac{7}{5}$.

$$\frac{3}{5} + \frac{4}{5} = \frac{7}{5}$$

Then we convert the improper fraction to a mixed number.

$$\frac{7}{5} = \frac{5}{5} + \frac{2}{5} = 1\frac{2}{5}$$

We find that **$1\frac{2}{5}$ casseroles** remained.

When adding mixed numbers, the fraction part of the answer may be an improper fraction.

$$1\frac{2}{3} + 2\frac{2}{3} = 3\frac{4}{3} \quad \longleftarrow \quad \text{Improper fraction}$$

We convert the improper fraction to a whole number or mixed number and add it to the whole-number part of the answer.

$$3\frac{4}{3} = 3 + \frac{3}{3} + \frac{1}{3}$$
$$= 3 + 1\frac{1}{3}$$
$$= 4\frac{1}{3}$$

Example 3

A three-person crew worked for $2\frac{1}{2}$ hours to repair a broken water line. The customer will be billed for how many hours of work?

Each person worked $2\frac{1}{2}$ hours, so we add $2\frac{1}{2} + 2\frac{1}{2} + 2\frac{1}{2}$. We get the sum $6\frac{3}{2}$. The fraction part of $6\frac{3}{2}$ is an improper fraction. We find that $\frac{3}{2}$ equals $1\frac{1}{2}$. We add $1\frac{1}{2}$ to 6.

$$6\frac{3}{2} = 6 + \frac{2}{2} + \frac{1}{2}$$
$$= 6 + 1\frac{1}{2}$$
$$= 7\frac{1}{2}$$

The customer will be billed for **$7\frac{1}{2}$ hours** of work.

Convert each improper fraction into a whole number or a mixed number:

a. $\frac{2}{2}$ b. $\frac{5}{2}$ c. $\frac{5}{3}$ d. $\frac{9}{4}$

e. $\frac{3}{2}$ f. $\frac{3}{3}$ g. $\frac{6}{3}$ h. $\frac{10}{3}$

i. $\frac{4}{2}$ j. $\frac{4}{3}$ k. $\frac{7}{3}$ l. $\frac{15}{4}$

Add. Simplify each answer.

m. $\frac{4}{5} + \frac{4}{5}$ n. $8\frac{1}{3} + 8\frac{1}{3} + 8\frac{1}{3}$

o. $\frac{5}{8} + \frac{3}{8}$ p. $7\frac{4}{8} + 8\frac{7}{8}$

q. (Analyze) What is the perimeter of a square with sides $2\frac{1}{2}$ inches long?

Written Practice

Distributed and Integrated

1. It takes Lee 20 minutes to walk to school. What time should he leave for school if he wants to arrive at 8:10 a.m.?
(10)

2. To improve her physical condition, Rebeka swims, bikes, and runs. Every day Rebeka swims 40 lengths of a pool that is 25 meters long. How far does Rebeka swim each day?
(13)

3. Cordelia has read $\frac{1}{3}$ of a 240-page book. How many pages has she read? What percent of the book has she read?
(Inv. 2, 34)

4. (Represent) It took $\frac{4}{5}$ of an hour for Cruz to finish his math homework. Felipe finished his math homework in $\frac{3}{4}$ of an hour. Draw pictures to compare these fractions. Who finished his homework in the shortest time?
(26)

*5. Arrange these fractions in order from least to greatest:
(15, 46)
$$\frac{5}{5}, \frac{3}{4}, \frac{2}{6}, \frac{1}{2}$$

6. (Analyze) A number is divisible by 4 if it can be divided by 4 without leaving a remainder. The numbers 8, 20, and 32 are all divisible by 4. What number between 10 and 20 is divisible by both 4 and 6?
(14, 29)

7. Use a fraction and a decimal number to name the
(53) shaded portion of this square.

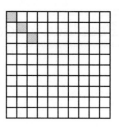

8. Which digit in 16.43 is in the tenths place?
(53)

*9. (**Represent**) The length of the notebook paper was 0.279 meter. Write
(55) 0.279 with words.

*10. (**Connect**) Use a mixed number and a decimal number to name the
(25) point on this number line marked by the arrow.

*11. Arrange these numbers in order from least to greatest:
(56)
$$1.37 \quad 3.17 \quad 1.73 \quad 3.71$$

*12. (**Verify**) A jewelry designer used 81 grams of gold alloy to make
(47) 10 identical earrings. What was the weight in grams of the gold
alloy in each earring? Use estimation to explain why your answer
is reasonable.

13. The length of $\overline{RT}$ is 100 millimeters. If the length of $\overline{RS}$ is 30
(RF24) millimeters, then how long is $\overline{ST}$?

R   S   T

*14. Change 13% and 0.7 to fractions with a denominator of 100.
(58)

15. 407
(44) $\times$ 819

*16. Find the area of the rectangles shown. Copy these rectangles onto your
(59) paper. Then draw square units inside each rectangle and count the units.

a.

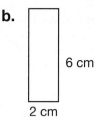

b.

17. $600 \div (60 \div 6)$
(7, 42)

*18. Find the perimeter of the triangle.
(60)

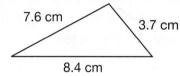

19. If each side of a regular hexagon is 4 inches long, then what is the
(21) perimeter of the hexagon?

20. $341 + 5716 + 98 + 492 + 1375$
(11)

*21. Seven meters is how many centimeters?
(61)

22. $\frac{1}{4} + \left(3 + 4\frac{1}{4}\right)$
(28)

23. $3\frac{1}{6} + 2\frac{2}{6} + 1\frac{3}{6}$
(28)

24. $20w = 300$
(17, 42)

*25. Separate $\frac{11}{4}$ into fractions equal to 1 plus a proper fraction. Then write
(62) the result as a mixed number.

26. Tsubasa found $30,000 of misplaced money. The grateful owner gave
(34) Tsubasa one tenth of the money as a reward. How much money did
Tsubasa receive?

27. (Conclude) In this figure there are three triangles.
(24) Triangle *WYZ* is a right triangle. Which triangle
appears to be an obtuse triangle?

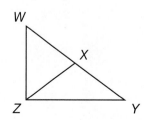

28. A coin is tossed once.
(45)

    a. List all the possible outcomes.

    b. What fraction describes the probability of each outcome?

29. (**Represent**) Write 0.625 with words.
(55)

*30. Sylvia worked at the flower shop during the weekend. She worked
(62) $2\frac{1}{2}$ hours on Friday; $6\frac{1}{2}$ hours on Saturday, and $1\frac{1}{2}$ hours on Sunday. Altogether, how many hours did Sylvia work during the weekend?

Early Finishers

Real-World Connection

Doubles tennis tournaments are played on a rectangular tennis court that measures 12 yards wide and 26 yards long. Find the distance around the outside of the tennis court in feet.

California Mathematics Content Standards

NS 2.0, 2.3 Solve simple problems, including ones arising in concrete situations, involving the addition and subtraction of fractions and mixed numbers (like and unlike denominators of 20 or less), and express answers in the simplest form.

MR 3.0, 3.2 Note the method of deriving the solution and demonstrate a conceptual understanding of the derivation by solving similar problems.

• How to Write an Improper Fraction as a Mixed Number

When the numerator of a fraction is greater than its denominator, the fraction is called an *improper fraction*. $\frac{5}{2}$ is an improper fraction. We usually write an improper fraction as a mixed number.

A mixed number is a whole number plus a fraction. We write $\frac{5}{2}$ as the mixed number $2\frac{1}{2}$. It represents the number $2 + \frac{1}{2}$.

To change an improper fraction to a mixed number, we can use a diagram, we can make fractions equal to 1, or we can divide. Let's look at the improper fraction $\frac{7}{3}$.

Use a Diagram:

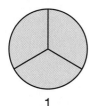 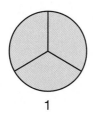 

1   1 $\frac{1}{3}$

We divide each unit into 3 equal parts, and we shade 7 parts.

The number of whole units that are shaded is 2 and $\frac{1}{3}$ of the last unit is shaded. So $\frac{7}{3} = 2\frac{1}{3}$.

Make Fractions Equal to 1:

Since $\frac{3}{3}$ equals 1, we can decompose $\frac{7}{3}$ to form fractions equal to 1.

$$\frac{7}{3} = \frac{3}{3} + \frac{3}{3} + \frac{1}{3} = 1 + 1 + \frac{1}{3} = 2\frac{1}{3}$$

Use Division:

$\frac{7}{3}$ means $7 \div 3$. We divide 3 into 7 two times with a remainder of 1:

$$7 \div 3 = 2 \text{ R } 1$$

The "2 R 1" means that we can take 2 times 3, which is 6, and then add 1 to get 7. This means that there are two 3's in 7 and a part of 3 left over.

What part of 3 is left over? The "R 1" also means that 1 part of 3 is left over. This can be written as:

$$7 \div 3 = 2\frac{1}{3}$$

Let us consider an alternate explanation of what the quotient means. The 7 we divided is seven $\frac{1}{3}$'s. We divided by 3 to make groups of three $\frac{1}{3}$'s. The 2 of the quotient means we can make 2 groups of three $\frac{1}{3}$'s. The remainder of 1 means that one 1/3 remains.

$$7/3 = 2\ 1/3$$

(**Represent**) Change each improper fraction to a mixed number:

a. $\frac{5}{4}$ **b.** $\frac{12}{5}$ **c.** $\frac{7}{2}$ **d.** $\frac{11}{8}$

63

California Mathematics Content Standards
NS 2.0, 2.4 Understand the concept of multiplication and division of fractions.
NS 2.0, 2.5 Compute and perform simple multiplication and division of fractions and apply these procedures to solving problems.
MR 2.0, 2.3 Use a variety of methods, such as words, numbers, symbols, charts, graphs, tables, diagrams, and models, to explain mathematical reasoning.

• Multiplying Fractions

facts	Power Up F
equivalent fractions	The following fractions are equal to one half: $\frac{1}{2}$, $\frac{2}{4}$, $\frac{3}{6}$, $\frac{4}{8}$. Read the fractions aloud and continue the pattern to $\frac{12}{24}$.
mental math	**a. Fractional Parts:** One fifth of 6 is $1\frac{1}{5}$. How much is $\frac{1}{5}$ of 7? $\frac{1}{5}$ of 8?
	b. Number Sense: A small pizza was cut into six equal slices. Margo ate one of the slices. What fraction of the pizza is left? (*Think:* $1 - \frac{1}{6}$)
	c. Number Sense: A large pizza was cut into ten equal slices. Tonya ate one of the slices. What fraction of the pizza is left? (*Think:* $1 - \frac{1}{10}$)
	d. Percent: The sale price is 10% off the regular price. How much is 10% of $200?
	e. Percent: The customer left a 20% tip for a $50 order. How much is 20% of $50?
	f. Estimation: Rae read for 86 minutes and then watched television for 27 minutes. Round each measurement to the nearest ten minutes and then add.
	g. Probability: Which is more likely: a coin landing heads up or a standard number cube landing on 2?
	h. Calculation: 500 ÷ 10, ÷ 2, + 5, ÷ 5, + 3, ÷ 3
problem solving	Choose an appropriate problem-solving strategy for this problem. Naomi has two number cubes. Each cube has sides labeled 1 through 6. Naomi plans to roll the two cubes and add the numbers that appear on top. What are the possible totals that Naomi can roll with two cubes? Explain your reasoning.

We have added and subtracted fractions. Adding and subtracting fractions involves counting same-sized parts. In this lesson we will multiply fractions. When we multiply fractions, the sizes of the parts change. Consider this multiplication problem: How much is one half of one half?

Model We can use fraction manipulatives to show one half of a circle. To find one half of one half, we divide the half circle in half. We see that the answer is one fourth.

$$\frac{1}{2} \qquad \frac{1}{4}$$

$$\frac{1}{2} \text{ of } \frac{1}{2} \text{ is } \frac{1}{4}$$

Using pencil and paper, the problem looks like this:

$$\frac{1}{2} \times \frac{1}{2} = \frac{1}{4}$$

Notice that the word *of* is another way to say "times." Also notice that we find the answer to a fraction multiplication problem by multiplying the numerators to get the numerator of the product and multiplying the denominators to get the denominator of the product.

Reading Math

When we multiply fractions, the product is stated in terms of the whole. While only one half of the half-circle is shaded, it is one fourth of the whole circle.

Example 1

Colvin found $\frac{1}{4}$ of a veggie quiche in the refrigerator and ate half of it. What fraction of the whole quiche did Colvin eat?

Model We can use the fraction manipulatives to show that one half of one fourth is one eighth.

$$\frac{1}{2} \times \frac{1}{4} = \frac{1}{8}$$

$\frac{1}{2}$ of $\frac{1}{4}$

Colvin ate $\frac{1}{8}$ of the whole quiche.

Example 2

What fraction is one half of three fourths?

Model First we use fraction manipulatives to show three fourths.

To find one half of three fourths, we may either divide each fourth in half or divide three fourths in half.

$\frac{1}{2}$ of $\frac{3}{4}$ $\qquad$ $\frac{1}{2}$ of $\frac{3}{4}$

Reading Math

One half of three fourths is three eighths of the whole circle.

Since one half of one fourth is one eighth, one half of three fourths is three eighths. We may also find one half of three fourths by multiplying.

one half $\quad$ of $\quad$ three fourths

$\downarrow \qquad \downarrow \qquad \downarrow$

$\dfrac{1}{2} \qquad \times \qquad \dfrac{3}{4} = \dfrac{3}{8}$

We multiplied the numerators to find the numerator of the product, and we multiplied the denominators to find the denominator of the product.

We can define the multiplication of two proper fractions as the area of a rectangle where the product of the fractions is a part of a unit square.

Example 3

a. What fraction of the whole square is shaded?

b. What is the area of the shaded rectangle?

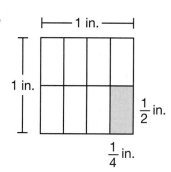

a. One of eight equal parts is shaded, so $\frac{1}{8}$ of the whole square is shaded.

b. To find the area of the shaded part, we use the formula $A = l \times w$.

$$A = l \times w$$
$$A = \frac{1}{2} \text{ in.} \times \frac{1}{4} \text{ in.}$$
$$A = \frac{1}{8} \text{ sq. in.}$$

Example 4

a. A nickel is what fraction of a dime?

b. A dime is what fraction of a dollar?

c. A nickel is what fraction of a dollar?

d. The answers to parts a–c show that one half of one tenth is what fraction?

a. $\dfrac{5}{10} = \dfrac{1}{2}$

b. $\dfrac{10}{100} = \dfrac{1}{10}$

c. $\dfrac{5}{100} = \dfrac{1}{20}$

d. $\dfrac{1}{2} \times \dfrac{1}{10} = \dfrac{1}{20}$

Example 5

Multiply: $\dfrac{2}{3} \times \dfrac{4}{5}$

We find two thirds of four fifths by multiplying.

$$\dfrac{2}{3} \times \dfrac{4}{5} = \dfrac{8}{15}$$

Lesson Practice

a. (Represent) Draw a semicircle (one half of a circle). Shade one half of the semicircle. The shaded part of the semicircle shows that $\frac{1}{2}$ of $\frac{1}{2}$ is what fraction?

b. (Analyze) A penny is what fraction of a dime? A dime is what fraction of a dollar? A penny is what fraction of a dollar? The answers to these questions show that $\frac{1}{10}$ of $\frac{1}{10}$ is what fraction?

c. What fraction is three fourths of one half?

d. What fraction is one half of one third?

e. What fraction is two fifths of two thirds?

Multiply:

f. $\dfrac{1}{3} \times \dfrac{2}{3}$

g. $\dfrac{3}{5} \times \dfrac{1}{2}$

h. $\dfrac{2}{3} \times \dfrac{2}{3}$

i. $\dfrac{1}{2} \times \dfrac{2}{2}$

j. Half of the students were girls, and one third of the girls wore red shirts. What fraction of the students were girls wearing red shirts?

k. What is the area of a square with sides $\frac{1}{2}$ inch long?

1. Show two ways to evaluate 6 (*x* − 2) when *x* = 8.
(40)

2. Rafael gave the clerk $10 for a book that cost $6.95 plus $0.42 tax.
(37) How much change should he receive?

3. Gema emptied a jar of 1000 pennies and put them into rolls of
(13) 50 pennies each. How many rolls did she fill?

4. The distance around the school track is $\frac{1}{4}$ mile. How many times must
(Inv. 1) Quinton run around the track to run 1 mile?

5. (**Analyze**) What even number greater than 20 and less than 30 is
(29) divisible by 3?

6. (**List**) Write the common factors of 10 and 15.
(16)

7. Compare: 44.4 ◯ 4.44
(56)

8. Which digit in 56,132 is in the same place as the 8 in 489,700?
(41)

9. Use both a fraction and a decimal number to name the unshaded portion
(53) of this group of circles.

10. (**Estimate**) Find the length of this segment to the
(32) nearest tenth of a centimeter.

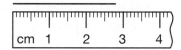

11. Which digit in 67.89 is in the hundredths place?
(53)

*12. (**Estimate**) Use a formula to estimate the area of a room that is 12 ft 8
(59) in. long and 15 ft 3 in. wide.

*13. Add or subtract:
(60)

    a.   4.37   **b.**   10.437

             2.4 $-\,3.2$

      $+\,5.76$

*14. How many yards are in one half of a mile?
(61)

15. $\dfrac{3744}{8}$ **16.**   30,000   **17.**   973
(17)   (11) $-\,29{,}925$ (43) $\times\,536$

*18. Convert each improper fraction into a whole number or mixed number.
(62)

    a. $\dfrac{12}{3}$ **b.** $\dfrac{13}{4}$ **c.** $\dfrac{9}{2}$

19.   \$0.65
(18) $\times$ 10

*20. After everyone had eaten, only one third of the lasagna was left. Tavon
(63)   ate one fourth of the leftover lasagna as a midnight snack. What
fraction of the whole lasagna did Tavon eat for a snack?

*21. One fourth of the swimmers at the beach were girls. One half of those
(63)   girls were floating on inflatable rafts. What fraction of the girls were
floating on rafts?

22. $7 - \left(3 + 1\dfrac{1}{3}\right)$ **23.** $5\dfrac{2}{3} + \left(3\dfrac{1}{3} - 2\right)$
(30, 51)   (28, 30, 46)

24. Use this information to answer parts **a** and **b:**
(Inv. 5).

      In the school election for president, Aaron received 239 votes,
      Brigit received 168 votes, and Chang received 197 votes.

    a. One other person ran for president and received 95 votes.
Altogether, how many votes were cast for president?

    b. The winner received how many more votes than the person who
came in second?

25. **Predict** A number cube is rolled once. What is the probability of each of these outcomes?
(45)

    a. The number will be 6 or less.

    b. The number will be greater than 6.

    c. The number will be even.

26. What is the place value of the 7 in $6.75?
(52)

*27. **Represent** Name the shaded portion of this square as a fraction, as a decimal number, and with words.
(53, 55)

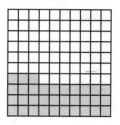

28. What mixed number is $\frac{1}{3}$ of 100?
(Inv. 2, 47)

29. **Interpret** The line graph shows temperatures at different times on a winter morning in Grand Forks, North Dakota. Use the graph to answer the questions that follow.
(49)

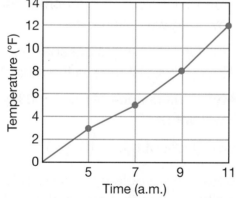

Morning Temperatures in Grand Forks

    a. During which two-hour period of time did the greatest temperature increase occur? What was that increase?

    b. **Explain** How many degrees below the freezing temperature of water was the 5 a.m. temperature? Explain your answer.

30. **Analyze** During summer vacation, Iluvia visited the skateboard park 3 more times than Shankeedra, and Shankeedra visited 7 fewer times than Leti. Shankeedra visited the park 15 times. How many times did Iluvia and Leti each visit the park?
(37)

LESSON
64

🖌 *California Mathematics Content Standards*

NS 2.0, 2.5 Compute and perform simple multiplication and division of fractions and apply these procedures to solving problems.

AF 1.0, 1.1 Use information taken from a graph or equation to answer questions about a problem situation.

MR 3.0, 3.3 Develop generalizations of the results obtained and apply them in other circumstances.

• Converting Units of Weight and Mass

facts	Power Up F
equivalent fractions	The following fractions are equal to one half: $\frac{1}{2}, \frac{2}{4}, \frac{3}{6}$. Read the fractions aloud and continue the pattern to $\frac{12}{24}$.

mental math

a. Powers/Roots: The symbol $\sqrt{}$ is a *square root* symbol. We read $\sqrt{25}$ as "the square root of 25." The expression $\sqrt{25}$ equals 5 because $5 \times 5 = 25$. What does $\sqrt{49}$ equal?

b. Number Sense: $1 - \frac{2}{3}$

c. Number Sense: $1 - \frac{3}{4}$

d. Number Sense: $1 - \frac{4}{5}$

e. Measurement: Lisa cut the 250-cm string into ten equal pieces. How long was each piece? (*Think:* 250 cm ÷ 10)

f. Estimation: Greg threw the baseball 55 feet 8 inches to the catcher. Round this distance to the nearest foot.

g. Probability: If the chance of rain is 30%, what is the chance it will not rain?

h. Calculation: 50% of 60, + 10, ÷ 5, + 2, × 10

problem solving

Choose an appropriate problem-solving strategy to solve this problem. Two figures are similar if they have the same shape. These two triangles are not similar. Draw a triangle that is similar to the top triangle and that has a perimeter of $4\frac{1}{2}$ inches. What length will you use for each side of the triangle?

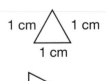

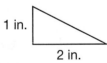

When you go to the doctor for a checkup, the doctor measures many things about you. The doctor might measure your height and your temperature. The doctor might also measure your blood pressure and heart rate. To measure your **weight** or **mass,** the doctor has you step onto a scale. Mass is a measure of how much matter an object contains, while weight is a measure of the force of gravity on an object.

To measure weight in the U.S. Customary System, we use units such as ounces (oz), pounds (lb), and tons (tn). One slice of bread weighs about 1 ounce. A shoe weighs about 1 pound. The weight of a small car is about 1 ton. To measure the mass of an object in the metric system, we use units such as milligrams (mg), grams (g), kilograms (kg), and metric tons (t).

The wing of a housefly weighs about 1 milligram. A paper clip weighs about 1 gram.

A pair of shoes weighs about 1 kilogram. A small car weighs about a metric ton.

This chart lists some common units of weight in the U.S. Customary System and units of mass in the metric system. The chart below also gives equivalences between different units.

Units of Weight

U.S. Customary System	Metric System
16 oz = 1 lb 2000 lb = 1 tn	1000 mg = 1 g 1000 g = 1 kg 1000 kg = 1 t
On Earth a kilogram weighs about 2.2 pounds, and a metric ton weighs about 2200 pounds.	

Example 1

A large female elephant weighs about 4 tons. About how many pounds does the elephant weigh?

One ton is 2000 pounds. Four tons is 4 times 2000 pounds. The large elephant weighs **about 8000 pounds.**

Example 2

The mass of the watermelon is about 6 kilograms. The mass of the watermelon is how many grams?

One kilogram is 1000 grams. Six kilograms is 6 times 1000 grams. The mass of the watermelon is about **6000 grams.**

Example 3

Jariah uses 2 ounces of cheese for one sandwich. If he makes 16 sandwiches, how many pounds of cheese does he use?

If one sandwich uses 2 ounces of cheese, 16 sandwiches would use 16 times 2 ounces or 32 ounces of cheese. Sixteen ounces is the same as one pound.

Jariah will use **2 pounds** of cheese for the 16 sandwiches.

Example 4

The cargo in a pickup truck weighs about $\frac{1}{2}$ ton. Mr. Sheridan unloaded $\frac{1}{4}$ of the cargo. About what fraction of a ton of cargo did he unload?

To find a fractional part of a whole, such as $\frac{1}{4}$ of $\frac{1}{2}$, we use multiplication.

$$\frac{1}{4} \text{ of } \frac{1}{2} = \frac{1}{4} \times \frac{1}{2}$$

To multiply two fractions, we multiply the numerators and multiply the denominators.

$$\frac{1}{4} \times \frac{1}{2} = \frac{1}{8}$$

Mr. Sheridan unloaded **about $\frac{1}{8}$ ton** of cargo.

Connect How many pounds is $\frac{1}{8}$ ton?

Example 5

Visit www. SaxonMath.com/ Int5ActivitiesCA for an online activity.

In which of the following situations could we use the expression $16 \times e$?

   A Conner has *e* pounds of lean ground meat.

   B Conner drives a car that weighs *e* tons.

   C A whale Conner saw while boating weighs *e* tons.

   D The amount of water Conner drinks each day is *e* ounces.

The expression $16 \times e$ represents 16 times *e*. Choice **A,** Conner has *e* pounds of lean ground meat can be represented by the expression because 16 oz = 1 lb.

Lesson Practice

  a. One half of a pound is how many ounces?

  b. If a pair of tennis shoes weighs about 1 kilogram, then one tennis shoe weighs about how many grams?

  c. Ten pounds of potatoes weighs how many ounces?

  d. Sixteen tons is how many pounds?

e. How many 500 mg vitamin tablets equal 1 gram?

f. **Multiple Choice** Which of the following situations could the equation x = 100 × 10m represent?

    A Lanisha used the equation to convert *m* milligrams to *x* grams.

    B Lanisha used the equation to convert *m* pounds to *x* tons.

    C Lanisha used the equation to convert *m* kilograms to *x* grams.

    D Lanisha used the equation to convert *m* pounds to *x* ounces.

Written Practice
Distributed and Integrated

1. Without dividing, decide which of these division problems will have a remainder.
(14)

$$\frac{57}{9} \qquad \frac{33}{6} \qquad \frac{35}{5} \qquad \frac{48}{8}$$

2. Anna Pavlova, a world-famous Russian ballerina, was born in 1881. George Balanchine, one of the founders of the New York City ballet, was born in 1904. How many years before the birth of George Balanchine was Anna Pavlova born?
(RF21)

3. **Estimate** Find the product of 307 and 593 by rounding both numbers to the nearest hundred before multiplying.
(50)

4. Three times a number *n* can be written "3*n*." If *n* equals the number 5, then what number does 3*n* equal?
(8, 12)

5. Roshaun calculates that a weekend is 48 hours long and that he sleeps for 16 hours each weekend, or $\frac{1}{3}$ of the time. What fraction of each weekend does Roshaun spend awake? What percent represents that fraction?
(Inv. 2, 48)

6. **Represent** Draw a circle and shade one eighth of it. What percent of the circle is shaded?
(Inv. 2, 58)

7. **Explain** Can 100 students arrange themselves in 7 different teams
(13) if there are to be the same number of students on each team? Explain
why or why not.

*8. From Yetty's house to the bus stop is 1.3 miles. From the bus stop to
(60) school is 12.9 miles. How far does Yetty travel from home to school
every day?

9. **Connect** Use a fraction and a decimal number to name
(53) the shaded part of this square.

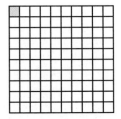

*10. Three yards is the same length as how many inches?
(61)

*11. During morning workouts the horse warmed up by trotting $\frac{4}{5}$ of a mile.
(62) Then the horse galloped $\frac{3}{5}$ of a mile. Altogether, how far did the horse
trot and gallop?

*12. **Represent** Use words to name the decimal number 16.21.
(55)

13. Write 1.5 with two decimal places.
(57)

*14. Multiply:
(63)   **a.** $\frac{1}{3} \times \frac{1}{2}$ **b.** $\frac{3}{4} \times \frac{2}{3}$ **c.** $\frac{4}{5} \times \frac{1}{3}$

15.   307
(44) $\times\ 593$

*16. **Estimate** Pape bought a pickup truck and discovered it weighed
(64) about 3 tons. About how many pounds does Pape's pickup truck
weigh?

17. $60\overline{)\$87.00}$
(42)

*18. **Estimate** A pair of shoes weighs about two pounds. About how
(64) many pounds would 12 pairs of these shoes weigh?

19. $2\frac{3}{10} + 1\frac{3}{10} + \frac{3}{10}$
(28)

*20. $9\frac{4}{8} + \left(4 - 1\frac{7}{8}\right)$
(28, 51)

21. $40 \times 50 \times 60$
(18)

22. $\$100 - (\$84.37 - \$12)$
(7)

23. Write "twenty-five cents"
(57)
    a. with a dollar sign.   **b.** with a cent sign.

24. **Represent** The average amount of precipitation received each year in
(Inv. 5) each of five cities is shown in the table. Choose an appropriate graph
for displaying the data, and then graph the data.

Average Annual Precipitation

City and State	Amount (to the nearest inch)
Albuquerque, NM	9
Barrow, AK	4
Helena, MT	12
Lander, WY	13
Reno, NV	8

*25. Suppose the 8 letter tiles below are turned over, mixed up, and that one
(45) tile is selected.

| T | C | B | F | M | R | J | N |

Which word best describes the following events: *likely, unlikely, certain,* or *impossible?*

a. The letter selected is a consonant.

b. The letter selected comes after S in the alphabet.

c. The letter selected is either G or H.

*26. One fourth of this square is shaded. Write the shaded
(53, 55) portion of the square as a decimal number. Then write the
decimal number with words.

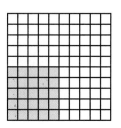

27. (Interpret) Tyronica and Lamar went fishing for trout. They caught 17
(Inv. 5)   trout that were at least 7 inches long. The distribution of lengths is shown
on the line plot below. Refer to this information to answer parts **a–c.**

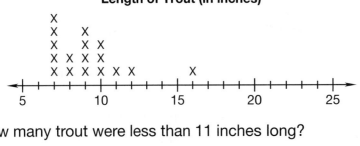

Length of Trout (in inches)

a. How many trout were less than 11 inches long?

b. Which lengths were recorded more than three times?

c. Which of the lengths, if any, are outliers?

28. (Analyze) Refer to the line plot in problem **27** to answer parts **a–c.**
(Inv. 5)

a. What is the median?

b. What is the mode?

c. What is the range?

29. (Explain) The star Fomalhaut is about 25 light years from Earth. The
(37)   star Gacrux is about 63 light years farther from Earth than Fomalhaut,
and the star Hadar is about 437 light years farther from Earth than
Gacrux. About how many light years distant from Earth is the star
Hadar? Explain how you found your answer.

*30. (Explain) One way to estimate the product of 76 × 4 is to round
(50)   76 to 80 and find the product of 80 × 4. Describe another way to
estimate the product of 76 × 4.

Real-World
Connection

In the community band, $\frac{3}{4}$ of the band members play brass instruments.
In the brass section, $\frac{2}{3}$ of the members play the trumpet. What fraction
of the band plays the trumpet?

If $\frac{1}{5}$ of the community is in the community band, what fraction of the
community plays the trumpet?

If the community is 240 people, how many people in the community
play the trumpet?

California Mathematics Content Standards
NS 1.0, **1.4** Determine the prime factors of all numbers through 50 and write the numbers as the product of their prime factors by using exponents to show multiples of a factor (e.g., 24 = 2 × 2 × 2 × 3 = 2³ × 3).
MR 2.0, 2.3 Use a variety of methods, such as words, numbers, symbols, charts, graphs, tables, diagrams, and models, to explain mathematical reasoning.
MR 3.0, 3.3 Develop generalizations of the results obtained and apply them in other circumstances.

• Prime and Composite Numbers

facts	Power Up C
mental math	**a. Percent:** 10% of 10
	b. Percent: 10% of 100
	c. Percent: 10% of 1000
	d. Fractional Parts: One third of 11 is $3\frac{2}{3}$. How much is $\frac{1}{3}$ of 13? $\frac{1}{3}$ of 14?
	e. Powers/Roots: $\sqrt{36}$
	f. Number Sense: $1 - \frac{2}{5}$
	g. Measurement: The door is 6 feet 7 inches tall. How many inches is that?
	h. Calculation: $8 \times 5, -10, \div 5, \times 7, -2, \div 5$

problem solving

Choose an appropriate problem-solving strategy to solve this problem. Gina, Bryce, and Shelley collected donations for the team trip. Gina collected $53.38. Bryce collected $22.89 less than Gina. Altogether, the three students collected $123.58. Find the amounts that Bryce and Shelley collected.

Focus Strategies: Make It Simpler; Write an Equation

(**Understand**) We are told that Gina, Bryce, and Shelley collected donations. We know how much Gina collected, the difference between Gina's and Bryce's amounts, and the total collected by all three. We are asked to find the amounts collected by Bryce and Shelley.

Plan The decimal places in the money amounts might be distracting, so we will *make the problem simpler* to more easily see a solution process. Then we will *write equations* to find each amount.

Solve We round the given amounts to the nearest ten dollars and perform a "trial solution." Gina collected about $50. Bryce collected about $20 less than Gina, so he collected about $50 − $20, or about $30. The total collection was about $120. We subtract Gina's and Bryce's amounts from the total to find the approximate amount collected by Shelley:

$$\$120 - \$50 - \$30 = \$40$$

We know that our solution process makes sense if we add the three approximate amounts for Gina, Bryce, and Shelley:

$$\$50 + \$30 + \$40 = \$120$$

Now we will use exact numbers in our solution. We can use a calculator to speed the process. First we calculate the amount Bryce collected:

$$\$53.38 - \$22.89 = \mathbf{\$30.49}$$

Now we subtract the amounts for Gina and Bryce from the total to find the amount for Shelley:

$$\$123.58 - \$53.38 - \$30.49 = \mathbf{\$39.71}$$

Check We know that our answers are reasonable because they are close to the rounded numbers we used when solving a simpler problem. Also, we find that the two amounts we found plus the amount we are given total $123.58, which equals the total given in the problem.

New Concept

Math Language

Since the product of zero and any number is zero, zero cannot be a factor of a composite number.

We have practiced listing the factors of whole numbers. Some whole numbers have many factors. Other whole numbers have only a few factors. In one special group of whole numbers, each number has exactly two factors.

Here, we list the first ten counting numbers and their factors. Numbers with exactly two factors are **prime numbers.** Numbers with more than two factors are **composite numbers.** The number 1 has only one factor and is neither prime nor composite.

Number	Factors	Type
1	1	
2	**1, 2**	**prime**
3	**1, 3**	**prime**
4	1, 2, 4	composite
5	**1, 5**	**prime**
6	1, 2, 3, 6	composite
7	**1, 7**	**prime**
8	1, 2, 4, 8	composite
9	1, 3, 9	composite
10	1, 2, 5, 10	composite

We often think of a prime number as a number that is not divisible by any other number except 1 and itself. Listing prime numbers will quickly give us a feel for which numbers are prime.

Example 1

The first three prime numbers are 2, 3, and 5. What are the next three prime numbers?

We list the next several whole numbers after 5. A prime number is not divisible by any number except 1 and itself, so we mark through numbers that are divisible by some other number.

6̶, 7, 8̶, 9̶, 1̶0̶, 11, 1̶2̶, 13, 1̶4̶, 1̶5̶, 1̶6̶, 17, 1̶8̶

The numbers that are not marked through are prime numbers. The next three prime numbers after 5 are **7, 11,** and **13.**

Every number in the shaded part of the following multiplication table has more than two factors. So every number in the shaded part is a composite number.

Thinking Skills

Conclude

Are all prime numbers odd numbers? Give one or more examples to support your answer.

	1	2	3	4	5	6	7	8	9	10	11
1	1	②	③	4	⑤	6	⑦	8	9	10	⑪
2	②	4	6	8	10	12	14	16	18	20	22
3	③	6	9	12	15	18	21	24	27	30	33
4	4	8	12	16	20	24	28	32	36	40	44
5	⑤	10	15	20	25	30	35	40	45	50	55
6	6	12	18	24	30	36	42	48	54	60	66
7	⑦	14	21	28	35	42	49	56	63	70	77
8	8	16	24	32	40	48	56	64	72	80	88

Prime numbers appear *only* in the row and column beginning with 1. We have circled the prime numbers that appear in the table. Even if the table was extended, prime numbers would appear only in the row and column beginning with 1.

(**Model**) We can use tiles to illustrate arrays, and we can use arrays to model the difference between prime and composite numbers. An **array** is a rectangular arrangement of numbers or objects in rows and columns. Here we show three different arrays for the number 12:

```
□ □ □ □        □ □ □ □ □ □      □ □ □ □ □ □ □ □ □ □ □ □
□ □ □ □        □ □ □ □ □ □             12 by 1
□ □ □ □           6 by 2
  4 by 3
```

Twelve is a composite number, which is demonstrated by the fact that we can use *different pairs* of factors to form arrays for 12. By turning the book sideways, we can actually form three more arrays for 12 (3 by 4, 2 by 6, and 1 by 12), but these arrays use the same factor pairs as the arrays already shown. For the prime number 11, however, there is only one pair of factors that forms an array:

```
□ □ □ □ □ □ □ □ □ □ □
        1 by 11
```

(**Generalize**) Explain how you can use factor pairs to identify prime numbers.

Example 2

Draw three arrays for the number 16. Use different factor pairs for each array.

The multiplication table can guide us. We see 16 as 4 × 4 and as 2 × 8, so we can draw a 4-by-4 array and a 2-by-8 array. Of course, we can also draw a 1-by-16 array. This time we arrange X's into arrays.

```
X X X X    X X X X X X X X    X X X X X X X X X X X X X X X X
X X X X    X X X X X X X X              16 by 1
X X X X          8 by 2
X X X X
  4 by 4
```

Activity

Identifying Composite and Prime Numbers

Materials needed:
- bag of 13 color tiles
- bag of 16 color tiles

Using your bag of 13 tiles, make as many different arrays as possible. Draw the arrays that you make using X's.

1. How many arrays did you make with 13 tiles?

2. Is 13 an example of a prime or composite number? Explain why.

Repeat the activity using the bag of 16 tiles.

3. How many arrays did you make using the bag of 16 tiles?

4. Is 16 an example of a prime or composite number? Explain why.

Lesson Practice

a. The first four prime numbers are 2, 3, 5, and 7. What are the next four prime numbers?

b. List all the factors of 21. Is the number 21 prime or composite? Why?

c. Which counting number is neither prime nor composite?

d. Draw two arrays of X's for the composite number 9. Use different factor pairs for each array.

Written Practice   *Distributed and Integrated*

1. What is the total cost of a $7.98 notebook that has 49¢ tax?
(57)

2. In Room 7 there are 6 rows of desks with 5 desks in each row. There are 4 books in each desk. How many books are in all the desks?
(37)

3. **Explain** Tavrean is twice as old as his sister. If Tavrean is 12 years old now, how old will his sister be next year? Explain how you found your answer.
(37)

4. Silviano saves half-dollars in a coin holder. How many half-dollars does
(34) it take to total $5?

5. (Analyze) Louisa put her nickel collection into rolls that hold 40 nickels
(37) each. She filled 15 rolls and had 7 nickels left over. Altogether, how
many nickels did Louisa have?

6. The number 7 has how many different factors?
(16)

7. Multiple Choice Which of these fractions is not equal to $\frac{1}{2}$?
(15)
$\quad$ **A** $\frac{6}{12}$ $\qquad$ **B** $\frac{7}{15}$ $\qquad$ **C** $\frac{8}{16}$ $\qquad$ **D** $\frac{9}{18}$

*8. (Justify) Shamal can swim 50 meters in half a minute. Lorena can
(56) swim 50 meters in 28.72 seconds. Which of the two girls can swim
faster? Explain how you know.

9. Evaluate $16y + 9$ for $y = 3$.
(8)

10. Which digit in 1.234 is in the thousandths place?
(55)

*11. (Represent) Use digits to write the decimal number ten and one
(55) tenth.

12. How many cents is $\frac{4}{5}$ of a dollar?
(Inv. 2)

13. Segment AB measures 50 millimeters. The length of $\overline{BC}$ is half the
(RF24) length of $\overline{AB}$. How long is $\overline{AC}$?

14. Compare: 12.3 $\bigcirc$ 12.30
(57)

15. On the Celsius scale, what temperature is 48° above the freezing point
(9) of water?

*16. Multiple Choice The height of a house is best measured in
(61)
$\quad$ **A** centimeters $\qquad$ **B** meters $\qquad$ **C** kilometers

17. $\quad$ $9.84
(44) $\times \quad 150$
$\overline{}$

18. $1.75 + 36¢ = $____
(57)

19. $1.15 − $0.80 = ____ ¢
(57)

*20. Add. Simplify each answer.
(62)
    a. $\frac{3}{5} + \frac{3}{5}$ **b.** $\frac{3}{4} + \frac{1}{4}$ **c.** $2\frac{1}{8} + 4\frac{2}{8}$

21. $39.00 ÷ 50
(42)

22. $\frac{13}{100} + \frac{14}{100}$
(28)

23. $7 - \left(6\frac{3}{5} - 1\frac{1}{5} \right)$
(28, 51)

*24. What is the area of a square with sides $\frac{1}{4}$ inch long?
(63)

*25. Linn's pair of shoes weighs two pounds. How many ounces do
(64)   Linn's shoes weigh?

*26. (List) Write all the factors of 28. Is the number 28 prime or composite?
(65)

*27. Draw three arrays for the number 18. Use different factor
(65)   pairs for each array.

*28. (Analyze) The fraction $\frac{2}{5}$ is equivalent to 0.4 and to 40%. Write 0.4 and
(58)   40% as unreduced fractions.

29. What is the name for a parallelogram that also has perpendicular
(33)   sides?

30. ✎ (Explain) England has had many rulers throughout its long history.
(22)   For example, Henry VI reigned from 1422 to 1461. Explain how to use
     rounding to estimate the length of Henry VI's reign.

California Mathematics Content Standards
NS 1.0, 1.4 Determine the prime factors of all numbers through 50 and write the numbers as the product of their prime factors by using exponents to show multiples of a factor (e.g., $24 = 2 \times 2 \times 2 \times 3 = 2^3 \times 3$).
MR 2.0, 2.3 Use a variety of methods, such as words, numbers, symbols, charts, graphs, tables, diagrams, and models, to explain mathematical reasoning.

• Prime Factorization

facts	Power Up F
estimation	Hold your fingers a decimeter apart. A centimeter apart. A millimeter apart.
mental math	**a. Fractional Parts:** One fifth of 11 is $2\frac{1}{5}$. How much is $\frac{1}{5}$ of 16? $\frac{1}{5}$ of 17?
	b. Time: What time is 1 hour 20 minutes after 11:10 p.m.?
	c. Measurement: How many ounces are in a pound?
	d. Estimation: Pam ran once around the block in 248 seconds. What is 248 seconds to the nearest minute?
	e. Powers/Roots: $\sqrt{9}$
	f. Number Sense: $1 - \frac{3}{10}$
	g. Number Sense: 6×23
	h. Calculation: 25% of 16, $\times$ 6, + 6, $\div$ 6, $\times$ 2, $\div$ 10
problem solving	Choose an appropriate problem-solving strategy to solve this problem. Risa stacked some small cubes together to form this larger cube. How many small cubes did Risa use? Explain how you arrived at your answer.

New Concept

Recall that a factor is a number that divides another number without a remainder. For example:

1 is a factor of 4 because $4 \div 1 = 4$.

2 is a factor of 4 because $4 \div 2 = 2$.

3 is not a factor of 4 because $4 \div 3 = 1$ R 1.

4 is a factor of 4 because $4 \div 4 = 1$.

In Lesson 65 we learned that a prime number has only two factors (1 and itself) and that a composite number has more than two factors. When we write a composite number as a product of its prime factors, we have written the **prime factorization** of the number.

There are two methods we can use to write the prime factorization of a number. The first method is called division by primes. To factor a number using **division by primes,** we divide the number by the smallest prime number that is a factor. For example, to write the prime factorization of 18, we first divide 18 by 2, its smallest prime factor.

$$2\overline{)18}^{\,9}$$

We continue dividing by prime numbers. Although 9 is not divisible by 2, the smallest prime number, 9 is divisible by 3, the next-smallest prime number. The quotient is 3. Notice how we "stack" the divisions.

$$3\overline{)9}^{\,3}$$
$$2\overline{)18}$$

We can again divide the quotient by 3.

$$3\overline{)3}^{\,1}$$
$$3\overline{)9}$$
$$2\overline{)18}$$

The quotient is 1, so the division is complete. By dividing by prime numbers, we have found the prime factorization of 18:

$$18 = 2 \cdot 3 \cdot 3$$

Example 1

Use division by primes to find the prime factorization of 12.

Because 12 is an even number, 12 is divisible by 2, the smallest prime number. So we begin dividing by 2.

$$3\overline{)3}$$
$$2\overline{)6}$$
$$2\overline{)12}$$

We have found the prime factorization of 12: **12 = 2 · 2 · 3.**

Another method we can use to write the prime factorization of a number is a factor tree. A **factor tree** is a diagram of the prime factorization of a number. To make a factor tree for a composite number, such as 36, we write two whole numbers whose product is 36, such as 9 · 4. These numbers form the first two "branches" of the factor tree.

The numbers 9 and 4 are not prime numbers, so we continue the process by factoring 9 into 3 · 3 and by factoring 4 into 2 · 2.

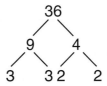

Since all of the factors at the ends of the branches are prime factors, the factor tree is complete. To write the prime factorization of a number, we arrange the factors in order from least to greatest.

$$36 = 2 \cdot 2 \cdot 3 \cdot 3$$

Example 2

Use a factor tree to find the prime factorization of 42.

We can begin the factor tree with several different pairs of numbers. For example, we could begin with 6 · 7, 3 · 14, or 2 · 21. All of these pairs of numbers will produce the same prime factors when the tree is complete. We choose 6 · 7 to begin.

The number 6 is not a prime number, so that branch of the tree must be continued. The number 7 is a prime number, so that branch of the tree is complete.

The factor tree is complete because all of the factors at the ends of the branches are prime factors. We write the prime factorization of 42 by writing the prime factors in order from least to greatest:

$$42 = \mathbf{2 \cdot 3 \cdot 7}$$

a. Which of these numbers are prime numbers?

1, 2, 3, 4, 5, 6, 7, 8, 9, 10, 11

b. **Represent** Use division by primes to find the prime factorization of 30.

c. **Represent** Use a factor tree to find the prime factorization of 24.

d. Write 72 as a product of prime factors.

Written Practice   *Distributed and Integrated*

1. **Formulate** Deion bought a dozen pretzels for 40¢ each. What was the total cost of the pretzels? Write an equation and find the answer.
(13, 57)

2. **Formulate** The total cost of 4 boxes of crayons was $10.00. If each box had the same price, what was the price per box? Write an equation and find the answer.
(13)

3. a. What fraction of this rectangle is shaded?
(19)

b. What percent of this rectangle is shaded?

c. What decimal part of this rectangle is shaded?

4. Lanelle has read $\frac{1}{3}$ of a 240-page book. How many pages does she still have to read to finish the book? What percent of the book does she still have to read?
(34, 48, 58)

*5. Separate $\frac{17}{5}$ into fractions equal to 1 plus a proper fraction. Then write the result as a mixed number.
(62)

*6. **Represent** Name the decimal number 12.25 with words.
(55)

7. Write a fraction that shows how many twelfths equal one half.
(15)

8. **List** Write the factors of 16.
(16)

*9. a. What fraction is one half of three eighths?
  (63)

  b. What fraction is one third of three fifths?

*10. Which digit in 436.2 is in the ones place?
  (55)

11. Write the quotient as a mixed number: $\dfrac{100}{3}$
  (47)

*12. A paper clip weighs about one gram. A box of paper clips contains
  (64) 100 paper clips.

  a. About how many grams does the box of paper clips weigh?

  b. About how much would ten boxes of paper clips weigh?

*13. (List) Write the first ten prime numbers.
  (65)

*14. Use division by primes to find the prime factorization of 18.
  (66)

15. $4.97
  (12) $\times$ 6
  ———————

16.   375
  (43) $\times$ 548
  ———————

17. $7)\overline{\$40.53}$
  (17)

*18. Use a factor tree to find the prime factorization of 32.
  (66)

19. $30m = 6000$
  (17, 42)

20. $3\frac{3}{8} + 1\frac{1}{8} + 4\frac{4}{8}$
  (46)

*21. $7\frac{3}{4} - \left(5 - 1\frac{1}{4}\right)$
  (28, 51)

22. Compare: $55.5 \bigcirc 5.55$
  (56)

23. $4\frac{1}{10} + 5\frac{1}{10} + 10\frac{1}{10}$
  (28)

24. $10 - \left(4 + 1\frac{1}{8}\right)$
(30, 51)

25. ⟮Analyze⟯ This rectangle is half as wide as it is long. What is the
(32) perimeter of the rectangle in millimeters?

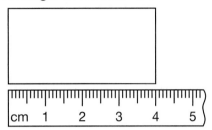

26. What is the area of the rectangle in problem **25** in square centimeters?
(59)

27. ⟮Represent⟯ Draw a spinner with four sectors labeled A, B, C, and D.
(45) Make the sizes of the sectors such that with one spin the probability
of outcome A is $\frac{1}{2}$, the probability of outcome B is $\frac{1}{4}$, and outcomes
C and D are equally likely.

28. ⟮Interpret⟯ Use the chart to solve parts **a–c**.
(50)

    a. ⟮Estimate⟯ Gibron mentally kept track of his
grocery purchases. As he placed each item in the
cart, he rounded the item's price to the nearest dollar
and then added the rounded amount to the total. Use
Gibron's method to estimate the total cost of these
seven items.

    b. ⟮Conclude⟯ Gibron does not want to spend much more
than $30 on groceries. He mentally keeps a running
total of his purchases. Does Gibron's calculation need
to be exact, or is an estimate acceptable?

    c. ⟮Conclude⟯ At the check-out line the clerk scans Gibron's
purchases and calculates the total cost of the items. Does
the clerk's calculation need to be exact, or is an estimate
acceptable?

29. The thermometer shows the temperature on a cold day on the
(9) continent of Antarctica. What was that temperature?

30. The first commuter train of the morning stops at Jefferson Station at
(10) 5:52 a.m. The second train of the morning stops at 6:16 a.m. How
many minutes after the first train arrives does the second train arrive?

Real-World Connection

Mrs. Lopez has a class of 24 students. She wants to divide the class evenly into groups of at least 4 students.

a. Write four different ways in which she could divide the class.

b. Is 24 a prime or composite number? Explain your answer.

c. How many students would have to join Mrs. Lopez's class in order to make the class size a prime number less than 30?

✎ *California Mathematics Content Standards*
NS 1.0, 1.3 Understand and compute positive integer powers of nonnegative integers; compute examples as repeated multiplication.
NS 1.0, (1.4) Determine the prime factors of all numbers through 50 and write the numbers as the product of their prime factors by using exponents to show multiples of a factor (e.g., $24 = 2 \times 2 \times 2 \times 3 = 2^3 \times 3$).
AF 1.0, (1.2) Use a letter to represent an unknown number; write and evaluate simple algebraic expressions in one variable by substitution.

• Exponents and Square Roots

Power Up

facts   Power Up G

equivalent fractions   The following fractions are equal to one half: $\frac{1}{2}, \frac{2}{4}, \frac{3}{6}$. Read the fractions aloud and continue the pattern to $\frac{12}{24}$.

mental math

    a. Measurement: 10% of a decimeter is a _____.

    b. Measurement: 10% of a centimeter is a _____.

    c. Powers/Roots: $\sqrt{64}$

    d. Number Sense: $640 \div 20$

    e. Geometry: An octagon has how many more sides than a pentagon?

    f. Time: How many days are in a leap year? In a common year?

    g. Probability: The answer choices are labeled A, B, and C, which means the probability of guessing correctly is $\frac{1}{3}$. What is the probability of guessing incorrectly?

    h. Calculation: $6 \times 8, -3, \div 5, \times 3, +1, \div 4$

problem solving   Choose an appropriate problem-solving strategy to solve this problem. Angie is playing a board game with her niece, Amber. For each turn, a player rolls two number cubes to determine how many spaces to move her game piece. Angie wants to move her piece 10 spaces. Make a table showing the ways Angie can roll a total of 10 with two number cubes.

First Cube	Second Cube

To show repeated addition, we may use multiplication.

$$5 + 5 + 5 = 3 \times 5$$

To show repeated multiplication, we may use an **exponent.**

$$5 \times 5 \times 5 = 5^3$$

In the **exponential expression** 5^3, the exponent is 3 and the **base** is 5. The exponent shows how many times the base is used as a factor.

$$5^3 = 5 \times 5 \times 5 = 125$$

Together, the base and exponent are called a **power.** Below are some examples of how expressions with exponents are read. The examples are "powers of three."

3^2 "three squared"

3^3 "three cubed"

3^4 "three to the fourth power"

3^5 "three to the fifth power"

We could read 3^2 as "three to the second power," but we usually say "squared" when the exponent is 2. The word *squared* is a geometric reference to a square. Here we illustrate "three squared":

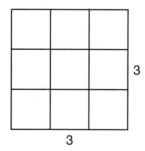

3

3

Each side is 3 units long, and the area of the square is 3^2 or 9 units.

Discuss If the side lengths of the square were 3 inches, we could record the area of the square as 9 in², which we read as "9 square inches." Explain why.

When the exponent is 3, we usually say "cubed" instead of "to the third power." The word *cubed* is also a geometric reference. Here we illustrate "three cubed":

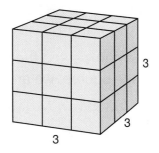

Each edge is three units long, and the number of blocks in the cube is 3^3 or 27 units.

(Discuss) In the cube model, are the units squares or cubes?

Example 1

Write 3^3 as a whole number.

We find the value of 3^3 by multiplying three 3's.

$$3^3 = 3 \times 3 \times 3 = \mathbf{27}$$

Example 2

Solve for *n*: $2n = 6$. What does n^2 equal?

The expression $2n$ means "2 times *n*" (or "$n + n$"). If $2n = 6$, then **$n = 3$**. The expression n^2 means "*n* times *n*." To find n^2 when *n* is 3, we multiply 3 by 3. So n^2 equals **9.**

Example 3

Write the prime factorization of 100. Use exponents to group the factors.

Using a factor tree or division by primes, we find the prime factorization of 100.

$$100 = 2 \cdot 2 \cdot 5 \cdot 5$$

We group the two 2's and the two 5's with exponents:

$$100 = \mathbf{2^2 \cdot 5^2}$$

Example 4

Which is greater, 3^3 or 5^2?

We must simplify the expressions before we can compare.

$$3^3 = 3 \cdot 3 \cdot 3 = 27 \qquad 5^2 = 5 \cdot 5 = 25$$

Compare 27 and 25. Since $27 > 25$, we find that $\mathbf{3^3 > 5^2}$.

If we know the area of a square, then we can find the length of each side. The area of this square is 25 square units. Each side must be 5 units long because $5 \times 5 = 25$.

When we find the length of the side of a square from the area of the square, we are finding a **square root.**

Example 5

**The area of this square is 36 cm².
How long is each side?**

The sides of a square have equal lengths, so we need to find a number that we can multiply by itself to equal 36.

$$\underline{} \times \underline{} = 36$$

We recall that $6 \times 6 = 36$, so each side of the square has a length of **6 centimeters.**

We use the square root symbol ($\sqrt{}$) to indicate the positive square root of a number.

$$\sqrt{36} = 6$$

We say, "The square root of thirty-six equals six."

Example 6

Find $\sqrt{100}$.

The square root of 100 is **10** because $10 \times 10 = 100$.

A **perfect square** has a whole-number square root. Here we shade the perfect squares on a multiplication table:

	1	2	3	4	5
1	1	2	3	4	5
2	2	4	6	8	10
3	3	6	9	12	15
4	4	8	12	16	20
5	5	10	15	20	25

The perfect squares appear diagonally on the multiplication table.

Example 7

What is the area of a square with sides 8 centimeters long?

The formula $A = s^2$ is used to find the area of a square, so we multiply 8 centimeters by 8 centimeters. Both the numbers and the units are multiplied.

$$8 \text{ cm} \cdot 8 \text{ cm} = (8 \cdot 8)(\text{cm} \cdot \text{cm}) = \textbf{64 cm}^2$$

We read 64 cm² as "64 square centimeters."

Lesson Practice

a. **Represent** This figure illustrates "five squared," which we can write as 5^2. There are five rows of five small squares. Draw a similar picture to illustrate 4^2.

b. This picture illustrates "two cubed," which we can write as 2^3. Two cubed equals what whole number?

Represent Write each power as a whole number. Show your work.

c. 3^4 d. 2^5 e. 11^2

f. Solve for m: $2m = 10$. Then find what m^2 equals.

Find each square root in problems **g–j.**

g. $\sqrt{1}$ h. $\sqrt{4}$ i. $\sqrt{16}$ j. $\sqrt{49}$

k. **Represent** Use a factor tree or division by primes to find the prime factorization of 180. Use exponents to group the factors.

l. **Justify** Which is greater, 4^3 or 8^2? Explain your reasoning.

Written Practice   *Distributed and Integrated*

*1. Gregorio bought a sheet of 39¢ stamps. The sheet had 5 rows of
(37, 57) stamps with 8 stamps in each row. How much did the sheet of stamps cost?

2. **Formulate** Ling is half the age of her brother, but she is 2 years older
(7, 37) than her sister. If Ling's brother is 18 years old, how old is her sister? Write one equation to solve this problem.

3. Tela was asked to run to the fence and back. It took her 23.4 seconds
(60) to run to the fence and 50.9 seconds to run back. How many seconds
did the whole trip take?

4. The classroom floor is covered with one-foot-square tiles.
(59) There are 30 rows of tiles with 40 tiles in each row.

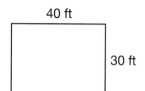

40 ft

30 ft

a. How many tiles cover the floor?

b. What is the area of the floor?

5. (Represent) Draw two circles. Shade $\frac{2}{8}$ of one circle and $\frac{1}{4}$ of the
(58) other circle. What percent of each circle is shaded?

*6. (Represent) What fraction is equal to one half of one fourth? Draw a
(63) model to show your work.

7. Which of the following angles appears to be
(20) **a.** obtuse? **b.** acute? **c.** right?

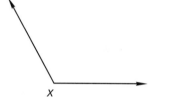
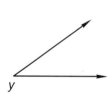
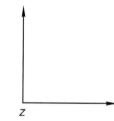

x y z

8. (List) Which numbers are factors of both 16 and 20?
(16)

9. Three times a number y can be written as $3y$. If $3y = 12$, then what
(8) number does $2y$ equal?

*10. The length of $\overline{AC}$ is 8.5 centimeters. If $\overline{AB}$ is 3.7 centimeters, then how
(60) long is $\overline{BC}$?

A B C

11. Compare: 12.0 ◯ 1.20
(56)

12. Rin found half of the lasagna from yesterday's lunch in the refrigerator.
(63) She ate one third of what she found. What fraction of the whole pan of
lasagna did Rin eat?

13. $6.48
(12)   ×   9

*14. Hugo weighed the cantaloupe at the grocery store and found
(64)   that its mass was 3 kilograms. The mass of cantaloupe is how
many grams?

*15. Draw two arrays of X's for the composite number 8. Use different
(65)   factor pairs for each array.

16. 5)$8.60
(17)

*17. Write 24 as a product of prime factors.
(66)

18.   378
(43)   × 296

19.   800
(18)   × 500

20. $30w = 9870$
(17, 42)

21. $12 + 1\frac{1}{2}$
(30)

*22. a. Write 4^3 as a whole number.
(67)

    b. Write 6^2 as a whole number.

23. $\dfrac{49}{99} + \dfrac{49}{99}$
(28)

24. Use this information to answer parts **a** and **b**:
(Inv. 5, 28)

*Akari did yard work on Saturday. He worked for $2\frac{1}{2}$ hours
in the morning and $1\frac{1}{2}$ hours in the afternoon. Akari's parents
paid him $5.50 for every hour he worked.*

    a. How many hours did Akari work in all?

    b. (**Explain**) How much money was Akari paid in all? Explain how
you found your answer.

25. **Interpret** Thirty-nine girls were asked to choose
(Inv. 5) their favorite form of exercise. Use the frequency
table below to answer parts **a** and **b**.

    a. What fraction of the girls chose swimming?

    b. What fraction of the girls chose an exercise
    other than bicycle riding or roller-skating?

Frequency Table

Type of Exercise	Frequency
Bicycle riding	5
Roller-skating	7
Soccer	6
Swimming	10
Walking	5
Basketball	2
Aerobic dancing	4

*26. Write 267,853 in expanded notation using powers of 10.
(67)

27. The bill for dinner was $14.85. Dannell wanted to leave a tip of about $\frac{1}{5}$
(Inv. 2,
50) of the bill. She rounded $14.85 to the nearest dollar and found $\frac{1}{5}$ of the
rounded amount. How much did Dannell leave as a tip?

28. **Represent** Draw a rhombus that has a right angle.
(33)

29. Chandi ran in the Chicago Marathon and finished the race in 3 hours
(10) 32 minutes 44 seconds. If she began the race at 7:59:10 a.m., what
time did she finish the race?

30. The table shows the temperatures that a number
(49) of students recorded at various times on Monday.
Display the data in a line graph.

Hourly Temperatures on Monday

Time	Temperature (°F)
8:00 a.m.	64
9:00 a.m.	65
10:00 a.m.	67
11:00 a.m.	69
12:00 p.m.	72
1:00 p.m.	76
2:00 p.m.	80
3:00 p.m.	85

68

• Order of Operations with Exponents

California Mathematics Content Standards

NS 1.0, 1.3 Understand and compute positive integer powers of nonnegative integers; compute examples as repeated multiplication.

NS 2.0, 2.2 Demonstrate proficiency with division, including division with positive decimals and long division with multidigit divisors.

AF 1.0, 1.2 Use a letter to represent an unknown number; write and evaluate simple algebraic expressions in one variable by substitution.

AF 1.0, 1.3 Know and use the distributive property in equations and expressions with variables.

MR 2.0, 2.4 Express the solution clearly and logically by using the appropriate mathematical notation and terms and clear language; support solutions with evidence in both verbal and symbolic work.

facts   Power Up D or E

mental math

   a. Powers/Roots: $\sqrt{81}$

   b. Number Sense: The cake was cut into 12 slices, and 5 slices have been eaten. What fraction of the cake remains?

   c. Number Sense: 10×10

   d. Number Sense: $10 \times 10 \times 10$

   e. Fractional Parts: One tenth of 23 is $2\frac{3}{10}$. How much is $\frac{1}{10}$ of 43? $\frac{1}{10}$ of 51?

   f. Estimation: David bought a pencil and a compass for $3.52. He paid the store clerk $6.78. If David used compatible numbers, approximately how much change would he receive?

   g. Probability: If the chance of rain is 60%, what is the chance it will not rain?

   h. Calculation: Find 25% of 40, + 1, × 3, − 1, ÷ 4

problem solving

Choose an appropriate problem-solving strategy to solve this problem. To decide which homework assignment to work on first, Jamie labeled 5 index cards as shown. She plans to turn the cards face down, mix them up, and then draw one card. What is the probability she will choose a subject other than math?

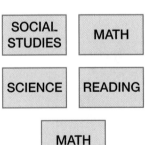

An expression or equation may contain more than one operation. Recall that we complete the operations by following the order of operations. We learned to work inside parentheses first, then multiply and divide from left to right, and then add and subtract from left to right.

Expressions and equations may also include powers and roots, which are also examples of operations. A power is a number raised to an exponent. So we must include powers and roots in the order of operations.

Order of Operations
1. Complete the operation(s) inside parentheses.
2. Simplify powers and roots.
3. Multiply and divide in order from left to right.
4. Add and subtract in order from left to right.

One way to remember the order of operations is to remember the sentence "Please excuse my dear Aunt Sally." The first letter of each word in the sentence reminds us of the order of operations.

Please	Parentheses
Excuse	Exponents (and roots)
My Dear	Multiplication and Division (from left to right)
Aunt Sally	Addition and Subtraction (from left to right)

Example 1

Simplify: $55 - 4^2 \cdot 3$.

Follow the order of operations.

$55 - 4^2 \cdot 3$ Write the expression. There are no parentheses to work inside of, so simplify all powers and roots.

$55 - 16 \cdot 3$ Multiply and divide in order from left to right.

$55 - 48$ Add and subtract in order from left to right.

7 The expression $55 - 4^2 \cdot 3$ simplifies to **7**.

Example 2

Simplify: $(12 - 8) + 2^3 \cdot \sqrt{25}$.

Follow the order of operations.

$(12 - 8) + 2^3 \cdot \sqrt{25}$ Write the expression. Work inside of the parentheses first.

$4 + 2^3 \cdot \sqrt{25}$ Simplify all powers and roots.

$4 + 8 \cdot 5$ Multiply and divide from left to right.

$4 + 40$ Add and subtract from left to right.

44 The expression $(12 - 8) + 2^3 \cdot \sqrt{25}$ simplifies to **44.**

Example 3

Evaluate $9^2 - 3a$ when $a = 10$ by following the order of operations.

$9^2 - 3a$ When we evaluate an expression, we substitute a number for a letter. Write the expression, then substitute 10 for a.

$9^2 - 3(10)$ Follow the order of operations. Simplify powers and roots.

$81 - 3(10)$ Multiply and divide.

$81 - 30$ Add and subtract.

51

We find that $9^2 - 3a$ equals **51** when $a = 10$.

Example 4

Show two ways to evaluate $5(m + n)$ when $m = 7$ and $n = 2$.

Follow the order of operations.

$5(m + n)$ Write the expression. Substitute 7 for m and 2 for n.

$5(7 + 2)$ Complete the operation inside parentheses first.

$5(9)$ Multiply.

45

Use the Distributive Property.

$5(m + n)$ Write the expression. Substitute 7 for m and 2 for n.

$5(7 + 2)$ Distribute the 5 by multiplying 7 by 5 and 2 by 5.

$5(7) + 5(2)$ Multiply.

$35 + 10$ Add.

45

We find that $5(m + n)$ equals **45** when $m = 7$ and $n = 2$.

Lesson Practice   Simplify each expression by following the order of operations. Justify each step of your solution.

a. $19 - (12 + 3)$

b. $4^2 \div 8$

c. $1 + \sqrt{16} \times 3$

d. $27 + 9 \div 3^2$

e. $16 - (2 + 3) \cdot 2$

f. $\sqrt{64} \div (2^2 + 4)$

Evaluate. Justify each step of your solution.

g. $4c + 1$ when $c = 3$

h. $45 - 5z$ when $z = 8$

i. $7^2 - 6h$ when $h = 5$

j. $q + 6^2 \div t$ when $q = 18$ and $t = 9$

Find each square root:

k. $\sqrt{4}$

l. $\sqrt{16}$

Written Practice   *Distributed and Integrated*

1. (**Analyze**) Gizmos come in a carton. A carton holds 6 packages. Each
(37) package holds 10 small boxes. Each small box holds 12 gizmos. How many gizmos come in a carton?

*2. The four friends took a break from playing games to eat a snack. They
(62) had six granola bars to share. How many granola bars will each person receive if they are shared equally?

3. (**Formulate**) Alejandro bought 7 pounds of sunflower seeds for $3.43.
(13) What was the price for 1 pound of sunflower seeds? Write an equation and find the answer.

4. Compare: $\dfrac{3}{6} \bigcirc \dfrac{6}{12}$
(15)

5. Write a mixed number to name the number of shaded circles in
(27) each diagram:

a.

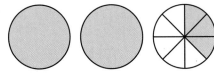

b.

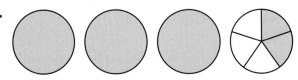

6. (Connect) Use a fraction and a decimal number to name the point
(54) marked by the arrow on this number line.

7. (Represent) Beyonce ran the 100-meter dash in 11.02 seconds. Use
(55) words to name the decimal number 11.02.

*8. A five-pound sack of sugar weighs how many ounces?
(64)

9. Segment *RT* measures 4 inches. If $\overline{RS}$ is $2\frac{1}{4}$ inches long, then how long
(51) is $\overline{ST}$?

10.   7
(30)
   $+ 1\frac{3}{4}$

11.   4
(51)
   $- 2\frac{1}{4}$

12.   30.1
(60)
   $- 14.2$

*13. (Classify) Which of the following numbers are prime numbers?
(65)   3   6   9   11   14   17

14. $12.98
(18) $\times$ 40

15. 16.2 + 1.25
(60)

16. $6)\overline{\$45.54}$
(29)

*17. If $3m = 12$, what does m^2 equal?
(67)

18. 12×12
(39)

*19. Simply: $48 - 2^3 \cdot 4$
(68)

*20. Use division by primes to find the prime factorization of 45.
(66)

21. Write the quotient as a mixed number: $\dfrac{18}{5}$.
(47)

22. Write a decimal number equal to 2.5 that has three decimal places.
(57)

23. The perimeter of a certain square is 24 inches.
(59)

    a. How long is each side of the square?

    b. What is the area of the square?

24. Show two ways to correct the money amount shown on this sign.
(57)

*25. Evaluate $6^2 + 4p$ when $p = 3$ by following the order or operations.
(68)

26. **a.** One foot is what fraction of a yard?
(58, 61)

    b. One foot is what percent of a yard?

27. (**Represent**) Draw a circle and shade $\frac{1}{2}$ of it. What percent of the circle
(58) is shaded?

28. The clock on the left shows a morning time. The clock on the right
(10) shows an evening time that same day. What elapsed time is shown by
the clocks?

Start

End

29. The average body temperature of a hummingbird is about 104°F.
(5, 9) The average body temperature of a crocodile is about 22°F cooler. A crocodile has an average body temperature of about what number of degrees?

*30. Four students ran a 1-mile relay race. Each student ran an equal
(61) distance. How many yards did each student run?

California Mathematics Content Standards

NS 1.0, 1.2 Interpret percents as a part of a hundred; find decimal and percent equivalents for common fractions and explain why they represent the same value; compute a given percent of a whole number.

NS 2.0, 2.3 Solve simple problems, including ones arising in concrete situations, involving the addition and subtraction of fractions and mixed numbers (like and unlike denominators of 20 or less), and express answers in the simplest form.

MR 2.0, 2.3 Use a variety of methods, such as words, numbers, symbols, charts, graphs, tables, diagrams, and models, to explain mathematical reasoning.

• Finding Equivalent Fractions by Multiplying by 1

facts	Power Up F
equivalent fractions	The following fractions are equal to one half: $\frac{1}{2}$, $\frac{2}{4}$, $\frac{3}{6}$. Read the fractions aloud and continue the pattern to $\frac{12}{24}$.
mental math	**a. Percent:** 10% of $100
	b. Percent: 10% of $10
	c. Powers/Roots: $\sqrt{100}$
	d. Number Sense: $3\frac{1}{2} + 3\frac{1}{2}$
	e. Probability: Janet wrote the name of each month on separate cards. She then turned the cards over and mixed them up. If she picks up one card, what is the probability it will be the card labeled "May"?
	f. Time: Six years is how many months?
	g. Fractional Parts: The sale price is $\frac{1}{3}$ off the regular price. What is the discount on a desk that is regularly priced at $120?
	h. Calculation: $\frac{1}{3}$ of 12, × 5, − 2, ÷ 2, × 5, − 1, ÷ 4

problem solving

Choose an appropriate problem-solving strategy to solve this problem. All squares are similar. Each side of this square is 1 centimeter long. Draw a square with sides twice as long. Calculate the perimeter of each square. Then estimate how many of the smaller squares could fit inside the square you drew. Explain how you arrived at your answer.

1 cm

1 cm

When a number is multiplied by 1, the value of the number does not change. This property is called the **Identity Property of Multiplication**. We can use this property to find **equivalent fractions**. Equivalent fractions are different names for the same number. For example, $\frac{1}{2}$, $\frac{2}{4}$, $\frac{3}{6}$, and $\frac{4}{8}$ are equivalent fractions. To find equivalent fractions, we multiply a number by different fraction names for 1.

$$\frac{1}{2} \times \frac{2}{2} = \frac{2}{4} \qquad \frac{1}{2} \times \frac{3}{3} = \frac{3}{6} \qquad \frac{1}{2} \times \frac{4}{4} = \frac{4}{8}$$

As we see above, we can find fractions equivalent to $\frac{1}{2}$ by multiplying by $\frac{2}{2}$, $\frac{3}{3}$, and $\frac{4}{4}$. By multiplying $\frac{1}{2}$ by $\frac{5}{5}$, $\frac{6}{6}$, $\frac{7}{7}$, and so on, we find more fractions equivalent to $\frac{1}{2}$:

$$\frac{1}{2} \times \frac{n}{n} = \frac{5}{10}, \frac{6}{12}, \frac{7}{14}, \frac{8}{16}, \frac{9}{18}, \frac{10}{20} \cdots$$

Example 1

By what name for 1 should $\frac{3}{4}$ be multiplied to make $\frac{6}{8}$?

$$\frac{3}{4} \times \frac{?}{?} = \frac{6}{8}$$

To change $\frac{3}{4}$ to $\frac{6}{8}$, we multiply by $\frac{2}{2}$. The fraction $\frac{2}{2}$ is equal to 1, and when we multiply by 1, we do not change the value of the number. Therefore, $\frac{3}{4}$ equals $\frac{6}{8}$.

Example 2

Write a fraction equal to $\frac{2}{3}$ that has a denominator of 12.

$$\frac{2}{3} = \frac{?}{12}$$

We can change the name of a fraction by multiplying by a fraction name for 1. To make the 3 a 12, we multiply by 4. So the fraction name for 1 that we will use is $\frac{4}{4}$. We multiply $\frac{2}{3} \times \frac{4}{4}$ to form the equivalent fraction $\frac{8}{12}$.

$$\frac{2}{3} \times \frac{4}{?} = \frac{?}{12}$$

$$\frac{2}{3} \times \frac{4}{4} = \frac{8}{12}$$

Example 3

Write a fraction equal to $\frac{1}{3}$ that has a denominator of 12. Then write a fraction equal to $\frac{1}{4}$ that has a denominator of 12. What is the sum of the two fractions you made?

We multiply $\frac{1}{3}$ by $\frac{4}{4}$ and $\frac{1}{4}$ by $\frac{3}{3}$.

$$\frac{1}{3} \times \frac{4}{4} = \frac{4}{12} \qquad \frac{1}{4} \times \frac{3}{3} = \frac{3}{12}$$

Then we add $\frac{4}{12}$ and $\frac{3}{12}$ to find their sum.

$$\frac{4}{12} + \frac{3}{12} = \frac{7}{12}$$

Example 4

Write $\frac{3}{4}$ as a fraction with a denominator of 100. Then write that fraction as a percent.

To change fourths to hundredths, we multiply by $\frac{25}{25}$.

$$\frac{3}{4} \times \frac{25}{25} = \frac{75}{100}$$

The fraction $\frac{75}{100}$ is equivalent to **75%**.

(**Verify**) Why did we multiply by $\frac{25}{25}$?

(**Lesson Practice**) Find the fraction name for 1 used to make each equivalent fraction:

a. $\frac{3}{4} \times \dfrac{?}{?} = \frac{9}{12}$

b. $\frac{2}{3} \times \dfrac{?}{?} = \frac{4}{6}$

c. $\frac{1}{3} \times \dfrac{?}{?} = \frac{4}{12}$

d. $\frac{1}{4} \times \dfrac{?}{?} = \frac{25}{100}$

(**Analyze**) Find the numerator that completes each equivalent fraction:

e. $\frac{1}{3} = \frac{?}{9}$

f. $\frac{2}{3} = \frac{?}{15}$

g. $\frac{3}{5} = \frac{?}{10}$

h. (**Analyze**) Write a fraction equal to $\frac{1}{2}$ that has a denominator of 6. Then write a fraction equal to $\frac{1}{3}$ that has a denominator of 6. What is the sum of the two fractions you made?

i. Write $\frac{3}{5}$ as a fraction with a denominator of 100. Then write that fraction as a percent.

1. Gaby bought 10 hair ribbons for 49¢ each and a package of barrettes
(37, 57) for $2.39. How much did she spend in all?

2. (**Analyze**) On the shelf there are three stacks of books. In the
(38) three stacks there are 12, 13, and 17 books. If the number of books
in each stack were made the same, how many books would be in
each stack?

*3. Arrange these numbers in order from least to greatest. Then find the
(56, 60) difference between the least and greatest numbers.

$$32.16 \qquad 32.61 \qquad 31.26 \qquad 31.62$$

4. What is the largest four-digit even number that has the digits 1, 2, 3,
(RF2) and 4 used only once each?

5. Use one unit to name each measure:
(35)

    a. 2 hours 20 minutes = ＿＿ minutes

    b. 3 feet 7 inches = ＿＿ inches

    c. 1 pound 13 ounces = ＿＿ ounces

*6. (**List**) Write all the factors of 36. Is 36 prime or composite?
(65)

*7. Use a factor tree to find the prime factorization of 40.
(66)

*8. (**Connect**) Use a mixed number and a decimal number to name the
(54) point marked by the arrow on this number line.

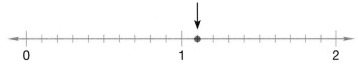

*9. Find each square root:
(67)
    a. $\sqrt{25}$ **b.** $\sqrt{9}$ **c.** $\sqrt{36}$ **d.** $\sqrt{64}$

10. The length of $\overline{PQ}$ is $1\frac{1}{4}$ inches. The length of $\overline{QR}$ is $1\frac{3}{4}$ inches. How long
(46) is $\overline{PR}$?

11. ✏️ (Explain) Seven twelfths of the months have 31 days, and the rest
(48) have fewer than 31 days. What fraction of the months have fewer than
31 days? Explain how you know.

12. $60.45 - 6.7$
(60)

*13. Show two ways to evaluate $4(x + y)$ when $x = 6$ and $y = 3$.
(68)

14. $3d = \$20.01$
(17)

*15. Write $\frac{7}{10}$ as a fraction with a denominator of 100. Then write that
(69) fraction as a percent.

16.   506
(44) $\times$ 478

17. $\frac{4690}{70}$
(42)

18. $30.75
(12) $\times$ 8

*19. Multiply:
(63)

  a. $\frac{2}{3} \times \frac{1}{4}$

  b. $\frac{1}{2} \times \frac{3}{5}$

  c. $\frac{3}{4} \times \frac{3}{4}$

*20. $\frac{4}{5} + \frac{4}{5}$
(62)

*21. Write a fraction equal to $\frac{1}{2}$ that has a denominator of 8. Then write a
(69) fraction equal to $\frac{1}{4}$ that has a denominator of 8. What is the sum of the
two fractions you made?

*22. $16\frac{2}{3} + 16\frac{2}{3}$
(62)

*23. (Analyze) If each side of a square is 1 foot, then the perimeter of the
(58, 61) square is how many inches? Each side of a square is what percent of
the square's perimeter?

*24. **a.** What is the area of the square in problem **23** in square feet?
(59, 61)

  b. What is the area in square inches?

25. (**Interpret**) The line graph shows the average monthly temperatures
(49) during summer in Portland, Maine. Use the graph to answer the
questions that follow.

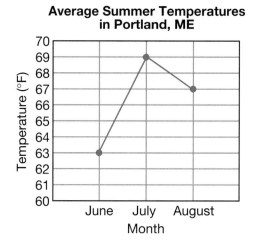

**Average Summer Temperatures
in Portland, ME**

a. What number of degrees represents the range of the
   temperatures?

b. How many months have an average temperature that is greater
   than 70°F?

c. The coldest average monthly temperature in Portland, Maine, occurs
   during January. The average temperature that month is 47° lower
   than the average July temperature. What is the average monthly
   temperature during January in Portland, Maine?

26. Name the coin that is equal to half of a half-dollar.
(Inv. 1)

27. Use a centimeter ruler to measure this rectangle. Then
(32, 59) answer parts **a** and **b**.

a. What is the perimeter of the rectangle?

b. What is the area of the rectangle?

28. Multiple Choice Three students are volunteer tutors. Last month
(37) Detrina tutored for 3 more hours than Denzel, and Tere tutored for
2 fewer hours than Detrina. Denzel tutored for 7 hours.

Which expression can be used to find the amount of time Tere spent
tutoring last month?

A $7 + 3 + 2$ **B** $7 - (3 + 2)$ **C** $(7 + 3) - 2$ **D** $7 - 3 - 2$

29. Name a parallelogram that is both a rectangle and a rhombus.
(33)

30. The number of miles a salesperson drove each day for one week is
(Inv. 5) shown below. Find the median, mode, and range of the data.

Day	Miles
Monday	41
Tuesday	67
Wednesday	13
Thursday	44
Friday	25

California Mathematics Content Standards

NS 1.0, 1.2 Interpret percents as a part of a hundred; find decimal and percent equivalents for common fractions and explain why they represent the same value; compute a given percent of a whole number.

NS 2.0, 2.3 Solve simple problems, including ones arising in concrete situations, involving the addition and subtraction of fractions and mixed numbers (like and unlike denominators of 20 or less), and express answers in the simplest form.

SDAP 1.0, 1.3 Use fractions and percentages to compare data sets of different sizes.

• Writing Fractions and Decimals as Percents

facts Power Up G

mental math A number is divisible by 4 if the number formed by the last two digits is a multiple of 4. For example, 1324 is divisible by 4 because 24 is divisible by 4, but 1342 is not. Use this information to answer problems **a–d.**

   a. Number Sense: Is 1234 divisible by 4?

   b. Number Sense: Is 3412 divisible by 4?

   c. Number Sense: Is 2314 divisible by 4?

   d. Number Sense: Is 4132 divisible by 4?

   e. Number Sense: $100 \div 4$

   f. Number Sense: $200 \div 4$

   g. Number Sense: $300 \div 4$

   h. Calculation: $\frac{1}{4}$ of 36, + 1, × 2, ÷ 4, × 3, − 1, ÷ 7

problem solving Choose an appropriate problem-solving strategy to solve this problem. Adam, Barbara, Conrad, and Debby were posing for a picture, but the photographer insisted that only three people could pose at one time. List the combinations of three people that are possible. (In this problem, different arrangements of the same three people are not considered different combinations.)

New Concept

Math Language

Percent means "per hundred."

A percent is a fraction that has a denominator of 100. For example, $25\% = \frac{25}{100}$. A fraction that has a denominator of 100 can be written as a percent by writing the numerator and writing a percent sign (%). For example, $\frac{80}{100} = 80\%$.

Example 1

Write $\frac{7}{100}$ as a percent.

To write a fraction that has a denominator of 100 as a percent, we write the numerator of the fraction and a percent sign. So we write $\frac{7}{100}$ as **7%**.

Example 2

Write $\frac{1}{10}$ as a percent.

We can write a fraction that has a denominator of 100 as a percent by writing the numerator and a percent sign (%). Since the fraction $\frac{1}{10}$ does not have a denominator of 100, we may change $\frac{1}{10}$ to an equivalent fraction that has a denominator of 100.

$$\frac{1}{10} = \frac{?}{100}$$

We multiply $\frac{1}{10}$ by $\frac{10}{10}$.

$$\frac{1}{10} \cdot \frac{10}{10} = \frac{10}{100}$$

We write the fraction $\frac{10}{100}$ as **10%**.

Example 3

In a class of 24 students, 12 students ride to and from school on a bus. What percent of the students in the class ride the bus?

Twelve of 24 students ride a bus. We write this fact as a fraction and reduce.

$$\frac{12}{24} = \frac{1}{2}$$

To write $\frac{1}{2}$ as a fraction that has a denominator of 100, we multiply $\frac{1}{2}$ by $\frac{50}{50}$.

$$\frac{1}{2} \cdot \frac{50}{50} = \frac{50}{100}$$

We find that **50%** of the students ride a bus.

Example 4

Write 0.19 as a percent.

The decimal number 0.19 is nineteen hundredths.

$$0.19 = \frac{19}{100}$$

A fraction that has a denominator of 100 can be written as a percent by writing the numerator and a percent sign (%).

$$\frac{19}{100} = 19\%$$

We find that 0.19 equals **19%**.

Example 5

Write 0.03 as a percent.

The decimal number 0.03 is three hundredths.

$$0.03 = \frac{3}{100}$$

Three hundredths is equivalent to **3%**.

Example 6

Write 0.6 as a percent.

The decimal number 0.6 is six tenths. If we place a zero in the hundredths place, we write an equivalent decimal number in hundredths.

$$0.6 = 0.60$$

Sixty hundredths is equivalent to **60%**.

Notice that when a decimal number is changed to a percent, the decimal point is shifted two places to the right. Shifting the decimal point two places to the right is a useful way to change a decimal number to a percent.

Lesson Practice

Write each fraction as a percent:

a. $\frac{9}{100}$ **b.** $\frac{73}{100}$ **c.** $\frac{5}{10}$

d. $\frac{17}{50}$ **e.** $\frac{4}{25}$ **f.** $\frac{4}{5}$

g. Nine students in a class of twenty students play soccer. What percent of the students in the class play soccer?

h. During a 30-minute study period, Mario read a book for 12 minutes. For what percent of the time did Mario read a book during the study period?

Write each decimal as a percent:

i. 0.35 **j.** 0.81 **k.** 0.24

l. 0.7 **m.** 0.2 **n.** 0.9

Written Practice *Distributed and Integrated*

1. Write the standard form for the following:
(36)
$(7 \times 100{,}000) + (8 \times 10{,}000) + (5 \times 1{,}000) + (3 \times 100) + (9 \times 1)$

2. **Formulate** The troop hiked 57 miles in 3 days. The troop averaged
(13, 38) how many miles per day? Write an equation and find the answer.

*3. When the decimal number six and thirty-four hundredths is subtracted
(55, 60) from nine and twenty-six hundredths, what is the difference?

4. **List** Which factors of 6 are also factors of 12?
(16)

5. **Analyze** If $3n = 18$, then what number does $2n$ equal?
(37)

*6. What is the area of a square with sides 10 cm long?
(59)

10 cm

7. Compare: $4.5 \bigcirc 4.500$
(57)

8. Arrange these fractions in order from least to greatest:
(15, 46, 62)
$$\frac{2}{3}, \frac{1}{2}, \frac{4}{3}, \frac{3}{8}, \frac{5}{5}$$

*9. **Analyze** One half of the 64 squares on the board were black. The
(34, 58, 63) other half were red. One half of the black squares had checkers on
them. None of the red squares had checkers on them.

   a. How many squares on the board were black?

   b. How many squares had checkers on them?

   c. What fraction of the squares had checkers on them?

   d. What percent of the squares had checkers on them?

*10. Write 48 as a product of prime factors.
(66)

11. $24.86 - 9.7$
(60)

*12. Write each power as a whole number. Show your work.
(67)
   a. 4^3 **b.** 8^2 **c.** 5^3

13. $8m = \$36.00$ **14.** $50w = 7600$
(17, 23)   (17, 42)

*15. Simplify each expression by following the order of operations.
(68) Justify each step of your solution.

  a. $24 - (4 + 7) \cdot 2$

  b. $35 + \dfrac{24}{2^2}$

16. $\begin{array}{r} 638 \\ \times\ 570 \\ \hline \end{array}$
(44)

17. $3\dfrac{1}{3}$
(46) $+\ 1\dfrac{2}{3}$

*18. Find the fraction name for 1 used to make each equivalent fraction:
(69)

  a. $\dfrac{2}{3} \times \dfrac{?}{?} = \dfrac{8}{12}$

  b. $\dfrac{3}{4} \times \dfrac{?}{?} = \dfrac{15}{20}$

  c. $\dfrac{1}{3} \times \dfrac{?}{?} = \dfrac{3}{9}$

  d. $\dfrac{2}{5} \times \dfrac{?}{?} = \dfrac{6}{15}$

19. $\begin{array}{r} 4 \\ -\ 1\dfrac{2}{5} \\ \hline \end{array}$
(51)

20. $\dfrac{1}{2}$ of $\dfrac{3}{5}$
(63)

21. $\dfrac{1}{3} \times \dfrac{2}{3}$
(63)

22. $\dfrac{1}{2} \times \dfrac{6}{6}$
(63)

23. The table shows the cost of general admission tickets to a concert. Use
(1) the table to answer the questions that follow.

Number of Concert Tickets	1	2	3	4
Cost	$35	$70	$105	$140

  a. **Generalize** Write a rule that describes how to find the cost of any number of tickets.

  b. **Predict** A group of 10 friends would like to attend the concert. What will be the total ticket cost for the group of friends?

*24. Refer to this rectangle to answer parts **a** and **b**.
(21, 59, 63)

  a. What is the area of the rectangle?

  b. Draw a rectangle that is similar to the rectangle but has sides twice as long.

$\dfrac{3}{4}$ in.

$\dfrac{3}{8}$ in.

25. a. Which number on the spinner is the most unlikely
   (45)   outcome of a spin?

b. Which outcomes have probabilities that exceed $\frac{1}{4}$
   with one spin of the spinner?

26. a. A nickel is what fraction of a quarter?
   (63)

b. A quarter is what fraction of a dollar?

c. A nickel is what fraction of a dollar?

d. The answers to parts **a–c** show that one fifth of one fourth is
   what fraction?

*27. Write the following decimals as percents:
   (70)
   a. 0.27   **b.** 0.09   **c.** 0.5

28. The table below shows the number of goals scored by the top
(Inv. 5)   four teams in the soccer league. Display the data in a pictograph.
   Remember to include a key.

**Goals Scored by
Soccer Teams**

Team Name	Goals
Goal Diggers	20
Buckies	16
Ball Hounds	15
Hornets	12

29. The record low temperature in the state of Alaska was −80°F and
   (9)   occurred in Prospect Creek Camp in 1971. The record low temperature
   in the state of New Hampshire was −47°F and occurred on Mount
   Washington in 1934. Which temperature is colder? What number of
   degrees represents the range of those two temperatures?

30. **Explain** Victor and Luis ran a race. Victor began running 3
   (37)   seconds before Luis began running, and Luis completed the race 1
   second before Victor completed the race. Victor ran for 32 seconds.
   For how many seconds did Luis run? Explain how you know your
   answer is correct.

California Mathematics Content Standards
SDAP 1.0, 1.2 Organize and display single-variable data in appropriate graphs and representations (e.g., histogram, circle graphs) and explain which types of graphs are appropriate for various data sets.
MR 2.0, 2.6 Make precise calculations and check the validity of the results from the context of the problem.
MR 3.0, 3.3 Develop generalizations of the results obtained and apply them in other circumstances.

INVESTIGATION 7

Focus on

Displaying Data

Data that are gathered and organized may be displayed in various types of charts and graphs. One type of graph is a **bar graph.** A bar graph uses rectangles, or bars, to display data. Below we show the activity and frequency table from Investigation 5 and a bar graph that displays the data.

> **Math Language**
>
> A bar graph can be horizontal or vertical. This graph is a vertical bar graph.

Activity Number: 4, 3, 3, 4, 2, 5, 6, 1, 3, 4, 5, 2, 2,
6, 3, 3, 4, 3, 2, 4, 5, 3, 5, 5, 6

Frequency Table

Activity	Frequency
1	1
2	4
3	7
4	5
5	5
6	3

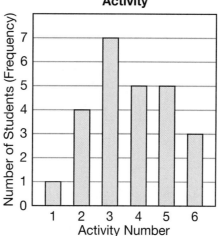

Notice how the information from the frequency table is presented in the bar graph. The scale across the bottom of the bar graph, the horizontal axis, lists all the possible activity numbers. It shows the same values as the first column of the frequency table. The scale along the left side of the bar graph, the vertical axis, lists the number of students. The height of a bar tells how often the activity shown below the bar was chosen. In other words, it tells the frequency of the activity.

Now we will practice making bar graphs using a new situation. Twenty children in a class were asked how many siblings (brothers and sisters) they each had. The data from their responses, as well as a frequency table to organize the data, are shown below.

Number of siblings: 2, 3, 0, 1, 1, 3, 0, 4, 1, 2,
0, 1, 1, 2, 2, 3, 0, 2, 1, 1

Frequency Table

Number of Siblings	Tally	Frequency
0	IIII	4
1	IIII II	7
2	IIII	5
3	III	3
4	I	1

1. (**Represent**) Copy and complete this bar graph to display the data.

Number of Siblings of Students in the Class

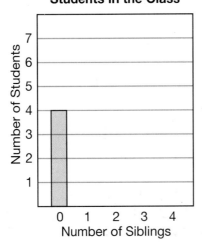

In Investigation 5 we made frequency tables with data grouped in intervals of equal size. Recall that ABC Market offered turkeys with these weights (in pounds):

11, 18, 21, 23, 16, 20, 22, 14, 16, 20, 17,
19, 13, 14, 22, 19, 22, 18, 20, 12, 25, 23

Histograms

Here is the frequency table for these data using intervals of 4 pounds, starting with the interval 10–13 lb:

Frequency Table

Weight	Tally	Frequency
10–13 lb	III	3
14–17 lb	IIII	5
18–21 lb	IIII III	8
22–25 lb	IIII I	6

To graph data grouped in intervals, we can make a **histogram,** which is a type of bar graph. In a histogram the widths of the bars represent the selected intervals, and there are no spaces between the bars. Below is a histogram for the turkey weight data. The intervals in the histogram match the intervals in the frequency.

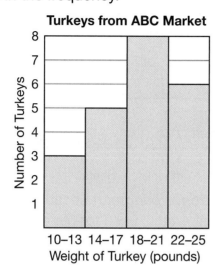

Turkeys from ABC Market

2. (**Represent**) Create a frequency table and histogram for the turkey weight data using these weight intervals:

11–13 lb, 14–16 lb, 17–19 lb, 20–22 lb, 23–25 lb

Stem-and-Leaf Plots

Another way to display these turkey weights is in a **stem-and-leaf plot.** The "stems" are the tens digits of the weights. The "leaves" for each stem are the ones digits of the weights that begin with that tens digit. Here is the stem-and-leaf plot for the first row of weights in the list. Notice that the leaves are listed in increasing order.

Stem	Leaf
1	1 4 6 6 7 8
2	0 0 1 2 3

3. (**Represent**) Make a stem-and-leaf plot for the second row of weights in the list.

4. Use the information in the stem-and-leaf plots for the first and second rows of the list of weights to make a stem-and-leaf plot for the weights of all 22 turkeys.

Numerical data represent such quantities as ages, heights, weights, temperatures, and points scored. But data also come in **categories** or **classes.** People, concepts, and objects belong to categories. Examples of categories include occupations, days of the week, after-school activities, foods, and colors.

Suppose Angela asked the students in her class to name their favorite type of juice and displayed the data in this frequency table and bar graph:

Frequency Table

Juice	Frequency
Grape	9
Cranberry	5
Apple	6
Orange	4

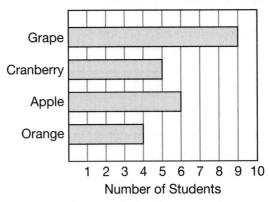

Favorite Juice of Students in Class

The bar graph Angela made is called a *horizontal bar graph* because the bars run horizontally. The categories that Angela used for her data are types of juice: grape, cranberry, apple, and orange.

Sixty students were asked to give their position among the children in their family. Their responses were put into the four categories shown in this frequency table:

Frequency Table

Category	Frequency
Only child	22
Youngest child	16
Oldest child	14
Middle child	8

5. **Represent** Make a horizontal bar graph for the data in the table above. Be sure to label each bar along the vertical side of the graph with one of the four categories. Along the bottom of the graph, use even numbers to label the number of students.

Pictographs

Recall that a **pictograph** uses symbols, or **icons,** to compare data that come from categories. An icon can represent one data point or a group of data points. In pictographs we include a **legend** to show what the icon represents.

Suppose 92 children were asked to choose their favorite sandwich from grilled cheese, tuna fish, and sliced turkey. The data that was collected is displayed in the following pictograph:

Favorite Sandwich	
Grilled Cheese	🥖 🥖 🥖 🥖 🥖 🥖 🥖 🥖 🥖 🥖
Tuna Fish	🥖 🥖 🥖 🥖 🥖 🥖 🥖 🥖
Sliced Turkey	🥖 🥖 🥖 🥖 🥖

Key: 🥖 = 4 students

Interpret We count 8 symbols for tuna fish in the pictograph. To find how many children 8 symbols represents, we read the legend and find that we should multiply the number of symbols by 4. So 8 × 4, or 32, children prefer tuna fish.

6. How many children prefer grilled cheese?

7. How many children prefer sliced turkey?

8. Draw a second pictograph for the food preferences in which each symbol represents 8 children.

Circle Graphs

Sometimes we are interested in seeing how one category breaks down into parts of a whole. The best kind of graph for this is a **circle graph**. A circle graph is sometimes called a **pie chart**.

Interpret The following circle graph shows how Greg spends a typical 24-hour day during the summer:

Greg's Day

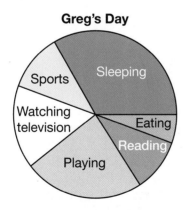

Math Language

A *circle graph* displays data that represent all of the parts of a whole. In this graph, the whole is one day.

9. Which two activities together consume most of Greg's time? Which of the activities consumes the least amount of Greg's time?

10. Which activity consumes about the same amount of time as sports?

11. Which activities consume more time than sports?

12. List activities that together consume about 12 hours.

We can make a circle graph to show the following data.

Election Results: Class President (24 voters)

Candidate	Votes Received
Gia	$\frac{3}{8}$
Yuliana	$\frac{1}{2}$
Jordy	$\frac{1}{8}$

A circle graph is the most appropriate way to display the data because a circle graph is a way to display parts of a whole. In the given data set, 24 voters represent the whole, and the fraction of votes each candidate received represent the parts of that whole.

To display the data in a circle graph, we first divide a circle. Since all three fractions can be expressed as eighths, we will divide the circle into 8 equal parts. We also rename $\frac{1}{2}$ as eighths.

$$\frac{1}{2} \times \frac{4}{4} = \frac{4}{8}$$

Now we can graph the election results.

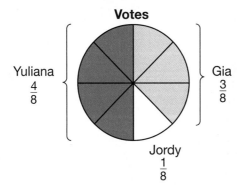

Gia received $\frac{3}{8}$ of the votes, so we label three parts of the circle with her name. Yuliana received $\frac{4}{8}$ of the votes, so we label four parts of the circle with her name. Jordy received $\frac{1}{8}$ of the votes, so we label one part of the circle with his name. We then add a title for our graph.

Connect Why can we check our work by adding the fractions and comparing the sum to 1?

13. **(Represent)** What type of graph is most appropriate for displaying the following data?

In Ms. Escobar's fifth grade class, $\frac{3}{4}$ of the students are boys, and $\frac{1}{4}$ of the students are girls.

Display the data in the type of graph you chose.

14. **(Classify)** Which type of graph would be most appropriate for each set of data? Explain why you chose that type of graph.

a. **How I Spent My $20 Allowance**

Activity and Cost	
Movie	$8.00
Board Game	$10.00
Snack	$2.00

b. **Population of Selected Towns**

Town	Population
Shorewood	1240
Greenway	1345
East Bend	4736

c. **Afternoon Temperature**

Time	Temperature (°F)
12:30 p.m.	68
1:30 p.m.	70
2:30 p.m.	73
3:30 p.m.	77
4:30 p.m.	76
5:30 p.m.	74

Investigate Further

a. In which month were you born? Create a horizontal bar graph that displays the birth months of your classmates.

b. In which season were you born: winter, spring, summer, or fall? (Use December 22, March 22, June 22, and September 22 as the first day of each season.) Create a histogram that displays the seasons in which your classmates were born.

c. Track local high temperatures for a week and make a line graph of the daily high temperatures. Write two problems involving temperature changes that could be solved using the line graph you made.

d. Survey 10 friends about their favorite color, and make a pictograph of the data. Write two problems that could be solved using the pictograph you made.

e. Select four classroom items that weigh between 100 grams and 1 kilogram. Using a scale or balance, determine the items' actual weights. Choose a type of graph to best display the data you have collected. After creating the graph, explain why you chose this particular type of graph.

California Mathematics Content Standards
NS 2.0, 2.3 Solve simple problems, including ones arising in concrete situations, involving the addition and subtraction of fractions and mixed numbers (like and unlike denominators of 20 or less), and express answers in the simplest form.
MR 3.0, 3.3 Develop generalizations of the results obtained and apply them in other circumstances.

• Reducing Fractions, Part 1

facts	Power Up G
equivalent fractions	The following fractions are equal to one half: $\frac{1}{2}$, $\frac{2}{4}$, $\frac{3}{6}$. Read the fractions aloud and continue the pattern to $\frac{12}{24}$.
mental math	**a. Number Sense:** Is 2736 divisible by 4?
	b. Number Sense: Is 3726 divisible by 4?
	c. Number Sense: $\frac{1}{3}$ of 10
	d. Number Sense: $\frac{1}{3}$ of 100
	e. Geometry: Each side of the square is $2\frac{1}{2}$ inches long. What is the perimeter of the square?
	f. Time: How many seconds is 10 minutes 25 seconds?
	g. Probability: A spinner is divided into five equal-sized sectors labeled A, B, C, D, and E. With one spin, what is the probability of the spinner landing on A or B?
	h. Calculation: $\sqrt{25}$, $+ 3$, $\times 4$, $+ 1$, $\div 3$
problem solving	Choose an appropriate problem-solving strategy to solve this problem. Isaac erased some digits in a multiplication problem and gave it to Albert as a problem-solving exercise. Copy Isaac's multiplication problem and find the missing digits for Albert.

$$\begin{array}{r} 3\_ \\ \times \_ \\ \hline 333 \end{array}$$

New Concept

In Lesson 69 we practiced making equivalent fractions by multiplying by a fraction name for 1. We changed the fraction $\frac{1}{2}$ to the equivalent fraction $\frac{3}{6}$ by multiplying by $\frac{3}{3}$.

$$\frac{1}{2} \times \frac{3}{3} = \frac{3}{6}$$

Multiplying by $\frac{3}{3}$ made the **terms** of the fraction greater. The terms of a fraction are the numerator and the denominator. The terms of $\frac{1}{2}$ are 1 and 2. The terms of $\frac{3}{6}$ are 3 and 6.

Generalize State a rule for writing an equivalent fraction using multiplication.

Sometimes we can make the terms of a fraction smaller by dividing by a fraction name for 1. Here we change $\frac{3}{6}$ to $\frac{1}{2}$ by dividing both terms of $\frac{3}{6}$ by 3:

$$\frac{3}{6} = \frac{3 \div 3}{6 \div 3} = \frac{1}{2}$$

Generalize State a rule for writing an equivalent fraction using division.

Changing a fraction to an equivalent fraction with smaller terms is called **reducing.** We reduce a fraction by dividing both terms of the fraction by the same number.

Math Language

Reducing a fraction is also referred to as writing a fraction in *lowest terms* or writing a fraction in *simplest form*.

Example 1

Reduce the fraction $\frac{6}{8}$ by dividing both the numerator and the denominator by 2.

We show the reducing process below.

$$\frac{6 \div 2}{8 \div 2} = \frac{3}{4}$$

Model We can use fraction manipulatives to show equivalent fractions. The reduced fraction $\frac{3}{4}$ has smaller terms than $\frac{6}{8}$. We can see from the picture below, however, that $\frac{3}{4}$ and $\frac{6}{8}$ are equivalent fractions.

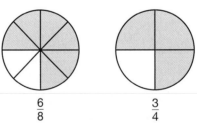

$$\frac{6}{8} \qquad\qquad \frac{3}{4}$$

Not all fractions can be reduced. Only fractions whose terms can be divided by the same number can be reduced.

Example 2

Which of these fractions cannot be reduced?

   A $\frac{2}{6}$ **B** $\frac{3}{6}$ **C** $\frac{4}{6}$ **D** $\frac{5}{6}$

We will consider each fraction:

  A The terms of $\frac{2}{6}$ are 2 and 6. Both 2 and 6 are even numbers, so they can be divided by 2. The fraction $\frac{2}{6}$ can be reduced to $\frac{1}{3}$.

  B The terms of $\frac{3}{6}$ are 3 and 6. Both 3 and 6 can be divided by 3, so $\frac{3}{6}$ can be reduced to $\frac{1}{2}$.

  C The terms of $\frac{4}{6}$ are 4 and 6. Both 4 and 6 are even numbers, so they can be divided by 2. The fraction $\frac{4}{6}$ can be reduced to $\frac{2}{3}$.

  D The terms of $\frac{5}{6}$ are 5 and 6. The only whole number that divides both 5 and 6 is 1. Since dividing by 1 does not make the terms smaller, the fraction $\frac{5}{6}$ cannot be reduced.

  The answer to the question is **D**.

Example 3

Add and reduce the answer: $\dfrac{1}{8} + \dfrac{5}{8}$.

We add $\frac{1}{8}$ and $\frac{5}{8}$.

$$\frac{1}{8} + \frac{5}{8} = \frac{6}{8}$$

The terms of $\frac{6}{8}$ are 6 and 8. We can reduce $\frac{6}{8}$ by dividing each term by 2.

$$\frac{6 \div 2}{8 \div 2} = \frac{3}{4}$$

Model We can use fraction manipulatives to show that the sum of $\frac{1}{8}$ and $\frac{5}{8}$ is $\frac{3}{4}$.

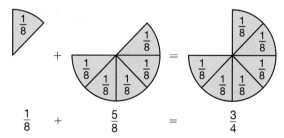

$$\frac{1}{8} \quad + \quad \frac{5}{8} \quad = \quad \frac{3}{4}$$

Example 4

Jenna has a box of beads that are all the same size and shape but different colors. The box has 4 red beads, 6 yellow beads, and 20 blue beads. Without looking, Jenna chose one bead from the box.

   a. What are all the possible outcomes?

   b. What is the probability that the bead Jenna chose was blue?

   a. There are three different colors of beads, so the possible outcomes are **red bead, yellow bead, and blue bead.**

   b. Since 20 of the 30 beads are blue, the probability that Jenna chose a blue bead is $\frac{20}{30}$. We reduce this ratio to $\frac{2}{3}$.

Example 5

Subtract and reduce the answer: $5\frac{5}{6} - 2\frac{1}{6}$.

First we subtract.

$$5\frac{5}{6} - 2\frac{1}{6} = 3\frac{4}{6}$$

Then we reduce $3\frac{4}{6}$. We reduce a mixed number by reducing its fraction.

(**Model**) We can use fraction manipulatives to reduce $3\frac{4}{6}$.

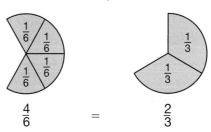

$$\frac{4}{6} \qquad = \qquad \frac{2}{3}$$

Since the fraction $\frac{4}{6}$ reduces to $\frac{2}{3}$, the mixed number $3\frac{4}{6}$ reduces to $3\frac{2}{3}$.

If an answer contains a fraction that can be reduced, we should reduce the fraction. Be alert for this as you work the problems in the problem sets.

Lesson Practice

   a. Reduce $\frac{8}{12}$ by dividing both 8 and 12 by 4.

   b. Multiple Choice Which of these fractions cannot be reduced?

   A $\frac{2}{8}$ **B** $\frac{3}{8}$ **C** $\frac{4}{8}$

Add, subtract, or multiply as indicated. Remember to write the fractions in simplest form.

   c. $\frac{3}{8} - \frac{1}{8}$ **d.** $\frac{3}{10} + \frac{3}{10}$ **e.** $\frac{2}{3} \times \frac{1}{2}$

f. In Example 4, what is the probability that Jenna chose a yellow bead?

Rewrite each mixed number with a reduced fraction:

g. $1\frac{3}{9}$ **h.** $2\frac{6}{9}$ **i.** $2\frac{5}{10}$

Find each sum or difference. Remember to write the fractions in lowest terms.

j. $1\frac{1}{4} + 2\frac{1}{4}$ **k.** $1\frac{1}{8} + 5\frac{5}{8}$ **l.** $5\frac{5}{12} - 1\frac{1}{12}$

Written Practice
Distributed and Integrated

1. In 1973, at the age of 31, author Isabel Allende began writing her first
(RF21) novel. In what year was Isabel Allende born?

2. Andre surveyed his classmates to see what their favorite fruit was.
(Inv. 7) The results are displayed in this frequency table. Construct a horizontal bar graph to display the information.

Frequency Table

Fruit	Frequency
Banana	5
Apple	7
Orange	6
Peach	6

3. Arrange these decimal numbers in order from least to greatest:
(56)
$$2.13, \ 1.32, \ 13.2, \ 1.23$$

4. One fourth of the 36 students earned A's on the test. One third of the
(34) students who earned A's scored 100%.

a. How many students earned A's?

b. How many students scored 100%?

c. What fraction of the students scored 100%?

*5. If $3n = 24$, then what does n^2 equal?
(67)

6. **Connect** Use a fraction, a decimal number, and a
(58) percent to name the shaded portion of this square.

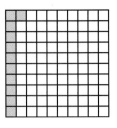

*7. Evaluate. Justify each step of your solution.
(68)
    a. $6^2 - 4m$ when $m = 5$ **b.** $x + \dfrac{4^2}{y}$ when $x = 12$ and $y = 8$

*8. Three hundred pennies have a mass of about 1kg. Yolanda has 900
(64) pennies. About how many grams is this?

9. $\overline{AB}$ is 3.5 centimeters. $\overline{BC}$ is 4.6 centimeters. Find $\overline{AC}$.
(60)

           A B C

*10. $\dfrac{3}{4} + \dfrac{3}{4} + \dfrac{3}{4}$ ***11.** $\dfrac{3}{3} + \dfrac{2}{2}$ ***12.** $3\dfrac{5}{8} + 4\dfrac{6}{8}$
(62)   (62)   (62)

*13. Find the numerator that completes each equivalent fraction:
(69)
    a. $\dfrac{3}{4} = \dfrac{?}{16}$ **b.** $\dfrac{2}{5} = \dfrac{?}{20}$ **c.** $\dfrac{2}{3} = \dfrac{?}{18}$

*14. Write the following fractions as percents:
(70)
    a. $\dfrac{1}{10}$ **b.** $\dfrac{5}{10}$

*15. **Multiple Choice** Which of these fractions cannot be reduced?
(71)
    A $\dfrac{7}{12}$ **B** $\dfrac{7}{14}$ **C** $\dfrac{7}{28}$ **D** $\dfrac{7}{70}$

16. $\dfrac{1}{2} \times \dfrac{2}{2}$ **17.** 401.3 **18.** $\$5.67$ **19.** 347
(63)   (60) $-\,264.7$ (18) $\times\quad 80$ (43) $\times\,249$

20. 50×50 **21.** $(\$5 + 4\text{¢}) \div 6$
(18)   (7, 57)

22. $64{,}275 \div 8$ **23.** $60w = 3780$
(23)   (17, 42)

24. Use the rectangle below to answer parts **a–c**.
(32, 59)

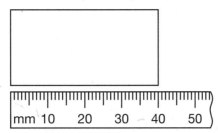

a. How long is the rectangle?

b. If the rectangle is half as wide as it is long, then what is the perimeter of the rectangle?

c. What is the area of the rectangle in square millimeters?

*25. Add, subtract, or multiply as indicated. Remember to reduce
(71) your answers.

a. $\frac{3}{4} - \frac{1}{4}$
b. $\frac{4}{5} \times \frac{1}{2}$
c. $\frac{3}{6} + \frac{1}{6}$

26. a. An inch is what fraction of a foot?
(61, 63)

b. A foot is what fraction of a yard?

c. An inch is what fraction of a yard?

d. The answers to parts **a–c** show that $\frac{1}{12}$ of $\frac{1}{3}$ is what fraction?

*27. Multiple Choice The mass of a dollar bill is about
(64)

A 1 milligram   **B** 1 gram   **C** 1 kilogram

28. This square inch is divided into quarter-inch squares.
(59, 63)

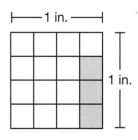

a. What fraction of the square inch is shaded?

b. What is the area of the shaded region?

c. [Explain] Did you use inches or square inches to label the answer in problem **b?** Explain why.

29. [Explain] Coy has four identical stacks of coins. Each stack
(13, 22) contains one dime, two nickels, and six pennies. What is a reasonable estimate of the total amount of money in those stacks? Explain your answer.

*30. Lindsey lives 1.2 kilometers from her school. Shamika lives
(37, 60) 0.2 fewer kilometers from school than Lindsey, and Vashon lives
0.4 fewer kilometers from school than Shamika. Which student
or students live more than half of a kilometer from school?

*Real-World
Connection*

In 2000 a baseball stadium with a retractable roof was built in Houston,
Texas. The construction cost for the ballpark was about $250,000,000.
Write two hundred fifty million in expanded notation using powers of 10.

California Mathematics Content Standards
NS 1.0, **1.2** Interpret percents as a part of a hundred; find decimal and percent equivalents for common fractions and explain why they represent the same value; compute a given percent of a whole number.
NS 1.0, **1.5** Identify and represent on a number line decimals, fractions, mixed numbers, and positive and negative integers.
NS 2.0, **2.3** Solve simple problems, including ones arising in concrete situations, involving the addition and subtraction of fractions and mixed numbers (like and unlike denominators of 20 or less), and express answers in the simplest form.
MR 2.0, 2.3 Use a variety of methods, such as words numbers, symbols, charts, graphs, tables, diagrams, and models, to explain mathematical reasoning.

• Writing Percents as Fractions and Decimals

facts   Power Up D or E

mental math

    a. Time: How many minutes is $2\frac{1}{2}$ hours?

    b. Estimation: Which is the more reasonable estimate for the height of a flagpole, 6 km or 6 m?

    c. Number Sense: Is 5172 divisible by 4?

    d. Percent: 10% of 250

    e. Fractional Parts: How much is $\frac{1}{2}$ of 12? $\frac{1}{3}$ of 12? $\frac{1}{4}$ of 12?

    f. Money: Peter purchased a sandwich for $3.25, a bag of pretzels for $1.05, and a juice for $1.20. What was the total cost?

    g. Geometry: If each side of a hexagon is 4 inches long, what is the perimeter of the hexagon? Express your answer in feet.

    h. Calculation: $\sqrt{36}$, $+1$, $\times 7$, $+1$, $\div 5$, -2, $\div 2$

problem solving

Choose an appropriate problem-solving strategy to solve this problem. Triangles *A* and *B* are congruent. Triangle *A* was "flipped" to the right to form triangle *B*. Suppose triangle *B* is flipped down to form triangle *C*. Draw triangles *A, B,* and *C*.

Now suppose that the triangle *C* you drew is flipped to the left to form triangle *D*. Draw triangle *D*.

We can use decimal squares to show how to change a percentage to a fraction. A decimal square is a grid with 100 squares.

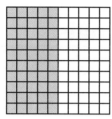 

$$50\% = \frac{50}{100} = \frac{1}{2} \qquad 75\% = \frac{75}{100} = \frac{3}{4}$$

To write a percent as a fraction, we remove the percent sign and write the number as the numerator of a fraction that has a denominator of 100. Then, if possible, we reduce the fraction.

Example 1

In the children's section of a library, 13% of the books are nonfiction books. Write 13% as a fraction.

We remove the percent sign and write a fraction with 13 as the numerator and 100 as the denominator.

$$13\% = \frac{13}{100}$$

The factors of 13 are 1 and 13, and the factors of 100 are 1, 2, 4, 5, 10, 20, and so on. Since 13 and 100 do not have common terms, $\frac{13}{100}$ cannot be reduced.

Example 2

Find the reduced fraction that is equivalent to 8%.

We remove the percent sign and write a fraction with 8 as the numerator and 100 as the denominator.

$$8\% = \frac{8}{100}$$

We reduce the fraction by dividing both the numerator and the denominator by 2, which is a common factor of 8 and 100.

$$\frac{8 \div 2}{100 \div 2} = \frac{4}{50}$$

We again reduce the fraction by dividing both the numerator and the denominator by 2, which is again a common factor of 4 and 50.

$$\frac{4 \div 2}{50 \div 2} = \frac{2}{25}$$

We find that 8% is equivalent to the fraction $\frac{2}{25}$.

Example 3

Write 55% in decimal form.

Fifty-five percent means $\frac{55}{100}$, which can be written as **0.55**.

Model Use a grid to show 55%.

Example 4

Write 100% in decimal form.

To write a percent as a fraction, we remove the percent sign and write the number as the numerator of a fraction that has a denominator of 100.

$$100\% = \frac{100}{100}$$

We reduce $\frac{100}{100}$ by recalling that the quotient of any number divided by itself is 1. So we find that the decimal form of 100% is **1**.

Example 5

Draw a number line divided into tenths. Place 50%, $\frac{3}{10}$, $\frac{80}{100}$, and 100% on the number line. Then write the numbers in order from least to greatest.

All of the given numbers are greater than 0 and less than or equal to 1, so we label 0 and label 1 on a number line. To show tenths, we divide the distance from 0 to 1 into ten unit segments.

We write an equivalent decimal number for each fraction or percent.

$$50\% = \frac{50}{100} = 0.50 = 0.5 \qquad \frac{3}{10} = \frac{30}{100} = 0.30 = 0.3$$

$$\frac{80}{100} = 0.80 = 0.8 \qquad 100\% = \frac{100}{100} = 1$$

Then we plot the decimal numbers.

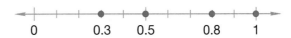

If we read the numbers on a number line from left to right, we read them in order from least to greatest. The numbers from least to greatest are $\frac{3}{10}$, **50%**, $\frac{80}{100}$, **100%**.

Lesson Practice

Write each percent as a fraction in simplest form:

a. 11% **b.** 99% **c.** 20%

d. 4% **e.** 78% **f.** 5%

Write each percent as a decimal:

g. 68% **h.** 10%

i. 34% **j.** 150%

k. 30% **l.** 225%

m. Draw a number line divided into tenths. Place 60%, $\frac{7}{10}$, 100%, and $\frac{10}{100}$ on the number line. Then write the numbers in order from greatest to least.

Written Practice *Distributed and Integrated*

1. One half of the students in a fifth grade class belong to an after-school club, and one fifth of those students belong to the math club. What fraction of the students belong to the math club? What percent of the students belong to the math club?
(63, 70)

2. Fred bought a car for $860 and sold it for $1300. How much profit did he make?
(RF17)

3. **Explain** Each hour from 4 p.m. to 8 p.m., an average of 79 guests arrived at a hotel. How many guests arrived during that time? Explain why your answer is reasonable.
(38)

4. The pickup truck could carry $\frac{1}{2}$ ton. How many pounds is $\frac{1}{2}$ ton?
(64)

*5. **List** Write the first ten composite numbers.
(65)

6. Multiple Choice Which shaded circle below is equivalent to the shaded circle at right?
(Inv. 2, 26)

A   B   C

7. Multiple Choice Which of these fractions does not equal one half?
(15)

    A $\frac{50}{100}$ **B** $\frac{1000}{2000}$ **C** $\frac{16}{30}$ **D** $\frac{6}{12}$

*8. Write $\frac{4}{5}$ as a fraction with a denominator of 100. Then write that fraction as a percent.
(69)

9. (List) Write the numbers that are factors of both 6 and 8.
(16)

10. Evaluate $7^2 + 4m$ when $m = 6$ by following the order of operations.
(68)

11. $\frac{2}{3} + \frac{2}{3} + \frac{2}{3}$ **12.** $\frac{3}{3} - \frac{2}{2}$
(62)   (46)

*13. $9\frac{4}{10} + 4\frac{9}{10}$ **14.** $4.6 + 3.27$
(62)   (60)

*15. Write these fractions as percents:
(70)   **a.** $\frac{14}{100}$ **b.** $\frac{3}{100}$

16. $\begin{array}{r} \$20.50 \\ \times 8 \\ \hline \end{array}$ **17.** $9\overline{)\$56.70}$
(12)   (23)

*18. $9^2 + \sqrt{9}$ **19.** $80\overline{)4650}$
(67)   (42)

20. Is the quotient of $98 \div 5$ a whole number or a mixed number? Write the quotient.
(47)

21. $\frac{3}{4}$ of $\frac{1}{2}$ ***22.** $\frac{3}{2} \times \frac{3}{4}$
(63)   (63)

*23. Rewrite each mixed number with a reduced fraction:
(71)   **a.** $1\frac{6}{8}$ **b.** $3\frac{4}{12}$

24. Use this information to answer parts **a** and **b**:

(10, 60)

It is 1.5 miles from Kiyoko's house to school. It takes Kiyoko 30 minutes to walk to school and 12 minutes to ride her bike to school.

    a. How far does Kiyoko travel going to school and back in 1 day?

    b. If Kiyoko leaves her house at 7:55 a.m. and rides her bike, at what time will she get to school?

*25. Of the six classes that went to the library, 70% of the students checked out a book. Write 70% as a reduced fraction.

(72)

26. Suppose the 7 letter tiles below are turned over, mixed up, then one tile is selected.

(45)

$$\boxed{A}\;\boxed{C}\;\boxed{A}\;\boxed{S}\;\boxed{L}\;\boxed{B}\;\boxed{E}$$

    a. What is the probability that the letter selected is A?

    b. What is the probability that the letter selected is a vowel?

    c. What is the probability that the letter selected comes before G in the alphabet?

27. Each angle of quadrilateral *ABCD* is a right angle. If $\overline{AB}$ is 10 ft and $\overline{BC}$ is 5 ft, what is the area of the quadrilateral?

(59)

28. Multiple Choice Which of these terms does not apply to quadrilateral *ABCD* in problem **27**?

(33)

    A rectangle   **B** parallelogram   **C** rhombus

*29. Write each percent as a decimal number or a whole number:

(72)

    a. 48%   **b.** 2%   **c.** 200%

30. **(Formulate)** This table shows the diameters of four planets, rounded to the nearest five hundred miles. Display the data in a horizontal bar graph. Then write two questions that can be answered using your graph.

(Inv. 7)

Planet Diameters
(rounded to the nearest 500 miles)

Planet	Diameter (miles)
Mercury	3000
Venus	7500
Earth	8000
Mars	4000

California Mathematics Content Standards
NS 2.0, **2.3** Solve simple problems, including ones
arising in concrete situations, involving the addition
and subtraction of fractions and mixed numbers
(like and unlike denominators of 20 or less), and
express answers in the simplest form.
MR 2.0, 2.2 Apply strategies and results from simpler
problems to more complex problems.

• Greatest Common Factor (GCF)

facts   Power Up F

mental math

 a. **Measurement:** How many inches is $2\frac{1}{2}$ feet?

 b. **Geometry:** What is the area of a square that is 3 inches on each side?

 c. **Number Sense:** $124 \div 4$

 d. **Number Sense:** $412 \div 4$

 e. **Number Sense:** $1 - \frac{7}{10}$

 f. **Fractional Parts:** One third of 22 is $7\frac{1}{3}$. How much is $\frac{1}{3}$ of 23? $\frac{1}{3}$ of 25?

 g. **Probability:** Karl has a $1 bill, a $5 bill, and a $10 bill in his wallet. He does not know the order the bills are in. If Karl pulls one bill out of the wallet without looking, what is the probability it will *not* be a $1 bill?

 h. **Calculation:** $\sqrt{64}$, $\div 2$, $\times 3$, $\div 2$, $\times 4$, $\div 3$

problem solving

Choose an appropriate problem-solving strategy to solve this problem. Abdul stacked some small cubes together to form this larger cube. How many small cubes did Abdul stack together? Explain how you arrived at your answer.

Math Language

A factor of a number is also a divisor of that number. The greatest common factor (GCF) of two numbers is also the greatest common divisor (GCD) of those numbers.

We have practiced finding the factors of whole numbers. In this lesson we will practice finding **common factors** and the **greatest common factor** of two numbers. The greatest common factor of two numbers is the largest whole number that is a factor of both numbers. The letters **GCF** are sometimes used to stand for the term *greatest common factor.*

To find the greatest common factor of 12 and 18, we first list the factors of each. We have circled the common factors, or the numbers that are factors of both 12 and 18.

Factors of 12: ①, ②, ③, 4, ⑥, 12

Factors of 18: ①, ②, ③, ⑥, 9, 18

The common factors are 1, 2, 3, and 6.

The greatest of these common factors is 6.

Connect What is the greatest common factor of 4, 6, 12?

Example 1

Find the greatest common factor (GCF) of 8 and 20.

We list the factors of 8 and of 20 and then circle the common factors.

Factors of 8: ①, ②, ④, 8

Factors of 20: ①, ②, ④, 5, 10, 20

We see that there are three common factors. The greatest of the three common factors is **4.**

We may use the greatest common factor to help us reduce fractions.

Example 2

Use the GCF of 8 and 20 to reduce $\frac{8}{20}$.

In Example 1 we found that the GCF of 8 and 20 is 4. So we can reduce $\frac{8}{20}$ by dividing 8 by 4 and 20 by 4.

$$\frac{8 \div 4}{20 \div 4} = \frac{2}{5}$$

Find the greatest common factor (GCF) of each pair of numbers:

a. 6 and 9   **b.** 6 and 12   **c.** 15 and 100

d. 6 and 10   **e.** 12 and 15   **f.** 7 and 10

Reduce each fraction by dividing the terms of the fraction by their GCF:

g. $\dfrac{6}{9}$ **h.** $\dfrac{6}{12}$ **i.** $\dfrac{15}{100}$

Written Practice

Distributed and Integrated

1. Mr. MacDonald bought 1 ton of hay for his cow, Geraldine. Every day
(13, 64) Geraldine eats 50 pounds of hay. At this rate 1 ton of hay will last how many days?

2. A platypus is a mammal with a duck-like bill and webbed feet. A platypus
(61) is about $1\frac{1}{2}$ feet long. One and one half feet is how many inches?

3. **Verify** Jamar bought 3 shovels for his hardware store for $6.30 each.
(22, 37) He sold them for $10.95 each. How much profit did Jamar make on all 3 shovels? (Jamar's profit for each shovel can be found by subtracting how much Jamar paid from the selling price.) Use estimation to show that your answer is reasonable.

4. **Represent** Add the decimal number ten and fifteen hundredths to
(55, 60) twenty-nine and eighty-nine hundredths. Use words to name the sum.

5. **Explain** By what fraction name for 1 should $\frac{2}{3}$
(69) be multiplied to make $\frac{6}{9}$? Explain why. $\dfrac{2}{3} \times \dfrac{?}{?} = \dfrac{6}{9}$

6. **Represent** Draw a rectangle whose sides are all 1 inch long. What is
(32, 33, 59) the area of the rectangle?

7. **List** Write the numbers that are factors of both 9 and 12.
(16)

8. **Analyze** Write a fraction equal to $\frac{3}{4}$ that has a denominator of 12.
(62, 69) Then write a fraction equal to $\frac{2}{3}$ that has a denominator of 12. What is the sum of the fractions you wrote? Write your answer as a reduced fraction.

9. Which of these numbers are prime numbers?
(65)

   15   23   21   27   31

10. $1\frac{1}{5} + 2\frac{2}{5} + 3\frac{3}{5}$
(62)

11. $5 - \left(3\frac{5}{8} - 3\right)$
(30, 51)

12. $\$10 - 10¢$
(57)

13. $\$10 \div 4$
(23)

*14. Simplify each expression by following the order of operations:
(68)

   a. $28 - (8 + 9)$

   b. $\dfrac{3^3}{3^2}$

15. $24.6 + m = 30.4$
(60)

16. $w - 6.35 = 2.4$
(60)

*17. Twenty-three of the fifty students in the seventh grade band play a
(70) brass instrument. What percent of the band members play a brass
      instrument?

18. $7\overline{)43{,}859}$
(17)

*19. $15^2 - \sqrt{25}$
(67)

*20. Find each sum or difference. Remember to reduce your answers.
(71)

   a. $2\frac{3}{12} + 1\frac{5}{12}$

   b. $4\frac{7}{8} + 2\frac{5}{8}$

21. $\frac{1}{2}$ of $\frac{1}{5}$
(63)

*22. $\frac{3}{4} \times \frac{2}{2}$
(63)

*23. Write each percent as a fraction in simplest form:
(72)

   a. 40%

   b. 8%

*24. Find the greatest common factor (GCF) of each pair of numbers:
(73)

   a. 9 and 18

   b. 8 and 12

25. (Analyze) A standard number cube is rolled once. What is the
(45) probability that the upturned face is not 4?

26. To multiply 12 by 21, Tom thought of 21 as 20 + 1. Then he mentally
(39) calculated this problem:

$$(20 \times 12) + (1 \times 12)$$

   Try mentally calculating the answer. What is the product of 12
   and 21?

*27. Multiple Choice Fourteen books were packed in a box. The mass of
(64) the packed box could reasonably be which of the following?

   A 15 milligrams   **B** 15 grams   **C** 15 kilograms

*28. Reduce each fraction by dividing the terms of the fraction by their GCF:
(73)
     a. $\dfrac{9}{18}$ **b.** $\dfrac{8}{12}$

29. Compare: 500 mg $\bigcirc$ 1.0 g
(64)

30. **Explain**   Mr. Johnson is deciding which of two used cars to buy.
(22) The price of one is $7995 and the price of the other is $8499. Find the
approximate difference in price. Explain how to estimate by rounding.

Early Finishers

Real-World Connection

Bianca's goal is to jog 5 miles a week. So far this week she has jogged
$1\frac{1}{8}$ mi and $1\frac{5}{8}$ mi. How far has she jogged this week? How many more
miles does she need to jog this week to meet her goal? Remember to
reduce your answers.

California Mathematics Content Standards
SDAP 1.0, 1.1 Know the concepts of mean, median, and mode; compute and compare simple examples to show that they may differ.
MR 1.0, 1.1 Analyze problems by identifying relationships, distinguishing relevant from irrelevant information, sequencing and prioritizing information, and observing patterns.

• Mean, Median, Mode, and Range

facts   Power Up G

mental math

    a. **Money:** How many cents are in two and a half dollars?

    b. **Measurement:** The low temperature was 55°. The high temperature was 81°. What is the difference between the low and high temperatures?

    c. **Probability:** If one card is drawn from a full deck of 52 cards, what is the probability it will be a "heart"?

    d. **Percent:** 10% of 360 seconds

    e. **Fractional Parts:** $\frac{1}{3}$ of 360 seconds

    f. **Number Sense:** $3\frac{1}{3} + 1\frac{2}{3}$

    g. **Time:** 2 days 2 hours is how many hours?

    h. **Calculation:** $\sqrt{49}$, $+\, 3$, $\times\, 10$, $-\, 1$, $\div\, 9$, $-\, 1$, $\div\, 10$

problem solving   Choose an appropriate problem-solving strategy to solve this problem. It takes Sam about 5 minutes to walk around the block. He takes about 600 steps from start to finish. Sam travels about 15 feet in 6 steps. About how many feet does Sam travel when he walks around the block? Explain how you arrived at your answer.

New Concept

In Lesson 38 we found the **average** of a set of numbers, and in Investigation 5 we learned about the median, mode, and range of a set of numbers. In this lesson we will review these terms.

The average is also called the **mean.** To find a mean, we add and then divide. For example, suppose we wanted to know the mean number of letters in the following names: Andrei, Raj, Althea, Mary, Bedros, Ann, and Yolanda.

Name	Andrei	Raj	Althea	Mary	Bedros	Ann	Yolanda
Number of Letters	6	3	6	4	6	3	7

We first add the seven numbers: 6, 3, 6, 4, 6, 3, and 7. Then we divide the resulting sum by 7, the number of names.

Add: $6 + 3 + 6 + 4 + 6 + 3 + 7 = 35$

Divide: $35 \div 7 = 5$

The mean number of letters is 5. Notice that no name contains 5 letters. So the mean of a set of numbers does not have to be one of the numbers. In fact, the mean of a set of whole numbers can even be a mixed number.

Example 1

Find the mean of this data set: 2, 7, 3, 4, 3

We divide the sum of the data points (19) by the number of data points (5). We write the remainder as a fraction and find that the mean of the data set is $3\frac{4}{5}$.

$$\begin{array}{r} 3\frac{4}{5} \\ 5\overline{)19} \\ \underline{15} \\ 4 \end{array}$$

Example 2

Kayla tracked the number of days it rained each month during the school year and recorded the totals in a table.

Month	S	O	N	D	J	F	M	A	M
Number of Rainy Days	3	5	8	2	5	7	7	6	1

Find the median number of rainy days per school month.

We first put the data in numerical order: 1, 2, 3, 5, 5, 6, 7, 7, 8. The middle object in a row of objects has the same number of objects on its left as it has on its right.

$$\underbrace{1\ 2\ 3\ 5}_{\substack{\text{4 objects} \\ \text{to the left}}}\ ⑤\ \underbrace{6\ 7\ 7\ 8}_{\substack{\text{4 objects} \\ \text{to the right}}}$$

We see that the median is **5 days of rain.**

If a data set has an even number of data points, there are two middle numbers. In these cases the median is the average of the two middle numbers.

Example 3

Jordan recorded the number of inches of snow that fell during the first eight weeks of winter.

Week	1	2	3	4	5	6	7	8
Inches of Snow	2	5	1	6	9	8	3	10

Find the median number of inches of snow that fell during these weeks.

We arrange the numbers in numerical order to get the list 1, 2, 3, 5, 6, 8, 9, 10. The two middle numbers are 5 and 6. The median is the average of 5 and 6. We add 5 and 6 and then divide the resulting sum by 2.

$$1\ 2\ 3\ \boxed{5\ 6}\ 8\ 9\ 10$$

$$\frac{5 + 6}{2} = \frac{11}{2} = 5\frac{1}{2}$$

The median is **$5\frac{1}{2}$ inches of snow.**

Returning to our list of names at the beginning of this lesson, we find that the most common number of letters in a name is 6. There are three names with 6 letters: Andrei, Althea, and Bedros. If some data points occur more than once, then recall that the one that occurs most often is called the **mode.** There can be more than one mode for a data set.

Example 4

The bank manager recorded the number of new savings accounts during the first nine business days of the month.

Day	1	2	3	4	5	6	7	8	9
Number of New Accounts	3	5	8	2	5	7	7	6	1

Find the mode of this set of data.

The numbers 5 and 7 both appear twice. No other numbers appear more than once. So there are two modes, **5** and **7.**

Mean, median, and mode are different ways to describe the *center* of a data set. They are called **measures of central tendency.** We might also be interested in the **spread** of a data set. Spread refers to how the data are stretched out. The simplest measure of spread is the **range.** Recall that the range is the difference between the largest and smallest data points. In Example 4, the largest number of new accounts is 8 and the smallest is 1. So the range or spread for the data set is 7 because $8 - 1 = 7$.

 You may use spreadsheet software to enter a set of data such as sports scores or temperatures to determine its measures of central tendency.

Lesson Practice

Find the mean, median, mode, and range of each data set in problems **a–c.**

a. 3, 7, 9, 9, 4

b. 16, 2, 5, 7, 11, 13

c. 3, 10, 2, 10, 10, 1, 3, 10

d. (Analyze) Find the mean, median, mode, and range for the ages of the students in this table:

Name	Andrei	Raj	Althea	Mary	Bedros	Ann	Yolanda
Age	13	10	10	11	11	10	11

Written Practice — *Distributed and Integrated*

*1. The store pays 96¢ for a box of one dozen pencils and sells them for 20¢ each. How much profit does the store make on a dozen pencils?
(37, 57)

2. A small car weighs about 1 ton. If its 4 wheels carry the weight evenly, then each wheel carries about how many pounds?
(13, 64)

3. (List) Write the numbers that are factors of both 8 and 12.
(16)

*4. The first five prime numbers are 2, 3, 5, 7, and 11. What are the next three prime numbers?
(65)

5. By what fraction name for 1 should $\frac{3}{4}$ be multiplied
(69) to make $\frac{9}{12}$? How do you know?

$$\frac{3}{4} \times \frac{?}{?} = \frac{9}{12}$$

6. Write a fraction equal to $\frac{1}{2}$ that has a denominator of 6. Then write a
(62, 69) fraction equal to $\frac{2}{3}$ that has a denominator of 6. What is the sum of the
fractions you wrote?

7. Think of a prime number. How many different factors does it have?
(65)

8. Arrange these numbers in order from least to greatest:
(15, 46,
56)

$$0.5 \qquad \frac{5}{6} \qquad 1.1 \qquad \frac{2}{3} \qquad 0.25 \qquad \frac{3}{8}$$

9. **Analyze** One mile is 1760 yards. How many yards is $\frac{1}{8}$ mile?
(34, 61)

*10. Seven of the fourteen items that Julia bought at the grocery store
(70) were vegetables. What percent of Julia's grocery items were
vegetables?

11. $8.43 + 68¢ + $15 + 5¢
(57)

12. 6.505 − 1.4
(60)

13. $12 − 12¢
(57)

14. $18.07 × 6
(12)

15. 6w = $76.32
(17)

16. 2^6
(67)

17. Simplify by following the order or operations: $86 − 2^3 \cdot 4$.
(68)

*18. A bag of marbles has three blue marbles, four yellow marbles, two red
(45, 71) marbles, and three green marbles. Without looking, Concepcion draws
one marble. (Be sure to reduce each fraction).

a. What is the probability she will draw a yellow marble?

b. What is the probability she will draw a blue marble?

c. What is the probability she will draw a red marble?

*19. $\frac{3}{4}$ of $\frac{3}{4}$
(63)

*20. $\frac{3}{2} \times \frac{3}{2}$
(63)

*21. Draw a number line from 0 to 1 divided into tenths. Place
(72) 70%, $\frac{2}{10}$, $\frac{50}{100}$, and 100% on the number line. Then write
the numbers in order from least to greatest.

22. $3\frac{2}{3} + 1\frac{2}{3}$
(62)

23. $5 - \frac{1}{5}$
(51)

24. $\frac{7}{10} - \frac{7}{10}$
(28)

25. A babysitter began work in the evening at the time shown
(10) on the clock and worked for $6\frac{1}{2}$ hours. What time did the
babysitter finish work?

26. The sun is about 92,956,000 miles from Earth. Which digit in
(41) 92,956,000 is in the millions place?

*27. Use the GCF of 12 and 36 to reduce $\frac{12}{36}$.
(73)

*28. Yolanda spent the first week of summer signing up customers for a new
(74) paper route. She recorded the new customers each day in a table. Find
the mean number of customers she signed up each day.

Day	M	T	W	Th	F
Number of New Customers	6	5	7	8	4

*29. Find the mean, median, mode, and range of the following data:
(74)
$$7, 9, 5, 6, 9, 4, 9$$

30. The fraction $\frac{4}{5}$ is equivalent to 0.8 and to 80%. Write 0.8 and 80% as
(58)   unreduced fractions.

Real-World Connection

Noni surveyed 36 students in her class to find out whether they would rather learn more about the oceans or about space. Of the students surveyed, 20 wanted to learn more about the oceans.

a. Write a fraction to represent the part of the class that wanted to learn more about the oceans.

b. Find the greatest common factor of the numerator and denominator.

c. Use the GCF to reduce the fraction.

d. Find the fraction in lowest terms which represents the part of the class that wanted to learn more about space.

e. How many students who said they wanted to learn about the oceans would have to change their mind in order for 50% of the class choose each survey answer?

LESSON 75

• Parallelograms

California Mathematics Content Standards

MG 1.0, (1.1) Derive and use the formula for the area of a triangle and of a parallelogram by comparing it with the formula for the area of a rectangle (i.e., two of the same triangles make a parallelogram with twice the area; a parallelogram is compared with a rectangle of the same area by cutting and pasting a right triangle on the parallelogram).

MG 2.0, (2.2) Know that the sum of the angles of any triangle is 180° and the sum of the angles of any quadrilateral is 360° and use this information to solve problems.

facts   Power Up C

estimation   Hold your fingers one inch apart. Hold your hands one yard apart.

mental math

a. **Geometry:** What is the area of a square that is 4 inches on each side?

b. **Number Sense:** $\frac{1}{4}$ of 36

c. **Number Sense:** $\frac{1}{4}$ of 360

d. **Number Sense:** $\frac{1}{3}$ of 36

e. **Money:** The regular price of the backpack is $28. It is on sale for 25% off. What is 25% of $28?

f. **Time:** How many minutes is 4 hours 40 minutes?

g. **Measurement:** A football field is 120 yards long from goal post to goal post. How many feet is this?

h. **Calculation:** $\sqrt{81}$, $- 1$, $\times 10$, $+ 1$, $\div 9$, $- 9$

problem solving

Choose an appropriate problem-solving strategy to solve this problem. If rectangle 1 is rotated a quarter of a turn clockwise around point A, it will be in the position of rectangle 2. If it is rotated again, it will be in the position of rectangle 3. If it is rotated again, it will be in the position of rectangle 4. Draw the congruent rectangles 1, 2, 3, and 4.

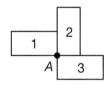

Figure J is a rectangle made from straws. Each angle of the rectangle has a measure of 90°. Figure K is a parallelogram that is formed by shifting the rectangle.

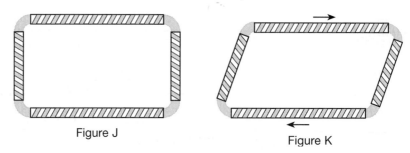

Figure J   Figure K

After the rectangle was shifted to form the parallelogram, two of the angle measures increased to more than 90°, and two of the angle measures decreased to less than 90°. Each angle increased or decreased *by the same amount.* For example, if two 90° angles of the rectangle were shifted to become 110° obtuse angles (an increase of 20° for each angle), the other two 90° angles of the rectangle would become 70° acute angles (a decrease of 20° for each angle). The following activity illustrates this relationship.

Activity 1

Angles of a Parallelogram

Materials needed:
- protractor
- paper
- two pairs of plastic straws (The straws within a pair must be the same length. The two pairs may be different lengths.)
- thread or lightweight string
- paper clip for threading the straws (optional)

Make a "straw" parallelogram by running a string or thread through two pairs of plastic straws. If the pairs of straws are of different lengths, alternate the lengths as you thread them (long-short-long-short).

Bring the two ends of the string together, pull until the string is snug but not bending the straws, and tie a knot.

You should be able to shift the sides of the parallelogram to various positions.

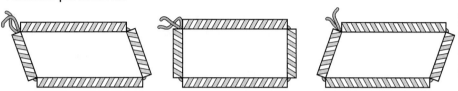

Lay the straw parallelogram on a desktop with a piece of paper under it. On the paper you will trace the parallelogram. Shift the parallelogram into a position you want to measure, hold the straws and paper still (this may require more than two hands), and carefully trace with a pencil around the *inside* of the parallelogram. Be sure to shift the sides so that the parallelogram is "leaning."

Set the straw parallelogram aside, and use a protractor to measure each angle of the traced parallelogram. Write the measure inside each angle. You may wish to trace and measure the angles of a second parallelogram with a different shape before answering the questions below.

1. What were the measures of the two obtuse angles of one parallelogram?

2. What were the measures of the two acute angles of the same parallelogram?

3. What was the sum of the measures of one obtuse angle and one acute angle of the same parallelogram?

If you traced two parallelograms, answer the three questions again for the second parallelogram.

Record several students' answers on the board.

(Conclude) Explain how the opposite angles of a parallelogram compare.

(Conclude) What is the sum of the angle measures of a parallelogram? How does this sum compare to the sum of the angle measures of a rectangle?

Recall from Lesson 33 that a parallelogram is a quadrilateral in which both pairs of opposite sides are parallel.

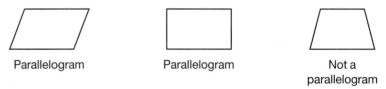

Parallelogram   Parallelogram   Not a parallelogram

Also recall that the dimensions of a rectangle are called the length and the width. When describing a parallelogram, we do not use these terms. Instead we use the terms **base** and **height.**

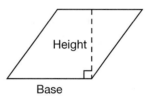

Notice that the height is not one of the sides of the parallelogram (unless the parallelogram is a rectangle). Instead, **the height is perpendicular to the base.**

Activity 2

Area of a Parallelogram

Materials needed:
- paper
- scissors
- straightedge

Cut a piece of paper to form a parallelogram as shown. You may use graph paper if available.

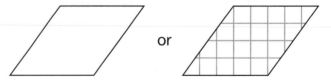

or

Then draw a segment perpendicular to two parallel sides of the parallelogram. The length of this segment is the height of the parallelogram. Cut the parallelogram into two pieces along the segment you drew.

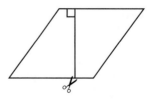

Finally, reverse the positions of the two pieces and fit them together to form a rectangle. The area of the original parallelogram equals the area of this rectangle.

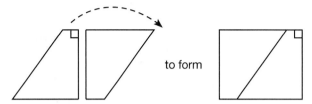

to form

To conclude this activity, answer these questions:

1. What dimensions of the original parallelogram match the length and width of this rectangle?

2. How would you find the area of the rectangle?

(**Discuss**) How would you find the area of the original parallelogram?

As we see in Activity 2, the area of the rectangle equals the area of the parallelogram we are considering. Thus, we find the area of a parallelogram by multiplying its base by its height.

> **Area of a parallelogram = base · height**
> $$A = bh$$

Example 1

A small city park has the dimensions shown. Find the perimeter and the area of the park.

The perimeter is the distance around the park. We add the lengths of the sides. Opposite sides of a parallelogram are the same length.

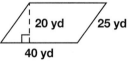

$$25 \text{ yd} + 40 \text{ yd} + 25 \text{ yd} + 40 \text{ yd} = \textbf{130 yd}$$

We multiply the base and height to find the area.

$$40 \text{ yd} \times 20 \text{ yd} = \textbf{800 sq. yd}$$

Example 2

In parallelogram **ABCD**, m∠**D** is 110°. Find the measures of angles **A**, **B**, and **C** in the parallelogram.

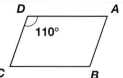

Since the sum of the angle measures of a parallelogram is 360° and opposite angles of a parallelogram have equal measures, we know that the sum of the measures of ∠A and ∠C is 360° − 110° − 110°, or 140°. The measure of each angle is 140° ÷ 2, or 70°.

So m∠A = **70°**, m∠B = **110°**, and m∠C = **70°**.

Lesson Practice

a. (**Conclude**) Find the measures of the angles marked *f, e,* and *d* in this parallelogram given m∠*g* = 75°.

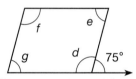

Figure *ABCD* is a parallelogram. Refer to this figure to find the measures of the angles in problems **b–d.**

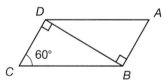

b. ∠A   **c.** ∠ADB   **d.** ∠ABC

(**Generalize**) Find the perimeter and area of each parallelogram. Dimensions are in centimeters.

e.
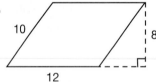

f.
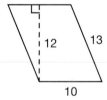

Written Practice — *Distributed and Integrated*

1. In 3 games Ren's bowling scores were 109, 98, and 135.
(38)

a. His highest score was how much more than his lowest score?

b. Find the average of the three bowling scores.

556 *Saxon Math* Intermediate 5

2. Write a fraction and a decimal to name the location of each point:
(54)

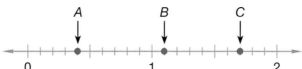

3. Liam is 5 feet 4 inches tall. How many inches is 5 feet 4 inches?
(35, 61)

*4. Write each percent as a decimal:
(72)

    a. 14%   **b.** 148%

5. (**Analyze**) Write a fraction equal to $\frac{2}{3}$ that has a denominator of 12.
(69) Then write a fraction equal to $\frac{1}{4}$ that has a denominator of 12. What is the sum of the two fractions you made?

*6. Use division by primes to find the prime factorization of 56.
(66)

*7. Reduce the fraction $\frac{10}{12}$ by dividing both 10 and 12 by 2.
(71)

*8. One fourth of the 24 members of an elementary school band can play
(34, 71) more than one instrument. One half of the band members who can play more than one instrument also practice playing those instruments every day.

    a. How many band members can play more than one instrument?

    b. How many band members who can play more than one instrument also practice every day?

    c. What fraction of the band members play more than one instrument and practice every day?

9. If the width of this rectangle is half its length, then what is
(32) the perimeter of the rectangle?

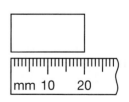

10. What is the area of the rectangle in problem **9**?
(32, 59)

*11. Find the greatest common factor (GCF) of 24 and 42.
(73)

12. 3.4 + 6.25
(60)

13. 6.25 − 3.4
(60)

14. (Represent) The figure at right illustrates four squared (4^2).
(67) Using this model, draw a figure that illustrates three squared (3^2).

15. $6\overline{)\$87.00}$
(23)

16. $40\overline{)2438}$
(42)

17. Divide 5280 by 9. Write the quotient as a mixed number with a reduced
(47) fraction.

18. $10 − ($5.80 + 28¢)
(7, 57)

19. $5\frac{3}{5} + \left(4 − 1\frac{3}{5}\right)$
(46, 51)

20. Reduce: $\frac{3}{6}$
(71)

21. $\frac{4}{3} \times \frac{1}{2}$
(63)

*22. Find the mean, median, mode, and range of the following data:
(74)
$$7 \quad 8 \quad 3 \quad 6 \quad 7 \quad 5$$

*23. Find the perimeter and area of the parallelogram.
(75)

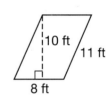

10 ft   11 ft   8 ft

*24. (Analyze) Use this information to answer parts **a** and **b**:
(13)
Rosa has a paper route. She delivers papers to 30 customers. At the end of the month she gets $6.50 from each customer. She pays the newspaper company $135 each month for the newspapers.

a. How much money does Rosa get each month from all her customers?

b. How much profit does she make each month for her work?

25. A standard number cube is rolled once.
(45)

    a. What is the probability that the upturned face is an even number?

    b. Describe a different event that has the same probability.

*26. **(Interpret)** The histogram below shows how many books some
(Inv. 7) students read during the last year.

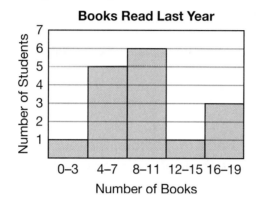

    a. How many students read 12 books or more?

    b. How many students read 15 books or fewer?

*27. Find the measures of angles *A*, *B*, and *C*.
(75)

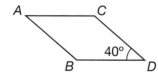

28. Write 15% as a fraction. Then reduce the fraction by dividing both
(58, 71) terms by 5.

29. Compare: $\frac{1}{2} \times \frac{1}{2} \bigcirc \frac{1}{2}$
(Inv. 1,
63)

30. **Explain** Parts of the shorelines of four Great Lakes form a
(22, 37) national boundary between the United States and Canada.

**U.S. and Canada Shared
Shorelines**

Shoreline	Length (miles)
Lake Superior	2730
Lake Huron	3830
Lake Erie	871
Lake Ontario	871

Estimate the total length of the shorelines. Then explain why your
estimate is reasonable.

Early Finishers

Real-World Connection

For five days in a row, Roberto recorded the number of visits that were
made to his classroom website. The least number of visits in a day
was 7. The greatest number of visits in a day was 14. The mode of
the group of data is 9. The median is 9, and the mean is 10. Use this
information to find the number of visits made to the classroom website
during each of the five days.

California Mathematics Content Standards

MG 1.0, (1.1) Derive and use the formula for the area of a triangle and of a parallelogram by comparing it with the formula for the area of a rectangle (i.e., two of the same triangles make a parallelogram with twice the area; a parallelogram is compared with a rectangle of the same area by cutting and pasting a right triangle on the parallelogram).

MG 1.0, 1.4 Differentiate between, and use appropriate units of measures, for two- and three-dimensional objects (i.e., find the perimeter, area, volume).

• Area of a Triangle

facts	Power Up H
estimation	Hold two fingers one centimeter apart. Hold your hands one meter apart.

mental math

a. **Measurement:** 1 cm = ___ mm

b. **Measurement:** 1 m = ___ cm

c. **Number Sense:** Is 3828 divisible by 4?

d. **Number Sense:** Is 2838 divisible by 4?

e. **Time:** Lili'uokalani was the name of the last Queen of Hawaii. She lived for eight decades. How many years is eight decades?

f. **Estimation:** Choose the more reasonable estimate for the height of a desk: 3 in. or 3 ft.

g. **Probability:** Jenna wrote the letters of the alphabet on separate pieces of paper and put them into a bag. If she chooses one piece of paper from the bag without looking, what is the probability it will be the letter *X*?

h. **Calculation:** $\sqrt{9}$, × 9, + 1, ÷ 4, + 3, × 8, + 1, ÷ 9

problem solving

Choose an appropriate problem-solving strategy to solve this problem. In Lesson 49 we found that there are 6 ways to roll a total of 7 with two number cubes. In Lesson 67 we found that there are 3 ways to roll a total of 10 with two number cubes. Which number, 7 or 10, has a greater probability of being rolled with one toss of two number cubes?

Ted performed an experiment in which he rolled two number cubes 100 times and recorded the total each time. Out of the 100 rolls, 16 rolls resulted in a 7. What is a reasonable guess for the number of times Ted rolled a 10?

A triangle has a **base** and a **height** (or **altitude**).

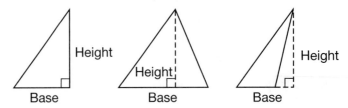

The base and the height of a triangle share a special relationship—their intersection forms a right or 90° angle. In other words, the base and the height of a triangle are perpendicular. The height of a triangle is not necessarily a side length.

To use formulas for finding the area of a triangle, we substitute the dimensions of the base (*b*) and the height (*h*).

$$\text{Area } (A) \text{ of a triangle} = \frac{1}{2}bh$$

$$\text{Area } (A) \text{ of a triangle} = \frac{bh}{2}$$

Discuss The formulas shown above are used to find the area of a triangle. How are the formulas different? Why do both formulas produce the same answer?

Example 1

A flower garden in the shape of a triangle has the dimensions shown. What is the area of the garden?
(Use $A = \frac{1}{2}bh$.)

The base and height are perpendicular dimensions. Since one angle of this triangle is a right angle, the base and height are the perpendicular sides, which are 8 meters and 4 meters long.

$$\text{Area} = \frac{1}{2} \cdot 8 \text{ m} \cdot 4 \text{ m}$$
$$= 16 \text{ m}^2$$

The area of the garden is **16 m²**.

Example 2

Thinking Skill

Explain

Why isn't one of the sides of this triangle its height?

Find the area of this triangle.
(Use A = $\frac{bh}{2}$.)

8 cm

10 cm

We find the area of the triangle by multiplying the base by the height and then dividing the product by 2. The base and height are perpendicular dimensions. In this figure the base is 10 cm, and the height is 8 cm.

$$\text{Area} = \frac{10 \text{ cm} \times 8 \text{ cm}}{2}$$
$$= \frac{80 \text{ cm}^2}{2}$$
$$= \mathbf{40 \text{ cm}^2}$$

You may wish to use drawing software to observe the relationship between the shape of the triangle and its area. Consider different types of triangles and their area and perimeter.

Lesson Practice Find the area of each triangle. Dimensions are in feet.

a.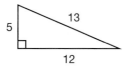

b.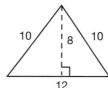

c.

d.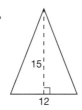

e.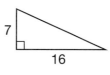

Written Practice *Distributed and Integrated*

1. *(10, 37)* **Justify** Javier was paid $34.50 for working on Saturday. He worked from 8 a.m. to 2 p.m. How much money did he earn per hour? Explain why your answer is reasonable.

2. *(50)* Estimate the product of 396 and 507 by rounding to the nearest hundred before multiplying.

3. *(1)* **Conclude** What is the next number in this counting sequence?

..., 3452, 3552, 3652, _____, ...

4. Multiple Choice Most adults are between 5 and 6 feet tall. The
(61) height of most cars is about

    A 4 to 5 feet   **B** 8 to 10 feet   **C** 40 to 50 feet

5. When sixty-five and fourteen hundredths is subtracted from eighty and
(55, 60) forty-eight hundredths, what is the difference?

6. If one side of a regular octagon is 12 inches long, then what is the
(21) perimeter of the octagon?

7. Multiple Choice Which of these numbers is not a prime number?
(65)
    A 11   **B** 21   **C** 31   **D** 41

*8. a. Find the greatest common factor (GCF) of 20 and 30.
(73)

    b. Use the GCF of 20 and 30 to reduce $\frac{20}{30}$.

9. a. Round $37.62 to the nearest ten cents.
(52)

    b. Round $486.59 to the nearest hundred dollars.

    c. Round $79.43 to the nearest ten dollars.

10. Write each decimal as a percent:
(70)
    a. 0.37   **b.** 0.06   **c.** 0.4

11. a. What number is $\frac{1}{3}$ of 12?
(Inv. 2)

    b. What number is $\frac{2}{3}$ of 12?

*12. Reduce: $\frac{6}{12}$ ***13.** Compare: $2^3 \bigcirc 3^2$
(71)   (67)

14. $\frac{5}{7} + \frac{3}{7}$ **15.** $\frac{4}{4} - \frac{2}{2}$ **16.** $\frac{2}{3} \times \square = \frac{6}{9}$
(62)   (46)   (69)

*17. **Explain** A new store opened downtown and a tally was kept of
(74) how many customers came each day during the first six days. Use the
information in the table to find the median of the data. Then explain
what the median means in this situation.

Day of Week	M	T	W	Th	F	S
Number of Customers	78	72	65	70	69	78

*18. Figure *ABCD* is a parallelogram. Refer to this figure to find the
(75) measures of angles *B* and *C*.

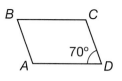

19. $8.47
(18) × 70

20. 6) 43,715
(17)

21. $\frac{2640}{30}$
(42)

22. 367
(43) × 418

23. $3\frac{1}{4} + 3\frac{1}{4}$
(71)

*24. Lakin's front yard is the shape of a triangle. Use the
(76) diagram to determine how many square feet of grass
the family should buy to cover the front yard.

*25. Find the area of the triangle at right:
(76)

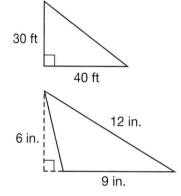

26. **Analyze** Find the probability that with one spin the spinner
(45, 71) will not stop on A. Write the answer as a reduced fraction.

*27. **Interpret** The circle graph below displays the favorite colors of
(Inv. 7) a number of students in a recent survey. Use the graph to answer
parts **a–c.**

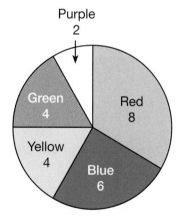

a. How many students are represented in the graph?

b. What fraction of the students name red as their favorite color?

c. What percent of the students named blue as their favorite color?

28. Write 22% as a fraction. Then reduce the fraction by dividing both
(58, 71) terms by 2.

29. In Alaska, the height of Mt. McKinley is 890 meters taller than the
(37) height of Mt. Foraker and 1198 meters taller than the height of
Mt. Blackburn. The height of Mt. Blackburn is 4996 meters. What is
the height of Mt. Foraker?

30. **Justify** In 1957, a satellite named *Sputnik* was the first satellite
(5, 22) launched into space. In 1976, a spacecraft named *Viking I* was the first
spacecraft to land on the planet Mars. About how many years after the
launch of *Sputnik* did *Viking I* land on Mars? Explain how you made your
estimate.

LESSON 77

California Mathematics Content Standards

NS 2.0, **2.2** Demonstrate proficiency with division, including division with positive decimals and long division with multidigit divisors.

AF 1.0, **1.2** Use a letter to represent an unknown number; write and evaluate simple algebraic expressions in one variable by substitution.

• Units of Capacity

facts   Power Up H

mental math

a. Time: What is the time 2 hours 15 minutes after 7:45 a.m.?

b. Number Sense: 100 ÷ 4

c. Number Sense: 1000 ÷ 4

d. Geometry: What is the area of a square that is 5 inches on each side?

e. Money: Brian had $10.00. He spent $6.80 on football collector cards. How much money did Brian have left?

f. Percent: 50% of $51

g. Measurement: The square table was 99 cm on each side. What is the perimeter of the table?

h. Calculation: $\sqrt{49}$, × 5, − 10, ÷ 5, − 5

problem solving

Choose an appropriate problem-solving strategy to solve this problem. Kasey built this rectangular prism with 1-inch cubes. How many 1-inch cubes did Kasey use? Explain how you arrived at your answer.

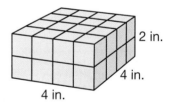

2 in.

4 in.

4 in.

New Concept

Thinking Skill

Analyze

A liter is a little more than a quart. About how many liters are equal to 1 gallon?

When we buy milk, water, or fruit juice at the store, we are buying a quantity of liquid. In the U.S. Customary System, liquid quantities are measured in ounces (oz), pints (pt), quarts (qt), and gallons (gal). In the metric system, liquid quantities are measured in **liters** (L) and milliliters (mL). Here we show some common containers of liquids:

Milk

Water

Juice

$\frac{1}{2}$ gallon   2 liters   1 quart

Thinking Skill

Discuss

The U.S. Customary System also includes units of measure for smaller amounts. For example, 1 tablespoon = $\frac{1}{2}$ ounce and 1 teaspoon = $\frac{1}{6}$ ounce. Three teaspoons are equal to 1 tablespoon. Explain why.

These cartons and bottles are said to have **capacity**. A container's capacity refers to the amount of liquid it can hold. Many containers in the U.S. Customary System are related by a factor of 2. One gallon is 2 half gallons. A half gallon is 2 quarts. A quart is 2 pints. A pint is 2 cups. We show these relationships in the following diagram:

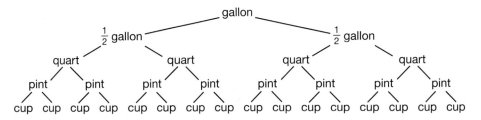

The table below shows some common units of liquid measure. The table also shows equivalences between the units.

Equivalence Table for Units of Liquid Measure

U.S. Customary System	Metric System
16 oz = 1 pt 2 pt = 1 qt 4 qt = 1 gal	1000 mL = 1 L
A liter is about 2 ounces more than a quart.	

Example 1

Math Language

The word *ounce* is used to describe a weight as well as an amount of liquid. The liquid measurement *ounce* is often called a **fluid ounce**. Although *ounce* has two meanings, a fluid ounce of water does weigh about 1 ounce.

One quart of juice is how many ounces of juice?

The table tells us that a quart is 2 pints and that each pint is 16 ounces. Since 2 times 16 is 32, 1 quart is the same as **32 ounces.**

Formulate Express the relationship of one quart to 32 ounces as an equation. Then use your equation to find the number of ounces equivalent to two quarts.

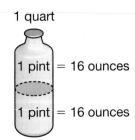

1 quart

1 pint = 16 ounces

1 pint = 16 ounces

Example 2

A half gallon of milk is how many quarts of milk?

A whole gallon is equal to 4 quarts. A half gallon is equal to half as many quarts. A half gallon equals **2 quarts.**

Connect What is the name of the unit of measurement that is equal to one half of one fourth of a gallon?

Example 3

In the table below, we see the number of pints in 1 gallon, 2 gallons, and 3 gallons.

Gallons	1	2	3	4	5
Pints	8	16	24	?	?

How many pints are equal to 4 gallons? 5 gallons? $5\frac{1}{2}$ gallons?

One gallon equals 8 pints, so 4 gallons equal **32 pints** and 5 gallons equal **40 pints.** Since half a gallon is half of 8 pints, we find that $5\frac{1}{2}$ gallons equal **44 pints.**

Example 4

A half liter equals 500 mL. How many milliliters is $3\frac{1}{2}$ liters?

Each liter is 1000 mL, so $3\frac{1}{2}$ liters is 3000 mL + 500 mL = **3500 mL.**

Lesson Practice

a. One fourth of a dollar is a quarter. What is the name for one fourth of a gallon?

b. How many pints is $\frac{1}{2}$ quart?

c. How many milliliters equal 2 liters?

d. A cup is one half of a pint. A cup is how many ounces?

e. Jane was making a large recipe that called for a quart of water, but she only had a 1-cup container to use for measuring. How many times must Jane fill her container to make the recipe?

Written Practice *Distributed and Integrated*

1. Alycia left for school at a quarter to eight in the morning and arrived home
(10) $7\frac{1}{2}$ hours later. What time was it when Alycia arrived home?

*2. Mark has 5 coins in his pocket that total 47¢. How many dimes are in
(52) his pocket?

3. (Represent) Use digits to write the number twenty-three million, two
(41) hundred eighty-seven thousand, four hundred twenty.

4. a. What number is $\frac{1}{3}$ of 24?
(Inv. 2)

  b. What number is $\frac{2}{3}$ of 24?

5. Use a factor tree to find the prime factorization of 54.
(66)

6. a. What is the greatest common factor (GCF) of 4 and 8?
(73)

  b. Use the GCF of 4 and 8 to reduce $\frac{4}{8}$.

7. Simplify each expression by following the order of operations.
(68) Justify each step of your solution.

  a. $6 + 3(4 - 2) + 5^2$ **b.** $\frac{4^3}{2^3}$

8. Find the reduced fractions that are equivalent to the following percents:
(72)
  a. 8%   **b.** 20%   **c.** 70%

9. Write a decimal number equal to the mixed number $1\frac{7}{10}$.
(58)

*10. Find the mean and median of this set of data:
(74)
                    7   5   6   11   11

*11. Find the perimeter and area of the parallelogram.
(75)

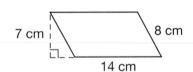

*12. Find the area of the triangle.
(76)

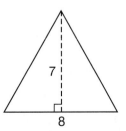

*13. $16^2 + \sqrt{16}$ **14.** 6.25×4 **15.** $6w = \$14.58$
(67)   (12)   (17)

16. (Analyze) Write a fraction equal to $\frac{1}{3}$ that has a denominator of 24.
(62, 69) Then write a fraction equal to $\frac{3}{4}$ that has a denominator of 24. What is the sum of the two fractions you wrote?

17. Reduce: $\frac{6}{8}$
(71)

18. $\frac{3}{4} = \frac{\square}{12}$
(69)

*19. a. A pint is how many cups?
(77)

    b. How many ounces are in a cup?

    c. How many ounces are in a pint?

20. $3\frac{3}{4}$
(46) $+ 1\frac{1}{4}$
———

21. 5
(51) $- 1\frac{1}{4}$
———

22. Compare: $0.1 \bigcirc 0.01$
(56)

23. The multiplication $3 \times \frac{1}{2}$ means $\frac{1}{2} + \frac{1}{2} + \frac{1}{2}$. So $3 \times \frac{1}{2}$ equals what mixed
(62) number?

24. Use the information and the table below to answer parts
(Inv. 5) **a–b.**

Mr. and Mrs. Minick took their children, Muncel and Douglas, to a movie. Ticket prices are shown in the table.

Movie Ticket Prices

Age	Price
Adults	$10.00
Ages 9–12	$8.50
Under 9	$6.50

    a. Muncel is 12 years old and Douglas is 8 years old. What is the total cost of all four tickets?

    b. Before 5 p.m., all tickets are $6.50. How much money would the Minicks save by going to the movie before 5 p.m. instead of after 5 p.m.?

25. Multiple Choice Which of these figures is an illustration of an object
(RF27) that "takes up space"?

    A △   **B** ▢   **C** ▱   **D** ⬡

26. Estimate the area in square feet of a room that is 14 ft 2 in. long and
(50, 59) 10 ft 3 in. wide.

27. **Interpret** The pie chart at right shows how a family's
(Inv. 7) monthly expenses are divided.

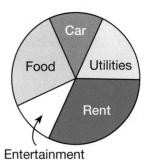

a. Which expense consumes about one third of the
budget?

b. About what fraction of the budget does food
consume?

28. What is the perimeter of a rhombus with sides 2.4 centimeters
(33, 60) long?

*29. One liter equals 1000 milliliters. How many milliliters are in 3 liters?
(77) How many milliliters are in $4\frac{1}{2}$ liters?

30. **Interpret** The line graph shows the average monthly temperatures
(49) during autumn in Knoxville, Tennessee. Use the graph to answer the
questions that follow.

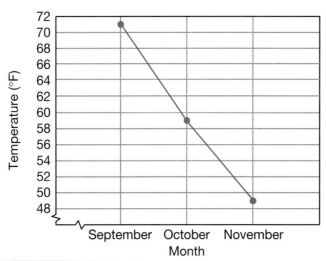

Average Autumn Temperatures in Knoxville, TN

a. What number of degrees represent the range of the
temperatures?

b. How many degrees warmer or cooler is the October temperature
than the September temperature?

c. How many degrees warmer or cooler is the October temperature
than the November temperature?

California Mathematics Content Standards
NS 1.0, (1.2) Interpret percents as a part of a hundred; find decimal and percent equivalents for common fractions and explain why they represent the same value; compute a given percent of a whole number.
NS 2.0, 2.4 Understand the concept of multiplication and division of fractions.
NS 2.0, 2.5 Compute and perform simple multiplication and division of fractions and apply these procedures to solving problems.
MR 2.0, 2.4 Express the solution clearly and logically by using the appropriate mathematical notation and terms and clear language; support solutions with evidence in both verbal and symbolic work.

• Multiplying Fractions and Whole Numbers

facts   Power Up H

mental math

    a. Measurement: The book weighs 2 lb 8 oz. How many ounces does the book weigh?

    b. Measurement: How many pounds are in 1 ton? In 2 tons? In 3 tons?

    c. Number Sense: Is 4218 divisible by 4?

    d. Number Sense: Is 8124 divisible by 4?

    e. Percent: What number is 50% of 5?

    f. Estimation: Choose the more reasonable estimate for the mass of a basketball: 1 kilogram or 1 gram.

    g. Probability: The sides of a number cube are labeled 1 through 6. If the cube is rolled once, what is the probability it will *not* land on 6?

    h. Calculation: $\sqrt{16}$, $\times\, 2$, $+\, 2$, $\div\, 10$, $-\, 1$, $\times\, 5$

problem solving

Choose an appropriate problem-solving strategy to solve this problem. Luis is building a fence to enclose his rectangular garden. The length of the garden is 18 feet. Luis has purchased 54 feet of fencing. If Luis uses all the fencing materials he purchased, what are the dimensions of the garden?

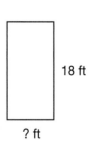

18 ft

? ft

New Concept

We have found a fraction of a whole number by dividing the whole number by the denominator of the fraction.

$\frac{1}{3}$ of 6 is 2. (6 ÷ 3 = 2)

The model below illustrates that $\frac{1}{3}$ of 6 rectangles is 2 rectangles.

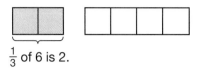

$\frac{1}{3}$ of 6 is 2.

Reading Math

When we multiply with fractions, the answer is stated in terms of the whole.

How can we model $\frac{1}{3}$ of 2? If we divide two whole rectangles into three parts each, then there are 6 parts in all, and $\frac{1}{3}$ of 6 parts is 2 parts. We see that 2 parts is $\frac{2}{3}$ of a whole rectangle.

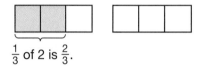

$\frac{1}{3}$ of 2 is $\frac{2}{3}$.

An arithmetic method for finding $\frac{1}{3}$ of 2 is to multiply.

What number is $\frac{1}{3}$ of 2?

$$\frac{1}{3} \text{ of } 2$$
$$\downarrow \quad \downarrow \quad \downarrow$$
$$\frac{1}{3} \times \frac{2}{1}$$

Notice that we wrote the whole number 2 as a fraction, $\frac{2}{1}$. Since 2 divided by 1 is 2, the fraction $\frac{2}{1}$ equals 2. Writing the whole number as a fraction gives us a numerator and a denominator to multiply. The product is:

$$\frac{1}{3} \times \frac{2}{1} = \frac{2}{3}$$

Now we check for reasonableness. We know that $\frac{1}{2}$ of 2 is 1. Since $\frac{1}{3}$ is less than $\frac{1}{2}$, $\frac{1}{3}$ of 2 must be less than 1, and $\frac{2}{3}$ is less than 1.

Here is another way to check our answer. Recall the Commutative Property of Multiplication. This property tells us that changing the order of factors does not affect the product. So another way to approach this problem is to switch the positions of $\frac{1}{3}$ and 2.

$$\frac{1}{3} \times 2$$

We may reverse the order of factors when we multiply.

$$2 \times \frac{1}{3}$$

Since $2 \times \frac{1}{3}$ means $\frac{1}{3} + \frac{1}{3}$, we again find that the product is $\frac{2}{3}$.

Example 1

What number is $\frac{2}{3}$ of 4?

We know that $\frac{2}{3}$ of 4 is greater than 2 because $\frac{1}{2}$ of 4 is 2, and $\frac{2}{3}$ is greater than $\frac{1}{2}$. We also know that $\frac{2}{3}$ of 4 is less than 4. We multiply to find the answer.

$$\frac{2}{3} \text{ of } 4$$

$$\downarrow \downarrow \downarrow$$

$$\frac{2}{3} \times \frac{4}{1} = \frac{8}{3} = 2\frac{2}{3}$$

We converted the improper fraction to a mixed number. Since $2\frac{2}{3}$ is greater than 2 but less than 4, the answer is reasonable. We can check the answer by reversing the order of factors.

$$4 \times \frac{2}{3} \quad \text{means} \quad \frac{2}{3} + \frac{2}{3} + \frac{2}{3} + \frac{2}{3}$$

Again we get $\frac{8}{3}$, which equals $2\frac{2}{3}$.

Example 2

The base of a triangle is 8 inches long. The height of the triangle is 2 inches. Use the formula $A = \frac{1}{2}bh$ to find the area of the triangle.

First we write the formula, and then substitute for b and h.

$$A = \frac{1}{2}b \; h$$
$$\downarrow \quad \downarrow$$
$$A = \frac{1}{2}(8)(2)$$

The expression $A = \frac{1}{2}bh$ represents the product of three factors. We may multiply the factors in any order.

$A = \frac{1}{2}(16)$ Multiply 8 and 2.

$A = \frac{1}{2}\left(\frac{16}{1}\right)$ Write 16 as an improper fraction.

$A = \frac{1 \times 16}{2 \times 1}$ Multiply.

$A = \frac{16}{2}$ Use division to reduce.

$A = 8$ The area of the triangle is **8 in²**.

(**Connect**) In this example, multiplication was used to find $\frac{1}{2}$ of 16. What operation could have been used instead of multiplication? Explain your answer.

Example 3

The 28 students in Mr. Bennett's class are attending a class picnic. Fifty percent of the students are playing volleyball, and the remainder of the students are playing softball. How many students are playing volleyball?

One way to find a percent of a number is to change the percent to a fraction, and then multiply. So to find 50% of 28 students, we first change 50% to a fraction in simplest form.

$$50\% = \frac{50}{100}$$

We change 28 to the improper fraction $\frac{28}{1}$, and then we multiply.

$$\frac{1}{2} \cdot \frac{28}{1} = \frac{28}{2} = 14$$

At the class picnic, **14 students** were playing volleyball.

Lesson Practice

Multiply. Simplify answers when possible. Reverse the order of factors to check your answer.

a. $\frac{1}{3} \times 4$ **b.** $\frac{3}{5} \times 2$ **c.** $\frac{2}{3} \times 7$

d. What number is $\frac{1}{5}$ of 4?

e. What number is $\frac{1}{6}$ of 5?

f. What number is $\frac{2}{3}$ of 5?

g. (**Model**) Sketch rectangles to model $\frac{1}{3}$ of 4. Begin by drawing four rectangles and then divide each rectangle into thirds. Then find $\frac{1}{3}$ of the total number of parts.

h. The base of a triangle is 6 inches and its height is 5 inches. What is the area of the triangle?

i. Kirsten is hosting a meeting for a club that has 36 members. Seventy-five percent of the members will attend a morning meeting, and the rest of the members will attend an after-school meeting. How many members will attend the morning meeting?

Written Practice   *Distributed and Integrated*

1. Three families are equally sharing the $2475 cost of renting a large
(13) home on a lake. What is each family's share of the cost?

2. Write each percent as a fraction in simplest form:
(72)

    a. 60%   **b.** 6%

3. A pair of Sebastian's dress shoes weighs about a kilogram. A kilogram
(64) is how many grams?

4. (**Estimate**) Write the product of 732 and 480 by rounding the numbers
(50) to the nearest hundred before multiplying.

5. Multiple Choice At which of these times do the hands of a clock
(10, 20) form an acute angle?

    A 3:00   **B** 6:15   **C** 9:00   **D** 12:10

6. Arrange these decimal numbers in order from least to greatest:
(56)

$$0.1, 0.01, 1.0, 1.01$$

7. a. Find the common factors of 8 and 12.
(73)

    b. Use the GCF of 8 and 12 to reduce $\frac{8}{12}$.

8. a. What number is $\frac{1}{4}$ of 80?
(Inv. 1)

    b. What number is $\frac{3}{4}$ of 80?

9. $\frac{1}{2} \times \square = \frac{3}{6}$ **10.** Reduce: $\frac{4}{6}$
(69)   *(71)*

11. (**Connect**) Name the total number of shaded circles as
(58) a mixed number and as a decimal number.

12. 9.9 + 6.14 + 7.5 + 8.31
(60)

13. $10 − 59¢   **14.** $30\overline{)672}$ **15.** 5 × 68¢ = $____
(57)   *(17)*   *(57)*

*16. Find the measures of the angles *A, B,* and *C* in this parallelogram:
(75)

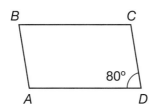

17. $10 - 3\frac{1}{3}$
(51)

18. $\frac{3}{4} \times \frac{5}{4}$
(63)

*19. Find the area of the triangle.
(76)

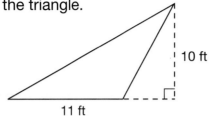

10 ft

11 ft

*20. **a.** How many quarts are in a gallon?
(77)

b. How many pints are in a quart?

c. How many cups are in a pint?

21. **Multiple Choice** Which angle in this figure appears to
(20) be a right angle?

A ∠AOB **B** ∠BOC

C ∠BOD **D** ∠AOD

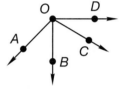

22. (**Analyze**) Use the grocery receipt to answer parts **a–e.**
(Inv. 5,
60, 74)

a. How much money was spent on eggs, juice, and cereal?

b. What was the average (mean) price of the eight items?

c. What is the median price of the eight items?

d. What is the mode of the prices?

e. What is the range of the eight prices?

```
Milk . . . . . . . 1.94
Milk . . . . . . . 1.94
Milk . . . . . . . 1.94
Milk . . . . . . . 1.94
Apple juice . . 1.38
Apple juice . . 1.38
Eggs . . . . . . 3.10
Cereal . . . . . 3.98
─────────────────
TOTAL     17.60
```

*23. Multiply. Simplify answers when possible. Reverse order of factors to
(78) check your answer.

a. $\frac{3}{4} \times 7$ **b.** $\frac{2}{5} \times 3$

24. Find the perimeter of this right triangle. Units are in inches.
(46)

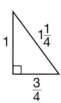

1     $1\frac{1}{4}$

$\frac{3}{4}$

25. (**Analyze**) Write 90% as a fraction. Then reduce the fraction by dividing
(58, 71) both terms by 10. What decimal number does the fraction equal?

26. On the Fahrenheit scale, how many degrees are between the
(9) temperature at which water freezes and the temperature at which water
boils?

27. (**Explain**) A full moon, crescent moon, and new moon are examples
(50) of phases of our moon. It takes the moon about $29\frac{1}{2}$ days to complete
one cycle of phases. Estimate the number of cycles of phases the moon
completes in one year, and explain why your estimate is reasonable. (*Hint:*
1 year is about 365 days.)

*28. a. What number is $\frac{1}{4}$ of 3?
(78)
  b. What number is $\frac{4}{5}$ of 8?

*29. The maximum depth in feet of three natural lakes is shown in the table.
(Inv. 5)
  a. (**Represent**) Display the data in a vertical bar graph. Remember to include a
    legend.

Lake	Continent	Maximum Depth in feet
Victoria	Africa	275
Nipigon	North America	540
Reindeer	North America	710

  b. (**Formulate**) Write two conclusions about the data.

30. The wall-to-wall carpeting in a family room needs to be replaced. The
(59) room measures 16 feet long by 12 feet wide by 8 feet high. What area
represents the amount of carpeting that will be replaced?

*Real-World
Connection*

Suri is planning a party with up to 80 people. She would like to serve
punch to every guest.

  a. If Suri serves each guest 1 cup of punch, how many gallons of punch will
    she need?

  b. If Suri serves each guest $1\frac{1}{2}$ cups of punch, how many gallons of punch
    will she need?

California Mathematics Content Standards
NS 2.0, 2.4 Understand the concept of multiplication and division of fractions.
MR 2.0, 2.3 Use a variety of methods, such as words, numbers, symbols, charts, graphs, tables, diagrams, and models, to explain mathematical reasoning.

• Using Manipulatives and Sketches to Divide Fractions

Power Up

facts	Power Up H
estimation	Hold two fingers one centimeter apart. Hold your hands one yard apart.
mental math	**a. Measurement:** How many centimeters are in one meter?
	b. Powers/Roots: 3^2
	c. Fractional Parts: $\frac{1}{4}$ of 20
	d. Fractional Parts: $\frac{1}{4}$ of 200
	e. Fractional Parts: $\frac{1}{5}$ of 16
	f. Percent: Steve deposits 25% of his earnings into savings. If Steve earns $20.00, how much will he deposit?
	g. Geometry: What is the area of a rectangular tabletop that is 5 feet long and 2 feet wide?
	h. Calculation: $\sqrt{49}$, -2, $\div 2$, -2
problem solving	Choose an appropriate problem-solving strategy to solve this problem. Carlos, Bao, and Sherry drew straws. Carlos's $3\frac{3}{4}$-inch straw was a quarter inch longer than Bao's straw and half an inch shorter than Sherry's straw. How long were Bao's and Sherry's straws?

New Concept

Model In this lesson we will use fraction manipulatives and make sketches to help us divide fractions. First let us think about what dividing fractions means.

The expression

$$\frac{3}{4} \div \frac{1}{8}$$

means "How many one eighths are in three fourths?" For example, how many one-eighth slices of pizza are in three fourths of a pizza?

Using manipulatives, we place three fourths on our desk.

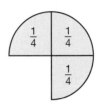

If we cover the three fourths with eighths, we can see that there are 6 one eighths in three fourths.

$$\frac{3}{4} \div \frac{1}{8} = 6$$

Example 1

How many one eighths are in one half?

(Model) This is a division question. It could also be written as:

$$\frac{1}{2} \div \frac{1}{8}$$

Using our fraction manipulatives, we place one half on our desk.

To find how many one eighths are in one half, we cover the half with eighths and then count the eighths.

The answer is 4. There are **4 one eighths** in one half.

Example 2

Divide: $\frac{3}{4} \div \frac{1}{4}$

(Model) This problem means, "How many one fourths are in three fourths?" We make three fourths of a circle using fourths. Then we count the fourths.

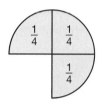

There are 3 one fourths in three fourths.

$$\frac{3}{4} \div \frac{1}{4} = \mathbf{3}$$

Example 3

Divide: $1 \div \frac{1}{3}$

This problem means, "How many one thirds are in one?" Using our manipulatives, we want to find the number of one-third pieces needed to make one whole circle.

There are 3 one thirds in one.

$$1 \div \frac{1}{3} = \mathbf{3}$$

We can use the image of a clock face to help us sketch models for twelfths and sixths. We draw a circle and make twelve tick marks where the numbers 1 through 12 are positioned. To show twelfths, we draw segments from the center of the circle to each of the tick marks. To show sixths, we draw segments only to the tick marks for 2, 4, 6, 8, 10, and 12.

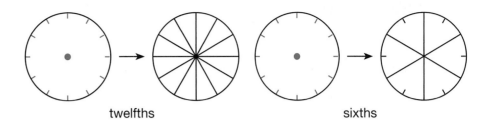

twelfths   sixths

Example 4

Make a sketch to show the division $\frac{1}{4} \div \frac{1}{12}$. What is the quotient?

Represent We draw a circle divided into twelfths. Then we lightly shade $\frac{1}{4}$ of the circle. To find how many $\frac{1}{12}$'s are in $\frac{1}{4}$, we count the number of $\frac{1}{12}$'s in the shaded portion of the circle. We find that the quotient is **3**.

$\frac{1}{4} \div \frac{1}{12} = 3$

Lesson Practice   **Represent** Make sketches to answer problems **a** and **b**.

   a. How many one sixths are in one half?

   b. How many one twelfths are in one third?

Find each quotient. Try to solve the problems mentally.

   c. $\frac{2}{3} \div \frac{2}{3}$ **d.** $1 \div \frac{1}{4}$ **e.** $\frac{2}{3} \div \frac{1}{3}$ **f.** $1 \div \frac{1}{2}$

Written Practice   *Distributed and Integrated*

1. **Represent** Draw a rectangle. Shade all but two fifths of it. What
(58)   percent of the rectangle is shaded?

2. **Analyze** Write a three-digit prime number using the digits 4, 1, and
(65)   0 once each.

3. Find the length of this segment in centimeters and in millimeters:
(32)

4. **(Analyze)** Tisha counted her heartbeats. Her heart beat 20 times in
(37) 15 seconds. At that rate, how many times would it beat in 1 minute?

5. **Multiple Choice** In this quadrilateral, which segment
(20) appears to be perpendicular to $\overline{AB}$?

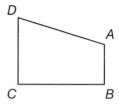

    A $\overline{BC}$ **B** $\overline{CD}$ **C** $\overline{DA}$

6. a. Find the common factors of 6 and 9.
(73)
    b. Use the GCF of 6 and 9 to reduce $\frac{6}{9}$.

7. a. What number is $\frac{1}{5}$ of 60?
(Inv. 2)
    b. What number is $\frac{2}{5}$ of 60?

8. $\overline{AB}$ is $1\frac{1}{4}$ inches. $\overline{BC}$ is $2\frac{1}{4}$ inches. Find $\overline{AC}$.
(71)

9. Arrange these numbers in order from least to greatest:
(56)
$$0.1, \ 0, \ 0.01, \ 1.0$$

10. Four quarts of water is how many pints of water?
(77)

11. Three liters equals how many milliliters?
(77)

12. Divide 100 by 6 and write the quotient as a mixed number. Then rewrite
(47, 71) the quotient by reducing the fraction part of the mixed number.

13. Find the measure of $\angle A$ in the diagram below.
(31)

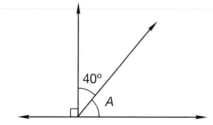

*14. Jesse sharpened three of the twelve pencils. What percent of the
(70) pencils did Jesse sharpen?

15. 396
(44) $\times$ 405

*16. Draw a number line from 0 to 1 divided into tenths. Place 30%, $\frac{8}{10}$,
(72)   70%, and $\frac{50}{100}$ on the number line. Then write the numbers in order from
greatest to least.

17. $9\overline{)3605}$
(23)

*18. Figure *QRST* is a parallelogram and triangles *QRT* and *STR* are
(75)   congruent. Refer to this figure to find the measure of angles *R*, *S*, and *T*.

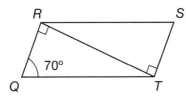

a. m∠R =   **b.** m∠S =   **c.** m∠T =

19. Reduce: $\frac{15}{20}$ **20.** $3 - \left(2\frac{2}{3} - 1\right)$
(71)   (30, 51)

21. (Analyze) Write a fraction equal to $\frac{3}{5}$ that has a denominator of 10.
(62, 69)   Then write a fraction equal to $\frac{1}{2}$ that has a denominator of 10. What is
the sum of the two fractions you wrote?

*22. Find the area of this triangle:
(76)

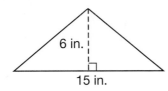

6 in.

15 in.

*23. Forty percent of the 25 softball players plan to also participate in track.
(78)   How many of the softball players plan to be in track?

24. Use this information to answer parts **a** and **b:**
(37)
    *Stan is 6 inches taller than Roberta. Roberta is 4 inches shorter
    than Pedro. Pedro is 5 feet 3 inches tall.*

    a. How tall is Roberta?

    b. How tall is Stan?

*25. Make sketches to help you answer parts **a** and **b**.
₍₇₉₎

    a. How many $\frac{1}{4}$'s are in $\frac{1}{2}$?

    b. How many one eights are in one fourth? (This could be written as $\frac{1}{4} \div \frac{1}{8}$).

26. If you toss a coin 50 times, about how many times would you expect it
₍₄₅₎ to land heads up?

27. The scores of Gaynell's first seven tests are listed below. Use this
₍₇₄₎ information to answer parts **a–c**.

90, 85, 80, 90, 95, 90, 100

    a. What is the range of the scores?
₍₇₄₎

    b. ✎ (**Justify**) What is the mode of the scores? How do you know?
₍₇₄₎

    c. ✎ (**Justify**) What is the median score? How do you know?
₍₇₄₎

28. Coretta has 2 more letters in her last name than Justin has in his last
₍₃₇₎ name. Rachel has 3 fewer letters in her last name than Justin has.
Rachel has 5 letters in her last name. How many letters does Coretta
have in her last name?

*29. Find each quotient. Try to solve the problems mentally.
₍₇₉₎
    a. $1 \div \frac{1}{5}$ **b.** $\frac{3}{4} \div \frac{1}{4}$ **c.** $\frac{5}{6} \div \frac{5}{6}$

30. (**Estimate**) At Central Middle School, 154 students are enrolled in
₍₂₂₎ Grade 6, 147 students are enrolled in Grade 7, and 133 students are
enrolled in Grade 8. What is a reasonable estimate of the number of
students enrolled in Grades 6–8?

LESSON

80

California Mathematics Content Standards

NS 1.0, **1.4** Determine the prime factors of all numbers through 50 and write the numbers as the product of their prime factors by using exponents to show multiples of a factor (e.g., $24 = 2 \times 2 \times 2 \times 3 = 2^3 \times 3$).

NS 2.0, **2.3** Solve simple problems, including ones arising in concrete situations, involving the addition and subtraction of fractions and mixed numbers (like and unlike denominators of 20 or less), and express answers in the simplest form.

• Reducing Fractions, Part 2

facts   Power Up H

mental math

a. **Measurement:** How many grams equal one kilogram?

b. **Measurement:** A pair of shoes weighs about one kilogram. One shoe weighs about how many grams?

c. **Percent:** 25% of 16

d. **Percent:** 25% of 160

e. **Fractional Parts:** $\frac{1}{3}$ of 16 hours

f. **Powers/Roots:** 4^2

g. **Estimation:** Kelvin walked 490 m to the bank, then 214 m to the grocery store, and then 306 m back home. Round each distance to the nearest hundred meters; then add to find the approximate distance Kelvin walked.

h. **Calculation:** $\sqrt{81}, -2, \div 2, -1, \times 2, -5$

problem solving

Choose an appropriate problem-solving strategy to solve this problem. Judy erased some of the digits in a multiplication problem. She then gave it to Frank as a problem-solving exercise. Copy Judy's multiplication problem and find the missing digits for Frank.

New Concept

The equivalent fractions pictured below name the same amount. We see that $\frac{4}{8}$ is equivalent to $\frac{1}{2}$.

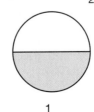

$\frac{1}{2}$

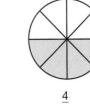

$\frac{4}{8}$

Lesson 80   587

We can reduce $\frac{4}{8}$ by dividing 4 and 8 by 2.

$$\frac{4 \div 2}{8 \div 2} = \frac{2}{4}$$

If we reduce $\frac{4}{8}$ by dividing both terms by 2, we find that $\frac{4}{8}$ is equal to $\frac{2}{4}$. However, fractions should be reduced to **lowest terms.** The fraction $\frac{2}{4}$ can also be reduced, so we reduce again.

$$\frac{2 \div 2}{4 \div 2} = \frac{1}{2}$$

The fraction $\frac{4}{8}$ reduces to $\frac{2}{4}$, which reduces to $\frac{1}{2}$. We reduce twice to find that $\frac{4}{8}$ equals $\frac{1}{2}$.

We can avoid the need to reduce more than once if we divide by the **greatest common factor** (GCF) of the terms. The GCF of 4 and 8 is 4. If we reduce $\frac{4}{8}$ by dividing both terms by 4, we reduce only once.

$$\frac{4 \div 4}{8 \div 4} = \frac{1}{2}$$

Example 1

There are 4 blue marbles and 8 white marbles in a bag. If one marble is taken from the bag, what is the probability that the marble selected is white?

Since 8 of the 12 marbles are white, the probability of selecting a white marble is $\frac{8}{12}$. Since 8 and 12 are divisible by 2, we may reduce $\frac{8}{12}$ by dividing both terms by 2. This gives us $\frac{4}{6}$, which also can be reduced.

Reduce Twice

$$\frac{8 \div 2}{12 \div 2} = \frac{4}{6}$$

$$\frac{4 \div 2}{6 \div 2} = \frac{2}{3}$$

We save a step if we reduce by the GCF of the terms. The GCF of 8 and 12 is 4. If we divide 8 and 12 by 4, then we reduce only once.

Reduce Once

$$\frac{8 \div 4}{12 \div 4} = \frac{2}{3}$$

The probability that the marble selected is white is $\frac{2}{3}$.

Example 2

The value of a dime is 40% of the value of a quarter. Write 40% as a reduced fraction.

We first write 40% as the fraction $\frac{40}{100}$. Since the numerator and denominator both end in zero, we know they are divisible by 10.

$$\frac{40 \div 10}{100 \div 10} = \frac{4}{10}$$

Since the terms of $\frac{4}{10}$ are both even, we can continue to reduce by dividing both terms by 2.

$$\frac{4 \div 2}{10 \div 2} = \frac{2}{5}$$

The GCF of 40 and 100 is 20. So we could have reduced $\frac{40}{100}$ in one step by dividing both terms by 20.

$$\frac{40 \div 20}{100 \div 20} = \frac{2}{5}$$

Another way to reduce a fraction is to write the factors of each term of the fraction, and then cross off the common factors.

Example 3

Reduce: $\frac{12}{18}$

We begin by writing the prime factorizations of the numerator and the denominator.

$$\frac{12}{18} = \frac{2 \cdot 2 \cdot 3}{2 \cdot 3 \cdot 3}$$

We then reduce both $\frac{2}{2}$ and $\frac{3}{3}$ to $\frac{1}{1}$. We show this by crossing off each factor that has been reduced and writing a 1 in its place.

$$\frac{12}{18} = \frac{\overset{1}{\cancel{2}} \cdot 2 \cdot \overset{1}{\cancel{3}}}{2 \cdot \underset{1}{\cancel{3}} \cdot 3}$$

We multiply the remaining factors in each term to find the simplest form of the fraction. We find that $\frac{12}{18}$ equals $\frac{1 \cdot 2 \cdot 1}{1 \cdot 1 \cdot 3}$, which reduces to $\frac{2}{3}$.

Lesson Practice

Reduce each fraction to lowest terms:

a. $\frac{4}{12}$ **b.** $\frac{6}{18}$ **c.** $\frac{16}{24}$

d. $\frac{4}{16}$ **e.** $\frac{12}{16}$ **f.** $\frac{60}{100}$

Solve. Reduce each answer to lowest terms.

g. $\frac{7}{16} + \frac{1}{16}$ **h.** $\frac{3}{4} \times \frac{4}{5}$ **i.** $\frac{19}{24} - \frac{1}{24}$

Write each percent as a reduced fraction:

j. 25%   **k.** 60%   **l.** 90%

Write the prime factorization of the numerator and the denominator of each fraction. Then reduce the fraction.

m. $\dfrac{6}{10}$ **n.** $\dfrac{8}{12}$ **o.** $\dfrac{30}{36}$

Written Practice
Distributed and Integrated

1. (20, 21) **Represent** Draw a pair of horizontal parallel segments. Make the lower segment longer than the upper segment. Make a quadrilateral by connecting the endpoints.

2. (50) **Estimate** Find the difference of 6970 and 3047 by rounding the numbers to the nearest thousand and then subtracting.

3. (24) **Classify** Classify each triangle by angles:

a.   **b.** 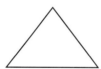   **c.**

Classify Classify each triangle by sides:

d.   **e.**   **f.**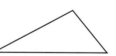

4. (70) Gloria practices the piano one hour each day. Today Gloria has practiced for 45 minutes. What percent of an hour has Gloria practiced? What percent of an hour does she still have to practice?

5. (58) Name the shaded portion of this square as a fraction, as a decimal number, and as a percent.

*6. a. What number is $\frac{1}{3}$ of 120?
(78)

   b. What number is $\frac{2}{3}$ of 120?

*7. Find the perimeter and area of the parallelogram.
(75)

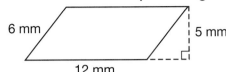

6 mm   5 mm

12 mm

8. (List) Write these fractions in order from least to greatest:
(15, 46, 62)

$$\frac{9}{18}, \frac{8}{7}, \frac{7}{16}, \frac{6}{6}, \frac{5}{8}$$

9. (Connect) To what mixed number is the arrow pointing?
(25)

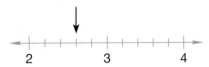

2   3   4

Multiply to find each product in problems **10** and **11**. Then reverse the order of factors to check your answers.

*10. $\frac{2}{3} \times 2$
(78)

*11. $\frac{3}{4}$ of 4
(78)

12. $3 - \left(2\frac{3}{5} - 1\frac{1}{5}\right)$
(28, 51)

13. $4.7 + 3.63 + 2.0$
(60)

14. 301.4
(60) $- 143.5$

15. 476
(44) $\times\ 890$

*16. Find the area of the triangle.
(76)

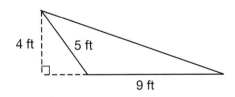

4 ft   5 ft

9 ft

17. $40\overline{)3480}$
(42)

18. $\$42.36 \div 6$
(23)

19. 22^2
(67)

20. a. What are the common factors of 60 and 100?
(16, 73)

   b. Use the GCF of 60 and 100 to reduce $\frac{60}{100}$.

21. Write a fraction equal to $\frac{3}{4}$ that has a denominator of 12. Then write a
(69)   fraction equal to $\frac{2}{3}$ that has a denominator of 12. Subtract the second
       fraction from the first fraction.

22. Since $\frac{3}{4} + \frac{3}{4} + \frac{3}{4} = \frac{9}{4}$, how many $\frac{3}{4}$'s are in $\frac{9}{4}$?
(Inv. 1)

*23. **a.** How many one sixths are in one third?
(79)
       b. How many one tenths are in one fifth?

24. (Interpret) Use the graph below to answer parts **a–c**.
(Inv. 5,
 74)

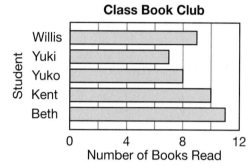

Class Book Club

a. How many more books must Yuki read to reach the goal of
       12 books?

b. Each book must have 180 pages or more. Kent has read at least
       how many pages so far?

c. What is the median number of books read by the five students?

25. What is the probability of rolling a number less than five with one toss of
(45, 71) a standard number cube? Write the probability as a reduced fraction.

*26. A quart is called a quart because it is a quarter of a gallon. What
(58, 77) percent of a gallon is a quart?

*27. Sixteen of the 24 students in Ms. Oliva's class are eating in the
(80)   cafeteria. What fraction are eating in the cafeteria? What fraction are
       not eating in the cafeteria?

*28. (Explain) For exercise, Jia walks $1\frac{1}{2}$ miles each morning and
(37, 62) $2\frac{1}{2}$ miles each evening. At that rate, how many days will it take Jia to
       walk 100 miles? Explain how you found your answer.

*29. A quarter is 25% of the value of a dollar. Write 25% as a reduced fraction.
(80)

*30. **(Represent)** A difference of 100° on the Celsius scale
(9, Inv. 7) is a difference of 180° on the Fahrenheit scale. So
a 10° change on the Celsius scale is an 18° change
on the Fahrenheit scale. Copy this thermometer on
your paper, and label the remaining tick marks on
the Fahrenheit scale.

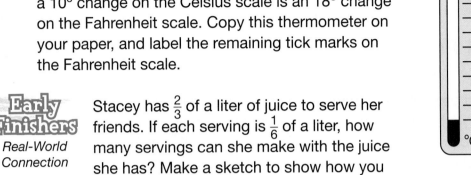

Early Finishers

Real-World Connection

Stacey has $\frac{2}{3}$ of a liter of juice to serve her
friends. If each serving is $\frac{1}{6}$ of a liter, how
many servings can she make with the juice
she has? Make a sketch to show how you
solved the problem.

California Mathematics Content Standards
AF 1.0, **1.5** Solve problems involving linear functions with integer values; write the equation; and graph the resulting ordered pairs of integers on a grid.
SDAP 1.0, **1.4** Identify ordered pairs of data from a graph and interpret the meaning of the data in terms of the situation depicted by the graph.
SDAP 1.0, **1.5** Know how to write ordered pairs correctly; for example, (x, y).

Focus on

Patterns and Functions

In Lesson 1 we introduced sequences as counting patterns that continue indefinitely. In each of the examples we looked at, we either counted up or down by a fixed amount. But there are many other possible patterns that can determine the terms of a sequence. Rather than adding or subtracting a fixed number, we could also multiply by a fixed number to produce the next terms.

Example 1

Math Language

Each number in a sequence is a term of the sequence. The first four terms of the given sequence are 3, 6, 12, and 24.

What rule seems to describe this sequence? Find the next two terms in the sequence.

$$3, 6, 12, 24, \underline{\quad}, \underline{\quad}, \ldots$$

Since $3 \times 2 = 6$, $6 \times 2 = 12$, and $12 \times 2 = 24$, we **multiply by 2** to find the next terms. Thus, the fifth term of the sequence is 24×2, or **48**, and the sixth term is 48×2, or **96.**

A sequence that counts up (adds) or counts down (subtracts) by the same amount is called an **arithmetic sequence.** A sequence that increases by multiplying by the same number or decreases by dividing by the same number is called a **geometric sequence.**

For problems **1–4** below, decide whether the sequence is arithmetic or geometric. Then write the next three terms.

1. 43, 49, 55, 61, \underline{\quad}, \underline{\quad}, \underline{\quad}, ...

2. 2, 4, 8, 16, \underline{\quad}, \underline{\quad}, \underline{\quad}, ...

3. 50, 48, 46, 44, \underline{\quad}, \underline{\quad}, \underline{\quad}, ...

4. 2, 6, 18, 54, \underline{\quad}, \underline{\quad}, \underline{\quad}, ...

5. Sally has saved $55. Each month she plans to add $8 to her savings. If she does not spend any of the money she saves, how much will Sally have after one month? Two months? Three months? What kind of sequence are we making?

6. The fruit fly population in an experiment doubled every week. If the experiment began with 50 fruit flies, what was the population after one week? Two weeks? Three weeks? What kind of sequence are we making?

Another kind of pattern found in sequences is **repetition.** This means that the terms of the sequence repeat themselves. The number of terms in a repeating unit is called the **period.**

Example 2

> **What appears to be the period of the following sequence? List the next three terms.**
>
> $$4, 5, 8, 4, 5, 8, 4, 5, \underline{\quad}, \underline{\quad}, \underline{\quad}, \ldots$$
>
> In this sequence, the unit "4, 5, 8" appears to be repeating, so the period is **three.** Since the last term given is 5, the next three terms would be **8, 4, 5.**

Science has demonstrated that the human brain searches for patterns in events and objects. Since the sun rises every day in the east and sets in the west, we expect the same to occur tomorrow. If we see a pattern in a section of floor tiles, we assume that the pattern continues over the whole floor. We might make similar assumptions about sequences. However, if the part of the sequence we are looking at is not large enough, we might assume a pattern that is not actually there. For example, if we see that a sequence begins with

$$4, 6, 4, 6, \ldots$$

we might assume that the sequence has a period of two and that the alternating 4's and 6's will continue. But those terms are also the beginning of the sequence

$$4, 6, 4, 6, 2, 4, 6, 4, 6, 2, \ldots$$

which seems to fit a very different pattern. Without clear information about the structure of a sequence, we must be aware that the patterns we see might not really be there.

7. Assuming the following sequence has a period of three, write the next three terms:

   $$4, 5, 9, 4, 5, 9, 4, \underline{\quad}, \underline{\quad}, \underline{\quad}, \ldots$$

8. Assuming the following sequence has a period of four, write the next three terms:

   $$5, 2, 3, 6, 5, 2, \underline{\quad}, \underline{\quad}, \underline{\quad}, \ldots$$

9. Assuming the following sequence has a period of four, write the next three terms:

   $$B, U, L, B, \underline{\quad}, \underline{\quad}, \underline{\quad}, \ldots$$

10. Assuming the sequence in problem **9** has a period of three, write the next three terms.

There are many types of patterns that sequences can follow. In the next example, we look at another kind of pattern.

Example 3

What pattern does this sequence appear to follow?

1, 0, 1, 0, 0, 1, 0, 0, 0, 1, ...

First one 0 separates 1's; then two 0's; then three 0's. It is reasonable to predict that there will be four more 0's before the next 1 that appears in the sequence.

1, 0, 1, 0, 0, 1, 0, 0, 0, 1, 0, 0, 0, 0, 1, ...

| 1 | 2 | 3 | 4 | zeros |

This sequence of 0's and 1's has 1's separated by an increasing number of 0's.

We can predict that there will then be five more 0's between 1's, six more 0's, and so on.

For problems **11–15**, describe the pattern that the sequence appears to follow. Then write the next few terms that seem to fit the pattern.

11. 1, 1, 2, 2, 3, 3, ...

12. 0, 2, 0, 4, 0, 6, 0, ...

13. A, B, D, E, G, H, ...

14. ⊤, ⊣, ⊥, ⊢, ⊤, ...

15. 1, 2, 1, 2, 3, 1, 2, 3, 4, ...

Some patterns can be seen more easily by recording the increase or decrease between terms.

Example 4

What are the next three terms in this sequence?

0, 1, 3, 6, 10, ...

We first find the difference between successive terms.

$$\overset{+2}{}\quad\overset{+3}{}\quad\overset{+4}{}$$
1, 3, 6, 10, ...

The increasing difference from one term to the next also forms a sequence. This sequence may be continued.

$$\overset{+2}{}\quad\overset{+3}{}\quad\overset{+4}{}\quad\overset{+5}{}\quad\overset{+6}{}\quad\overset{+7}{}$$
1, 3, 6, 10, _____, _____, _____, ...

We add 5 to 10 and get 15 for the next term. We add 6 to 15 and get 21 for the following term. We add 7 to 21 and get 28. We have found the next three terms.

1, 3, 6, 10, **15, 21, 28,** ...

Find the next three terms in each sequence:

16. 1, 4, 9, 16, 25, _____, _____, _____, ...

17. 2, 3, 5, 8, 12, _____, _____, _____, ...

Example 5

> Suppose the first two terms of a sequence are 3 and 4, and that we always get the next term by adding the previous two terms together. The third term would be 3 + 4 = 7. Find the fourth, fifth, and sixth terms of the sequence:
>
> **3, 4, 7,** _____, _____, _____, ...
>
> We find each term by adding the two preceding terms. Three and 4 were added to get the third term, 7. Now we add 4 and 7 to find the fourth term, 11.
>
> 3, 4, 7, _11_, _____, _____, ...
>
> We continue adding the two preceding terms. The sum of 7 and 11 is 18. The sum of 11 and 18 is 29.
>
> **3, 4, 7, 11, 18, 29,** ...

18. A famous sequence in mathematics is the **Fibonacci sequence,** which follows a pattern similar to the sequence in Example 5. Many patterns found in nature fit the Fibonacci sequence. Below we show the first six terms of the Fibonacci sequence. Find the next three terms.

1, 1, 2, 3, 5, 8, _____, _____, _____, ...

We have studied patterns in sequences. There are also patterns between pairs of numbers. Below we show a **function** table that shows the relationship between gallons and quarts. A function table can be written vertically or horizontally, as shown.

Gallons (x)	Quarts (y)
1	4
2	8
3	12
4	16
5	20

Gallons	1	2	3	5
Quarts	4	8	12	20

Math Language

A **function** is a rule that describes a relationship between two sets of data. For each number in the first set, there is only one corresponding number in the second set.

We can use words, a formula, an equation, or a graph to represent a function.

19. Use words to describe the rule of the function table above.

20. (**Formulate**) Write an equation to represent the rule. Use g for gallons and q for quarts.

We can graph the function if we use the pairs of numbers in the table as **ordered pairs.**

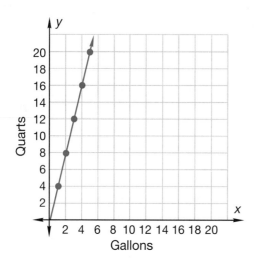

Math Language

This is a graph of a **linear function.** The graph of a linear function is a line.

21. How can we use *x* and *y* to write an equation for this function?

Predict Eight gallons of milk is how many quarts of milk? What ordered pair represents your prediction?

Example 6

Write the ordered pairs for this graph in a table. Then write an equation to represent the data. Finally, name a situation that the equation and the graph could represent.

x	y
1	3
2	?
3	?
4	?
5	?

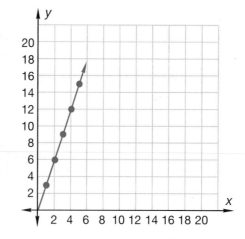

We can write the ordered pairs using the points on the graph. Read the x-axis first. Then read the y-axis. One point is $x = 1$ and $y = 3$. We write this as **(1, 3).** We can make a table to organize the ordered pairs.

Ordered Pairs

x	y
1	3
2	6
3	9
4	12
5	15

Look at the relationship shared by each pair of numbers. If we multiply each value for x by 3, the result is each value of y. Since this rule works for each pair of numbers, we can write the equation $3x = y$ or $y = 3x$ to represent the data. We usually write the y on the left side of the equal sign, so we write **$y = 3x$** to represent the data.

Now we can think of a situation that is represented by the equation. We need a situation where we multiply by 3. One possibility is the perimeter of an equilateral triangle. Since all of the sides of an equilateral triangle have the same length, we can find its perimeter using the formula $P = 3s$, where P = the perimeter and s = the length of each side. Since $P = 3s$ has the same relationship as $y = 3x$, the equation and graph can represent the **perimeter of an equilateral triangle.**

(**Connect**) Name another situation that has the same relationship as y = 3x. Explain your reasoning.

Example 7

Look at the equations below. Choose the equation that represents changing a number of quarts (q) to a number of pints (p). Then write ordered pairs for the equation and graph the pairs.

$$q = 2p \qquad p = 2q$$

Since 2 pints = 1 quart, the correct equation is not $q = 2p$ because when we substitute a number of pints for p, the result is twice as many quarts.

Instead, we need to multiply the number of quarts by 2 to find the number of pints, so we choose the equation **$p = 2q$.**

We can now write ordered pairs for the equation and then graph the pairs: **(1, 2), (2, 4), (3, 6), (4, 8), (5, 10).** We draw a line through the points because the relationship is continuous.

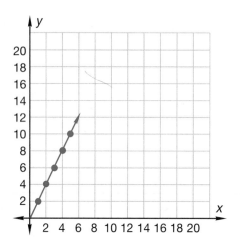

Verify Explain why this graph is the graph of a linear function.

22. **Explain** Which equation represents data in this table? Explain your reasoning.

x	y
1	6
2	8
3	10
4	12
5	14

$y = 6x$ or $y = 2x + 4$

23. Write a table of ordered pairs for this equation:

$$y = 3x + 2$$

24. Write a table of ordered pairs for the graph below. Then use x and y to write an equation that represents the graph. Name a situation that the equation and the graph could represent.

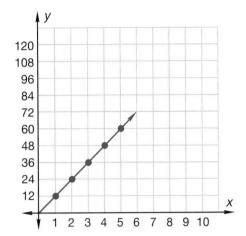

a. Explain why the equation $y = 3x - 2$ represents this pattern of cubes. Then create a set of ordered pairs for the equation and graph the result.

Position (x)   1   2   3   4   5   6

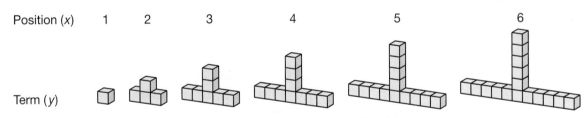

Term (y)

b. We can use toothpicks to build the following pattern.

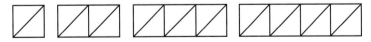

Explain why the equation $y = 4x + 1$ represents this pattern. Then create a set of ordered pairs for the equation and graph the results.

California Mathematics Content Standards

AF 1.0, 1.2 Use a letter to represent an unknown number; write and evaluate simple algebraic expressions in one variable by substitution.

MR 3.0, 3.2 Note the method of deriving the solution and demonstrate a conceptual understanding of the derivation by solving similar problems.

• Understanding Two-Step Equations

A two-step equation tells us how two operations are used to relate one variable to another variable. The equation $y = 4x + 2$ is a two-step equation that shows us how to find the value of y when we know the value of x. It means that we multiply the value of x by 4 and then add 2 to find the value of y.

Example 1

> **A taxi ride that costs $2 plus $4 per mile can be represented by the equation $y = 4x + 2$, where y is the cost in dollars and x is the number of miles. What is the cost of a 5-mile taxi ride?**
>
> We know that x is 5, so we multiply 4×5 and then subtract 2.
>
> $y = 4(5) - 2$
>
> $y = 20 - 2$
>
> $y = 18$
>
> When x is 5, y is 18. So the taxi ride costs **$18.**

Example 2

> **What will be the cost of a 3-mile taxi ride to the airport, a 7-mile taxi ride to the hotel, and then a 9-mile taxi ride to the museum?**
>
> We can make a table of the x- and y-values to find the answer.
>
> $4x + 2 = y$
>
> | x | y |
> |-----|-----|
> | 3 | 14 |
> | 7 | 30 |
> | 9 | 38 |
>
> "Multiply x by 4 and add 2" is the rule for the related data in this table.
>
> When x is 3, y is 14; when x is 7, y is 30; and when x is 9, y is 38. So the 3-mile taxi ride cost **$14,** the 7-mile taxi ride cost **$30,** and the 9-mile taxi ride cost **$38.**

Evaluate Find 3 more ordered pairs of x- and y-values that satisfy the equation $y = 4x + 2$.

California Mathematics Content Standards
NS 2.0, **2.3** Solve simple problems, including ones arising in concrete situations, involving the addition and subtraction of fractions and mixed numbers (like and unlike denominators of 20 or less), and express answers in the simplest form.
MR 2.0, 2.3 Use a variety of methods, such as words, numbers, symbols, charts, graphs, tables, diagrams, and models, to explain mathematical reasoning.

• Simplifying Improper Fractions

facts	Power Up H
estimation	Hold your hands about one foot apart. Hold your hands about one yard apart.

mental math

a. **Measurement:** One mile is how many feet?

b. **Fractional Parts:** $\frac{1}{4}$ of 30

c. **Fractional Parts:** $\frac{1}{4}$ of 300

d. **Powers/Roots:** 5^2

e. **Time:** After school James walks his dog for 30 minutes and then starts his homework. James is halfway through his daily walk. How long before James starts his homework?

f. **Percent:** 10% of $300

g. **Estimation:** Choose the more reasonable estimate for the diameter of a CD: 12 centimeters or 12 millimeters.

h. **Calculation:** 30×30, $+ 100$, $\div 2$, $- 100$, $\div 4$

problem solving

Choose an appropriate problem-solving strategy to solve this problem. List the possible arrangements of the letters A, E, and R. What percent of the possible arrangements spell English words?

New Concept

We have learned two ways to simplify fractions. We have converted improper fractions to whole numbers or mixed numbers, and we have reduced fractions. In some cases we need to use both ways to simplify a fraction. Consider the following story:

After the party some pizza was left over. There was $\frac{3}{4}$ of a pizza in one box and $\frac{3}{4}$ of a pizza in another box. Altogether, how much pizza was in the two boxes?

In this problem about combining, we add $\frac{3}{4}$ to $\frac{3}{4}$.

$$\frac{3}{4} + \frac{3}{4} = \frac{6}{4}$$

We see that the sum is an improper fraction. To convert an improper fraction to a mixed number, we divide the numerator by the denominator and write the remainder as a fraction.

$$\frac{6}{4} \rightarrow \begin{array}{r} 1\frac{2}{4} \leftarrow \text{remainder} \\ \leftarrow \text{fraction} \\ 4\overline{)6} \\ \underline{4} \\ 2 \end{array}$$

The improper fraction $\frac{6}{4}$ is equal to the mixed number $1\frac{2}{4}$. However, $1\frac{2}{4}$ can be reduced.

$$1\frac{2}{4} = 1\frac{1}{2}$$

The simplified answer to $\frac{3}{4} + \frac{3}{4}$ is $1\frac{1}{2}$.

(Discuss) Use fractions to explain why $1\frac{2}{4} = \frac{6}{4}$.

Example 1

Write $\frac{8}{6}$ as a mixed number in lowest terms.

To convert $\frac{8}{6}$ to a mixed number, we divide 8 by 6 and get $1\frac{2}{6}$. Then we reduce $1\frac{2}{6}$ by dividing both terms of the fraction by 2.

$$\overset{\text{Convert}}{\frac{8}{6} = 1\frac{2}{6}} \longrightarrow \overset{\text{Reduce}}{1\frac{2}{6} = \mathbf{1\frac{1}{3}}}$$

(Verify) Use fractions to explain why $1\frac{2}{6} = \frac{8}{6}$.

Example 2

The dictionary is $1\frac{7}{8}$ in. thick, and the thesaurus is $1\frac{3}{8}$ in. thick. If the two books are side by side, how thick are they altogether?

We add $1\frac{7}{8}$ and $1\frac{3}{8}$ to get $2\frac{10}{8}$. We convert the improper fraction $\frac{10}{8}$ to $1\frac{2}{8}$ and add it to the 2 to get $3\frac{2}{8}$. Finally, we reduce the fraction to get $\mathbf{3\frac{1}{4}}$.

$$\overset{\text{Add}}{1\frac{7}{8} + 1\frac{3}{8} = 2\frac{10}{8}} \longrightarrow \overset{\text{Convert}}{2\frac{10}{8} = 3\frac{2}{8}} \longrightarrow \overset{\text{Reduce}}{3\frac{2}{8} = 3\frac{1}{4}}$$

(Justify) Use fractions to explain why $2\frac{10}{8} = 3\frac{2}{8}$.

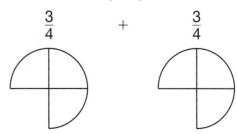

Activity

Modeling Improper Fractions

Materials needed:
- fraction manipulatives from Investigations 1 and 2

Use your fraction manipulatives to model each problem below. Write the mixed-number or whole-number answer for each problem. For example, model $\frac{3}{4} + \frac{3}{4}$ this way:

$$\frac{3}{4} \qquad + \qquad \frac{3}{4}$$

Then combine the pieces to show that $\frac{3}{4} + \frac{3}{4} = 1\frac{1}{2}$.

1. $\frac{1}{2} + \frac{1}{2} + \frac{1}{2}$　　　　　**2.** $\frac{3}{4} + \frac{3}{4}$

3. $\frac{5}{8} + \frac{5}{8}$　　　　　**4.** $\frac{2}{3} + \frac{2}{3}$

Lesson Practice　Simplify each fraction or mixed number:

a. $\frac{6}{4}$　　　**b.** $\frac{10}{6}$　　　**c.** $2\frac{8}{6}$　　　**d.** $3\frac{10}{4}$

e. $\frac{10}{4}$　　　**f.** $\frac{12}{8}$　　　**g.** $4\frac{14}{8}$　　　**h.** $1\frac{10}{8}$

Perform each indicated operation. Simplify your answers.

i. $1\frac{5}{6} + 1\frac{5}{6}$　　　**j.** $2\frac{3}{4} + 4\frac{3}{4}$　　　**k.** $\frac{5}{3} \times \frac{3}{2}$

l. **Connect** Each side of this square is $\frac{5}{8}$ inch long. What is the perimeter of the square? Show your work.

$\frac{5}{8}$ in.

Written Practice　*Distributed and Integrated*

1. **Analyze** Laquinta's rectangular garden is twice as long as it is wide.
(59) Her garden is 10 feet wide.

　a. What is the perimeter of her garden?

　b. What is the area of the garden?

2. **Multiple Choice** In which of these numbers does the 1 mean $\frac{1}{10}$?
(55)
　A 12.34　　　**B** 21.43　　　**C** 34.12　　　**D** 43.21

3. Arrange these numbers in order from least to greatest:
(56, 58)
$$1, 0, \frac{1}{2}, 0.3$$

*4. Two quarts of juice is how many ounces of juice?
(77)

5. **a.** A quarter is what fraction of a dollar?
(13, 19)

    b. How many quarters equal 1 dollar?

    c. How many quarters equal 3 dollars?

*6. Reduce each fraction to lowest terms:
(80)

    a. $\frac{8}{12}$ **b.** $\frac{18}{27}$ **c.** $\frac{12}{16}$ **d.** $\frac{15}{25}$

7. Multiple Choice If $a = 3$, then $2a + 5$ equals which of the
(8) following?

    A 10   **B** 11   **C** 16   **D** 28

8. Find the area of the triangle.
(76)

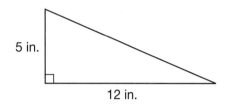

5 in.

12 in.

*9. Write a fraction equal to $\frac{1}{2}$ that has a denominator of 6. Then write a
(69) fraction equal to $\frac{1}{3}$ that has a denominator of 6. Subtract the second
fraction from the first fraction.

*10. **a.** Find the common factors of 20 and 50.
(73)

    b. Use the GCF of 20 and 50 to reduce $\frac{20}{50}$.

*11. $\frac{3}{5}$ of 4   ***12.** $\frac{1}{2} \div \frac{1}{12}$ **13.** $3\frac{7}{8} - 1\frac{1}{8}$
(78)   (79)   (71)

14. $2250 \div 50$ **15.** $5\overline{)225}$
(42)   (17)

*16. Evaluate. Justify each step of your solution.
(68)

    a. $8^2 - 4m$ when $m = 6$

    b. $q + 9^2 \div t$ when $q = 16$ and $t = 3$

17. $4\overline{)\$8.20}$ **18.** $20^2 - \sqrt{100}$ **19.** $\begin{array}{r} \$12.75 \\ \times \quad\quad 80 \\ \hline \end{array}$
(23)   (67)   (18)

20. Divide 100 by 8 and write the quotient as a mixed number. Then rewrite
(47, 71) the quotient by reducing the fraction part of the mixed number.

*21. How many one eighths are in one fourth?
(79)

*22. Since $\frac{2}{3} + \frac{2}{3} + \frac{2}{3} = 2$, how many $\frac{2}{3}$'s are in 2?
(79)

23. The diagram below shows the distance from Marysville to three other
(Inv. 7) towns. Use the information to answer the questions that follow.

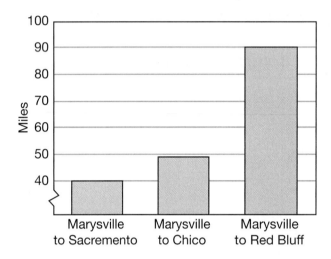

a. The distance from Marysville to Red Bluff is about how many miles
greater than the distance from Marysville to Sacramento?

b. The distance from Marysville to Chico is about how many miles less
than the distance from Marysville to Red Bluff?

*24. Simplify each fraction or mixed number:
(62, 81)
   a. $\frac{8}{3}$ **b.** $\frac{8}{6}$ **c.** $2\frac{6}{4}$ **d.** $3\frac{10}{6}$

*25. Perform each indicated operation. Simplify your answers.
(81)
   a. $2\frac{4}{6} + 2\frac{4}{6}$ **b.** $3\frac{5}{8} + 2\frac{7}{8}$ **c.** $\frac{5}{4} \times \frac{4}{3}$

26. In an 8-hour endurance race for automobiles, a car dropped out of the
(RF21) race after 5 hours 32 minutes. If the race ended at midnight, what time
was it when the car dropped out?

27. **Explain** On Sunday evening, Alonso studied for $\frac{3}{4}$ of an hour and
(81) read a mystery book for $1\frac{3}{4}$ hours. How many hours did Alonso spend
studying and reading on Sunday evening? Explain why your answer is
reasonable.

*28. Neftalen made $3\frac{1}{4}$ dozen oat bran muffins, and his sisters and their
(71) friends ate $\frac{3}{4}$ of a dozen muffins after they arrived home from school.
How many dozen muffins were not eaten?

29. (**Estimate**) The highest scoring regular season game in the National
(50) Basketball Association happened in 1983 when the Denver Nuggets
defeated the Detroit Pistons 186–184. About how many points
altogether were scored during that game?

30. (**Represent**) The temperature atop Mt. Wilson was recorded at 3-hour
(49) intervals, as shown in the table below. Display the data in line graph.

**Temperature on
Mount Wilson**

Time	Temperature
6:00 a.m.	4° C
9:00 a.m.	6° C
noon	9° C
3:00 p.m.	11° C
6:00 p.m.	8° C

(**Formulate**) Write two questions based on your graph.

LESSON

82

✎ *California Mathematics Content Standards*

NS 2.0, 2.2 Demonstrate proficiency with division, including division with positive decimals and long division with multidigit divisors.
MR 2.0, 2.4 Express the solution clearly and logically by using the appropriate mathematical notation and terms and clear language; support solutions with evidence in both verbal and symbolic work.
MR 2.0, 2.6 Make precise calculations and check the validity of the results from the context of the problem.

• Dividing by Two-Digit Numbers

facts	Power Up H
mental math	In the expression 3(40 + 6), the sum of 40 and 6 is multiplied by 3. By using the *Distributive Property,* we can first multiply each addend and then add the partial products.

$$3(40 + 6)$$

$$120 + 18 = 138$$

Use the Distributive Property to solve problems **a** and **b**.

   a. Number Sense: 3(20 + 7)

   b. Number Sense: 4(30 + 6)

   c. Powers/Roots: 6^2

   d. Time: What time is 30 minutes before 11:18 a.m.?

   e. Number Sense: Reduce the fractions $\frac{2}{4}$, $\frac{2}{6}$, $\frac{2}{8}$, and $\frac{2}{10}$.

   f. Number Sense: $\frac{1}{3}$ of 100

   g. Measurement: The classroom is 8 yards wide. How many feet is that?

   h. Calculation: $\sqrt{81}$, + 1, × 5, − 2, ÷ 4

problem solving	Choose an appropriate problem-solving strategy to solve this problem. Marissa is covering a 5-foot-by-3-foot bulletin board with blue and gold construction paper squares, making a checkerboard pattern. Each square is 1 foot by 1 foot. Copy this diagram on your paper, and complete the checkerboard pattern. What is the total area of the bulletin board? How many squares of each color does Marissa need?

5 ft

3 ft

B	G			
G	B			
B				

New Concept

In this lesson we will begin dividing by two-digit numbers. Dividing by two-digit numbers is necessary to solve problems like the following:

One hundred forty-four players signed up for soccer. If the players are separated into 12 equal teams, how many players will be on each team?

When we divide by a two-digit number, we continue to follow the four steps of division: divide, multiply, subtract, and bring down. When we divide by two-digit numbers, the "divide" step takes a little more thought because we have not memorized the two-digit multiplication facts.

Example 1

Thinking Skill

Verify

Why do we write the digit 1 in the quotient above the 5?

Divide: 150 ÷ 12

We begin by breaking the division into a smaller division problem. Starting from the first digit in 150, we try to find a number that 12 will divide into at least once. Our first smaller division is $12\overline{)15}$. We see that there is one 12 in 15, so we write "1" in the tens place above the digit 5 of the number 15. Then we multiply, subtract, and bring down.

$$\begin{array}{r} 1 \\ 12\overline{)150} \\ \underline{12} \\ 30 \end{array}$$

Now we begin a new division. This time we find $12\overline{)30}$. If we are not sure of the answer, we may need to try more than once to find the number of 12's in 30. We find that there are two 12's in 30. We write "2" in the ones place above the 0. Then we multiply and subtract. Since there is no digit to bring down, we are finished. The answer is **12 R 6.**

$$\begin{array}{r} 12 \text{ R } 6 \\ 12\overline{)150} \\ \underline{12} \\ 30 \\ \underline{24} \\ 6 \end{array}$$

Thinking Skill

Connect

Why can we use multiplication to check division?

To check our answer, we multiply 12 by 12 and then add the remainder, which is 6.

$$\begin{array}{r} 12 \quad \text{quotient} \\ \times\ 12 \quad \text{divisor} \\ \hline 144 \\ +\quad 6 \quad \text{remainder} \\ \hline 150 \quad \text{dividend} \end{array}$$

There are some "tricks" we can use to make dividing by two-digit numbers easier. One trick is to think of dividing by only the first digit.

Example 2

Divide: $32\overline{)987}$

We begin by breaking the division into the smaller division problem $32\overline{)98}$. Instead of thinking, "How many 32's are in 98?" we can use the first-digit trick and think, "How many 3's are in 9?" We see $32\overline{)98}$ but we think "$3\overline{)9}$." We try 3 as an answer. Since we are really finding $32\overline{)98}$, we write the 3 above the 8 of 98. Then we multiply 3 by 32, subtract, and bring down.

$$\begin{array}{r} 30\text{ R }27 \\ 32\overline{)987} \\ \underline{96} \\ 27 \\ \underline{0} \\ 27 \end{array}$$

Now we begin the new division, $32\overline{)27}$. Since there is not one 32 in 27, we write "0" in the ones place of the quotient; then we multiply and subtract. There are no digits to bring down, so we are finished. The answer is **30 R 27**. We can check our answer by multiplying 30 by 32 and then adding the remainder, 27.

$$\begin{array}{rl} 32 & \text{divisor} \\ \times\ 30 & \text{quotient} \\ \hline 960 & \\ +\ 27 & \text{remainder} \\ \hline 987 & \text{dividend} \end{array}$$

Example 3

A school principal is planning a field trip for 329 students, teachers, and parents. The principal needs to reserve buses for the trip. Each bus can hold 23 passengers. How many buses should the principal reserve?

$$\begin{array}{r} 14 \\ 23\overline{)329} \\ \underline{23} \\ 99 \\ \underline{92} \\ 7 \end{array}$$

We divide 329 by 23 to find the number of buses.

The remainder of the division is 7, which represents the number of people who will not have a ride if 14 buses are reserved. So we must increase the quotient. The principal should reserve **15 buses.**

Connect Why is the remainder in this problem important?

Lesson Practice

Divide:

a. $11\overline{)253}$ **b.** $21\overline{)253}$ **c.** $31\overline{)403}$

d. $12\overline{)253}$ **e.** $12\overline{)300}$ **f.** $23\overline{)510}$

g. One hundred forty-four players signed up for soccer. If the players are separated into 12 equal teams, how many players will be on each team?

Divide. Use the first-digit trick to help with the "divide" step.

h. $30\overline{)682}$ **i.** $32\overline{)709}$ **j.** $43\overline{)880}$

k. $22\overline{)924}$ **l.** $22\overline{)750}$ **m.** $21\overline{)126}$

n. If an amusement park ride can run every 8 minutes, and there are 75 minutes left until the park closes, how many more times can the ride be run today?

o. In problem **n,** the quotient included a remainder. Was the remainder important? Explain why or why not.

Written Practice
Distributed and Integrated

1. Write each precent as a decimal:
(72)
    a. 26%   **b.** 18%   **c.** 170%   **d.** 239%

2. Find the mean, median, mode, and range of this data set:
(74)

        12   8   10   16   23   5   17

3. When the decimal number three and twelve hundredths is subtracted
(55, 60) from four and twenty-five hundredths, what is the difference?

4. a. How many dimes are in $1?
(13, 19)

    b. How many dimes are in $5?

*5. What number is $\frac{2}{3}$ of 150?
(78)

*6. A half gallon of milk is how many quarts of milk?
(77)

7. Find the measures of the angles marked *A, B,* and *C* in this
(75) parallelogram:

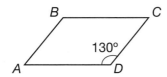

8. (**Analyze**) Write a fraction equal to one third that has a denominator of
(69) six. Then subtract that fraction from five sixths. Remember to reduce the answer.

9. a. What fraction of this rectangle is shaded? Reduce
(58, 71) the answer.

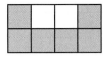

b. What percent of this rectangle is shaded?

*10. Solve. Reduce each answer to lowest terms.
(80)
a. $\frac{5}{8} + \frac{1}{8}$ **b.** $\frac{3}{4} \times \frac{2}{3}$ **c.** $\frac{15}{16} - \frac{3}{16}$

*11. Compare: $\frac{3}{5} + \frac{3}{5} + \frac{3}{5}$ ◯ $3 \times \frac{3}{5}$
(78)

12. Multiple Choice In this drawing, which angle appears
(20) to be obtuse?

A $\angle ABC$ **B** $\angle ABD$

C $\angle BDC$ **D** $\angle DAB$

*13. $\frac{1}{8} \times 3$ ***14.** $\frac{3}{8} \div \frac{1}{8}$
(78) (79)

*15. a. How many $\frac{1}{4}$'s are in 1?
(71, 78)

b. $\frac{1}{6} \times 4$

16. $\frac{1}{4} + \frac{1}{4}$ **17.** $\frac{7}{8} - \frac{1}{8}$ **18.** $5 - 1\frac{3}{10}$
(71) (71) (51)

*19. There are 208 students in the fifth grade at Brackenridge Elementrary.
(82) The science teacher is taking them on a field trip to visit Morro Rock,
an extinct volcano peak, where they hope to see Peregrine falcons
in their protected home. The students will travel on buses that can
hold 42 people. How many buses will be needed for all the fifth grade
students?

*20. Divide:
(82)
a. $13\overline{)342}$ **b.** $21\overline{)384}$ **c.** $11\overline{)341}$

21. 30^2 **22.** 340×607 **23.** $9\overline{)\$7.65}$
(67) (44) (17)

24. **Interpret** Use the school schedule below to answer parts **a** and **b**.
Inv. 5

School Schedule	
Reading	8:00–8:50
Math	8:50–9:40
Recess	9:40–10:10
Language	10:10–10:50
Science	10:50–11:30
Lunch	11:30–12:30

    a. How many total minutes are spent each morning in Reading and Language?

    b. If students come back for 2 hours 10 minutes after lunch, then at what time does school end?

25. Room 16 is 30 feet long and 30 feet wide. What is the floor area of the room?
(59)

26. **Conclude** Write the next three terms of this arithmetic sequence:
(Inv. 8)

$$\frac{1}{2}, 1, 1\frac{1}{2}, 2, 2\frac{1}{2}, 3, \underline{\quad}, \underline{\quad}, \underline{\quad}, \dots$$

*27. **Analyze** Without looking, Jevonte chose one marble from a bag
(45, 71) containing 2 red marbles, 3 white marbles, and 10 black marbles. Find the probability that the marble Jevonte chose was black. Write the answer as a reduced fraction.

*28. Find the perimeter of this rectangle:
(81)

$\frac{5}{8}$ in.

$1\frac{5}{8}$ in.

*29. A portion of this square inch is shaded. What is the area of the shaded rectangle?
(72, 76)

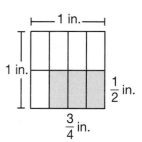

Lesson 82   **615**

30. The year 1983 was the 200th anniversary of the world's first hot air balloon
(37) flight. Fifty-six years after that flight, the world's first pedaled bicycle was
invented. In what year was the pedaled bicycle invented?

*Real-World
Connection*

Dala and Marcela just finished decorating their room. They have $\frac{3}{4}$ of
a gallon of paint left in one bucket and $\frac{1}{2}$ of a gallon of paint in another
bucket.

   a. Use your fraction manipulatives to find out how much paint they have
   altogether.

   b. They also used several rolls of wallpaper border. They have $\frac{15}{8}$ rolls left.
   Simplify the number of rolls of wallpaper to determine how many rolls
   they have left.

✎ **California Mathematics Content Standards**

AF 1.0, 1.1 Use information taken from a graph or equation to answer questions about a problem situation.

SDAP 1.0, 1.4 Identify ordered pairs of data from a graph and interpret the meaning of the data in terms of the situation depicted by the graph.

SDAP 1.0, 1.5 Know how to write ordered pairs correctly; for example, (x, y).

• Comparative Graphs

facts	Power Up H
estimation	Hold your hands about one yard apart. Hold your hands about one inch apart.

mental math

a. **Measurement:** One mile is how many feet?

b. **Number Sense:** 6(20 + 3)

c. **Number Sense:** 7(30 + 5)

d. **Number Sense:** Reduce the fractions $\frac{2}{8}$, $\frac{4}{8}$, and $\frac{6}{8}$.

e. **Number Sense:** $33\frac{1}{3} + 33\frac{1}{3}$

f. **Probability:** To determine who will give the first speech, Alan, Bill, Christie, and Denise put their names in a hat. The teacher will draw one name. What is the probability that either Alan's or Christie's name will be drawn?

g. **Estimation:** Choose the more reasonable estimate for the width of a street: 25 inches or 25 feet.

h. **Calculation:** 50% of $\sqrt{36}$, × 4, ÷ 2, × 6

problem solving

Choose an appropriate problem-solving strategy to solve this problem. Nicole reads the package of fertilizer and sees that it contains enough to cover 225 square meters. Nicole's yard has the dimensions shown at right. The rectangle in the middle of the yard represents an area where fertilizer will not be used. How many packages does Nicole need to purchase to fertilize the yard? Explain your reasoning.

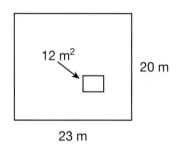

New Concept

Comparative graphs can be used to display two or more sets of related data.

Example 1

Thinking Skill

Analyze

How many bars can a bar graph have?

Bar graphs usually do not have a great number of bars. Why not?

The average daily high temperature in January and July for five cities is displayed in the comparative vertical bar graph below.

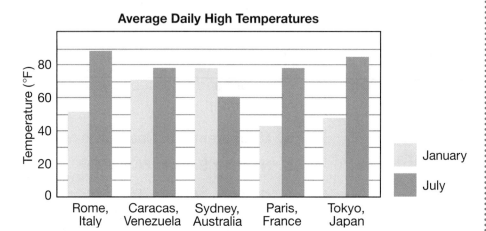

Average Daily High Temperatures

a. **In which city was the average July high temperature highest?**

b. **In which city was the average January high temperature lowest?**

c. **Which city had the smallest range between these temperatures? Do you know why?**

d. **For which city is the average January high temperature greater than the average July high temperature? Do you know why?**

a. The tallest dark blue bar appears above **Rome, Italy.** The average July high temperature is about 89°F in Rome.

b. The shortest light blue bar appears above **Paris, France.** The average January high temperature is about 42°F in Paris.

c. The smallest difference in heights of the bars occurs above **Caracas, Venezuela.** Caracas is near the equator, and temperatures in locations near the equator do not vary much throughout the year.

d. We look for the city that has a light blue bar that is taller than its dark blue bar. We find **Sydney, Australia.** Australia is warmer in January than in July because it is south of the equator, where January is in the summer and July is in the winter.

Example 2

We can use a double-line graph to show how two or more things change in relation to one another. For example, the double-line graph below shows the change in population of the cities of Austin, Texas, and Pittsburgh, Pennsylvania, from 1950 to 2000. The legend to the right tells which line belongs to which city.

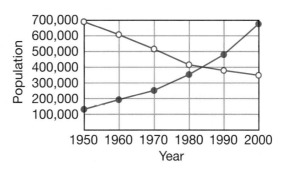

a. What was Austin's approximate population in 1970?

b. Approximately how much did Pittsburgh's population decrease between 1950 and 2000?

a. The line graph with solid dots represents Austin's population. For 1970, the dot is about halfway between 200,000 and 300,000, which means the population was **about 250,000.**

b. In the 50-year period, Pittsburgh's population declined from about 700,000 to about 350,000. Subtracting, we find that the decrease was **approximately 350,000.**

$$700,000 - 350,000 = 350,000$$

Example 3

Compare line m and line k. Which line represents the perimeter of a square? Which line represents the perimeter of an equilateral triangle?

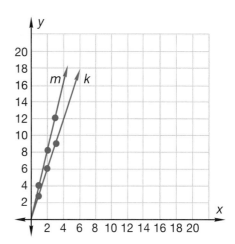

We look at line *m* and write a table of ordered pairs for the points on the line. We notice that every *y*-coordinate is four times greater than every *x*-coordinate. This relationship is the same relationship that is shared by the perimeter of a square and the lengths of its four sides. **So line *m* and the equation *y* = 4*x* represent the perimeter of a square.**

line *m*

x	y
1	4
2	8
3	12

We now verify that line *k* represents the perimeter of an equilateral triangle. We look at line *k* and write a table of ordered pairs for the points on the line.

line *k*

x	y
1	3
2	6
3	9

We notice that every *y*-coordinate is three times greater than every *x*-coordinate. This relationship is the same relationship that is shared by the perimeter of an equilateral triangle and the lengths of its three sides. **So line *k* and the equation *y* = 3*x* represent the perimeter of an equilateral triangle.**

Lesson Practice

a. Lana, Felicia, Alberto, and José each take two quizzes. Each quiz has ten questions. The scores on the quizzes are shown in the table below. Make a comparative **horizontal** bar graph to show the scores. There should be two bars for each student.

Student	Quiz 1	Quiz 2
Lana	8	8
Felicia	3	6
Alberto	6	7
José	7	10

b. For a science project, Mekelle and Bernardo each planted a seed. A record of the height of each seedling is shown below. Display the data in a double-line graph.

	Week 1	Week 2	Week 3	Week 4
Mekelle's Seedling	1 cm	5 cm	11 cm	20 cm
Bernardo's Seedling	2 cm	4 cm	10 cm	16 cm

c. Write a table of ordered pairs for the points on this line, write an equation to represent the relationship of the data, and then name a real-world conversion that the graph could represent.

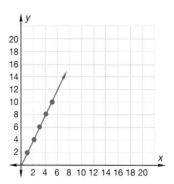

1. Find the area of the triangle.
(76)

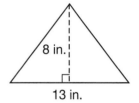

8 in.

13 in.

2. **Analyze** Shandi won $10,000. She will be paid $20 a day until she
(13, 42) receives the entire $10,000.

    a. How many days will she be paid $20?

    b. Is that greater or less than a year?

3. **Multiple Choice** Which of these numbers is divisible by both
(14) 4 and 5?

    A 15   **B** 16   **C** 20   **D** 25

4. Arrange these numbers in order from least to greatest:
(56, 58)
$$0.5, \frac{3}{2}, 1, 10\%, 0, 1.1$$

5. **a.** How many half-gallon cartons of milk equal 1 gallon?
(77)

    b. How many half-gallon cartons of milk equal 3 gallons?

6. **Represent** Use digits to write the number one million, three hundred
(41) fifty-four thousand, seven hundred sixty.

7. **Analyze** Write a fraction equal to $\frac{1}{2}$ that has a denominator of 6. Then
(69, 71) subtract that fraction from $\frac{5}{6}$. Remember to reduce the answer.

8. a. What fraction of the circles are shaded? Reduce the fraction.
(19, 71)

    b. What percent of the circles are shaded?

*9. Write each percent as a reduced fraction:
(80)
    a. 50%   **b.** 75%   **c.** 80%

10. Write the length of the segment below as a number of centimeters and
(32) as a number of millimeters.

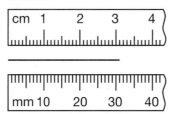

*11. $\frac{2}{5}$ of 3
(78)

12. $\frac{2}{5} + \frac{2}{5} + \frac{2}{5}$
(62)

13. $1\frac{1}{4} + 1\frac{1}{4}$
(71)

14. $3\frac{5}{6} - 1\frac{1}{6}$
(71)

*15. Stefano has folding lap trays that are $1\frac{3}{4}$ inches thick when folded up.
(81) If Stefano stacks all four trays on top of each other in the cabinet, how
tall will the stack of four trays be?

16. $10 − (57¢ + $2.48)
(7, 57)

17. 42 × 5 × 36
(44)

18. $6.15 × 10
(18)

19. 40)‾2760‾
(42)

20. 4w = 276
(17)

*21. $\frac{1}{2} \div \frac{1}{10}$
(79)

22. $\frac{1}{2} \times \frac{6}{8}$
(63, 71)

*23. Two hundred ten people came to participate in the cancer walk.
(82) Fourteen tents were set up for people to take shade under. If the total
number of people were divided evenly among all the tents, how many
people would be at each of the tents?

24. Use this information to answer parts **a** and **b**.
(37)

When Jenny was born, her dad was 29 years old. Her brothers are Omar and Monty. Omar is 2 years older than Jenny and 2 years younger than Monty. Monty is 10 years old.

   a. How old is Jenny?   **b.** How old is Jenny's dad?

25. $\sqrt{25} - \sqrt{9}$ **26.** $3^2 + 4^2$
(67)   (67)

27. (List) A dime is tossed and then a quarter is tossed. One possible
(45) outcome is dime:heads, quarter:tails. List the three other possible outcomes.

28. **a.** What fraction of a quart is a pint?
(63, 77)

    b. What fraction of a gallon is a quart?

    c. What fraction of a gallon is a pint?

    d. The answers to parts **a–c** show that one half of one fourth equals what fraction?

*29. The service club at the high school held a canned food drive at the
(83) school for one week in the fall and one week in the spring. Display the data below in a double line graph.

	M	T	W	Th	F
Fall Drive	26	32	30	28	41
Spring Drive	33	29	38	40	47

*30. For two consecutive Fridays, the students in Coach DeLeon's P.E.
(83) classes held free-throw contests. The number of shots made by the top four shooters are shown in the table below. Make a comparative bar graph to show the results.

Free Throws Made

Student	1st Friday	2nd Friday
Jorge M.	16	20
Sammy L.	12	15
Anthony C.	18	16
Thomas G.	20	24

✎ *California Mathematics Content Standards*
NS 2.0, 2.2 Demonstrate proficiency with division, including division with positive decimals and long division with multidigit divisors.
MR 2.0, 2.1 Use estimation to verify the reasonableness of calculated results.

• Estimating the First Digit of a Quotient

---

facts	Power Up H
mental math	**a. Number Sense:** $9(30 + 2)$
	b. Number Sense: $8(30 + 4)$
	c. Number Sense: Reduce the fractions $\frac{2}{6}$, $\frac{3}{6}$, and $\frac{4}{6}$.
	d. Measurement: An adult horse can weigh about half a ton. Half a ton equals how many pounds?
	e. Percent: 10% of $500
	f. Powers/Roots: 7^2
	g. Probability: Manny plans to flip a coin 50 times and record the results. Is it certain, likely, unlikely, or impossible that *all* the coin flips will be tails?
	h. Calculation: $\frac{1}{3}$ of 60, $+ 1$, $\div 3$, $\times 5$, $+ 1$, $\div 4$
problem solving	Choose an appropriate problem-solving strategy to solve this problem. A permutation is an arrangement of numbers or objects in a particular order. For example, if we take the combination (1, 2, 3) from the set of counting numbers, we can form six permutations. Four of the permutations are (1, 2, 3), (1, 3, 2), (2, 1, 3), and (2, 3, 1). What are the remaining two permutations for these three numbers?

In Lesson 82, we learned a method to help us divide by two-digit numbers. The problems in that lesson were chosen so that using the first digit to guess the division answer would work. However, this method does not always work. In this lesson we will learn another strategy for two-digit division.

Using the first-digit trick for $19\overline{)59}$, we would follow this process:

We see: We think: We try the guess, but the guess is too large:

$$\begin{array}{c} ? \\ 19\overline{)59} \end{array} \longrightarrow \begin{array}{c} ⑤ \\ 1\overline{)5} \end{array} \qquad \begin{array}{c} 5 \\ 19\overline{)59} \\ ㊙95 \end{array}$$

Our guess, 5, is incorrect because there are not five 19's in 59. Our guess is too large. So we will **estimate**. To estimate, we mentally round both numbers to the nearest 10. Then we use the first-digit trick with the rounded numbers.

We see: We round: We think: We try:

$$19\overline{)59} \longrightarrow 20\overline{)60} \longrightarrow \begin{array}{c} ③ \\ 2\overline{)6} \end{array} \begin{array}{c} 3\ \text{R}\ 2 \\ 19\overline{)59} \\ \underline{57} \\ 2 \end{array}$$

Example

Divide: $19\overline{)595}$

We begin by breaking the division into the smaller division problem $19\overline{)59}$. We round to $20\overline{)60}$ and focus on the first digits, $2\overline{)6}$. We guess 3, so we write the 3 above the 9 of 59. Then we multiply 3 by 19, subtract, and bring down. The next division is $19\overline{)25}$. We may estimate to help us divide. We write "1" in the answer, and then we multiply and subtract.

The answer is **31 R 6**. To check our answer, we multiply 31 by 19 and add the remainder, which is 6.

Lesson Practice   Divide:

a. $19\overline{)792}$ **b.** $30\overline{)600}$ **c.** $29\overline{)121}$

d. $29\overline{)900}$ **e.** $48\overline{)829}$ **f.** $29\overline{)1210}$

g. $28\overline{)896}$ **h.** $18\overline{)782}$ **i.** $39\overline{)1200}$

Written Practice

Distributed and Integrated

1. Find the GCF of each pair of numbers:
(73)
    a. 9 and 12   **b.** 4 and 8   **c.** 12 and 18

2. (**Analyze**) Write fractions equal to $\frac{1}{2}$ and $\frac{3}{5}$ with denominators of 10.
(62, 69) Then add the fractions. Remember to convert the answer to a mixed number.

3. a. How many quarts of milk are in 1 gallon?
(77)
    b. How many quarts of milk are in 6 gallons?

4. Find the sum when the decimal number fourteen and seven tenths is
(55, 60) added to the decimal number four and four tenths.

5. Name the shaded portion of this rectangle as a decimal
(58) number, as a reduced fraction, and as a percent.

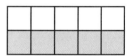

*6. Simplify each improper fraction or mixed number:
(81)
    a. $\frac{14}{4}$ **b.** $\frac{10}{8}$ **c.** $2\frac{9}{6}$ **d.** $3\frac{12}{10}$

7. Multiple Choice In this rectangle, which segment is
(20) parallel to $\overline{AB}$?

    A $\overline{BC}$ **B** $\overline{CD}$

    C $\overline{BD}$ **D** $\overline{DA}$

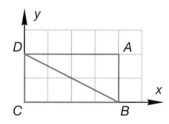

8. Classified by angles, what type of triangle is triangle *BCD*?
(24)

*9. Divide. Use the first-digit trick to help with the "divide" step.
(82)
    a. $24\overline{)316}$ **b.** $34\overline{)478}$ **c.** $41\overline{)895}$

10. $\frac{5}{6} + \frac{5}{6}$ **11.** $\frac{5}{6} \times 2$
(62)   (78)

*12. $\frac{2}{5} \div \frac{1}{10}$ ***13.** $\frac{1}{12} + \frac{7}{12}$
(79)   (28, 80)

*14. A survey was conducted in the small community. All the students in the
(83) elementary school, middle school, and high school were asked whether
they like Math or English more this school year. The comparative bar
graph shows the percentages of all the votes.

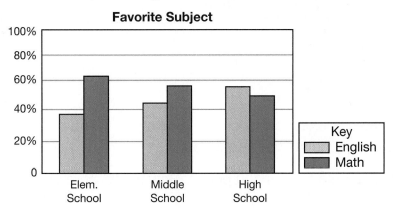

a. Which group enjoyed Math most? Which group enjoyed Math
least?

b. Which group enjoyed English more? Which group enjoyed English
less?

*15. $\dfrac{2}{3} \times \dfrac{3}{4}$
(63, 80)

*16. Divide:
(84)
    a. $40\overline{)800}$ **b.** $28\overline{)134}$ **c.** $18\overline{)767}$

17. $8.36 - 4.7$ **18.** 40^2 **19.** $\sqrt{36} + \sqrt{64}$
(60)   (67)   (67)

*20. Divide:
(84)
    a. $38\overline{)782}$ **b.** $29\overline{)696}$ **c.** $48\overline{)1240}$

21. $5n = 240$ **22.** $1 \div \dfrac{1}{3}$
(17)   (79)

23. $\dfrac{3}{4} \times 3$ **24.** $\dfrac{3}{5} \times \square = \dfrac{60}{100}$
(78)   (69)

25. The table below lists ways Manuel can earn extra credit in Social
(Inv. 5) Studies. Use the table to answer questions that follow.

Extra Credit

Magazine report	35 points
TV report	50 points
Book report	75 points
Museum report	100 points

a. Manuel has done a book report, two magazine reports, and a
TV report. How many points has he earned?

b. Manuel wants to earn a total of 400 points. How many more points
does he need?

26. (Analyze) A bag contains 3 red marbles, 5 white marbles, 2 blue marbles,
(45, 71) and 6 orange marbles. A marble is drawn without looking. Find the probability
that the marble is orange. Write the answer as a reduced fraction.

27. The area of this square is 25 square inches.
(59)

a. How long is each side of the square?

b. What is its perimeter?

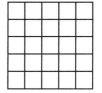

*28. (Generalize) What is the next term of the sequence below? Describe
(21, Inv. 8) the pattern in words.

29. a. (List) Write the factors of 16 in order from
(16, 74, 67) least to greatest.

b. Is the number of factors odd or even?

c. What is the median of the factors?

d. What is $\sqrt{16}$?

30. (Explain) Yvonne is car shopping. One model she likes costs
(50) $23,460. Another model she likes costs $24,575. What is a reasonable
estimate of the cost difference of those two models? Explain how you
found your answer.

LESSON
85

California Mathematics Content Standards
NS 2.0, 2.4 Understand the concept of multiplication and division of fractions.
MR 2.0, 2.3 Use a variety of methods, such as words, numbers, symbols, charts, graphs, tables, diagrams, and models, to explain mathematical reasoning.

• Reciprocals

facts   Power Up H

**mental
math**

    a. Measurement: 3 × (2 pounds 4 ounces)

    b. Measurement: 3 × (4 pounds 6 ounces)

    c. Measurement: One mile equals how many feet?

    d. Measurement: Half a pound equals how many ounces?

    e. Number Sense: Reduce the fractions $\frac{2}{10}$, $\frac{4}{10}$, $\frac{6}{10}$, and $\frac{8}{10}$.

    f. Number Sense: $33\frac{1}{3} + 66\frac{2}{3}$

    g. Probability: The sides of a number cube are labeled 1 through 6. If the cube is rolled once, what is the probability that the number will be a 5 or 6?

    h. Calculation: $\frac{1}{2}$ of 5, × 2, × 5, × 4

**problem
solving**
Choose an appropriate problem-solving strategy to solve this problem. Two cups equals a pint. Two pints equals a quart. Two quarts equals a half gallon. Two half gallons equals a gallon. One pint and one quart is a total of how many cups?

New Concept

If we switch the numerator and denominator of a fraction, the new fraction is the **reciprocal** of the first fraction. The reciprocal has the same terms, but their positions are reversed. When we switch the positions of the numerator and denominator, we **invert** the fraction.

The reciprocal of $\frac{2}{3}$ is $\frac{3}{2}$.

The reciprocal of $\frac{3}{2}$ is $\frac{2}{3}$.

Counting numbers also have reciprocals. Recall that a counting number may be written as a fraction by writing a 1 under the counting number. So the counting number 2 may be written as $\frac{2}{1}$. To find the reciprocal of $\frac{2}{1}$, we invert the fraction and get $\frac{1}{2}$.

Since $2 = \frac{2}{1}$, the reciprocal of 2 is $\frac{1}{2}$.

Notice that the product of $\frac{1}{2}$ and 2 is 1.

$$\frac{1}{2} \times 2 = \frac{1}{2} \times \frac{2}{1} = 1$$

The product of any counting number and its reciprocal is 1.

$$\frac{2}{3} \times \frac{3}{2} = \frac{6}{6} = 1 \qquad \frac{1}{2} \times \frac{2}{1} = \frac{2}{2} = 1$$

Verify Think of a fraction and write it on your paper. Then, write the reciprocal of the fraction. Now multiply the fraction and its reciprocal. What is the product?

Notice that reciprocals appear when we ask these division questions:

How many $\frac{1}{2}$'s are in 1? Answer: 2 (or $\frac{2}{1}$)

How many $\frac{1}{3}$'s are in 1? Answer: 3 (or $\frac{3}{1}$)

How many $\frac{1}{4}$'s are in 1? Answer: 4 (or $\frac{4}{1}$)

How much of 4 is in 1? Answer: $\frac{1}{4}$

The reciprocal also appears as the answer to this question:

How many $\frac{2}{3}$'s are in 1? Answer: $1\frac{1}{2}$ (or $\frac{3}{2}$)

One $\frac{2}{3}$ + half of $\frac{2}{3}$ =   1

When we divide 1 by any number (except 0), the answer is the reciprocal of the number.

Example 1

What is the reciprocal of $\frac{5}{6}$?

The reciprocal of $\frac{5}{6}$ is $\frac{6}{5}$. We leave the answer as an improper fraction.

Thinking Skill

Model

Use the fraction manipulatives to show the reciprocal of $\frac{1}{4}$.

Thinking Skill

Model

Use the fraction manipulatives to show how many $\frac{2}{5}$'s are in 1.

Example 2

What is the product of $\frac{1}{3}$ and its reciprocal?

The reciprocal of $\frac{1}{3}$ is $\frac{3}{1}$. To find the product, we multiply.

$$\frac{1}{3} \times \frac{3}{1} = 1$$

The product of any fraction and its reciprocal is 1.

Example 3

What is the reciprocal of 4?

To find the reciprocal of a counting number, we may first write the counting number as a fraction by writing a 1 under it. To write 4 as a fraction, we write $\frac{4}{1}$. The reciprocal of $\frac{4}{1}$ is $\frac{1}{4}$.

Example 4

Divide: $1 \div \frac{3}{4}$

This problem means, "How many $\frac{3}{4}$'s are in 1?" When we divide 1 by any number other than zero, the quotient is the reciprocal. So the answer to this division is the reciprocal of $\frac{3}{4}$, which is $\frac{4}{3}$, or $1\frac{1}{3}$. We check the answer by multiplying the quotient $\frac{4}{3}$ by the divisor $\frac{3}{4}$.

$$\frac{4}{3} \times \frac{3}{4} = \frac{12}{12} = 1$$

The result is the original dividend, 1, so the answer is correct.

Lesson Practice

Write the reciprocal of each number in problems **a–l**. Leave improper fractions as improper fractions.

a. $\frac{4}{5}$ **b.** $\frac{6}{5}$ **c.** 3 **d.** $\frac{7}{8}$

e. $\frac{3}{8}$ **f.** 5 **g.** $\frac{3}{10}$ **h.** $\frac{5}{12}$

i. 2 **j.** $\frac{1}{5}$ **k.** 10 **l.** 1

m. How many $\frac{3}{5}$'s are in 1? **n.** Divide: $1 \div \frac{4}{5}$

o. (**Analyze**) Think of a fraction and write it down. Then write its reciprocal. Multiply the two fractions and reduce your answer. What is the product? (Be sure to show your work.)

p. Is the following sentence true or false? If the product of two numbers is 1, then the two numbers are reciprocals.

1. Two fathoms deep is 12 feet deep. How deep is 10 fathoms?
(37)

2. ✏️ **Explain** When Nekell babysits, she is paid $6.50 per hour. If she
(37) babysits Saturday from 10:30 a.m. to 3:30 p.m., how much money will she be paid? Explain how you found your answer.

3. **Represent** Use digits to write the number one hundred fifty-four million,
(41) three hundred forty-three thousand, five hundred fifteen.

4. a. How many quarter-mile laps does Oluwaposi have to run to
(79) complete 1 mile?

   b. How many quarter-mile laps does Oluwaposi have to run to complete 5 miles?

5. **Analyze** Write a fraction equal to $\frac{3}{4}$ that has a denominator of 8. Add
(62, 69) that fraction to $\frac{5}{8}$. Remember to convert the answer to a mixed number.

6. What mixed number names the number of shaded
(27, 71) hexagons?

7. The Flanagans' new home has a rectangular backyard 45 ft by
(75) 60 ft. They want to put a fence around the whole yard, so they must figure the perimeter. Then they want to buy 1-foot grass squares to cover the entire yard, so they must figure the area. Draw a diagram of the backyard and determine the amount of fencing and number of squares of grass they need.

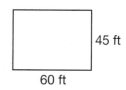

8. Compare: $\frac{1}{2}$ of 2 $\bigcirc$ 2 $\times \frac{1}{2}$
(15)

*9. Fifteen different swimming classes are offered for the summer at the
(82) city pool. Ananda's job is to put the 135 people who signed up into the different classes. If she is able to divide them evenly, how many people will be in each class?

10. *AB* is 3.2 cm. *BC* is 1.8 cm. *CD* equals *BC*. Find *AD*.
(60)

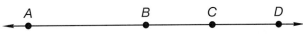

*11. $1\frac{3}{4} + 1\frac{3}{4}$
(81)

12. $5\frac{7}{8} - 1\frac{3}{8}$
(28, 71)

*13. $3 \times \frac{3}{8}$
(78, 81)

14. $10 - (\$1.25 + 35¢)$
(7, 57)

*15. Even though they are twins, Anthony and Rodrigo are different heights
(83) and have had growth spurts at different times. The double line graph
shows their heights at various ages.

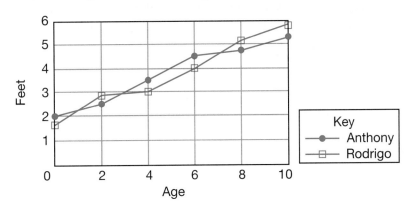

a. At which ages was Anthony taller?

b. At which ages was Rodrigo taller?

c. At which ages were Anthony and Rodrigo about the same height?

16.   416
(44) $\times\, 740$

*17. Divide:
(84)
    a. $19\overline{)635}$ **b.** $28\overline{)697}$ **c.** $39\overline{)858}$

*18. Write the reciprocal of each number. Leave improper fractions as
(85) improper fractions.
    a. $\frac{3}{5}$ **b.** $\frac{1}{6}$ **c.** $\frac{5}{8}$ **d.** $\frac{7}{12}$

19. $80\overline{)9600}$
(42)

20. $5m = \$12.00$
(17, 23)

*21. $\frac{5}{2} \times \frac{2}{3}$
(63, 81)

22. $\frac{2}{3} \div \frac{1}{3}$
(79)

23. $\frac{2}{3} \div \frac{1}{6}$
(79)

*24. **a.** What is the reciprocal of $\frac{2}{3}$?
(85)

b. What is the product of $\frac{3}{4}$ and its reciprocal?

c. What is the reciprocal of 7?

*25. (Conclude) Assuming that the sequence below repeats with period 3,
(Inv. 8) write the next 5 terms.

$$4, 4, 1, 4, 4, \ldots$$

26. The days of the week are Sunday, Monday, Tuesday, Wednesday,
(74) Thursday, Friday, and Saturday. Make a list of the number of letters in
each name. Friday, for instance, has 6 letters and Saturday has 8. Refer
to your list of numbers to answer parts **a–d.**

a. What number is the median?

b. What number is the mode?

c. What is the range?

d. Find the mean, and write it as a mixed number.

*27. Divide: $1 \div \frac{3}{7}$
(85)

28. On a very cold day, the high temperature was 19°F. The low temperature
(9) was –4°F. What was the range of temperatures that day in Minneapolis?

29. Yesterday it took Clanatia $\frac{1}{4}$ of an hour to walk to school and $\frac{1}{4}$ of an
(71) hour to walk home from school. In simplest form, what fraction of one
hour did Clanatia spend walking to and from school yesterday?

*30. (Explain) A square room is 121 square feet. What is the length of each
(67) side? Explain how you found your answer.

*Real-World
Connection*

Most of 61 students were placed in equal groups. However, 5 students
were not part of a group. If there were 7 equal groups, how many
students were in each group?

🖊 *California Mathematics Content Standards*

NS 2.0, 2.2 Demonstrate proficiency with division, including division with positive decimals and long division with multidigit divisors.

MR 3.0, 3.2 Note the method of deriving the solution and demonstrate a conceptual understanding of the derivation by solving similar problems.

• Why Can't We Divide by Zero?

There are a few rules in math that are important to learn and understand. One of them is that division by zero is NOT allowed.

Why is this true? Below are two explanations that show why we cannot divide by zero.

Explanation 1: Think about making zero equal parts.

We know a fraction represents division. The fraction $\frac{2}{3}$ can be shown by this picture:

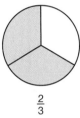

$$\frac{2}{3}$$

We divided a unit into 3 equal parts and took 2 of the parts. But how do we draw a picture for $\frac{2}{0}$? It is not possible for us to divide a unit into 0 equal parts.

Explanation 2: Think about the related multiplication problem.

All division problems can be written as multiplication problems:

$$8 \div 4 = 2 \text{ is the same as } 8 = 4 \times 2$$

If we could divide by 0, the problem $2 \div 0 = \underline{?}$ would have to be the same as $2 = 0 \times \underline{?}$. Is there a number that we can multiply by zero to get 2? The Zero Property of Multiplication says we cannot do this because any number multiplied by 0 equals 0.

Both explanations show that division by zero does not work. However, the division of zero is allowed.

Why is this true? Below is a picture of a circle representing zero with no shaded parts:

Now notice what happens to the same circle if we divide it by 2, 3, and 4:

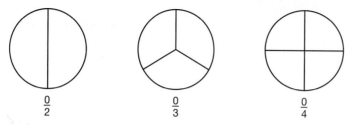

$$\frac{0}{2} \qquad \frac{0}{3} \qquad \frac{0}{4}$$

We take a number of parts equal to the numerator. In each of these cases, the number of parts we take is equal to zero. It is possible to divide zero by a nonzero number because the quotient will equal zero.

Explain Use one of the explanations given in this lesson to tell whether $\frac{0}{2}$ is possible.

LESSON
86

California Mathematics Content Standards
NS 2.0, 2.4 Understand the concept of multiplication and division of fractions.
NS 2.0, 2.5 Compute and perform simple multiplication and division of fractions and apply these procedures to solving problems.
MR 1.0, 1.2 Determine when and how to break a problem into simpler parts.
MR 2.0, 2.6 Make precise calculations and check the validity of the results from the context of the problem.

• Using Reciprocals to Divide Fractions

facts	Power Up H
mental math	**a. Money:** 3 × ($6 and 25¢)
	b. Money: 5 × ($3 and 25¢)
	c. Money: One dollar is how many quarters?
	d. Measurement: How many quarts are in a gallon?
	e. Powers/Roots: 8^2
	f. Probability: The sides of a number cube are labeled 1 through 6. If the cube is rolled once, what is the probability of rolling a number less than 5?
	g. Estimation: Choose the more reasonable estimate for the mass of a hamster: 90 grams or 90 kilograms.
	h. Calculation: $\frac{1}{3}$ of 90, + 3, ÷ 3, × 9

problem solving

Choose an appropriate problem-solving strategy to solve this problem. The circle graph at right is based on year 2004 estimates published by the Census Bureau. The graph shows the percentage of United States residents that belong to each of four age groups. Each percentage of population is nearly 3 million residents. Use that estimate to find the approximate number of U.S. residents who are 65 years of age or older.

U.S. Population by Age

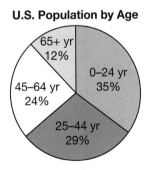

New Concept

Reciprocals can help us solve division problems such as the following:

$$\frac{1}{2} \div \frac{2}{3}$$

Math Language

Two numbers whose product is 1 are called *reciprocals*.

This problem means "How many $\frac{2}{3}$'s are in $\frac{1}{2}$?" However, since $\frac{2}{3}$ is more than $\frac{1}{2}$, the answer is less than 1. So we change the question to

"How much of $\frac{2}{3}$ is in $\frac{1}{2}$?"

"How much of ⬙ is in ◐ ?"

This problem is different from the problems we have been solving. To solve this problem, we will use another method. This method uses reciprocals to help us find the answer. We begin by asking a different question: "How many $\frac{2}{3}$'s are in 1?" Once we know how many $\frac{2}{3}$'s are in 1, then we can find how much of $\frac{2}{3}$ is in $\frac{1}{2}$.

Step 1: How many $\frac{2}{3}$'s are in 1? The answer is $\frac{3}{2}$, which is the reciprocal of $\frac{2}{3}$.

Step 2: The number of $\frac{2}{3}$'s in $\frac{1}{2}$ is *half* the number of $\frac{2}{3}$'s in 1. In other words, what is $\frac{1}{2}$ of $\frac{3}{2}$? So we multiply $\frac{3}{2}$ by $\frac{1}{2}$.

$$\frac{1}{2} \times \frac{3}{2} = \frac{3}{4}$$

This method changes the division problem into a multiplication problem. Instead of dividing $\frac{1}{2}$ by $\frac{2}{3}$, we end up multiplying $\frac{1}{2}$ by the reciprocal of $\frac{2}{3}$.

$$\frac{1}{2} \div \frac{2}{3} = ?$$
$$\frac{1}{2} \times \frac{3}{2} = \frac{3}{4}$$

(Discuss) The answer $\frac{3}{4}$ represents part of what whole? Explain.

Example 1

Divide: $\frac{2}{3} \div \frac{1}{2}$

We are finding the number of $\frac{1}{2}$'s in $\frac{2}{3}$. The number of $\frac{1}{2}$'s in 1 is $\frac{2}{1}$. So the number of $\frac{1}{2}$'s in $\frac{2}{3}$ is $\frac{2}{3}$ of $\frac{2}{1}$.

We multiply $\frac{2}{3}$ by the reciprocal of the second fraction, $\frac{1}{2}$. We simplify the answer $\frac{4}{3}$ to get **1$\frac{1}{3}$**.

$$\frac{2}{3} \div \frac{1}{2}$$
$$\frac{2}{3} \times \frac{2}{1} = \frac{4}{3}$$
$$= 1\frac{1}{3}$$

Example 2 . . . .

Divide: $2 \div \frac{2}{3}$

We are finding the number of $\frac{2}{3}$'s in 2. The number of $\frac{2}{3}$'s in 1 is $\frac{3}{2}$. So the number of $\frac{2}{3}$'s in 2 is twice that many.

We write the whole number 2 as the fraction $\frac{2}{1}$. Then we multiply $\frac{2}{1}$ by the reciprocal of $\frac{2}{3}$. Finally, we simplify the answer and find that the number of $\frac{2}{3}$'s in 2 is **3.**

$$\frac{2}{1} \div \frac{2}{3}$$

$$\frac{2}{1} \times \frac{3}{2} = \frac{6}{2}$$

$$= 3$$

Justify Why is the answer reasonable? Use $1 \div \frac{2}{3}$ in your explanation.

Example 3 . . . .

Solve each word problem. Then name the operation you used to solve the problem, and explain why you chose that operation.

a. One-half of an 8-foot length of ribbon is to be used for an art project. What length of ribbon will be used for the project?

b. How many lengths of ribbon, each $\frac{1}{2}$ foot long, can be cut from an 8-foot length of ribbon?

a. We use multiplication to find part of a whole.

$$\frac{1}{2} \cdot 8 = \frac{1}{2} \cdot \frac{8}{1} = \frac{8}{2} = 4$$

A **4-foot** length of ribbon will be used for the art project.

b. We use division to find the number of equal parts in a whole.

$$8 \div \frac{1}{2} = \frac{8}{1} \cdot \frac{2}{1} = \frac{16}{1} = 16$$

An 8-foot length of ribbon can be divided into **16** $\frac{1}{2}$-foot lengths.

Lesson Practice Divide:

a. $\frac{1}{3} \div \frac{1}{2}$

b. $\frac{2}{3} \div \frac{3}{4}$

c. $\frac{2}{3} \div \frac{1}{4}$

d. $\frac{1}{2} \div \frac{1}{3}$

e. $\frac{3}{4} \div \frac{2}{3}$

f. $3 \div \frac{3}{4}$

g. $2 \div \frac{1}{3}$

h. $3 \div \frac{2}{3}$

i. $10 \div \frac{5}{6}$

j. How many $\frac{1}{3}$'s are in $\frac{3}{4}$?

k. How much of $\frac{3}{4}$ is in $\frac{1}{3}$?

Solve each word problem. Then name the operation you used to solve the problem, and explain why you chose that operation.

l. How many lengths of string, each $\frac{1}{4}$ foot long, can be cut from a 6-foot length of string?

m. One half of a 6-foot length of string is to be used to wrap a package. What length of string will be used to wrap the package?

Written Practice — Distributed and Integrated

1.
(20, 21)
Represent Draw a pair of horizontal line segments. Make them the same length. Then draw two more line segments to make a quadrilateral.

2.
(10, 37)
Nathan worked on his homework from 3:30 p.m. to 6 p.m. For how many *minutes* did Nathan work on his homework?

3.
(53)
Represent Write a decimal number equal to the mixed number $3\frac{9}{10}$.

4.
(72)
Write the following percents as decimals and as reduced fractions:
a. 80%   **b.** 48%   **c.** 12%

5.
(76)
Find the area of this triangle.

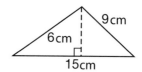

6. a.
(86)
How many apples weighing $\frac{1}{3}$ pound each would it take to total 1 pound?

b. How many apples weighing $\frac{1}{3}$ pound each would it take to total 4 pounds?

*7.
(49, 83)
Jeffrey and Samson both got a new puppy from the same litter. A record of each puppy's weight for the first four months is shown below. Display the data in a double-line graph.

	Month 1	Month 2	Month 3	Month 4
Jeffrey's Puppy	6 lb	7 lb	9 lb	10 lb
Samson's Puppy	6 lb	8 lb	10 lb	13 lb

8. Name the shaded portion of this square as a decimal number,
(58) as a reduced fraction, and as a percent.

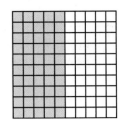

9. Multiple Choice Which of these numbers does not equal $\frac{1}{2}$?
(15)
    A 0.5   **B** 50%   **C** $\frac{6}{12}$ **D** 0.05

*10. Divide:
(84)
    a. $18\overline{)426}$ **b.** $29\overline{)135}$ **c.** $38\overline{)932}$

11. a. How many $\frac{3}{4}$'s are in 1?
(85)
    b. Divide: $1 \div \frac{2}{3}$

*12. Divide:
(86)
    a. $\frac{2}{3} \div \frac{5}{6}$ **b.** $\frac{3}{4} \div \frac{1}{3}$ **c.** $9 \div \frac{3}{5}$

13. 4^3 **14.** $8 \times \$125$
(67)   (12)

15. $\sqrt{100} - \sqrt{64}$ ***16.** $293 \div 13$
(67)   (82)

*17. $24\overline{)510}$ ***18.** $3\frac{5}{8} + 1\frac{7}{8}$
(82)   (81)

19. $5 - 1\frac{2}{5}$ **20.** $\frac{1}{3}$ of 5
(51)   (78)

*21. Divide:
(86)
    a. $\frac{1}{3} \div \frac{1}{6}$ **b.** $\frac{5}{6} \div \frac{2}{3}$ **c.** $4 \div \frac{3}{4}$

*22. $\frac{6}{10} \div \frac{1}{5}$
(79)

*23. **Analyze** Write a fraction equal to $\frac{2}{5}$ that has a denominator of 10. Add
(69, 71) that fraction to $\frac{1}{10}$. Remember to reduce your answer.

24. **Estimate** Estimate the area of a window that is 3 ft 10 in.
(50, 59) wide and 2 ft 11 in. tall.

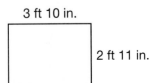

25. (Predict) A penny, nickel, dime, and quarter are tossed at the same
(45) time. Which word best describes the following events—*likely, unlikely, certain,* or *impossible?*

    a. All of the upturned faces are heads.

    b. At least one of the upturned faces is heads.

    c. None of the upturned faces are heads or tails.

26 Use the information and the table below to answer parts **a–c.**
(Inv. 5, 50).
    Sumi, Anais, and Melanie bought decorations for the party. This is a list of the items they purchased.

Napkins	....$2.19
Plates	......$1.19
Balloons	....$3.87
Streamers	..$1.39

    a. (Estimate) Describe how to estimate the total cost of the items. What is your estimate?

    b. What was the total cost of the decorations?

    c. If the girls share the cost evenly, how much will each girl pay?

27. (Conclude) Assuming that the sequence below repeats with period 5,
(Inv. 8) write the next 5 terms.

$$4, 4, 1, 4, 4, \ldots$$

28. (Analyze) In the 1988 Summer Olympic games in Seoul,
(60) South Korea, U.S. athlete Florence Griffith-Joyner won three gold medals in track events. "Flo-Jo," as she was called, finished the 200-meter run in 21.34 seconds, breaking the previous Olympic record of 21.81 seconds. By how much did Florence Griffith-Joyner break the previous Olympic record?

*29. (Represent) The lengths of several suspension bridges in
(Inv. 7) North America are shown in the table.

**Suspension Bridges
(North America)**

Bridge	Location	Length (ft)
Tacoma Narrows	Tacoma, WA	2800
Golden Gate	San Francisco Bay, CA	4200
A. Murray Mackay	Halifax, Nova Scotia	1400

Name an appropriate type of graph for the data. Explain your choice, and then graph the data.

30. These thermometers show the average daily maximum and minimum
   (9) temperatures during the month of January. When compared to
   the lower temperature, how many degress warmer is the higher
   temperature?

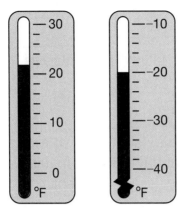

*Real-World
Connection*

The map below shows the location of several places in town where the
mail truck stops. Refer to the map to complete parts **a** and **b**.

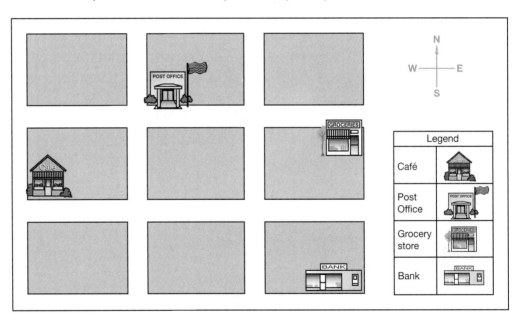

   a. How many blocks would the mail truck travel if it took the shortest path
   to the bank from the cafe?

   b. Compare the shortest distance between the post office and the bank
   to the shortest distance between the grocery store and the cafe.

🖊 *California Mathematics Content Standards*

NS 2.0, 2.5 Compute and perform simple multiplication and division of fractions and apply these procedures to solving problems.

MR 3.0, 3.2 Note the method of deriving the solution and demonstrate a conceptual understanding of the derivation by solving similar problems.

• How Dividing Fractions is Related to Multiplication

To divide fractions we apply the "invert and multiply" procedure as shown below:

$$\frac{1}{3} \div \frac{3}{4} = \frac{1}{3} \times \frac{4}{3} = \frac{4}{9}$$

We can verify that $\frac{1}{3} \div \frac{3}{4} = \frac{4}{9}$ by inverse operations. Recall that the dividend equals the product of the quotient and the divisor. In this problem $\frac{1}{3}$ is the dividend, $\frac{3}{4}$ is the divisor, and $\frac{4}{9}$ is the quotient.

$\frac{1}{3} \overset{?}{=} \frac{4}{9} \times \frac{3}{4}$ Does the dividend equal the product of the quotient and divisor?

$\frac{1}{3} = \frac{12}{36}$ Multiply the fractions

$\frac{1}{3} = \frac{1}{3}$ Reduce the product

Through multiplication, we have verified that $\frac{4}{9}$ is the correct quotient.

Discuss In a division problem involving fractions, how do you find the missing quotient?

Apply Find the quotient of each problem and then check your answer using multiplication.

    a. $\frac{1}{5} \div \frac{2}{3}$

    b. $\frac{2}{7} \div \frac{1}{3}$

    c. $\frac{7}{8} \div \frac{1}{3}$

California Mathematics Content Standards
SDAP 1.0, 1.3 Use fractions and percentages to compare data sets of different sizes.
MR 2.0, 2.3 Use a variety of methods, such as words, numbers, symbols, charts, graphs, tables, diagrams, and models, to explain mathematical reasoning.

• Comparing Data

Power Up

facts   Power Up H

mental math

a. Measurement: $3 \times$ (2 ft 4 in.)

b. Measurement: $4 \times$ (3 ft 4 in.)

c. Powers/Roots: 9^2

d. Estimation: Choose the more reasonable estimate for the amount of water in a drinking glass: 300 milliliters or 3 liters.

e. Number Sense: Reduce the fractions $\frac{2}{10}$, $\frac{2}{12}$, $\frac{2}{14}$, and $\frac{2}{16}$.

f. Percent: Chad has hiked 25% of the 4-mile trail. How many miles does he have left to hike?

g. Probability: Nine of the ten boxes contain a hidden prize. Latrisha will choose one box to open. Is it certain, likely, unlikely, or impossible that she will get a prize?

h. Calculation: $\frac{1}{4}$ of 400, $\div$ 2, $-$ 5, $\div$ 5, $\times$ 4, $\div$ 6

problem solving   Choose an appropriate problem-solving strategy to solve this problem. Some 1-inch cubes were used to build this rectangular solid. How many 1-inch cubes were used?

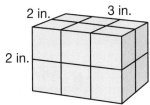

New Concept

A **ratio** is a way of comparing two numbers by division.

If there are 12 boys and 18 girls in a class, then the ratio of boys to girls in the class is 12 to 18.

We often write ratios as fractions. We write the terms of the ratio in order from top to bottom.

The ratio 12 to 18 is written as $\frac{12}{18}$.

We read the ratio $\frac{12}{18}$ by saying "twelve to eighteen."

We reduce ratios just as we reduce fractions. Since 12 and 18 are both divisible by 6, we divide each term of $\frac{12}{18}$ by 6.

$$\frac{12 \div 6}{18 \div 6} = \frac{2}{3}$$

So the ratio of boys to girls in the class is $\frac{2}{3}$ (two to three). This means that for every two boys in the class, there are three girls.

Example 1

There were 12 girls and 16 boys in the class. What was the ratio of boys to girls?

First we place the numbers in the correct order. We are asked for the ratio of boys to girls. Since we follow the order from top to bottom, we write the number of boys as the numerator and the number of girls as the denominator.

$$\frac{\text{boys}}{\text{girls}} \quad \frac{16}{12}$$

Unlike fractions, we do not write ratios as mixed numbers. The top number of a ratio may be greater than the bottom number. However, we do reduce ratios. Since the terms of the ratio, 16 and 12, are both divisible by 4, we reduce the ratio as follows:

$$\frac{16 \div 4}{12 \div 4} = \frac{4}{3}$$

The ratio of boys to girls in the class was $\frac{4}{3}$.

Connect What is the ratio of girls to boys?

Ratios can often be used to describe data sets. We can use fractions and percents to compare data sets of different sizes.

Example 2

Kendra has collected 40 sports trading cards, and 8 of those cards are hockey cards. Walt has collected 24 sports trading cards, and 6 of those cards are hockey cards. Which collection contains the greater percent of hockey trading cards?

The ratios in this problem compare the number of hockey trading cards to the total number of trading cards. We first write the ratios as fractions in simplest form.

Kendra's collection: $\frac{8}{40} = \frac{1}{5}$ Walt's collection: $\frac{6}{24} = \frac{1}{4}$

One way to compare fractions is to change the fractions to percents.

$$\text{Kendra's collection: } \frac{1}{5} = \frac{20}{100} = 20\%$$

$$\text{Walt's collection: } \frac{1}{4} = \frac{25}{100} = 25\%$$

We find that because 25% > 20%, **Walt's trading collection** contains the greater percent of hockey cards.

Example 3

This season, a middle school soccer team played 16 games and won 10. Last season, the team played 27 games and won 15. During which season, this year's or last year's, did the team win a greater share of its games?

The ratios in this problem represent games won to games played. We first write the ratios as fractions in simplest form.

$$\frac{10}{16} = \frac{5}{8} \qquad \frac{15}{27} = \frac{5}{9}$$

We can use unit fractions to compare the ratios because the numerator of each fraction is the same.

$$\text{Since } \frac{1}{8} > \frac{1}{9}, \text{ we know that } \frac{5}{8} > \frac{5}{9}.$$

The soccer team won a greater share of its games **this season** when it won 10 of 16 games.

Lesson Practice

There were 20 prairie dogs and 30 jackrabbits on Henry's ranch.

a. What was the ratio of jackrabbits to prairie dogs?

b. What was the ratio of prairie dogs to jackrabbits?

There were 8 red socks and 10 blue socks in Tevin's drawer.

c. What was the ratio of red socks to blue socks?

d. What was the ratio of blue socks to red socks?

e. **Explain** Two seasons ago, a middle school flag football team played 8 games and won 6. Last season, the team played 10 games and won 8. During which season did the team win a greater share of its games? Explain how you know.

Written Practice *Distributed and Integrated*

1. **Estimate** The saying "A pint's a pound the world around" means that a pint of water weighs about a pound. About how much does 2 quarts of water weigh?
(64)

2. At a grocery store, apples are sold by the pound. What is the cost of
(37) 4 pounds of apples if 3 pounds costs $2.55?

*3. The total rainfall in 2000 and 2005 for five cities is displayed in the
(83) comparative vertical bar graph below.

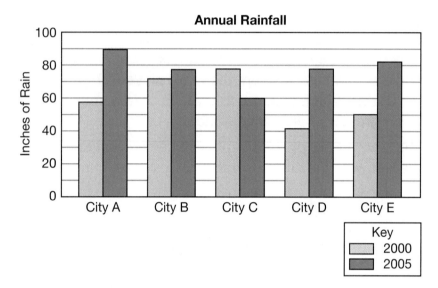

a. Which city received the most rain in 2005?

b. Which city received the least rain in 2000?

c. Which city had the largest range between its two rainfall amounts?

d. Which city had the smallest range between its two rainfall amounts?

4. Name the shaded portion of this group as a decimal
(58) number, as a reduced fraction, and as a percent.

5. a. (**Analyze**) How many plums weighing $\frac{1}{5}$ pound each
(79) would it take to total 1 pound?

b. How many plums weighing $\frac{1}{5}$ pound each would it take to total 3 pounds?

*6. Divide:
(84) **a.** $29\overline{)792}$ **b.** $50\overline{)1000}$ **c.** $18\overline{)682}$

7. Compare: $\frac{2}{3}$ of 3 $\bigcirc$ $3 \times \frac{2}{3}$
(78)

8. Multiple Choice If $3n = 18$, then $2n + 5$ equals which of the
(37) following?

    A 23   **B** 17   **C** 31   **D** 14

*9. a. The product of any number and its reciprocal is _____.
(85)

    b. What is the reciprocal of $\frac{4}{5}$?

    c. What is the reciprocal of $\frac{3}{4}$?

*10. Divide:
(86)

    a. $4 \div \frac{3}{4}$ **b.** $\frac{2}{5} \div \frac{1}{3}$ **c.** $\frac{1}{2} \div \frac{1}{4}$

11. $\quad 1\frac{3}{5}$ **12.** $\quad 4\frac{5}{8}$
(81)   (80)

    $+\, 2\frac{4}{5}$ $-\, \frac{1}{8}$

*13. Mrs. Brown's flower garden has 30 flowers, but it also has 12 weeds.
(87)

    a. What is the ratio of flowers to weeds?

    b. What is the ratio of weeds to flowers?

*14. $1 \div \frac{1}{8}$ **15.** $\frac{8}{10} \times \frac{5}{10}$ **16.** $\frac{1}{5} \div \frac{1}{10}$
(79)   (80)   (79)

17. $12.34 - (5.67 - 0.8)$
(60)

*18. Catalina's fruit bowl had 8 apples and 6 oranges in it.
(87)

    a. What is the ratio of apples to oranges?

    b. What is the ratio of oranges to apples?

19. 10×56¢   **20.** $6 \times 78 \times 900$
(57)   (18)

*21. $31\overline{)970}$ **22.** $9^2 - \sqrt{9}$
(82)   (67)

23. (**Analyze**) Write fractions equal to $\frac{3}{4}$ and $\frac{1}{6}$ that have denominators of 12.
(69)   Then add the fractions.

24. Refer to the picture below to answer parts **a–c.**
(32, 59)

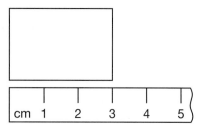

   a. How long is the rectangle?

   b. The rectangle is 1 centimeter longer than it is wide. What is the perimeter of the rectangle?

   c. What is the area of the rectangle?

*25. a. Write the next three terms of the repeating sequence below.
(Inv. 8)
   b. What is the period of the sequence?

   $$E, \textrm{w}, \textrm{ƨ}, \textrm{m}, E, \underline{\quad}, \underline{\quad}, \underline{\quad}, \ldots$$

Refer to the spinner to answer parts **a–c.**

26. a. If you spin this spinner 60 times, about how many times would you expect it to stop on 2?
(45)

   b. What percent of the spinner's face is region 2?

   c. What decimal part of the spinner's face is region 3?

27. Montana became a state in 1889, which was 98 years after Vermont became a state. Utah became a state 105 years after Vermont. In what year did Utah become a state?
(37)

28. ✎ **Explain** A teacher must divide a class of 31 students into four teams. If possible, the same number of students are to be on each team. What is a reasonable estimate of the number of students that will be on each team? Explain your answer.
(50)

29. **Justify** Antonia Novello was born on August 23, 1944, and began serving as the Surgeon General of the United States on March 9, 1990. How old was she when she became Surgeon General? Explain why your answer is reasonable.
(10)

30. A square field that is one hectare is 10,000 square meters. Describe how to use a calculator to find the length of each side of the field. How long is each side?
(67)

California Mathematics Content Standards
NS 2.0, **2.1** Add, subtract, multiply, and divide with decimals; add with negative integers; subtract positive integers from negative integers; and verify the reasonableness of the results.
MR 2.0, 2.3 Use a variety of methods, such as words, numbers, symbols, charts, graphs, tables, diagrams, and models, to explain mathematical reasoning.

• Representing Integers

facts   Power Up H

mental math

   a. Number Sense: $5(30 + 4)$

   b. Number Sense: $5(34)$

   c. Number Sense: Reduce the fractions $\frac{3}{12}, \frac{10}{12},$ and $\frac{9}{12}$.

   d. Measurement: How many ounces are in a pound? How many ounces are in a pint?

   e. Powers/Roots: 10^2

   f. Estimation: A pencil costs 69¢, a protractor costs $1.29, and a compass costs $2.99. Round the cost of each item to the nearest ten cents and then add.

   g. Percent: Lacey is studying a list of 800 words for the upcoming spelling bee. She has studied only 25% of the words. How many words has Lacey studied?

   h. Calculation: $5^2, -1, \div 3, +2, \times 10$

problem solving

Choose an appropriate problem-solving strategy to solve this problem. The circle graph at right is based on year 2004 estimates published by the Census Bureau. The graph shows the percentage of United States residents that belong to each of four age groups. Each percentage of population is nearly 3 million residents. Use that estimate to determine how many more residents are in the 25–44 age group than are in the 45–64 age group.

U.S. Population by Age

- 65+ yr 12%
- 0–24 yr 35%
- 45–64 yr 24%
- 25–44 yr 29%

The set of integers contains positive whole numbers, their opposites, and zero. Whenever we write a negative integer, we write its sign. Whenever we write a positive integer, we do not write its sign. An integer with no sign is a positive integer.

Examples of Negative Integers
-2 -6 -11 -1

Examples of Positive Integers
3   10   1   7

We can use our understanding of science to help understand how to add and subtract positive and negative integers. For example, we know that some particles have electrical charges. Some have a positive charge ($+$), some have a negative charge ($-$), and some are neutral because they have the same number of positive and negative charges. To find the charge of a particle, we cross off a positive charge ($+$) and a negative charge ($-$), and continue crossing off positive-negative pairs until no more remain.

Example 1

Find whether the following collection of charges is positive or negative.

Before

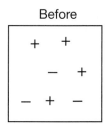

To find out whether the charges are positive or negative, we pair up and cross out every positive sign ($+$) with a negative sign ($-$) until there are no more pairs left.

After

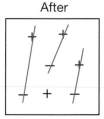

One positive remains.

We find that the collection of charges is **positive.**

Example 1 shows that if there are more positives than negatives, the result is positive.

Example 2

Find whether the following collection of charges is positive or negative. Then state by how much the charge is positive or negative.

Before

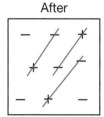

Again we pair up and cross out every positive sign (+) with a negative sign (−), until there are no more pairs left.

After

Three negatives remain.

We find that the collection has a charge of **three negatives.**

Example 2 shows that if there are more negatives than positives, the result is negative.

Example 3

Find whether the following collection of charges is positive or negative.

Before

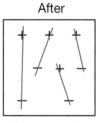

After pairing up and crossing out every positive sign with a negative sign, we find that there are no signs left.

After

Neither positive nor negative

The collection of charges is **neither positive nor negative.**

Example 3 shows that if there are the same number of positives and negatives, the result is neither positive nor negative. We can use the idea of crossing off positive and negative charges to add integers.

Example 4

Add: −4 + 6

Both −4 and 6 are addends. We write four negative signs (−) to represent −4 because it is a negative integer. We write six positive signs (+) to represent 6 because it is a positive integer. (Remember that a number without a sign is always a positive number.)

Use signs to represent the addends.

Cross off positive/negative pairs.

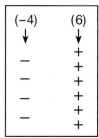 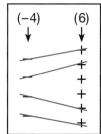

Two positives remain.

We find that because two positives remain, −4 + 6 = +2. The simplest way to write a positive number such as +2 is to write the number without the positive sign. So −4 + 6 = **2.**

Example 5

Add: 2 + (−5)

Math Symbols

Parentheses are used in the expression 2 + (−5) to help us recognize that + is an operation sign and − is the sign of the addend.

Use signs to represent the addends.

Cross off positive/negative pairs.

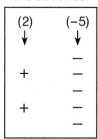 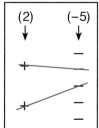

Three negatives remain.

We find that because three negatives remain, 2 + (−5) = **−3.**

Lesson Practice Cross off positive/negative pairs. Then write the number of positives or negatives that remain.

a.

$-$	$+$
	$+$
$-$	$+$

b.

$+$	$-$
$+$	$-$
$+$	$-$
	$-$
	$-$

Write $+$ and $-$ signs to represent each addend. Cross off positive/negative pairs, and then write the sum.

c. $-2 + 1$ **d.** $2 + (-1)$ **e.** $-3 + 3$

f. $2 + (-6)$ **g.** $-2 + 5$ **h.** $4 + (-9)$

i. $-5 + 3$ **j.** $13 + (-8)$ **k.** $-10 + 12$

l. **(Represent)** What addition equation is represented by problem **a?**

m. **(Represent)** What addition equation is represented by problem **b?**

Written Practice   *Distributed and Integrated*

1. **(List)** Write all of the prime numbers less than 50 that end with the
(65) digit 1.

2. What number is missing in this division problem?
(6)
$$\square \div 8 = 24$$

*3. Write the reciprocal of each number. Leave improper fractions as
(85) improper fractions.

   a. $\dfrac{2}{5}$ **b.** $\dfrac{3}{6}$ **c.** $\dfrac{4}{7}$

4. **(Represent)** Write a decimal number equal to the mixed number $4\dfrac{9}{10}$.
(58)

5. Seventy-six trombone players led the parade. If they marched in 4
(13) equal rows, how many were in each row?

6. a. A dime is what fraction of a dollar?
(79)

    b. How many dimes are in $1?

    c. How many dimes are in $4?

7. Multiple Choice Which of the following means, "How many 19's are
(82) in 786?"

    A $19 \div 786$ **B** $786 \div 19$ **C** 19×786

8. a. How many $\frac{1}{4}$'s are in 1?
(79)

    b. How many $\frac{1}{3}$'s are in 1?

*9. a. How many $\frac{1}{3}$'s are in $\frac{1}{2}$?
(86)

    b. How many $\frac{2}{3}$'s are in $\frac{3}{4}$?

10. Multiple Choice If $\overline{LN}$ is perpendicular to $\overline{JM}$, then $\angle JNL$
(20) is what type of angle?

    A acute   **B** right   **C** obtuse

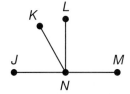

*11. The kitchen cabinet contains 14 glasses and 8 cups.
(87)

    a. What is the ratio of glasses to cups?

    b. What is the ratio of cups to glasses?

12. $1010 - (101 - 10)$
(7)

13. Find the exterior angle measurement for this angle:
(Inv. 3)

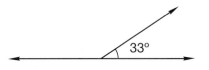

14. 25^2 ***15.** $19\overline{)786}$
(67)   (84)

*16. $\sqrt{36} + \sqrt{64}$ ***17.** $38\overline{)1200}$
(67)   (84)

18. $\frac{5}{6} + \frac{5}{6} + \frac{5}{6}$ **19.** $\frac{5}{6} \times 3$
(81)   (81, 78)

20. Reduce: $\frac{8}{12}$
(80)

21. Find the exterior angle measurement for this angle:
(Inv. 3)

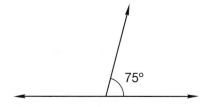

75°

22. $\frac{1}{3}$ of $\frac{3}{4}$
(63)

23. (**Analyze**) Write a fraction equal to $\frac{2}{3}$ that has a denominator of 12.
(69, 71) Subtract that fraction from $\frac{11}{12}$. Remember to reduce the answer.

24. (**Interpret**) The graph below shows Monty's height on his birthday from
(49) ages 9 to 14. Use this graph to answer parts **a** and **b.**

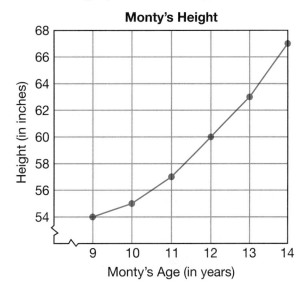

Monty's Height

a. How many inches did Monty grow between his twelfth and fourteenth birthdays?

b. On which birthday was Monty 5 feet tall?

25. The sides of this square are one yard long. Since 1 yard
(21, 33, 59) equals 3 feet, the sides are also 3 feet long. Refer to this
figure to answer parts **a–c.**

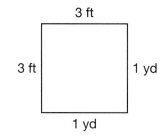

3 ft

3 ft   1 yd

1 yd

    a. Multiple Choice Which of these terms does not
    describe the figure?

        A rectangle   **B** parallelogram

        C pentagon   **D** regular quadrilateral

    b. What is the perimeter of the square in feet? What is the perimeter
    in yards?

    c. What is the area of the square in square feet? What is the area in
    square yards?

26. a. Compare: 1 yd $\bigcirc$ 3 ft
(59, 61)

    b. Compare: 1 sq. yd $\bigcirc$ 9 sq. ft

27. ✎ **Explain** In a fifth grade class, $\frac{7}{8}$ of the students wore sneakers on
(48) Friday. What fraction of the class did not wear sneakers on Friday?
Explain why your answer is reasonable.

28. ✎ **Explain** In 4 different rooms of a museum, a curator is planning to
(38, 50) display a collection of 152 archeological objects. Estimate the number
of objects in each room if each room is to contain the same number
of objects. Explain why your estimate is reasonable.

29. When an opossum is active, its body temperature is about 95°F. When
(9) it is hibernating, its body temperature decreases by about 44°F. What is
the body temperature of a hibernating opossum?

30. Javier and Beth were both born in 1997. Javier was born on October
(RF21) 29. Beth was born on December 1. How many days after the birth of
Javier was Beth born?

*Real-World
Connection*

Rahul was working an end-of-year exam and got the following problem
wrong. What mistake did he make in working the problem? What is the
correct answer in simplest form?

$$\frac{8}{7} \div \frac{9}{6} = \frac{7}{8} \times \frac{6}{9} = \frac{42}{72} = \frac{21}{36} = \frac{7}{12}$$

LESSON
89

• Adding Integers

California Mathematics Content Standards
NS 1.0, 1.5 Identify and represent on a number line decimals, fractions, mixed numbers, and positive and negative integers.
NS 2.0, 2.1 Add, subtract, multiply, and divide with decimals; add with negative integers; subtract positive integers from negative integers; and verify the reasonableness of the results.
MR 2.0, 2.3 Use a variety of methods, such as words, numbers, symbols, charts, graphs, tables, diagrams, and models, to explain mathematical reasoning.

Power Up

facts   Power Up F

mental math

a. **Number Sense:** $4(30 + 4)$

b. **Number Sense:** $4(34)$

c. **Number Sense:** Reduce the fractions $\frac{4}{12}$, $\frac{6}{12}$, and $\frac{8}{12}$.

d. **Measurement:** How many ounces are in a pint?

e. **Measurement:** How many pints are in a quart?

f. **Measurement:** How many ounces are in a quart?

g. **Estimation:** Choose the more reasonable estimate for the weight of a pair of scissors: 10 oz or 10 lb.

h. **Calculation:** $\frac{1}{10}$ of 1000, $- 1$, $\div 9$, $+ 1$, $\times 4$, $+ 1$, $\div 7$

problem solving

Choose an appropriate problem-solving strategy to solve this problem. A **line of symmetry** divides a figure into mirror images. If a rectangle is longer than it is wide, then it has exactly two lines of symmetry: one lengthwise and one widthwise. The lines of symmetry for this rectangle are shown with dashes. On your paper, draw a rectangle that is longer than it is wide, and show its lines of symmetry.

New Concept

In Lesson 88 we learned that the idea of positive and negative electrical charges can be used to add integers. Another way to add integers is to use a number line.

A thermometer is an example of a number line. Suppose the temperature is 0°F. If the temperature decreases three degrees (−3) and then decreases three degrees (−3) again, the new temperature will be six degrees below zero (−6°F).

The first thermometer helps us see that when we add two negative numbers, the sum is a negative number.

Again suppose the temperature is 0°F. If the temperature decreases three degrees (−3) and then increases three degrees (+3), the new temperature will be zero degrees (0°F).

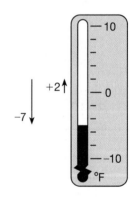

The numbers −3 and +3 are opposites. When we add opposites, the sum is zero.

We can also use the third thermometer to show the sum of two addends that have different signs. The beginning temperature is again 0°F. If the temperature increases two degrees (+2) and then decreases seven degrees (−7), the result is −5°F.

The result is a negative temperature because the temperature decreased more than it increased.

A thermometer is an example of a vertical number line. We can also use a horizontal number line to add integers.

Example 1

Add: +8 + (−6)

We begin at zero and move eight units in the positive direction (to the right). Then from +8 we move six units in the negative direction (to the left).

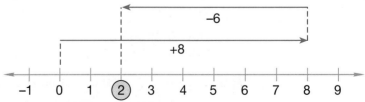

The sum of +8 and −6 is +2, which we write as **2.**

Example 2

Math Symbols

Parentheses are used in the expression $-1 + (-7)$ to help us recognize that $+$ is an operation sign and -7 is an addend.

Add: $-1 + (-7)$

We again begin at zero and move one unit in the negative direction, or to the left. Then from -1 we continue moving in the negative direction seven units to -8.

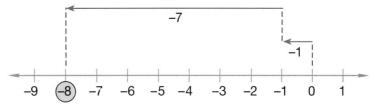

We find that $-1 + (-7) = $ **-8.**

Example 3

Add: $-6 + (+6)$

We begin at zero and move six units to the left. Then we move six units to the right.

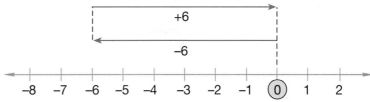

The result is **zero** because -6 and $+6$ are opposite numbers.

The number line below shows other examples of **opposite numbers.** In order for two numbers to be opposites, they must be the same distance from zero, but in opposite directions. On the number line we see that -3 and $+3$ and -5 and $+5$ are opposite numbers.

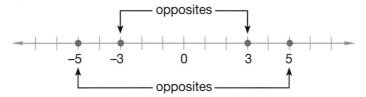

Example 4

Find the opposite of each number:

    a. -4 **b.** 9

The opposite of a number is written using the same digits but with the opposite sign.

    a. The opposite of -4 is $+4$, which is usually written as **4.**

    b. The opposite of 9 (which is a positive number) is **-9.**

Draw a number line from −10 to 10. Use the number line to find each sum.

a. −2 + (+1)

b. −4 + (−6)

c. 9 + (−3)

d. −1 + (+5)

Find each sum. Use mental math if you can.

e. −6 + 7

f. −5 + (−5)

g. 7 + (−10)

h. 10 + (−18)

Write a word to complete each sentence:

i. The opposite of a positive number is a _____ number.

j. The opposite of a negative number is a _____ number.

k. The sum of a number and its opposite is _____.

Find the opposite of each number:

l. −7

m. 11

n. 0

Written Practice   *Distributed and Integrated*

1. **Analyze** These three boxes of nails weigh
(38)   35 lb, 42 lb, and 34 lb. If some nails are moved from the heaviest box to the other two boxes so that all three boxes weigh the same, how much will each box weigh?

35 lb   42 lb   34 lb

2. **Analyze** Each finger of the human hand is formed by three bones,
(RF12)   except for the thumb, which is formed by two bones. The palm contains five bones, one leading to each finger. Not counting the bones in the wrist, the hand contains how many bones?

3. Name the shaded portion of this square as a decimal
(58)   number, as a reduced fraction, and as a percent.

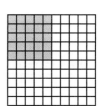

*4. What is the product of $\frac{2}{3}$ and its reciprocal?
(85)

5. **a.** A quarter is what fraction of a dollar?
(79)

    b. How many quarters equal $1?

    c. How many quarters equal $5?

*6. What is the reciprocal of $\frac{3}{4}$? What is the product of $\frac{3}{4}$ and its reciprocal?
(85)

7. **Multiple Choice** Which of the following means, "How many 25's are
(82) in 500?"

    A $25 \div 500$ **B** $500 \div 25$ **C** 25×500

8. **a.** What is the reciprocal of 6?
(85)

    b. What is the reciprocal of $\frac{1}{4}$?

*9. Divide:
(86)
    a. $5 \div \frac{3}{7}$ **b.** $\frac{1}{6} \div \frac{2}{3}$ **c.** $\frac{5}{6} \div \frac{2}{3}$

10. $(\$20 - \$4.72) \div 8$ **11.** $160 \times \$1.25$
(17)   (44)

*12. In the teachers' parking lot at the school, there were 18 cars and
(87) 12 pickup trucks.

    a. What is the ratio of cars to pickup trucks?

    b. What is the ratio of pickup trucks to cars?

13. 100^2 **14.** $31\overline{)140}$ ***15.** $27x = 567$
(67)   (84)   (17, 84)

16. Reduce: $\frac{15}{25}$ **17.** $1\frac{5}{6} + 1\frac{5}{6}$ **18.** $4\frac{5}{6} - 1\frac{1}{6}$
(80)   (81)   (71)

19. $\frac{3}{8}$ of 24   **20.** $3 \times \frac{4}{5}$ **21.** $\frac{9}{10} \div \frac{1}{10}$
(78)   (78, 81)   (79)

22. **(Analyze)** Write fractions equal to $\frac{3}{4}$ and $\frac{1}{6}$ that have denominators of 12.
(69) Subtract the smaller fraction from the larger fraction.

23. The giant pendulum swung back and forth 10 times in 123 seconds.
(47) The pendulum swung back and forth one time in how many seconds?

24. **Connect** Isabella used toothpicks to make this rectangle.
(59) Refer to this rectangle to answer parts **a** and **b**.

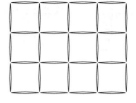

    a. How many toothpicks form the perimeter of this rectangle?

    b. The rectangle closes in an area covered with small squares. How many small squares cover the area of the rectangle?

25. Robert awoke on a cool fall morning and looked at the
(9) thermometer outside his window. What temperature is indicated on the thermometer?

26. Add: $-9 + 12$
(89)

27. $\sqrt{100} - \sqrt{36}$
(67)

28. Add: $-5 + 8$
(89)

29. Add: $-8 + 5$
(89)

30. The land area of Fort Worth is 139.2 square miles greater than the area
(37, 60) of Denver. The land area of Denver is 67.6 square miles greater than the area of Honolulu. The land area of Fort Worth is 292.5 square miles. What is the land area of Honolulu?

Real-World Connection

Cherise is going to bake a cake. She wants to make a smaller cake that is $\frac{2}{3}$ the size of the original recipe. If 3 cups of flour and 2 cups of milk are needed to make the cake in the recipe, how much flour and milk will she need to make the smaller cake?

California Mathematics Content Standards
NS 2.0, 2.1 Add, subtract, multiply, and divide with decimals; add with negative integers; subtract positive integers from negative integers; and verify the reasonableness of the results.
MR 2.0, 2.1 Use estimation to verify the reasonableness of calculated results.

• Adding and Subtracting Whole Numbers and Decimal Numbers

facts   Power Up F

mental math

   a. Number Sense: 6(40 + 6)

   b. Number Sense: 6(46)

   c. Number Sense: Reduce the fractions $\frac{4}{8}$, $\frac{4}{12}$, and $\frac{4}{16}$.

   d. Fractional Parts: $\frac{1}{3}$ of 19

   e. Measurement: The 1-liter bottle was full of water. Then Quincy poured out 350 mL. How many mL of water were left in the bottle?

   f. Measurement: Which U.S. Customary unit is nearly equal to a liter?

   g. Percent: Eric and Trey agree to each pay 50% of the $31 cost of the videogame. How much will each boy pay?

   h. Calculation: $\frac{1}{4}$ of 36, + 1, × 2, + 1, ÷ 3, × 7, + 1, ÷ 2

problem solving

At the store, Chris wants to be able to purchase any item that costs from 1¢ to 99¢ using exact change. What is the combination of the fewest quarters, dimes, nickels, and pennies that Chris needs?

Focus Strategy: Make it Simpler

(**Understand**) We are told that Chris wants to be able to purchase any item that costs from 1¢ to 99¢ using exact change. We are asked to find the combination of the fewest quarters, dimes, nickels, and pennies that Chris needs.

(**Plan**) We do not want to consider all 99 possible prices from 1¢ to 99¢ individually, so we look for a way to *make it simpler*. We approach the problem by thinking about each coin separately.

Solve We can start with pennies. We know Chris would need 4 pennies to pay for a 4¢ item with exact change. We cannot think of a price for which Chris would need 5 or more pennies, because 5 pennies can always be replaced with only 1 nickel.

Now we think, "What is the greatest number of nickels Chris would need?" We might see that two nickels have a value of 10¢. This means that Chris needs only 1 nickel, because 2 nickels can always be replaced with 1 dime.

For dimes, we think, "3 dimes can always be replaced with 1 quarter and 1 nickel, so Chris only needs 2 dimes." For quarters, Chris can use 3 quarters for a 75¢ item and 3 quarters plus some additional coins for an item costing from 76¢ to 99¢. So we find that the smallest set of coins Chris needs is **3 quarters, 2 dimes, 1 nickel, and 4 pennies.**

Check We know that our answer is reasonable because the coins we found can make all combinations from 1¢ to 99¢ using fewer pennies than equal a nickel, fewer nickels than equal a dime, and fewer dimes than equal a quarter.

We should also ask ourselves whether there are other possible answers. Can you find another combination of 10 coins that can be used to pay exact change for any price from 1¢ to 99¢?

New Concept

Sometimes we need to add whole numbers and decimal numbers in the same problem. Here is an example:

The Kubats hired a carpenter to cut an opening in their wall and to install a new door. The carpenter needed to order a frame for the door to cover the thickness of the wall. The carpenter knew that the siding was 1 inch thick, the wall stud was 3.5 inches thick, and the drywall was 0.5 inches thick.

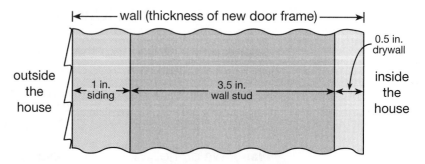

To find the thickness of the wall, the carpenter writes 1 inch as 1.0 inch, aligns the decimal points of all three measurements, and adds. He finds that a 5.0-inch-thick door frame is needed.

$$
\begin{array}{r}
1.0 \text{ in.} \\
3.5 \text{ in.} \\
+ \ 0.5 \text{ in.} \\
\hline
5.0 \text{ in.}
\end{array}
$$

The carpenter wrote the whole number 1 as the decimal number 1.0 so that he could align the decimal points before adding. Since a decimal point marks the end of a whole number, we may add a decimal point to the back (right-hand side) of a whole number. After placing the decimal point, we may also attach zeros to make arithmetic with the whole number easier.

Thinking Skill

Connect

Why do we line up the decimal points when we add or subtract decimals?

When adding whole numbers to decimal numbers, it might help to remember the game "Pin the Tail on the Donkey." The tail belongs on the back of the donkey, and the decimal point belongs on the back of the whole number. Remember this rule:

"Pin the decimal point on the back of the whole number."

Example 1

In a science experiment, the scientist placed food at the end of a short maze and placed a mouse at the beginning of the maze. The scientist timed how fast the mouse reached the food. The scientist repeated the experiment three times. The mouse's times were 6.2 seconds, 4.25 seconds, and 3 seconds. What was the total time of the three trials?

We find the total time by adding. To add digits with the same place value, we align decimal points. In this problem the whole number 3 has the same place value as the 6 and the 4. We place a decimal point to the right of the 3 and align decimal points. We may fill empty decimal places with zeros if we wish. The total elapsed time is **13.45 seconds.**

$$
\begin{array}{r}
6.20 \\
4.25 \\
+ \ 3.00 \\
\hline
13.45
\end{array}
$$

Verify Explain why the answer is reasonable.

Example 2

A computer that began a complex task 8 minutes ago needs 24.6 minutes altogether to complete the task. In how many minutes will the task be complete?

$$
\begin{array}{r}
24.6 \\
- \ 8.0 \\
\hline
16.6
\end{array}
$$

To find the remaining time, we subtract. We place a decimal point to the right of the whole number 8, and then align decimal points before subtracting. We may fill the empty decimal place with a zero if we wish. The task will be completed in **16.6 minutes.**

Verify Explain why the answer is reasonable.

Example 3

Which digit in 4.65 is in the same place as the 2 in 12?

The 2 in 12 is in the ones place. In 4.65 a decimal point separates the ones place and the tenths place, marking the end of the whole number and the beginning of the fraction. So the **4** in 4.65 is in the same place as the 2 in 12.

Lesson Practice   Find each sum or difference:

a. 4.3 + 2   **b.** 12 + 1.2

c. 6.4 + 24   **d.** 4 + 1.3 + 0.6

e. 5.2 + 0.75 + 2   **f.** 56 + 75.4

g. 8 + 4.7 + 12.1   **h.** 9 + 4.8 + 12

i. 4.75 − 2   **j.** 12.4 − 5

k. Which digit in 24.7 is in the same place as the 6 in 16?

l. Compare: 12 ◯ 12.0

Written Practice   *Distributed and Integrated*

1. Felix, Cleon, Teresa, and Camryn have been learning their math facts
(83) for practice tests. The scores for their first two practice tests are shown in the table below.

Student	Practice Test 1	Practice Test 2
Felix	72	75
Cleon	78	82
Teresa	70	79
Camryn	68	80

Make a comparative horizontal bar graph to show the scores. There should be two bars for each student.

2. (**Analyze**) Cuinton gave Venedict half of an apple. Venedict gave his
(58, 63) sister half of what he had. What fraction of the whole apple did Venedict's sister get? What percent of the whole apple did she get?

3. How much is $\frac{2}{3}$ of one dozen?
(78)

4. **Estimate** Write the product of 712 and 490 by rounding both
(50) numbers to the nearest hundred before multiplying.

*5. There were 24 students and 6 adult sponsors going on the field trip.
(87)

    a. What was the ratio of students to adults?

    b. What was the ratio of adults to students?

6. **Multiple Choice** Which of these means, "How many one tenths are
(79) there in three?"

    A $\frac{1}{10} \div 3$ **B** $3 \div \frac{1}{10}$ **C** $\frac{1}{10} \div \frac{3}{10}$

7. **Analyze** Write fractions equal to $\frac{1}{4}$ and $\frac{1}{5}$ that have denominators
(69) of 20. Then add the fractions.

*8.   **a.** $1 \div \frac{1}{10}$ **b.** $3 \div \frac{1}{10}$
(86)

*9. Which digit in 237.86 is in the same place as the 5 in 15?
(90)

10. The blossom of the saguaro cactus is the state flower of Arizona. A
(34, 78) saguaro cactus can weigh as much as 10 tons. About $\frac{3}{4}$ of a saguaro's
weight comes from the water it stores inside of it. If a saguaro cactus
weighs 10 tons, about how much of its weight is water?

*11. Find each sum or difference:
(90)

    a. $32.4 + 5$ **b.** $7 + 3.1 + 0.64$

    c. $3.98 - 2$ **d.** $52.7 - 39$

12. **Connect** Name the shaded portion of this square as a
(58) decimal number, as a reduced fraction, and as a percent.

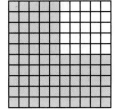

*13. $\frac{1}{3} \div \frac{1}{4}$
(86)

*14. $\frac{1}{4} \div \frac{1}{3}$
(86)

*15. $3 \div \frac{1}{2}$
(86)

16. $m + 1.4 = 3.75$
(60)

17. $m - 1.4 = 3.75$
(60)

18. $\frac{1}{10} \times \square = \frac{10}{100}$
(69)

19. Add: $-6 + 4 - 2$
(89)

20. $568 \div 15$
(84)

21. $30\overline{)427}$
(42)

22. $6m = \$30.24$
(17, 23)

23. $5 \times \left(\frac{2}{3} \times \frac{1}{2} \right)$
(63, 78, 81)

24. $5 - \left(1\frac{1}{4} + 2 \right)$ $3\frac{1}{4}$
(30, 51)

25. Compare: $\sqrt{100} \bigcirc 5^2$
(67)

26. (Analyze) At Walton School there are 15 classrooms. The numbers of
(74) students in each classroom are listed below. Use this information to
answer parts **a–c.**

20, 18, 30, 20, 22, 28, 31, 20, 27, 30, 26, 31, 20, 24, 28

a. What is the mode of the number of students in the classrooms?

b. What is the range?

c. What is the median number of students in the classrooms?

27. Add: $14 + (-6)$
(89)

28. Three classmates were born in July. Bruce's birthday is 6 days before
(37) Kosta's birthday and 14 days after Michelle's birthday. Michelle's
birthday is July 4. When is Kosta's birthday?

29. (Justify) Bryan estimates that his sport utility vehicle travels about
(50) 21 miles for every gallon of fuel it uses. Trina estimates that her car
will travel about 5 more miles for every gallon of fuel it uses. If each
person drives their vehicle for 500 miles, about how many fewer
gallons of fuel will Trina need to purchase? Explain why your answer is
reasonable.

30. **Interpret** Gold, iron, and aluminum are well-known examples of
(Inv. 7) metals. The melting temperatures of other metals are shown in the bar
graph below. Use the graph to answer the questions that follow.

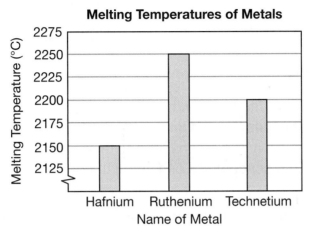

Melting Temperatures of Metals

a. What is the range in degrees Celsius of the melting temperatures?

b. Which of the three metals melts at the lowest temperature?

c. **Explain** The melting temperature of gold is 1064.43°C. About
how many degrees less than the melting temperature of ruthenium
is the melting temperature of gold? Explain why your estimate is
reasonable.

California Mathematics Content Standards

MG 1.0, 1.2 Construct a cube and rectangular box from two-dimensional patterns and use these patterns to compute the surface area for these objects.

MG 1.0, 1.3 Understand the concept of volume and use the appropriate units in common measuring systems (i.e., cubic centimeter [cm^3], cubic meter [m^3], cubic inch [in^3], cubic yard [yd^3]) to compute the volume of rectangular solids.

MG 1.0, 1.4 Differentiate between, and use appropriate units of measures for, two-and three-dimensional objects (i.e., find the perimeter, area, volume).

Focus on

Rectangular Solids

The **volume** of an object is the amount of space the object occupies. Geometric figures that occupy space include cubes, spheres, cones, cylinders, pyramids, and combinations of these shapes. In this investigation we will concentrate on finding the volume of rectangular solids.

The units we use to measure volume are **cubic units.** Here we illustrate the three types of units we use to measure distance, area, and volume.

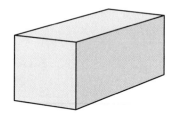

Rectangular solid

Math Language

We use cubic units to measure volume because cubes are three-dimensional and volume is a measure of the amount of three-dimensional space inside a figure.

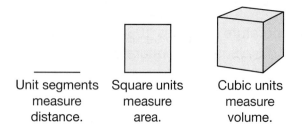

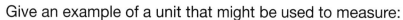

Unit segments measure distance.

Square units measure area.

Cubic units measure volume.

Give an example of a unit that might be used to measure:

1. the amount of molding around a room.

2. the amount of carpet on the floor of a room.

3. the maximum storage capacity of a room.

To find the volume of an object, we calculate the number of cubic units of space the object occupies.

Here we show a cubic inch and a cubic centimeter:

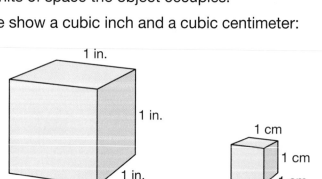

One cubic inch

One cubic centimeter

The solid at right is 3 cm long, 2 cm wide, and 2 cm high. There are 6 cubes in each layer of the solid. The solid has 2 layers, so there are 12 cubes in all. Since the cubes are 1-cm cubes, the volume is 12 cubic centimeters.

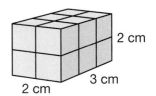

We can abbreviate cubic centimeters by writing "cm³". When we multiplied 3 cm × 2 cm × 2 cm, we multiplied both the units and the numbers.

$$(3 \text{ cm}) \cdot (2 \text{ cm}) \cdot (2 \text{ cm}) = (3 \cdot 2 \cdot 2)(\text{cm} \cdot \text{cm} \cdot \text{cm}) = 12 \text{ cm}^3$$

We read the result as "twelve cubic centimeters."

4. **Justify** Why is the answer labeled "cubic centimeters" and not "square centimeters"?

Example 1

What is the volume of this solid?

The solid is 4 inches long, 2 inches wide, and 3 inches high. For the bottom layer, we imagine a 4-by-2 rectangle of 1-inch cubes, which is 8 cubes. Three layers are needed for the whole solid. Since 3 × 8 = 24, the volume is **24 in³**.

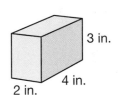

We found the number of cubes on the bottom layer and then multiplied that number by the number of layers, which is the height of the solid. We can find the number of cubes on the bottom layer by multiplying the length and width of the rectangular solid. Then we find the volume by multiplying by the height.

$$\text{Volume} = \text{length} \times \text{width} \times \text{height}$$
$$V = l \times w \times h$$

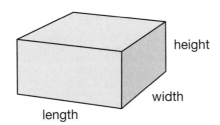

Example 2

Emma keeps the quilts she makes in a sturdy box.

a. **She plans to cover the top of the box with fabric. Choose a formula and use it to decide how much fabric she needs.**

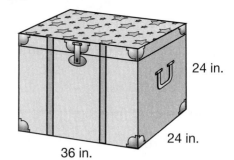

24 in.

24 in.

36 in.

b. **How much space is inside the box? Choose a formula and use it to determine the volume of the box.**

a. The top of the box is a rectangle. The fabric covers the area of the rectangle, so we use the area formula.

$$A = l \times w$$
$$A = 36 \text{ in.} \times 24 \text{ in.}$$
$$A = 864 \text{ sq. in.}$$

Emma needs a 36 in. by 24 in. rectangle of fabric, which is **864 in².**

b. The space inside the box is the volume of the box. We use the volume formula.

$$V = l \times w \times h$$
$$V = 36 \text{ in.} \times 24 \text{ in.} \times 24 \text{ in.}$$
$$V = 20{,}736 \text{ cu. in.}$$

The volume of the box is **20,736 in³.**

Find the volume of each rectangular solid:

5.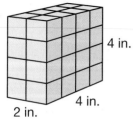

4 in.

4 in.

2 in.

6.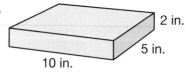

2 in.

5 in.

10 in.

7.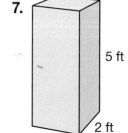

5 ft

2 ft

2 ft

8. Ella's closet is 3 feet wide, 2 feet deep, and 8 feet high. How many boxes that are 1-foot cubes could Ella fit into her closet?

9. In inches, a box of Kelvin's favorite wheat crackers measures $5\frac{1}{4}$ by $2\frac{1}{8}$ by $7\frac{5}{8}$. What is a reasonable estimate in cubic inches of the volume of the box? Explain how you made your estimate.

A container such as a cereal box is constructed out of a flat sheet of cardboard that is printed, cut, folded, and glued to create a colorful, three-dimensional container.

By cutting apart a cereal box, you can see the six panels or faces of the box at one time. Here we show one way to cut apart a box, but many arrangements are possible.

> **Math Language**
>
> A **net** is a pattern that can be folded to form a three-dimensional solid.

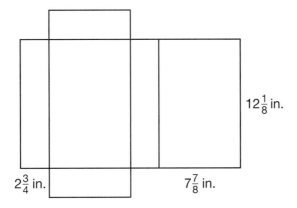

$12\frac{1}{8}$ in.

$2\frac{3}{4}$ in. $7\frac{7}{8}$ in.

We can estimate the areas of the rectangles by rounding the dimensions to whole numbers. For the given number of inches, we round $2\frac{3}{4}$ to 3, we round $7\frac{7}{8}$ to 8, and $12\frac{1}{8}$ to 12. We see that there are three different sizes of rectangles and two of each size.

We find the approximate area of each rectangle. Then we add and find that the approximate area of the outside surface of the box is

$$24 + 24 + 36 + 36 + 96 + 96 = 312 \text{ sq. in.}$$

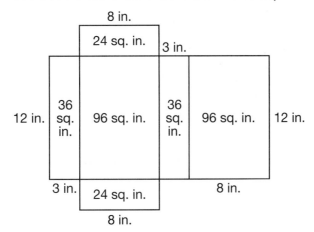

Example 3

For each statement below, use the terms *volume* or *surface area* in each blank.

    a. The air inside a box fill its ____.

    b. The painted parts of a cereal box cover its ____.

    c. If you fill a box with one-inch cubes, you can count to find the ____ of the box.

    d. If you cover the outside of a box with one-inch-square stickers, you can count to find the ____ of the box.

    e. Units used to measure the ____ of a box are square units.

    f. Units used to measure the ____ of a box are cubic units.

Explain Describe the difference between volume and surface area.

Construct a Rectangular Solid

Materials needed:
- **Lesson Activity 20**
- scissors
- tape
- ruler

Use the net from **Lesson Activity 20** to complete the following tasks.

1. **Model** Cut out the net, and then fold and tape it to make a rectangular solid.

2. **Discuss** Describe the faces.

3. Measure each face and record its measurements.

4. Use what you know about area to find the area of each face.

5. **Conclude** The sum of the areas of the individual faces is called the total surface area. What is the total surface area of the solid? Explain how you found your answer.

6. **Explain** Did you label your answer with square units or with cubic units? Explain why.

California Mathematics Content Standards

NS 1.0, **1.5** Identify and represent on a number line decimals, fractions, mixed numbers, and positive and negative integers.
AF 1.0, 1.3 Know and use the distributive property in equations and expressions with variables.

• Simplifying Decimal Numbers

facts
Power Up I

mental math

a. Time: Rudy turns eleven years old today. How many months old is Rudy?

b. Number Sense: Reduce the fractions $\frac{3}{6}$, $\frac{3}{9}$, $\frac{3}{12}$, and $\frac{3}{15}$.

c. Number Sense: $12\frac{1}{2} + 12\frac{1}{2}$

d. Measurement: Romy kicked the soccer ball 15 yards. How many feet is that?

e. Powers/Roots: 1^3

f. Probability: Juan plans to flip a coin 10 times and record the results. Is it certain, likely, unlikely, or impossible that at least one flip will be heads?

g. Calculation: $\sqrt{64}$, $\times 3$, $- 3$, $\div 3$, $\times 2$, $- 2$, $\div 2$, $\div 3$, $\div 2$

h. Evaluate: What is the value of the expression $a - 1$ when $a = 7$?

problem solving

Choose an appropriate problem-solving strategy to solve this problem. This table lists the years from 2009 to 2014 and the day of the week on which each year begins. Notice that each year begins one day of the week later than the first day of the previous year until 2013. Since 2012 is a leap year and has an additional day, the year 2013 begins an additional day later. Copy this table and continue it through the year 2023, which begins on a Sunday.

Year	First Day
2009	Thursday
2010	Friday
2011	Saturday
2012	Sunday
2013	Tuesday
2014	Wednesday

When we write numbers, we usually write them in simplest form. To **simplify** a number, we change the form of the number, but we do not change the value of the number. For example, we simplify fractions by reducing. We can often simplify decimal numbers by removing unnecessary zeros. We will explain this by simplifying 0.20.

The decimal number 0.20 has a 2 in the tenths place and a 0 in the hundredths place. The zero in the hundredths place means "no hundredths." If we remove this zero from 0.20, we get 0.2. The number 0.2 also has a 2 in the tenths place and "no hundredths." Thus, 0.20 equals 0.2. We say that 0.20 simplifies to 0.2.

> **We can remove zeros from the front of whole numbers and from the back of decimal numbers.**

We may remove zeros until we come to a digit that is not a zero or until we come to a decimal point. Below we have simplified 02.0100, 20.0, and 0.200 by removing unnecessary zeros.

	02.0100	20.0	0.200
Simplified →	2.01	20	0.2 or .2

In the center example, we took two steps to simplify 20.0. After removing the unnecessary zero, we also removed the decimal point. A decimal point can be removed when there is no fraction part to a number.

To simplify 0.200, we removed the two trailing zeros, leaving 0.2 as the simplified form.

In some situations we might want to attach zeros to a decimal number. The decimal point of a decimal number determines place value, not the number of digits. So attaching zeros at the end of a decimal number does not change place values.

Example 1

Otis added 3.75 to 2.75 and found that the sum was 6.50. Simplify the sum.

We may remove the ending zero(s) of a decimal number.

$$6.50 = \mathbf{6.5}$$

Example 2

Attach a zero to the end of 5 without changing the value of the number.

If we attach a zero to 5 without using a decimal point, we get 50, which does not equal 5. So we write the whole number 5 with a decimal point and then attach a zero.

$$5 = \mathbf{5.0}$$

Example 3

In a classroom science experiment, a snail moved at a rate of 1.20 centimeters per second. The experiment was repeated and the snail again moved at a rate of 1.20 centimeters per second. Write an expression to represent the total distance that the snail moved during the two experiments.

The rate is a decimal number that can be simplified, so we first write an equivalent decimal number for 1.20 centimeters.

$$1.20 \text{ cm} = 1.2 \text{ cm}$$

Now we write an expression to represent the total distance that the snail moved.

1.2 cm $\times$ f represents the distance during the first experiment.
1.2 cm $\times$ s represents the distance during the second experiment.

The expression $(1.2 \times f) + (1.2 \times s)$ represents the total distance in centimeters that the snail moved. We can use the Distributive Property to simplify the expression.

$$(1.2 \times f) + (1.2 \times s) = \mathbf{1.2(f + s)}$$

(**Evaluate**) What is the total distance the snail moved if $f = 20$ seconds and $s = 10$ seconds? Explain your reasoning.

Example 4

Draw a number line divided into tenths. Place $\frac{6}{10}$, $\frac{1}{5}$, 1.1, and 0.80 on the number line. Then write the numbers in order from greatest to least.

We draw a number line. To show tenths, we divide the distance from 0 to 1 into ten unit segments. We extend the number line beyond 1 because 1.1 > 1.

Since 1.1 is a decimal number in tenths, we write an equivalent decimal number in tenths for $\frac{6}{10}$, $\frac{1}{5}$, and 0.80.

$$\frac{6}{10} = 0.6 \qquad \frac{1}{5} = \frac{20}{100} = 0.20 = 0.2 \qquad 0.80 = 0.8$$

Then we plot the decimal numbers.

If we read the numbers on a number line from right to left, we read them in order from greatest to least. The numbers from greatest to least are **1.1, 0.80, $\frac{6}{10}$, $\frac{1}{5}$**.

Verify Explain why 0.80 = 0.8.

Lesson Practice

Simplify each decimal number:

a. 03.20   **b.** 0.320   **c.** 32.00   **d.** 3.020

Simplify each answer:

e. $\begin{array}{r} 3.65 \\ + 6.35 \\ \hline \end{array}$ **f.** $\begin{array}{r} 23.16 \\ - 19.46 \\ \hline \end{array}$ **g.** $\begin{array}{r} 4.28 \\ - 3.18 \\ \hline \end{array}$

h. Attach a zero to the end of 2.5 without changing its value.

i. Attach a zero to the end of 6 without changing its value.

j. Rewrite the expression shown below by applying the Distributive Property. Then evaluate the expression when $d = 10$ cm and $e = 100$. Make sure any decimal numbers you write are in simplest form.

$$(2.50 \times d) + (2.50 \times e)$$

k. Draw a number line divided into tenths. Place $\frac{2}{5}$, 1.2, $\frac{8}{10}$, and $\frac{20}{100}$ on the number line. Then write the numbers in order from least to greatest.

*1. There were 15 pennies and 10 nickels in Kordell's drawer. What was the
(87) ratio of pennies to nickels in his drawer?

2. When the ticket office opened at the basketball arena, fifty-two
(39) people were in line to buy tickets. Each ticket will cost $26.50. If each
person in line buys one ticket, what will be the total cost of all fifty-two
tickets?

3. **Explain** Jazmyn had 4 one-dollar bills, 3 quarters, 2 dimes, and
(37) 1 nickel. If she spent half of her money, how much money does she
have left? Explain how you found your answer.

4. How many $\frac{1}{8}$'s are in $\frac{1}{2}$?
(79)

5. Find the value of p that makes this equation true:
(40)
$$8 \times 39 = (8 \times p) + (8 \times 9)$$

6. When the decimal number eleven and twelve hundredths is subtracted
(55, 60) from twelve and eleven hundredths, what is the difference?

7. a. A quart is what fraction of a gallon?
(77, 79)

   b. How many quarts are in 1 gallon?

   c. How many quarts are in 4 gallons?

8. **Analyze** Write fractions equal to $\frac{2}{3}$ and $\frac{2}{5}$ that have denominators of 15.
(28, 69) Then subtract the smaller fraction from the larger fraction.

*9. Kaison rode her bicycle 2.3 miles to Gracie's house. Then Gracie's dad
(90) took both girls to the mall in his car. If the mall was twelve miles from
Gracie's house, how many total miles did Kaison travel to get from her
house to the mall?

*10. Compare: $\frac{1}{2} \div 2 \bigcirc 2 \div \frac{1}{2}$
(86)

*11. Simplify the following numbers by removing unnecessary zeroes:
(91)
   a. 4.070   **b.** 06.02   **c.** 08.30

*12. $3 \div \frac{2}{3}$ 13. $\frac{2}{3} \div 3$ 14. $\frac{7}{10} + \frac{7}{10}$
(86)   (86)   (28, 81)

*15. Simplify each answer:
(91)
   a. $\begin{array}{r} 48.73 \\ -\ 13.53 \\ \hline \end{array}$ **b.** $\begin{array}{r} 16.58 \\ +\ 13.42 \\ \hline \end{array}$ **c.** $\begin{array}{r} 21.64 \\ +\ 15.26 \\ \hline \end{array}$

16. ($10 − 19¢) ÷ 9   17. Add: 12 + (−4)
(7, 57)   (89)

18. 35^2 *19. $24\overline{)500}$ 20. Reduce: $\frac{50}{100}$
(67)   (82)   (80)

21. $12y = 1224$ 22. $5\frac{3}{4} - \left(3 - 1\frac{3}{4}\right)$
(82)   (7, 51, 71)

23. $1\frac{1}{4} + 1\frac{1}{4} + 1\frac{1}{4} + 1\frac{1}{4}$ 24. Add: −10 + 5
(46)   (89)

25. **a.** What is the length of each side of this square?
(32)
   b. What is the perimeter of this square?

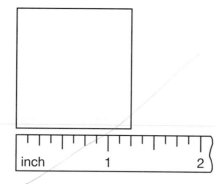

26. If the area of a square is 64 square inches, then what is the length
(59)   of each side?

27. What number is $\frac{1}{64}$ of 640?
(78, 82)

*28. **(Conclude)** What are the next three terms in this Fibonacci sequence?
(Inv. 8)

$$1, 1, 2, 3, 5, 8, 13, 21, \underline{\qquad}, \underline{\qquad}, \underline{\qquad}, \ldots$$

29. a. **(List)** Write the factors of 64 from least to greatest.
(16, 67, 74)

  b. Is the number of factors an odd or even number?

  c. What is the median of the factors?

  d. What is $\sqrt{64}$?

*30. There are 50 stars and 13 stripes on the United States flag. What is the
(87) ratio of stripes to stars on the flag?

• Rounding Mixed Numbers

California Mathematics Content Standards
NS 1.0, 1.5 Identify and represent on a number line decimals, fractions, mixed numbers, and positive and negative integers.
MG 1.0, 1.1 Derive and use the formula for the area of a triangle and of a parallelogram by comparing it with the formula for the area of a rectangle (i.e., two of the same triangles make a parallelogram with twice the area; a parallelogram is compared with a rectangle of the same area by cutting and pasting a right triangle on the parallelogram).
MR 2.0, 2.1 Use estimation to verify the reasonableness of calculated results.

facts   Power Up I

mental math

   a. Number Sense: Reduce the fractions $\frac{6}{8}$, $\frac{6}{9}$, and $\frac{6}{12}$.

   b. Fractional Parts: $\frac{1}{3}$ of 100

   c. Money: The price of the used car is $5000. To buy the car, Sanjay had to make a down payment (first payment) of 10% of the price. What is 10% of $5000?

   d. Money: Sanjay decided to make a greater down payment than was required. He made a down payment of $\frac{1}{5}$ of $5000. What is $\frac{1}{5}$ of $5000?

   e. Powers/Roots: 2^3

   f. Probability: The bag contains five tiles. Each tile had a vowel written on it. If Stuart reaches into the bag and pulls out one tile without looking, what is the probability it will be the letter *C*?

   g. Calculation: $\sqrt{100}$, × 2, × 50, − 1, ÷ 9

   h. Evaluate: What is the value of the expression $9 - b$ when $b = 0$?

problem solving

Choose an appropriate problem-solving strategy to solve this problem. Recall that a *permutation* is an ordered arrangement of objects. Adam, Barbara, and Conrad stood side by side to have their picture taken (A, B, C). Then Barbara and Conrad switched places (A, C, B). List the remaining possible side-by-side arrangements.

New Concept

The mixed number $7\frac{3}{4}$ is between 7 and 8. To round $7\frac{3}{4}$ to the nearest whole number, we decide whether $7\frac{3}{4}$ is nearer 7 or nearer 8. To help us understand this question, we can use this number line:

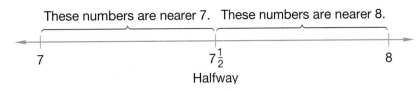
Thinking Skill

Discuss

Where is $7\frac{1}{4}$ on the number line? Where is $7\frac{1}{8}$?

We see that $7\frac{1}{2}$ is halfway between 7 and 8. Since $7\frac{3}{4}$ is between $7\frac{1}{2}$ and 8, we know that $7\frac{3}{4}$ is nearer 8 than 7. So $7\frac{3}{4}$ rounds up to **8.**

Example 1

Round $6\frac{2}{5}$ to the nearest whole number.

The mixed number $6\frac{2}{5}$ is between 6 and 7. We need to decide whether it is nearer 6 or nearer 7. The number $6\frac{1}{2}$ is halfway between 6 and 7. The number $6\frac{2}{5}$ is less than $6\frac{1}{2}$ because the numerator of $\frac{2}{5}$ is less than half the denominator. So we round $6\frac{2}{5}$ down to **6.**

Verify Explain why $6\frac{3}{5}$ is closer to 7 than 6.

Example 2

Math Language

A fraction bar is a grouping symbol. We must complete the operations above and below the bar before we can complete the division.

Kylie estimated the area of this triangle to be 20 in². Did Kylie make a reasonable estimate?

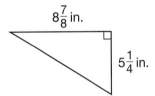

We will make an estimate of the area by rounding $8\frac{7}{8}$ inches to 9 inches and $5\frac{1}{4}$ inches to 5 inches. We then solve $A = \frac{bh}{2}$ by substitution.

$$A = \frac{(9 \text{ in.})(5 \text{ in.})}{2}$$

$$A = \frac{45 \text{ in}^2}{2}$$

$$A = 22\frac{1}{2} \text{ in}^2$$

Since our estimate of $22\frac{1}{2}$ in² is close to Kylie's estimate of 20 in², we find that **Kylie made a reasonable estimate.**

Explain To make our estimate, we substituted 9 for b and 5 for h. Would our estimate have been different if we substituted 5 for b and 9 for h? Explain why or why not.

Example 3

Estimate the perimeter of a rectangular picture frame that is $15\frac{1}{8}$ inches long and $10\frac{3}{4}$ inches wide.

We round $15\frac{1}{8}$ inches to 15 inches and we round $10\frac{3}{4}$ inches to 11 inches.

$$P = 2l + 2w$$
$$P = 2(15 \text{ in.}) + 2(11 \text{ in.})$$
$$P = 30 \text{ in.} + 22 \text{ in.}$$
$$P = 52 \text{ in.}$$

The perimeter of the frame is **about 52 inches.**

Lesson Practice

Round each mixed number to the nearest whole number:

a. $3\frac{2}{3}$ **b.** $7\frac{1}{8}$ **c.** $6\frac{3}{5}$

d. $6\frac{1}{4}$ **e.** $12\frac{5}{6}$ **f.** $25\frac{3}{10}$

g. Estimate the product of $9\frac{4}{5}$ and $5\frac{1}{3}$.

h. Estimate the sum of $36\frac{5}{8}$ and $10\frac{9}{10}$.

i. Estimate the area of the rectangle in Example 3.

j. On the number line below, estimate the location of $5\frac{1}{3}$, $4\frac{1}{4}$, $6\frac{3}{8}$, and $7\frac{2}{5}$ by rounding each number to the nearest whole number. Draw and label a point at each location.

Written Practice *Distributed and Integrated*

*1. (Justify) There were 12 dogs and 8 cats at the class pet show. What
(87) was the ratio of cats to dogs at the show? Explain how you found your answer.

2. a. (Conclude) What is the name of this solid?
(RF27)

b. How many faces does it have?

3. Lucia, Tameron, Elisa, and Alma planted tomato plants for a project. The height of the plants is shown in the table below. Make a comparative horizontal bar graph to show the growth of the four plants.

(83)

Growth of Tomato Plants

Student Name	Week 2	Week 4
Lucia	$10\frac{1}{2}$ in.	14 in.
Tameron	10 in.	$13\frac{1}{2}$ in.
Elisa	12 in.	17 in.
Alma	$11\frac{1}{4}$ in.	$16\frac{1}{2}$ in.

*4. Mrs. White's fourth grade class keeps a record of each day's weather. For the past twenty days, there have been thirteen sunny days and seven cloudy days.

(87)

a. What is the ratio of sunny to cloudy days?

b. What is the ratio of cloudy to sunny days?

5. **Connect** Refer to this number line to solve parts **a** and **b.**

(25)

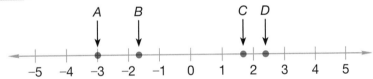

a. Which arrow could be pointing to $2\frac{1}{3}$ on the number line?

b. Which arrow is pointing to negative three?

6. A person who is a fast swimmer can swim at a rate of about 3 mph. A sea turtle can swim about 17 mph faster, and a sailfish can swim about 40 mph faster than a sea turtle. About how fast can a sailfish swim?

(37)

7. **Multiple Choice** If $\overline{LN}$ is perpendicular to $\overline{JM}$, then which of these angles is obtuse?

(20, 21)

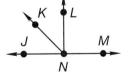

    A ∠JNK   **B** ∠KNL

    C ∠KNM   **D** ∠LNM

8. $6.5 + 2.47 + 0.875$

(60)

*9. Find each sum or difference:
(90)
   a. 4.7 + 6.82 + 3   **b.** 14.79 − 3.9

10. 23.45 − 1.2
(60)

*11. Simplify each decimal number:
(91)
   a. 06.70   **b.** 0.560   **c.** 51.00   **d.** 8.040

12. $1.25 × 7   **13.** 750 × 608
(12)   (44)

14. 364 ÷ 16   **15.** $7.20 ÷ 20   **16.** $3\frac{1}{2}$
(84)   (42)   (46)
                                                             $+ 1\frac{1}{2}$
                                                            _____

*17. Estimate the perimeter of a card table that is $31\frac{1}{2}$ inches on
(92)   each side.

18.   6
(51)
      $- 1\frac{1}{3}$
      _____

*19. Round each mixed number to the nearest whole number:
(92)
   a. $5\frac{3}{8}$ **b.** $2\frac{4}{5}$ **c.** $21\frac{3}{4}$

20. $\frac{4}{5}$ of 25   ***21.** $\frac{3}{4} \div \frac{2}{3}$
(78)   (86)

22. $\frac{7}{10} = \frac{\square}{100}$ **23.** Reduce: $\frac{30}{100}$
(69)   (80)

24. a. The thermometer on the left shows the record high
(9)   temperature in December. What is the temperature
         shown?

   b. The thermometer on the right shows the record low
         temperature in December. What is the temperature
         shown?

   c. What is the range of the two temperatures shown?

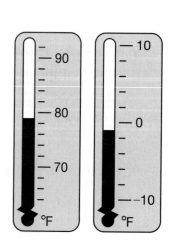

25. $9^2 + \sqrt{81}$
(67)

26. a. (List) Find the common factors of 70 and 100.
(73, 80)

   b. Use the GCF of 70 and 100 to reduce $\frac{70}{100}$.

27. Compare:
(63)

   a. $\frac{1}{2} \times \frac{1}{3} \bigcirc \frac{1}{2}$ **b.** $\frac{1}{2} \times \frac{1}{3} \bigcirc \frac{1}{3}$

*28. Add: $-4 + 5$
(89)

29. Add: $-2 + 9$
(89)

30. Arrange these decimal numbers in order from least to greatest:
(56)

   0.376   0.037   0.38   0.367

California Mathematics Content Standards

NS 2.0, **2.2** Demonstrate proficiency with division, including division with positive decimals and long division with multidigit divisors.
NS 2.0, 2.5 Compute and perform simple multiplication and division of fractions and apply these procedures to solving problems.
MR 1.0, 1.2 Determine when and how to break a problem into simpler parts.

• Why the Division Algorithm Works for Two-Digit Divisors

Long division also works with two-digit divisors.

We will see what happens step by step as we divide to understand why the long-division process works. This algorithm depends on place value.

The number 5232 is read "five thousand, two hundred thirty-two." This number is the same as $5000 + 200 + 30 + 2$. Its place value is:

5	2	3	2
thousands	hundreds	tens	ones

The Algorithm **What We Do** **What Is Happening**

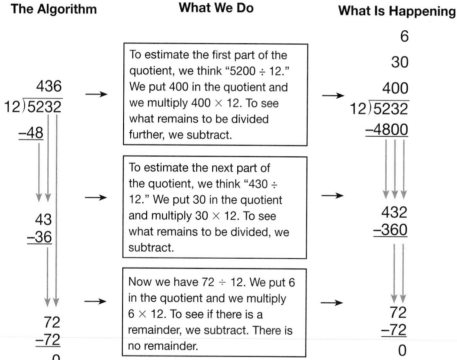

Notice that the quotient is made up of $400 + 30 + 6$ and is equal to 436.

The long-division process breaks a problem into parts. We estimate and divide part by part and subtract to see what is left. The process continues until nothing is left to divide.

Verify Since $5232 = 5000 + 200 + 32$, show that $\frac{5000}{12} + \frac{200}{12} + \frac{32}{12} =$ 436.

LESSON
93

California Mathematics Content Standards
NS 2.0, **2.1** Add, subtract, multiply, and divide with
  decimals; add with negative integers; subtract
  positive integers from negative integers; and
  verify the reasonableness of the results.
MR 3.0, 3.3 Develop generalizations of the results
  obtained and apply them in other circumstances.

• Subtracting Decimal Numbers Using Zeros

facts   Power Up I

mental   a. **Number Sense:** Reduce the fractions $\frac{5}{20}$, $\frac{5}{15}$, and $\frac{5}{10}$.
math
               b. **Powers/Roots:** 3^3

               c. **Money:** The total fee for 4 children to attend the summer
                  camp was $436. What was the cost per child?
                  (*Think:* $436 \div 4$)

               d. **Percent:** What is 50% of $100? 50% of $10?
                  50% of $1?

               e. **Time:** How many years are in a millennium? How many
                  years are in half of a millennium?

               f. **Estimation:** At the game, 329 fans wore red and 273 fans
                  wore orange. There were 947 fans altogether. Use compatible
                  numbers to estimate the number of fans that did not wear red
                  or orange.

               g. **Calculation:** $\frac{1}{3}$ of 6, $\times$ 2, + 1, $\times$ 5, $-$ 1, $\div$ 6

               h. **Evaluate:** What is the value of the expression $c + 2$ when
                  $c = 3$?

problem   Choose an appropriate problem-solving strategy to
solving   solve this problem. Barry erased some of the digits in
                a multiplication problem. He then gave it to Pablo as a
                problem-solving exercise. He told Pablo that there are two
                different possible solutions. Copy Barry's multiplication problem,
                and find both solutions for Pablo.

$$\begin{array}{r} 2\_ \\ \times \ \_ \\ \hline 2\_2 \end{array}$$

For some subtraction problems we need to add decimal places to perform the subtraction. If we subtract 0.23 from 0.4, we find there is an "empty" place in the problem.

$$0.4\_ \leftarrow \text{empty place}$$
$$-\ 0.23$$

We fill the empty place with a zero. Then we subtract.

$$
\begin{array}{r}
0.\overset{3}{\cancel{4}}\overset{1}{0} \\
-\ 0.23 \\
\hline
0.17
\end{array}
$$

Example 1

In a test of computing speed, a Brand X computer completed a task in 0.4 second. A Brand Y computer completed the same task in 0.231 fewer seconds. What length of time did the Brand Y computer take to complete the task?

To find the time difference, we subtract. We set up the problem by lining up the decimal points, remembering to write the first number on top. We fill empty places with zeros. Then we subtract. Brand Y completed the task in **0.169 second.**

$$
\begin{array}{r}
0.\overset{3}{\cancel{4}}\overset{9}{\cancel{0}}\overset{1}{0} \\
-\ 0.231 \\
\hline
0.169
\end{array}
$$

Explain How can you check the answer?

Example 2

A pedometer measures the distance a person has walked. Jayna is walking 3 kilometers to Rochelle's house. While waiting at a crosswalk, Jayna notices that her pedometer reads 1.23 kilometers. What distance does Jayna still need to walk to arrive at Rochelle's house?

This problem is similar to subtracting $1.23 from $3. We place the decimal point to the right of the 3, fill the decimal places with zeros, and subtract.

$$
\begin{array}{r}
\overset{2}{\cancel{3}}.\overset{9}{\cancel{0}}\overset{1}{0} \\
-\ 1.23 \\
\hline
1.77
\end{array}
$$

Jayna has **1.77 kilometers** left to walk.

Connect What would the answer be if it were a money amount?

Example 3

> In 2004, the land area of Laredo, Texas, was 83.44 square miles. In 1993, the land area was 44 sq. miles. Between 1993 and 2004, the city of Laredo added about how many square miles?
>
> The number 83.44 is between 83 and 84. We choose the compatible number 84 and subtract.
>
> $$84 \text{ sq. mi.} - 44 \text{ sq. mi.} = 40 \text{ sq. mi.}$$
>
> Laredo added **about 40 square miles** between 1993 and 2004.

Lesson Practice Subtract:

a. $0.3 - 0.15$ **b.** $0.3 - 0.25$

c. $4.2 - 0.42$ **d.** $3.5 - 0.35$

e. $10 - 6.5$ **f.** $6.5 - 4$

g. $1 - 0.9$ **h.** $1 - 0.1$

i. $1 - 0.25$ **j.** $2.5 - 1$

k. Audra poured 1.2 liters of cranberry juice from a full 2-liter container. How much cranberry juice was left in the container? Show your work.

l. The land area of Long Beach, California, is 50.4 square miles. The land area of Jersey City, New Jersey, is 14.9 square miles. About how much greater is the land area of Long Beach? Explain why your estimate is reasonable.

Written Practice *Distributed and Integrated*

1. There were 50 boys and 60 girls on the playground. What was the ratio
(87) of girls to boys on the playground?

2. The pizza was sliced into 6 equal pieces. Martin ate 2 pieces. What
(58, 71) fraction of the pizza did he eat? What percent of the pizza did he eat?

3. Write the reciprocal of each number:
(85)
    a. $\dfrac{3}{8}$ **b.** 6   **c.** $\dfrac{2}{5}$

*4. **Analyze** Maria ran 100 yards in 13.8 seconds. Taron ran 1 second
(90) slower than Maria. How long did it take Taron to run 100 yards?

5. **Connect** Name point X on the number line below as both a decimal
(25, 71) number and a reduced mixed number.

6. If $10n = 100$, then n^2 equals what number?
(67)

7. **Represent** Write the decimal number one thousand, six hundred
(55) twenty and three tenths.

8. **Estimate** A door was 6 ft 10 in. tall and 2 ft 11 in. wide. Estimate the
(50, 59) area of one side of the door.

9. **Analyze** Write a fraction equal to $\frac{3}{4}$ that has a denominator of 8. Then
(69) subtract that fraction from $\frac{7}{8}$.

*10. Attach a zero to the end of 7 without changing its value.
(91)

*11. Round each mixed number to the nearest whole number:
(92) **a.** $4\frac{2}{3}$ **b.** $2\frac{2}{5}$ **c.** $5\frac{7}{8}$

*12. $3.4 + 5$ ***13.** $7.25 - 7$ **14.** $\sqrt{25} - \sqrt{16}$
(90) (90) (67)

*15. Omar is two meters tall. His brother, Emiliano, is 1.62 meters tall.
(93) How much taller is Omar than Emiliano?

16. $28\overline{)952}$ **17.** $\$18.27 \div 9$
(84) (23)

18. $4\frac{5}{8} + 1\frac{7}{8}$ **19.** $5 - \left(2\frac{3}{5} - 1\right)$
(81) (30, 51)

20. $\frac{3}{4} \times \frac{1}{3}$ **21.** $\frac{3}{4} \div 3$
(80) (86)

22. $\frac{9}{10} = \frac{\square}{100}$ **23.** Reduce: $\frac{20}{100}$
(69) (80)

24. Use the table to answer the questions that follow.
(Inv. 8)

Gallons	1	2	3	4	5
Fluid Ounces	128	256	384	512	640

a. **Generalize** Write a rule that describes how to find the number of fluid ounces for any number of gallons.

b. **Predict** How many fluid ounces are in 8 gallons?

*25. Subtract:
(93)
    a. $0.4 - 0.23$ b. $8 - 3.9$ c. $4.6 - 2$

26. **Conclude** There is a pattern to the differences between successive
(Inv. 8) terms of this sequence:

$$3, 4, 7, 12, 19, \ldots$$

Assuming the pattern of differences continues, find the next three terms of the sequence.

27. A standard number cube is rolled once.
(45)

a. What is the probability that the upturned face is 3 or less?

b. Describe a different event that has the same probability.

28. Write two billion, six hundred million in expanded notation using
(41, 67) powers of 10.

29. Add: $-1 + 19$
(89)

30. In an election for class president, $\frac{3}{8}$ of the students voted for Tyra and $\frac{3}{8}$
(28) of the students voted for Aaliyah. In simplest form, what fraction of the students voted for Tyra or Aaliyah?

California Mathematics Content Standards

NS 1.0, **1.5** Identify and represent on a number line decimals, fractions, mixed numbers, and positive and negative integers.

MG 1.0, **1.1** Derive and use the formula for the area of a triangle and of a parallelogram by comparing it with the formula for the area of a rectangle (i.e., two of the same triangles make a parallelogram with twice the area; a parallelogram is compared with a rectangle of the same area by cutting and pasting a right triangle on the parallelogram).

MG 1.0, **1.3** Understand the concept of volume and use the appropriate units in common measuring systems (i.e., cubic centimeter [cm3], cubic meter [m3], cubic inch [in3], cubic yard [yd3]) to compute the volume of rectangular solids.

MR 2.0, 2.5 Indicate the relative advantages of exact and approximate solutions to problems and give answers to a specified degree of accuracy.

• Rounding Decimal Numbers to the Nearest Whole Number

facts	Power Up I
mental math	a. **Number Sense:** Reduce the fractions $\frac{3}{15}$, $\frac{5}{15}$, and $\frac{10}{15}$.
	b. **Fractional Parts:** $\frac{1}{3}$ of 15
	c. **Fractional Parts:** $\frac{2}{3}$ of 15
	d. **Percent:** 50% of 15
	e. **Geometry:** A soccer ball represents which geometric solid?
	f. **Estimation:** Choose the more reasonable estimate for the mass of a soccer ball: 15 oz or 15 kg.
	g. **Calculation:** $\sqrt{81}$, $\times 5$, -1, $\div 4$, $+1$, $\div 4$, -3
	h. **Evaluate:** What is the value of the expression $8 + d$ when $d = 9$?

problem solving

Choose an appropriate problem-solving strategy to solve this problem. Two cups equals a pint, and two pints equals a quart. Two quarts equals a half gallon. Two half gallons equals one gallon. A quart of milk was poured out of a full gallon container. How many pints of milk were still in the container?

In previous problem sets we have answered questions such as the following:

Is $7.56 closer to $7 or $8?

When we answer this question, we are rounding $7.56 to the nearest dollar. This is an example of rounding a decimal number to the nearest whole number. Using rounded numbers helps us to estimate.

A number written with digits after the decimal point is not a whole number. It is between two whole numbers. We will learn how to find which of the two whole numbers it is nearer. A number line can help us understand this idea.

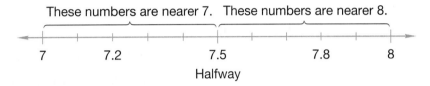

The decimal number 7.5 is halfway between 7 and 8. It is the same distance from 7.5 to 7 as it is from 7.5 to 8. The number 7.2 is less than halfway, so it is nearer 7. The number 7.8 is more than halfway, so it is nearer 8.

Although 7.5 is halfway between 7 and 8, we customarily round up if the digit after the decimal is 5 or more.

Example 1

Round 7.6 to the nearest whole number.

The decimal number 7.6 is greater than 7 but is less than 8. Halfway from 7 to 8 is 7.5. We can see on this number line that 7.6 is closer to 8 than it is to 7.

Since 7.6 is more than halfway, we round up to the whole number **8.**

Example 2

Estimate the product of 8.78 and 6.12.

Rounding decimal numbers with two decimal places is similar to rounding money. The decimal number 8.78 rounds to the whole number 9 just as $8.78 rounds to $9. Likewise, 6.12 rounds to the whole number 6. We multiply 9 by 6 and find that the product of 8.78 and 6.12 is **about 54.**

Example 3

Lorenzo estimated the area of this parallelogram to be 15 m². Did Lorenzo make a reasonable estimate?

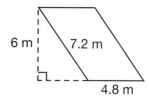

6 m | 7.2 m | 4.8 m

To find the area of a parallelogram, we multiply the base by the height and recall that the base and height of a parallelogram are perpendicular. We will make an estimate by rounding 4.8 m to 5 m.

We then solve $A = bh$ by substitution.

$$A = (5 \text{ m})(6 \text{ m})$$
$$A = 30 \text{ m}^2$$

Since our estimate of 30 m² is double Lorenzo's estimate, we decide that **Lorenzo did not make a reasonable estimate.**

(**Connect**) How can we rewrite (5 m)(6 m) to help recognize that the unit of the answer is m²?

Example 4

Thinking Skill

(**Verify**)

Which estimate will be closer to the exact answer, rounding to the nearest whole number or rounding to the nearest ten? Explain your answer.

A stop sign is an example of a regular polygon. All of the sides of a regular polygon have the same measure.

31.75 cm

What is a reasonable estimate of the perimeter of the sign?

The shape of a stop sign is a regular octagon. To estimate the perimeter, we round 31.75 cm to 32 cm and then multiply by 8.

$$P = 8s$$
$$P = 8 \times 32 \text{ cm}$$
$$P = 256 \text{ cm}$$

The perimeter of a stop sign is **about 256 cm.**

(**Estimate**) How could we perform a less accurate estimate mentally to verify that our multiplication is reasonable?

Example 5

Thinking Skill

Verify

Which estimate will be farther away from the exact volume of the storage space, rounding to the nearest whole number or rounding to the nearest tenth? Explain your answer.

The interior dimensions of a personal storage space are shown in the diagram. What is the approximate volume of storage space in cubic meters?

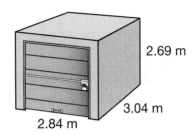

2.69 m

3.04 m

2.84 m

The shape of the space is a rectangular prism. We round each dimension to the nearest whole meter and then calculate the volume.

$$V = l \times w \times h$$
$$V = 3\,\text{m} \times 3\,\text{m} \times 3\,\text{m}$$
$$V = 27\,\text{m}^3$$

The volume of the storage space is **about 27 cubic meters.**

Justify Why is the answer labeled cubic meters and not square meters?

Lesson Practice

Round each money amount to the nearest dollar:

a. $6.24   **b.** $15.06   **c.** $118.59

d. Estimate the sum of $12.89 and $6.95.

Round each decimal number to the nearest whole number:

e. 4.75   **f.** 12.3   **g.** 96.41

h. 7.4   **i.** 45.7   **j.** 89.89

k. Estimate the product of 9.8 and 6.97.

l. **Analyze** Shateque ran one lap in 68.27 seconds. Round her time to the nearest second.

m. The illustration shows the dimensions of a small gift box. Estimate the volume of the box.

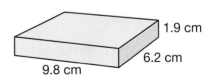

1.9 cm

6.2 cm

9.8 cm

n. What is a reasonable estimate of the area of this parallelogram? Explain why your estimate is reasonable.

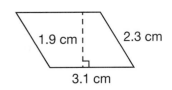

1.9 cm

2.3 cm

3.1 cm

o. On the number line below, estimate the location of 4.4, 3.25, 6.18, and 5.75. Draw and label a point at each location.

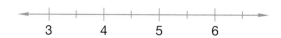

1. Ja'Von counted 60 peas and 20 carrot slices on his plate. What was the ratio of carrot slices to peas on his plate?
(87)

2. A package of 10 rolls costs $3.25. At that price, what would be the cost of 100 rolls?
(37)

3. Find the area of the triangle below.
(76)

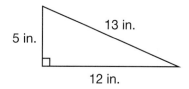

4. This rectangle was formed with pins 1 inch long.
(59)

    a. How many pins form the perimeter?

    b. How many small squares cover this rectangle?

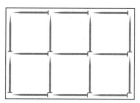

*5. Attach a zero to the end of 8 without changing the value of the number.
(91)

*6. a. (**Connect**) Which arrow could be pointing to $7\frac{3}{4}$ on the number line below?
(25)

    b. Which arrow could be pointing to negative 2?

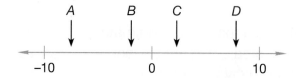

7. (Analyze) Write fractions equal to $\frac{5}{6}$ and $\frac{3}{4}$ that have denominators of
(69)   12. Then subtract the smaller fraction from the larger fraction.

8. Sun's new car has a sixteen gallon gas tank. How many quarts is
(77)   sixteen gallons?

****9. a.** Estimate the product of $6\frac{7}{8}$ and $4\frac{2}{5}$.
(92)
    b. Estimate the sum of $41\frac{3}{4}$ and $23\frac{3}{7}$.

****10.** $6.2 + 3 + 4.25$ **11.** $10^3 - 10^2$
(90)   (67)

****12.** $6.37 - 6$ **13.** 234×506
(90)   (44)

14. $10 \times \$1.75$ **15.** $\$17.50 \div 10$
(18)   (42)

****16.** Adrian ran the 400-meter dash in 54.7 seconds. Julian ran the same
(93)   race in 58.2 seconds. Adrian ran how many seconds faster than
    Julian?

17. Reduce: $\dfrac{40}{100}$
(80)

****18.** Round each money amount to the nearest dollar:
(94)
    a. $4.62   **b.** $21.78   **c.** $56.39   **d.** $111.11

19. $16w = 832$ ****20.** $\dfrac{5}{9} + \dfrac{5}{9} + \dfrac{5}{9}$
(17, 84)   (81)

21. $\dfrac{9}{10} \times \dfrac{9}{10}$ **22.** $\dfrac{2}{3} \div \dfrac{3}{4}$ ****23.** $3 \div \dfrac{3}{4}$
(63)   (86)   (86)

24. The flagpole is 10 yards tall. The flagpole is how many feet tall?
(61)

25. In many years, the first day of summer begins on June 21 and the
(10)   first day of winter begins on December 21. During those years, what is
    the elapsed time in days from the first day of summer to the first day of
    winter?

*26. a. What is the volume of this rectangular prism?
_(Inv. 9)

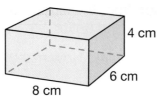

4 cm

6 cm

8 cm

b. How many faces does it have?

c. How many edges does it have?

*27. Estimate the volume of a rectangular prism with a length of 12.2 cm, a
₍₉₄₎ width of 9.6 cm, and height of 8.4 cm.

28. Multiple Choice For an art assignment, six students chose to draw
_(Inv. 7) a house, ten chose to draw a tree, two chose to draw a dog, and
seven chose to draw a person. Which of the following would **not** be an
appropriate choice of graph for this information?

   A pie chart   **B** bar graph   **C** line graph   **D** pictograph

29. The data below describe the first 30 minutes of the flight of a homing
₍₄₉₎ pigeon during a 100-mile race.

Elapsed Time in Minutes	0	10	20	30
Distance Traveled in Miles	0	7	14	22

a. **Represent** Display the data in a line graph.

b. **Explain** About how long will it take the pigeon to complete the
race? Explain your answer.

30. The length of the Wisconsin River is 30 miles longer than half the length
₍₃₇₎ of the North Canadian River in New Mexico and Oklahoma. The North
Canadian River is 800 miles long. What is the length of the Wisconsin
River?

LESSON
95

California Mathematics Content Standards
NS 2.0, 2.1 Add, subtract, multiply, and divide with decimals; add with negative integers; subtract positive integers from negative integers; and verify the reasonableness of the results.
MR 2.0, 2.3 Use a variety of methods, such as words, numbers, symbols, charts, graphs, tables, diagrams, and models, to explain mathematical reasoning.

• Subtracting Integers

facts	Power Up I
mental math	**a. Number Sense:** What is the reduced mixed number for $\frac{10}{4}$?
	b. Number Sense: What is the reduced mixed number for $\frac{10}{6}$?
	c. Number Sense: What is the reduced mixed number for $\frac{10}{8}$?
	d. Fractional Parts: $\frac{1}{5}$ of 15
	e. Fractional Parts: $\frac{2}{5}$ of 15
	f. Fractional Parts: $\frac{3}{5}$ of 15
	g. Calculation: $9^2 + 9 \div 10 + 9 \div 9$
	h. Evaluate: What is the value of the expression $3e$ when $e = 6$?

problem solving

Choose an appropriate problem-solving strategy to solve this problem. All squares are similar. Each side of this square is $\frac{1}{2}$ inch long. Draw a square with sides half as long and another square with sides twice as long. Calculate the sum of the perimeters of all three squares.

$\frac{1}{2}$ in.

New Concept

In Lesson 88 we learned that -3 and 3 are opposites because they are the same distance from zero on a number line, but on opposite sides of zero.

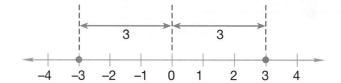

We can write the opposite of a positive number, such as +3, by writing − (+3). We can write the opposite of a negative number, such as −3, by writing − (−3). The expression −(+3) represents "the opposite of positive 3" which is the same as −3. The expression −(−3) represents "the opposite of negative 3," which is the same as 3.

We can use our understanding of opposites to find the answers to subtraction problems. Consider this subtraction problem:

$$5 - 2$$

Taking 2 away from 5 and naming 3 as the answer is one way to solve the problem. Another way to solve the same problem is to add the opposite of 2.

$$5 + (-2)$$

In both problems, the answer is 3. Subtracting a number by adding its opposite is called **algebraic addition.** We can use algebraic addition whenever we solve a subtraction problem.

Example 1

Subtract: −4 − (+6)

We will use algebraic addition. Instead of subtracting +6 from −4, we change the subtraction to an addition and we change +6 to its opposite.

$$-4 - (+6) = -4 + (-6)$$

Then we add. Since we know that the sum of two negative numbers is a negative number, we know that the sum of −4 and −6 is −10.

$$-4 + (-6) = -10$$

The answer to the subtraction is **−10.**

Example 2

Subtract: −3 − 2

In this example, 2 is being subtracted from −3, and the sign of 2, although it is not given, is positive (+). We find the answer using algebraic addition by changing the subtraction to an addition and changing +2 to its opposite.

$$-3 - 2 = -3 + (-2)$$

Again we recall that the sum of two negative numbers is a negative number. So we know that the sum of −3 and −2 is −5.

$$-3 + (-2) = -5$$

The answer to the subtraction is **−5.**

Example 3

Subtract: 7 − (−1)

We find the answer using algebraic addition by changing the subtraction to an addition and changing −1 to its opposite.

$$7 - (-1) = 7 + (+1)$$

Recall that because we do not need to write a positive sign (+) when we write a positive number, we can rewrite the expression 7 + (+1) as 7 + 1.

$$7 - (-1) = 8$$

The answer to the subtraction is **8.**

Example 4

Simplify this expression: −5 − (−4) − (+1)

When we have more than two terms to add or subtract, we simplify two of them from left to right (following the Order of Operations), then choose another two, and so on, until there is only one term left. In this example, we will simplify the −5 and −4 terms first. We will group them with brackets.

$$-5 - (-4) - (+1) = [-5 - (-4)] - (+1)$$

We will use algebraic addition to change the subtraction to an addition and change the −4 to its opposite. Then we add.

$$[-5 - (-4)] - (+1) = (-5 + 4) - (+1) = (-1) - (+1)$$

Now we have simplified down to two terms. Instead of subtracting +1 from −1, we will change the subtraction to an addition and change the +1 to its opposite. Then we add.

$$(-1) - (+1) = (-1) + (-1) = -2$$

The simplified expression is equal to **−2**.

Lesson Practice   Use algebraic addition to rewrite each subtraction as an addition. Then write the answer.

   a. −2 − 5   **b.** −7 − (+1)

   c. −1 − (−3)   **d.** 2 − 4

   e. 3 − (−2)   **f.** −6 − (+6)

   g. 4 − 7   **h.** 10 − (−9)

   i. −8 − (−8)   **j.** −5 − 3

Use algebraic addition to simplify the expressions in problems **k** and **l.**

   k. −6 + 3 − 7

   l. 4 − (−5−6)

   m. Which expression below is greater? Explain how you know.

   $$2 + (-10) \qquad 2 - (-10)$$

Written Practice   *Distributed and Integrated*

1. There were 60 deer and 40 antelope playing on the range. What was
(87) the ratio of deer to antelope playing on the range?

2. If a side of a regular octagon is 25 centimeters long, then the perimeter
(61) of the octagon is how many meters?

3. Find the perimeter and area of the parallelogram.
(75)

4. Find the area of the triangle.
(76)

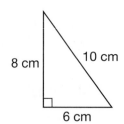

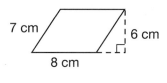

*5. Add a zero to the end of the following numbers without changing their values:
(91)
   a. 8   **b.** 3.9   **c.** 0.2   **d.** 0.13

*6. Subtract:
(93)
    a. $9 - 5.8$ **b.** $4.7 - 2.86$ **c.** $8.5 - 3$

7. **Explain** Is \$8.80 closer to \$8 or to \$9? Explain why.
(56)

*8. Estimate the difference when $7\frac{3}{4}$ is subtracted from $18\frac{7}{8}$.
(92)

9. The kite was at the end of 240 feet of string. How many yards of string is that?
(61)

*10. Round each number to the nearest whole number:
(94)
    a. 5.62   **b.** 19.39   **c.** 127.5

*11. $4 + 8.57 + 12.3$ ***12.** $16.37 - 12$
(90)   (90)

*13. Use algebraic addition to simplify each expression:
(95)
    a. $(-4) - (+3)$ **b.** $(-5) - (-2)$
    c. $(+5) - (2)$ **d.** $(+3) - (-4)$

14. 24^2 ***15.** $\dfrac{4300}{25}$
(67)   (82)

16. $14w = \$20.16$ **17.** $\sqrt{9} + \sqrt{16}$
(17, 84)   (67)

18. **Analyze** Write fractions equal to $\frac{5}{6}$ and $\frac{1}{4}$ that have denominators of
(69)   12. Then subtract the smaller fraction from the larger fraction.

19. $6\frac{3}{5} + 1\frac{3}{5}$ **20.** $8\frac{5}{6} - 1\frac{1}{6}$
(81)   (71)

21. $\dfrac{2}{10} \times \dfrac{5}{10}$ **22.** $2 \div \dfrac{4}{5}$ **23.** $\dfrac{9}{50} = \dfrac{\square}{100}$
(80)   (86)   (69)

24. Use this information to answer parts **a** and **b**.
(90)
       Becky ran two races at the track meet. She won the 100-meter
       race with a time of 13.8 seconds. In the 200-meter race she came
       in second with a time of 29.2 seconds.

    a. In the 200-meter race the winner finished 1 second faster than
       Becky. What was the winning time?

    b. Becky earned points for her team. At the track meet first place earns
       5 points, second place earns 3 points, and third place earns 1 point.
       How many points did Becky earn?

25. Reduce: $\dfrac{50}{100}$
(80)

26. Write the coordinates of points *A, B,* and *C.*
(Inv. 6)

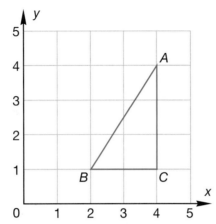

27. Temima has run the 100-meter race five times. Her times in seconds are
(74) listed below. What is the median of Temima's 100-meter race times?

14.0, 13.8, 13.7, 13.9, 14.1

*28. Simplify: $-(-4) - 7 - (+5) + 6$
(95)

29. Use an inch ruler to find the length and width of this rectangle.
(32) Then calculate the perimeter of the rectangle.

30. **Explain** Franco estimates that he has read $\dfrac{7}{10}$ of a book. What is
(48) a reasonable estimate of the fraction of the book that Franco has not read? Explain how you found your answer.

Early Finishers

Real-World Connection

Mr. Rollins is building a rectangular run for his dog. The run is 6.25 meters long and 4.5 meters wide.

a. Estimate the area of the dog run.

b. How many meters of fencing material will he need to build a fence around the dog run?

c. If the fencing is sold in sections that are each 2 meters long, then how many sections will Mr. Rollins need to buy?

LESSON
96

✎ *California Mathematics Content Standards*
NS 1.0, ①⑤ Identify and represent on a number line
decimals, fractions, mixed numbers, and positive
and negative integers.
NS 2.0, ②① Add, subtract, multiply, and divide with
decimals; add with negative integers; subtract
positive integers from negative integers; and verify
the reasonableness of the results.
AF 1.0, ①② Use a letter to represent an unknown
number; write and evaluate simple algebraic
expressions in one variable by substitution.
AF 1.0, ①④ Identify and graph ordered pairs in the
four quadrants of the coordinate plane.
AF 1.0, ①⑤ Solve problems involving linear functions
with integer values; write the equation; and graph
the resulting ordered pairs of integers on a grid.

• Solving Problems Involving Integers

facts	Power Up I
mental math	**a. Number Sense:** What is the reduced mixed number for $\frac{14}{4}$?
	b. Number Sense: What is the reciprocal of $\frac{5}{6}$?
	c. Fractional Parts: Tamara cooked $\frac{1}{4}$ of the dozen eggs for breakfast. How many eggs did she cook?
	d. Fractional Parts: In many parts of the country, school is in session for approximately $\frac{3}{4}$ of a year. How many months is $\frac{3}{4}$ of a year?
	e. Powers/Roots: $2^2 + 3^2$
	f. Geometry: A soup can represents which geometric solid?
	g. Time: Kelly boarded the school bus at 7:34 a.m. The bus arrived at school 23 minutes later. At what time did Kelly arrive at school?
	h. Evaluate: What is the value of the expression $4f - 3$ when $f = 7$?

problem solving

Choose an appropriate problem-solving strategy to solve this problem. Kerry is wearing a necklace with 30 beads strung in a red-white-blue-red-white-blue pattern. If she counts beads in the direction shown, starting with red, what will be the color of the one hundredth bead?

New Concept

Numbers that are greater than zero are **positive numbers.**
Numbers that are less than zero are **negative numbers.** Zero is
neither positive nor negative. On the following number line, we
show both positive and negative numbers.

We write negative numbers with a minus sign in front. Point *A* is at −3, which we read as "negative three." All of the numbers to the right of point *A* are greater than −3. Those numbers include −2, −1, 0, 1, 2, and so on. All of the numbers to the left of point *A* are less than −3. Those numbers include −4, −5, and so on. We can use a number line to compare in this way:

On a number line, the number farthest to the left is least and the number farthest to the right is greatest.

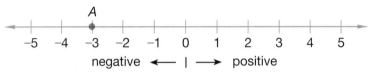

Thinking Skill

Connect

What is the freezing point of water on the Celsius scale? On the Fahrenheit scale?

One place we might see negative numbers is on a thermometer. On a very cold day the temperature may drop below zero. If the temperature is four degrees below zero, we might say the temperature is "minus four."

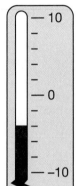

Example 1

The high temperature for the day was 6°C. The thermometer shows the low temperature during the night. How many degrees are there between the high and low temperatures?

The distance between tick marks is two degrees. Counting down from 0°, we find that the thermometer indicates a temperature of −12°C.

The high temperature was 6°C above zero, so the difference between the high and low temperatures was **18°.**

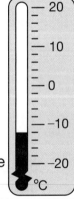

Example 2

Rick has a checking account. The amount of money in an account is called a balance. When he writes a check, the balance decreases. When he makes a deposit, the balance increases.

The balance in Rick's account is $7. If he writes a check for $10, what integer represents the balance in his account?

We can use a number line to illustrate the balance in Rick's account. We start at zero and move 7 units to the right to represent $7.

From 7 we move 10 units to the left to represent writing a check for $10. Writing a check is the same as taking dollars away.

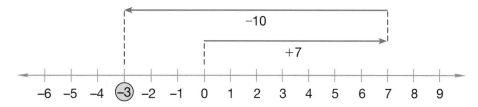

We find that the integer **−3** represents the balance in Rick's account.

(**Connect**) Write an equation to represent this problem.

Example 3

Evaluate 10 − (x + 5) when x = −4.

To evaluate an expression, we substitute for the missing number and then follow the order of operations.

$10 - (x + 5)$	Write the expression. Substitute -4 for x.
↓	
$10 - (-4 + 5)$	Work inside of the parentheses first.
↓	
$10 - (1)$	Subtract.
↓	
9	The expression $10 - (x + 5)$ simplifies to **9** when $x = -4$.

Math Symbols

We usually do not write the + sign when we write a positive number.

Example 4

Complete the function table. Write an equation to represent the ordered pairs in the table, and then graph the equation.

x	y
−2	−3
−1	
0	−1
1	
2	1

Since every *y*-value in the table is 1 less than its corresponding *x*-value, we write the equation **y = x − 1** to describe the relationship and complete the table.

y = x − 1

x	y
−2	−3
−1	−2
0	−1
1	0
2	1

We then plot points at (−2, −3), (−1, −2), (0, −1), (1, 0), and (2, 1) and draw a line.

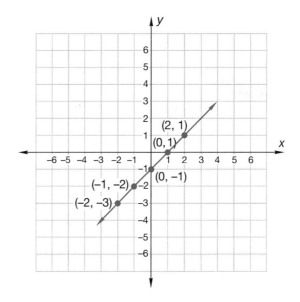

Connect Why does the equation represent a linear function?

Lesson Practice

a. Use digits and symbols to write the temperature that is twelve degrees below zero on the Fahrenheit scale.

b. What temperature is shown on this thermometer?

c. If the temperature shown on the thermometer is 14° lower than the high temperature for the day, then what is the high temperature?

d. If the temperature falls 3° from the temperature shown, what will the temperature be?

e. The balance in a checking account is $6. If a check is written for $10, what integer represents the number of dollars in the account?

f. Evaluate $5 - (x + 4)$ when $x = -4$.

g. Evaluate $8 + (q + 1)$ when $q = -3$.

h. Evaluate $2 + (5 - m)$ when $m = 7$.

i. Complete the function table. Write an equation to represent the ordered pairs in the table, and then graph the equation.

x	y
–2	–1
–1	
0	1
1	
2	3

Written Practice · *Distributed and Integrated*

1. **Represent** Draw two parallel segments that are horizontal. Make the
(20, 33) upper segment longer than the lower segment. Connect the endpoints of the segments to form a quadrilateral. What kind of quadrilateral did you draw?

2. "A pint's a pound the world around" means that a pint of water
(64, 77) weighs about a pound. About how much does a gallon of water weigh?

*3. **Estimate** Estimate the sum of $7\frac{1}{5}$ and $3\frac{7}{8}$ by rounding both
(92) numbers to the nearest whole number before adding.

4. **Analyze** There are 43 people waiting in the first line and 27 people
(38) waiting in the second line. If some of the people in the first line move to the second line so that there are the same number of people in each line, then how many people will be in each line? Does your answer represent the mean, median, mode, or range of the data?

5. Write these percents as fractions and as decimals:
(72)

    a. 48%   **b.** 80%   **c.** 6%

6. (**Represent**) Name the shaded part of this square as a
(58) decimal number, as a reduced fraction, and as a percent.

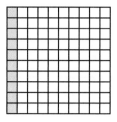

7. (**Analyze**) Write fractions equal to $\frac{1}{5}$ and $\frac{7}{8}$ that have denominators
(62, 69) of 40. Then add the fractions. Remember to convert the answer to a mixed number.

8. Reduce each fraction by dividing the terms of the fraction by their GCF:
(73)
    a. $\frac{12}{30}$ **b.** $\frac{8}{36}$ **c.** $\frac{12}{60}$

9. Simplify:
(91)
    a.   9.78   **b.**   28.79
            + 5.52   − 13.74

*10. What is a reasonable estimate of the perimeter of this scalene triangle?
(94)

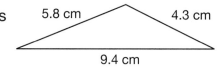

11. In a recent year, the United States produced 53.3 million metric tons of
(37, 60) wheat, which was 21.9 million metric tons more than France produced. That year, how many million metric tons of wheat did the United States and France produce altogether?

*12. 0.4 − 0.12   ***13.** 6.2 − 0.71
(93)   *(93)*

*14. Use algebraic addition to simplify each expression:
(95)
    a. $-\left(\frac{4}{6}\right)+\left(-\frac{1}{6}\right)$ **b.** $(0.4)-(-0.5)$

    c. $(-7)-(+6)$ **d.** $(-2)-(-1)-(+3)$

*15. The high temperature of the day was 92°F. The low temperature of the
(96) day was 24°F lower than the high temperature. If $h - 24$ represents the
low temperature of the day, where h is the high temperature, what is the
value of the expression when $h = 92$?

16. 540×780
(44)

17. $\dfrac{432}{6}$
(62)

18. $\dfrac{864}{12}$
(84)

19. $5 - \left(1\dfrac{2}{3} + 1\dfrac{2}{3} \right)$
(51, 62)

20. $\dfrac{5}{6} \times \left(3 \times \dfrac{2}{5} \right)$
(63, 78)

21. $2 \div \dfrac{1}{3}$
(85)

22. $\dfrac{1}{3} \div 2$
(86)

23. $\dfrac{12}{50} = \dfrac{\square}{100}$
(69)

24. This graph shows how Darren spends his time each school day. Use
(Inv. 7) the information in this graph to answer parts **a** and **b**.

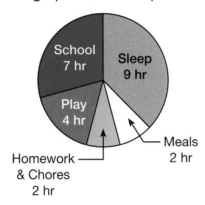

a. What is the total number of hours shown in the graph?

b. What fraction of the day does Darren spend sleeping?

*25. Freddy poured 1.4 liters of juice from a full 2-liter container. How much
(93) juice was left in the container?

*26. a. What temperature is shown on the thermometer?
(96)

    b. If the temperature shown on the thermometer is 19° lower
than the high temperature for the day, then what was the high
temperature?

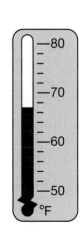

27. What is the volume of this rectangular solid if each block is a
(Inv. 9) one-inch cube?

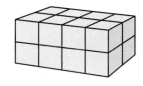

28. A fruit stand sells pineapples, strawberries, and kiwis.
(45) Purchases of fruit over a two-day period are recorded
at right.

Estimate the probability that someone who purchases
a piece of fruit will buy a pineapple.

Fruit	Number Sold
Pineapples	23
Strawberries	16
Kiwis	41

29. Arrange these numbers in order from least to greatest:
(56)

$$1.0 \quad \frac{1}{10} \quad 0.001 \quad \frac{1}{100}$$

30. The table shows the number of Super Bowl wins for five professional
(Inv. 7) football teams in the first 40 Super Bowls.

NFL Super Bowl

Team	Wins
Denver Broncos	2
Dallas Cowboys	5
Green Bay Packers	3
San Francisco 49ers	5
Tampa Bay Buccaneers	1

a. Choose an appropriate type of graph and then graph the data.

b. (**Formulate**) Write two questions that can be answered using your
graph.

California Mathematics Content Standards
AF 1.0, 1.2 Use a letter to represent an unknown number; write and evaluate simple algebraic expressions in one variable by substitution.
MR 3.0, 3.3 Develop generalizations of the results obtained and apply them in other circumstances.

• Writing Expressions

When writing expressions in math, the placement of parentheses matters.

Remember that the Associative Property applies to the operations of addition and multiplication.

$$a + (b + c) = (a + b) + c \qquad\qquad a \times (b \times c) = (a \times b) \times c$$

$$2 + (3 + 4) = (2 + 3) + 4 \qquad\qquad 2 \times (3 \times 4) = (2 \times 3) \times 4$$

$$2 + 7 = 5 + 4 \qquad\qquad\qquad 2 \times 12 = 6 \times 4$$

$$9 = 9 \qquad\qquad\qquad\qquad 24 = 24$$

The order in which we add or multiply does not change the answer. We will always arrive at the same answer. The placement of the parentheses does not change the answer. However, there are cases where placement of the parentheses becomes very important.

Remember that the Associative Property does *not* apply to the operations of subtraction and division.

$$(a - b) - c \neq a - (b - c) \qquad\qquad (a \div b) \div c \neq a \div (b \div c)$$

$$(6 - 3) - 2 \neq 6 - (3 - 2) \qquad\qquad (8 \div 4) \div 2 \neq 8 \div (4 \div 2)$$

$$3 - 2 \neq 6 - 1 \qquad\qquad\qquad 2 \div 2 \neq 8 \div 2$$

$$1 \neq 5 \qquad\qquad\qquad\qquad 1 \neq 4$$

We can change subtraction and division expressions so that the Associative Property will apply. We can change a subtraction expression so that we are adding negative numbers.

$$(6 - 3) - 2 = [6 + (-3)] + (-2) = 6 + [(-3) + (-2)] = 6 + (-5) = 6 - 5 = 1$$

We can change a division expression so that we are multiplying by a reciprocal.

$$(8 \div 4) \div 2 = (8 \times \tfrac{1}{4}) \times \tfrac{1}{2} = 8 \times (\tfrac{1}{4} \times \tfrac{1}{2}) = 8 \times \tfrac{1}{8} = 1$$

a. (Verify) Check that the Associative Property applies to addition by simplifying both sides of this equation.

$$(4 + 5) + (6 + 12) = [4 + (5 + 6)] + 12$$

b. (Verify) Check that the Associative Property applies to multiplication by simplifying both sides of this equation.

$$2 \times (3 \times 9) = (2 \times 3) \times 9$$

(Connect) The Commutative Property also applies only to addition and multiplication. How can the following subtraction and division problems be changed so that the Commutative Property will apply to them?

c. $6 - 3$ **d.** $8 \div 4$

e. $12 - 5$ **f.** $20 \div 4$

LESSON
97

California Mathematics Content Standards

NS 1.0, 1.2 Interpret percents as a part of a hundred; find decimal and percent equivalents for common fractions and explain why they represent the same value; compute a given percent of a whole number.

SDAP 1.0, 1.3 Use fractions and percentages to compare data sets of different sizes.

MR 2.0, 2.3 Use a variety of methods, such as words, numbers, symbols, charts, graphs, tables, diagrams, and models, to explain mathematical reasoning.

• Using Percent to Name Part of a Group

facts   Power Up I

mental math

    a. Number Sense: Simplify the improper fractions $\frac{7}{6}$, $\frac{8}{6}$, and $\frac{9}{6}$.

    b. Number Sense: What is the reciprocal of $\frac{1}{3}$?

    c. Fractional Parts: $\frac{1}{3}$ of 100

    d. Number Sense: $33\frac{1}{3} + 33\frac{1}{3}$

    e. Number Sense: $\frac{2}{3}$ of 100

    f. Powers/Roots: $3^2 - 1$

    g. Calculation: 10% of 500, × 10, ÷ 2, − 10, ÷ 4, + 3, ÷ 9

    h. Evaluate: What is the value of the expression $5g + 4$ when $g = 2$?

problem solving

Choose an appropriate problem-solving strategy to solve this problem. George was down to three clean socks—one red, one white, and one blue. How many combinations of two socks can George make from these three socks?

For each combination of two socks, George could choose between two permutations of the socks. For example, George could wear a red sock on his left foot and a white sock on his right foot (R, W), or he could switch the socks (W, R). List all the permutations of two socks George could make.

Percent is a word that means "out of 100." If we read that 50 percent of all Americans drive cars, we understand that 50 out of every 100 Americans drive cars. Likewise, the statement "Ten percent of the population is left-handed" means that 10 out of every 100 people are left-handed. When we say "percent," we speak as though there were 100 in the group. However, we may say "percent" even when there are more than or less than 100 in the group.

Like fractions, percents name parts of a whole. We have used fraction manipulatives to learn the percents that are equivalent to some fractions. In this lesson we will learn how to find percents for other fractions by renaming the fraction with a denominator of 100.

Example 1

Thinking Skill

Verify

What property of multiplication states that we can multiply any number by 1 and not change the value of the number?

If 8 of the 20 students are boys, what percent of the students are boys?

If we write the number of boys over the total number of students in the group, we get 8 boys over 20 total. If we multiply this fraction by a name for 1 so that the denominator becomes 100, the numerator will be the percent. So we multiply by $\frac{5}{5}$.

$$\frac{8 \text{ boys}}{20 \text{ total}} \times \frac{5}{5} = \frac{40 \text{ boys}}{100 \text{ total}}$$

This means that if there were 100 students, there would be 40 boys. Thus, **40 percent** of the students are boys.

Example 2

There were 400 beads in all. If 60 beads were red, what percent of the beads were red?

We have the fraction 60 beads over 400 total. We can partially reduce this fraction ratio to make the denominator equal 100. We do this by dividing each term by 4.

$$\frac{60 \text{ red beads} \div 4}{400 \text{ total} \div 4} = \frac{15 \text{ red beads}}{100 \text{ total}}$$

When the denominator is 100, the top number is the percent. Thus, **15 percent** of the beads were red.

Instead of using the word *percent*, we may use the percent sign (%). Using the percent sign, we write 15 percent as **15%**.

Some fractions are not easily renamed as parts of 100. Let's suppose that $\frac{1}{6}$ of the students earned an A on the test. What percent of the students earned an A?

$$\frac{1}{6} = \frac{?}{100}$$

Thinking Skill

Connect

What are the factors of 100?

Since 100 is not a multiple of 6, there is no whole number by which we can multiply the numerator and denominator of $\frac{1}{6}$ to rename it with a denominator of 100. However, we can find $\frac{1}{6}$ of 100% by multiplying and then dividing.

$$\frac{1}{6} \times 100\% = \frac{100\%}{6}$$

$$16\frac{4}{6}\% = 16\frac{2}{3}\%$$

$$6\overline{)100\%}$$
$$\underline{6}$$
$$40$$
$$\underline{36}$$
$$4$$

We find that $\frac{1}{6}$ equals $16\frac{2}{3}\%$.

Connect Explain how to write a quotient and a remainder as a mixed number.

Example 3

The team won $\frac{2}{3}$ of its games. Find the percent of games the team won.

We first multiply $\frac{2}{3}$ by 100%.

$$\frac{2}{3} \times 100\% = \frac{200\%}{3}$$

Then we divide 200% by 3 and write the quotient as a mixed number.

$$66\frac{2}{3}\%$$
$$3\overline{)200\%}$$
$$\underline{18}$$
$$20$$
$$\underline{18}$$
$$2$$

The team won **$66\frac{2}{3}\%$** of its games.

Example 4

In Mrs. Langston's fifth grade class, 14 out of 20 students belong to an after-school club. In Mr. Rodriguez's fifth grade class, 12 out of 16 students belong to an after-school club. Which class has the greater percent of students who belong to an after-school club?

The ratios in this problem compare the number of students who belong to an after-school club to the total number of students. We first write the ratios as fractions in simplest form.

$$\text{Mrs. Langston's class: } \frac{14}{20} = \frac{7}{10}$$

$$\text{Mr. Rodriguez's class: } \frac{12}{16} = \frac{3}{4}$$

One way to compare fractions is to change the fractions to percents.

$$\text{Mrs. Langston's class: } \frac{7}{10} = \frac{70}{100} = 70\%$$

$$\text{Mr. Rodriguez's class: } \frac{3}{4} = \frac{75}{100} = 75\%$$

We find that because 75% > 70%, **Mr. Rodriguez's class** has the greater percent of students who belong to an after-school club.

Lesson Practice

a. If 120 of the 200 students are girls, then what percent of the students are girls?

b. If 10 of the 50 apples are green, then what percent of the apples are green?

c. Sixty out of 300 is what percent?

d. Forty-eight out of 200 is what percent?

e. Thirty out of 50 is what percent?

f. If half of the people ate lunch, then what percent of the people ate lunch?

g. Five minutes is $\frac{1}{12}$ of an hour. Five minutes is what percent of an hour?

h. (**Explain**) In Ms. Viau's class, 11 out of 20 students are boys. In Mr. Jackson's class, 3 out of 5 students are boys. Which class has the greater percent of boys? Explain how you know.

1. The room was cluttered with 15 magazines and 25 newspapers. What
(87) was the ratio of magazines to newspapers cluttering the room?

2. **Analyze** About $\frac{1}{3}$ of the weight of a banana is the weight of the peel.
(34, 58) If a banana weighs 12 ounces, then the weight of the peel would
be about how many ounces? About what percent of the weight of a
banana is the weight of the peel?

3. **Analyze** What is the probability that a standard number cube, when
(45, 65) rolled once, will stop with a prime number on top?

4. Write the following fractions as decimals and as percents:
(70)
a. $\frac{8}{10}$ **b.** $\frac{40}{100}$ **c.** $\frac{1}{10}$

*5. Eleven of the twenty-five students taking a golf class are girls. What
(97) percent of the class is girls?

*6. There are 300 vehicles in the parking lot. If 75 vehicles were vans, what
(97) percent of the vehicles were vans?

7. Twenty-seven students entering a classroom seat themselves in rows
(14) with 6 students in each row except the last row. How many rows of
6 students will be seated in the classroom? How many students will be
seated in the last row?

8. **Explain** Mr. Alfredson's family loves to read. Last night
(37) Mr. Alfredson read a book for 15 more minutes than his son
and for 10 fewer minutes than his daughter. Mr. Alfredson read
for 30 minutes. Altogether, how many minutes did the family spend
reading? Explain why your answer is reasonable.

*9. Estimate the product of 12.34 and 4.8.
(94)

10. Estimate the perimeter and area of this rectangle by
(59, 92) first rounding the length and width to the nearest inch.

$7\frac{7}{8}$ in.

$4\frac{1}{4}$ in.

*11. Simplify: −(+3) − 5 + (−4) + 3
(95)

*12. 3 − 2.35   ***13.** 10 − 4.06   **14.** 4.35 + 12.6 + 15
(93)   (93)   (60)

*15. Mr. Perez's fifth grade science class recorded the temperature each
(96)   day for seven different cities for one week. The highest recorded
         temperature was 102°F. The lowest recorded temperature was 58°
         lower than the highest temperature. What was the lowest recorded
         temperature?

16. 2^5 **17.** Add: −2 + 7
(67)   (89)

18. $\sqrt{25} - \sqrt{9}$ **19.** $16x = 2112$
(67)   (17, 84)

20. $3\frac{2}{3} + \left(2 - \frac{2}{3} \right)$ **21.** $\frac{1}{2} \times \left(4 \times \frac{1}{4} \right)$
(46, 51)   (78)

22. $1 \div \frac{7}{5}$ **23.** $\frac{3}{2} \div \frac{2}{3}$
(86)   (86)

24. $\frac{4}{10} \times \frac{5}{10}$ **25.** Add: −9 + 9
(80)   (89)

26. Reduce: $\frac{500}{1000}$
(80)

27. **a.** What is the volume of this rectangular solid?
(Inv. 9)

         b. How many faces does it have?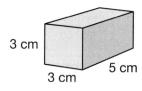

         c. How many vertices does it have?

28. Write the coordinates of each vertex of triangle *ABC*.
(Inv. 6)

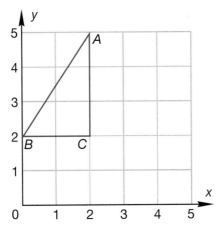

29. In a presidential election, each state is assigned a number of electoral
(Inv. 5) votes. To become president, a candidate must win 270 or more
electoral votes. The 2000 Census assigned these numbers of electoral
votes to four states.

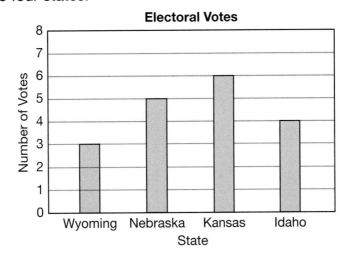

a. What number represents the median number of electoral votes of
these four states?

b. The state of California is assigned eleven times the number
of electoral votes as the state of Nebraska is assigned. How
many electoral votes are assigned to the state of California?

c. Suppose a candidate for president won 12 electoral votes by
winning three of the states shown in the graph. Which three states
did the candidate win?

30. Use an inch ruler to measure the sides of this triangle. Refer
(24, 32) to the illustration and measurements to answer parts **a–c.**

   a. How many inches long is each side of the triangle?

   b. What is the perimeter of the triangle?

   c. Classify the triangle by sides and by angles.

*Real-World
Connection*

Marc's batting average this year is .300. Last year his average was
.279. What is the difference between his average last year and his
current average? Nathan's batting average this year is .009 lower than
Marc's. What is Nathan's batting average?

California Mathematics Content Standards

NS 2.0, 2.1 Add, subtract, multiply, and divide with decimals; add with negative integers; subtract positive integers from negative integers; and verify the reasonableness of the results.

MR 2.0, 2.1 Use estimation to verify the reasonableness of calculated results.

MR 2.0, 2.3 Use a variety of methods, such as words, numbers, symbols, charts, graphs, tables, diagrams, and models, to explain mathematical reasoning.

• Multiplying Decimal Numbers

facts	Power Up I
mental math	**a. Number Sense:** Simplify the improper fractions $\frac{6}{4}$, $\frac{7}{4}$, and $\frac{8}{4}$.
	b. Number Sense: What is the reciprocal of $\frac{3}{4}$? The reciprocal of $\frac{1}{4}$?
	c. Percent: What is 50% of $20? 25% of $20? 10% of $20?
	d. Powers/Roots: $4^2 + 3^2$
	e. Estimation: Choose the more reasonable estimate for the capacity of a coffee cup: 300 mL or 300 L.
	f. Time: The movie began at 6:45 p.m. It ended 1 hour 50 minutes later. At what time did the movie end?
	g. Calculation: $\frac{1}{3}$ of 21, × 2, + 1, ÷ 3, × 6, + 2, ÷ 4
	h. Evaluate: What is the value of the expression $66 - 6h$ when $h = 1$?
problem solving	Choose an appropriate problem-solving strategy to solve this problem. Sasha used 1-inch cubes to build this rectangular soild. How many 1-inch cubes did Sasha use?

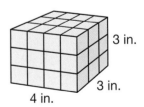

3 in.

3 in.

4 in.

New Concept

What is one tenth of one tenth? We will use pictures to answer this question.

The first picture at right is a square. The square represents one whole, and each column is one tenth of the whole. We have shaded one tenth of the whole.

one tenth

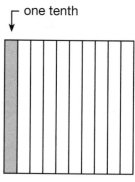

To find one tenth of one tenth, we divide each tenth into ten parts. In the second picture at right, we show each column divided into ten parts. One small square is shaded. We have shaded one tenth of one tenth of the whole. The shaded part is one hundredth of the whole.

one tenth of one tenth

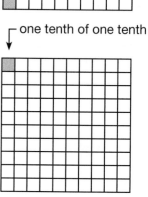

When we find one tenth of one tenth, we are multiplying. Here we show the problem written as a multiplication equation:

$$\frac{1}{10} \times \frac{1}{10} = \frac{1}{100}$$

tenths × tenths = hundredths

We can also write the same problem using decimal numbers.

$$\begin{array}{r} 0.1 \\ \times\ 0.1 \\ \hline 0.01 \end{array}$$

tenths × tenths = hundredths

When we set up a decimal multiplication problem, we do not line up the decimal points as we do in addition and subtraction. We just set up the problem as though it were a whole-number problem and then multiply. To place the decimal point in the answer, we first count the total number of decimal places in both factors. Then we insert a decimal point in the answer so that it has the same total number of decimal places as the factors.

Copy and study the following examples and solutions:

$$\begin{array}{r} 1 \\ 0.12 \\ \times\quad 6 \\ \hline 0.72 \end{array}$$

0.12   2 digits to right of decimal point

×   6   0 digits to right of decimal point

0.72   2 digits to right of decimal point

You can count the decimal places because fractions and decimals are related.

tenths × ones = tenths
$\frac{1}{10} \times 3 = \frac{3}{10}$
$0.1 \times 3 = 0.3$

tenths × tenths = hundredths
$\frac{3}{10} \times \frac{5}{10} = \frac{15}{100}$
$0.3 \times 0.5 = 0.15$

tenths × hundredths = thousandths
$\frac{3}{10} \times \frac{7}{100} = \frac{21}{1000}$
$0.3 \times 0.07 = 0.021$

$$
\begin{array}{r}
\overset{1}{} \\
25 \\
\times\; 0.3 \\
\hline
7.5
\end{array}
$$
25 — 0 digits to right of decimal point
× 0.3 — 1 digit to right of decimal point
7.5 — 1 digit to right of decimal point

$$
\begin{array}{r}
\overset{4}{} \\
0.15 \\
\times\; 0.9 \\
\hline
0.135
\end{array}
$$
0.15 — 2 digits to right of decimal point
× 0.9 — 1 digit to right of decimal point
0.135 — 3 digits to right of decimal point

The rule for multiplying decimal numbers is **"Multiply, then count."** We *multiply* the digits to get the answer. Then we *count* the total number of decimal places in the factors. Next, starting from the right side of the answer, we count the same number of digits as the number of decimal places and mark the decimal point.

In the chart below we have summarized the rules of decimal arithmetic for adding, subtracting, and multiplying.

Decimals Chart

Operation	+ or −	×
Memory cue	line up . ± . ‾‾‾‾ .	×; then count . − × . − ‾‾‾‾ . − −
You may need to … • Place a decimal point on the end of whole numbers. • Fill empty places with zero.		

We can apply these rules when we multiply larger numbers that include decimal places.

Example 1

There are 2.54 centimeters in 1 inch. How many centimeters are in 6 inches?

Since we know the number of centimeters in 1 inch, we multiply to find the number of centimeters in 6 inches.

$$
\begin{array}{r}
2.54 \\
\times\quad 6 \\
\hline
15.24
\end{array}
$$
2.54 — 2 decimal places
× 6 — 0 decimal places
15.24 — 2 decimal places

We place two decimal places in the product because there is a total of two decimal places in the factors, and we find that 6 inches = **15.24 cm.**

Verify How can we check that the answer is reasonable?

Example 2

There are about 39.37 inches in 1 meter. How many inches are in a half-meter?

We can think of a half-meter as 0.5. Then we can multiply 0.5 by 39.37 to find the number of inches.

$$
\begin{array}{rl}
39.37 & \text{2 decimal places} \\
\times\ \ 0.5 & \text{1 decimal places} \\
\hline
19.685 & \text{3 decimal places}
\end{array}
$$

We place three decimal places in the product because there are a total of three decimal places in the factors, and we find that a half-meter is **19.685 inches.**

Lesson Practice   Multiply:

a. 0.3
  × 4

b. 3
  × 0.6

c. 0.12
  × 12

d. 1.4
  × 0.7

e. 0.3×0.5

f. 1.2×3

g. 1.5×0.5

h. 0.25×1.1

i. Compare: $\dfrac{3}{10} \times \dfrac{3}{10} \bigcirc 0.3 \times 0.3$

j. What is the area of this square?

0.8 cm

k. There are 2.54 centimeters in 1 inch. How many centimeters are in half an inch?

l. There are about 39.37 inches in 1 meter. How many inches are in 3 meters?

Written Practice   *Distributed and Integrated*

1. Write 48 as a product of prime factors.
(66)

2. **Analyze** In Sovann's class there are twice as many boys as there are
(87)   girls. There are 18 boys in the class.

a. How many girls are in the class?

b. How many students are in the class?

c. What is the ratio of boys to girls in the class?

3. **Analyze** Marcia's last seven test scores were 85, 90, 90, 80, 80, 80,
(74)   and 75.

    a. Arrange the seven scores in order from least to greatest.

    b. What is the median of the scores?

    c. What is the mode of the scores?

4. **Represent** Write this sentence using digits and symbols:
(63)

        The product of one half and one third is one sixth.

5. Which digit is in the tenths place in 142.75?
(55)

*6. Simplify: $-(-7) + (-9) - (+3) + 4$
(95)

7. Draw four circles the same size. Shade 25% of the first circle,
(58)   50% of the second circle, 75% of the third circle, and 100% of
    the fourth circle. Write a fraction and a decimal to represent the
    sum of the shaded parts.

8. Round $4\frac{3}{10}$ to the nearest whole number.
(92)

*9. a. Round $10.49 to the nearest dollar.
(94)

    b. Round $9.51 to the nearest dollar.

10. a. **List** The first five multiples of 2 are 2, 4, 6, 8, and 10. What are the
(16)   first five multiples of 7?

    b. What are the common factors of 2 and 7?

11. **Connect** Which arrow could be pointing to 7.2 on this number line?
(54)

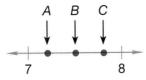

*12. **Estimate** Find the area and perimeter of this rectangle
(59, 94)   by first rounding the length and width to the nearest
    centimeter.

6.8 cm

3.9 cm

13. 6.4 + 2.87 + 4
(90)

*14. The low temperature for the night was 11°C. The thermometer shows
(96)   the high temperature for the day. How many degrees are there between
       the high and low temperatures?

15. $5.64 × 10
(18)

16. 976 × 267
(43)

17. (Analyze) All these ratios are equal. What is the quotient of each
(87)   division?

$$\frac{640}{32}, \frac{320}{16}, \frac{160}{8}, \frac{80}{4}$$

18. Write a fraction equal to $\frac{2}{3}$ with a denominator of 9. Then add $\frac{7}{9}$ to the
(62, 69)   fraction you wrote. Remember to convert the sum to a mixed number.

19. $5\frac{2}{5} + \left(3 - \frac{1}{3}\right)$
(51, 62)

20. $2 \times \left(\frac{1}{2} \times \frac{1}{3}\right)$
(63, 78)

*21. Will has completed $\frac{3}{8}$ of his display for the science fair. Find the percent
(97)   of work Will has completed on his display.

22. $\frac{4}{25} = \frac{\square}{100}$
(69)

*23. Multiply:
(98)
  a.   5
       × 0.7

  b.   3.2
       × 0.4

  c.   0.15
       ×   6

*24. Find the area of the parallelogram:
(75, 98)

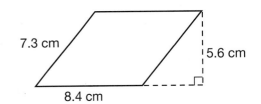

7.3 cm

5.6 cm

8.4 cm

25. Write the coordinates of each vertex of triangle *ABC*.
(Inv. 6)

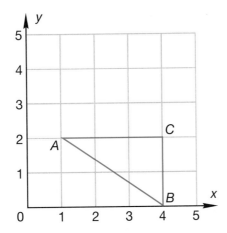

26. (**Conclude**) Determine a possible pattern for this sequence, and draw
(Inv. 8) the next figure.

27. a. What is the volume of a box of tissues with the dimensions
(Inv. 9) shown?

    b. How many vertices does the box have?

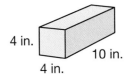

4 in.

10 in.

4 in.

28. In 2000, about 28% of the people living in Texas were under age 18.
(58, 80) Write 28% as a reduced fraction.

29. Multiple Choice Three friends ride the school bus each day. Amador
(37) rides for 5 fewer minutes than Lon, and Lon rides for 3 more minutes
than Yuuma. Amador rides for 4 minutes. Which expression can be
used to find the length of time Yuuma rides the bus?

    A $4 + 5 - 3$ **B** $3 - (5 - 4)$ **C** $5 + 3 - 4$ **D** $4 + 3 + 5$

30. Multiple Choice Two thirds of the 18 students in a study hall
worked to complete their homework. The other students in the study
hall read a book. Which diagram shows the number of students who
read a book?

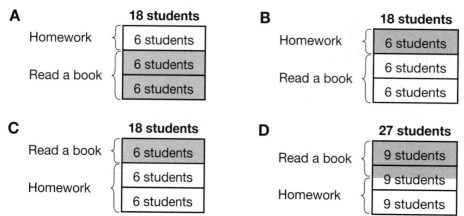

A   18 students
Homework { 6 students
Read a book { 6 students
             6 students

B   18 students
Homework { 6 students
Read a book { 6 students
             6 students

C   18 students
Read a book { 6 students
Homework { 6 students
           6 students

D   27 students
Read a book { 9 students
Homework { 9 students
           9 students

Real-World Connection

One hundred twenty-three students were surveyed to find out whether
they wanted to go on a field trip to the ocean or to the museum. Of the
students surveyed, $\frac{2}{3}$ wanted to go to the ocean and the rest wanted
to go to the museum. How many students wanted to go to the ocean
and how many wanted to go to the museum? Draw a circle graph
to represent the results of the survey.

California Mathematics Content Standards
NS 2.0, **2.1** Add, subtract, multiply, and divide with decimals; add with negative integers; subtract positive integers from negative integers; and verify the reasonableness of the results.
MR 2.0, 2.6 Make precise calculations and check the validity of the results from the context of the problem.

• Multiplying Decimal Numbers Using Zeros as Placeholders

facts   Power Up I

mental math

a. **Number Sense:** Simplify the improper fractions $\frac{10}{8}$, $\frac{11}{8}$, and $\frac{12}{8}$.

b. **Number Sense:** What is the reciprocal of $\frac{1}{2}$? The reciprocal of 2?

c. **Number Sense:** $\frac{1}{8}$ of 100

d. **Number Sense:** $12\frac{1}{2} + 12\frac{1}{2} + 12\frac{1}{2}$

e. **Number Sense:** $\frac{3}{8}$ of 100

f. **Measurement:** How many feet are in 33 yards? In $33\frac{1}{3}$ yards?

g. **Calculation:** $\sqrt{64}$, $\times$ 6, $\div$ 8, $\times$ 4, $\div$ 3

h. **Evaluate:** What is the value of the expression $7 + 7i$ when $i = 9$?

problem solving

Choose an appropriate problem-solving strategy to solve this problem. Two cups equals a pint. Two pints equals a quart. Two quarts equals a half gallon. Two half gallons equals a gallon. Imani used a gallon container that was full of water to fill a half-gallon container, a quart container, a pint container, and a cup container. How much water was left in Imani's gallon container?

New Concept

When we multiply decimal numbers, we follow the rule "Multiply, then count." We count the total number of decimal places in the factors. Then starting from the right-hand end of the product, we count over the same number of places and mark the decimal point.

Sometimes there are more decimal places in the factors than there are digits in the product. Look at this problem, for example:

$$
\begin{array}{r}
0.3 \\
\times\ 0.3 \\
\hline
.\ 9 \\
\end{array}
$$

There are two digits to the right of the decimal points in the factors. We count over two places in the product, but there is only one digit.

To complete the multiplication, we use a rule from the bottom of the decimals chart in Lesson 98. We "fill empty places with zero." Then we add a zero to the left of the decimal point.

Add a zero to the left of the decimal point.

$$
\begin{array}{r}
0.3 \\
\times\ 0.3 \\
\hline
0.\underline{09} \\
\end{array}
$$

Fill the empty place with zero.

Changing the problem 0.3 × 0.3 to a fraction problem may help us understand why we use zeros as placeholders. Since 0.3 equals $\frac{3}{10}$, we may write the multiplication problem like this:

$$\frac{3}{10} \times \frac{3}{10} = \frac{9}{100}$$

The product $\frac{9}{100}$ may be written as the decimal number 0.09.

Example 1

Multiply: 0.12 × 0.3

We set up the problem as though it were a whole-number problem. We follow the rule "Multiply, then count." We "fill empty places with zero" and get the product **0.036.**

Verify Explain why the answer is reasonable.

$$
\begin{array}{r}
0.12 \\
\times\ 0.3 \\
\hline
36 \\
\end{array}
$$
3 digits to the right of the decimal points

.036 Count over 3 places; fill the empty place with zero.

Example 2

Find the area of a square with sides of length 0.3 m.

We know that the formula for the area of a square is $A = s \times s$, or $A = s^2$. So we know that to find the area of the square, we multiply 0.3 m by 0.3 m.

$$
\begin{array}{r}
0.3 \\
\times\ 0.3 \\
\hline
9 \\
\end{array}
$$
Two digits to the right of the decimal points

We set up the problem as though it were a whole-number problem. We follow the rule, "Multiply, then count."

0.09 Count over 2 places; fill the empty place with zero.

We find the area of the square to be **0.09 m².**

Multiply:

a. $\begin{array}{r} 0.25 \\ \times\ 0.3 \\ \hline \end{array}$ **b.** $\begin{array}{r} 0.12 \\ \times\ 0.12 \\ \hline \end{array}$ **c.** $\begin{array}{r} 0.125 \\ \times\ 0.3 \\ \hline \end{array}$ **d.** $\begin{array}{r} 0.05 \\ \times\ 0.03 \\ \hline \end{array}$

e. 0.03×0.3 **f.** 3.2×0.03

g. 0.6×0.16 **h.** 0.12×0.2

i. 0.01×0.1 **j.** 0.07×0.12

k. What is the area of this rectangle?

0.2 m

0.4 m

Written Practice

Distributed and Integrated

1. The ratio of boys to girls in the auditorium was 4 to 5. If there were
(87) 40 boys in the auditorium, how many girls were there? (*Hint:* In this problem, the ratio 4 to 5 means that for every 4 boys there were 5 girls.)

2. This circle is divided into tenths. How many tenths does it
(19) take to equal one whole?

3. (**Analyze**) Tony had six coins in his pockets totaling 43¢. How many of
(57) the coins were nickels?

4. Write the numbers, 1.1, 0.7, $\frac{3}{10}$, and $\frac{4}{5}$ in order from greatest to least.
(91)

*5. Use algebraic addition to simplify each expression:
(95)
a. $(+4) - (+2)$ **b.** $(-9) - (-3)$

c. $(-6) + (-7)$ **d.** $8 - (-4)$

6. (**Analyze**) Write a fraction equal to $\frac{1}{2}$ that has a denominator of 10.
(69, 80) Then subtract that fraction from $\frac{9}{10}$. Remember to reduce the answer.

7. (**Analyze**) Inez and Felicia had three days to read a book. Inez read
(38) 40 pages the first day, 60 pages the second day, and 125 pages the third day. Felicia read the same book, but she read an equal number of pages each of the three days. How many pages did Felicia read each day?

8. Estimate the cost of 12 comic books priced at $1.95 each.
(50)

9. Estimate the quotient when 20.8 is divided by 6.87 by rounding both
(94) decimal numbers to the nearest whole number before dividing.

*10. **a.** Name the coordinates of each vertex of rectangle
(59, Inv. 6) *ABCD*

b. The area of rectangle *ABCD* is how many square units?

c. The perimeter of the rectangle is how many units?

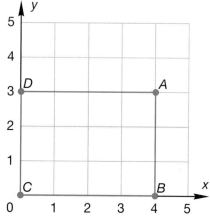

*11. Evaluate $16 - (x + 2)$ when $x = -6$.
(96)

*12. Refer to quadrilateral *ABCD* to answer parts **a–c.**
(20, 33)

a. Recall that a right angle is sometimes marked with a square in the corner. Both $\angle CDA$ and DCB are right angles. Which angle appears to be acute?

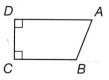

b. Which two sides are parallel?

c. What type of quadrilateral is quadrilateral *ABCD*?

13. $\dfrac{1}{100} + \dfrac{9}{100}$
(80)

14. $\dfrac{63}{100} - \dfrac{13}{100}$
(80)

15. $\dfrac{5}{10} \times \dfrac{5}{10}$
(80)

*16. $\dfrac{3}{5} \div \dfrac{3}{4}$
(86)

17. $3.76 + 12 + 6.8$
(90)

18. $12 - 1.25$
(93)

19. $\sqrt{64} + \sqrt{36}$
(67)

*20. In Mrs. Jones' class, 8 of the 24 students play soccer, while 12 of the
(97) 24 students play softball. Which sport has the greater percentage of participation? Show your comparison.

*21. There are 2.54 centimeters in one inch. How many centimeters are in
(98) 12 inches?

22. $14m = 5964$
(17, 84)

*23. Multiply:
(99)
   a.   0.09   **b.**   0.13   **c.**   0.38
        $\times$ 0.4 $\times$ 0.08 $\times$ 0.2

24. $\dfrac{7}{25} = \dfrac{\square}{100}$
(69)

25. (**Interpret**) The line graph shows temperatures at different times on an
(49) April afternoon in Mexico City, Mexico. Use the graph to answer the
   questions that follow.

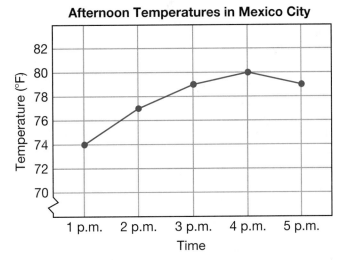

Afternoon Temperatures in Mexico City

  a. At which two times of the day was the temperature the same?

  b. During which one-hour period of time did the greatest temperature
     decrease occur? What was that decrease?

  c. The low temperature that day in Mexico City was 26° lower than
     the 4 p.m. temperature. What was the low temperature that
     day?

*26. Multiply:
(99)
    a. 0.03 × 0.3   **b.** 0.11 × 0.5

27. a. What is the volume of a box of cereal with these
(Inv. 9)   dimensions?

    b. How many edges does the box have?

10 in.

7 in.   2 in.

28. In a 100-meter dash, Tyrone ran fourteen hundredths of a second faster
(93)   than an opponent who ran the race in 13.02 seconds. How long did it
    take Tyrone to run the race?

29. a. Which of these letters has rotational symmetry?
(RF28)

T E N

    b. Which letters have reflective symmetry?

30.   (**Explain**) The number of votes cast in Dickenson County, Virginia,
(22) in the 2000 presidential election is shown in the table.

2000 Election Results
Dickenson County, Virginia

Candidate	Number of Votes
Bush (R)	3,122
Gore (D)	3,951

What is a reasonable estimate of the total number of votes cast for the
two candidates? Explain your answer.

Early Finishers

Real-World Connection

One ounce of 18-karat gold consists of 0.75 ounces of pure gold and
0.25 ounces of other metals. How many ounces of pure gold would
there be in an 18-karat gold bracelet that weighs 2.8 ounces?

California Mathematics Content Standards
NS 2.0, 2.1 Add, subtract, multiply, and divide with
    decimals; add with negative integers; subtract
    positive integers from negative integers; and verify
    the reasonableness of the results.
MR 2.0, 2.3 Use a variety of methods, such as words,
    numbers, symbols, charts, graphs, tables, diagrams,
    and models, to explain mathematical reasoning.
MR 3.0, 3.3 Develop generalizations of the results
    obtained and apply them in other circumstances.

• Multiplying with Multi-Digit Decimal Numbers

facts   Power Up I

mental math

   a. Number Sense: Simplify the improper fractions $\frac{15}{10}$, $\frac{20}{10}$, and $\frac{25}{10}$.

   b. Number Sense: What is the reciprocal of 3? The reciprocal of $\frac{3}{5}$?

   c. Percent: What is 25% of $100? 25% of $10? 25% of $1?

   d. Time: How many years are in two and a half centuries?

   e. Time: How many years are in two and a half millennia?

   f. Powers/Roots: $5^2 - 1^3$

   g. Measurement: The topmost shelf is 2 yards above the floor. How many inches is that?

   h. Evaluate: What is the value of the expression $j^2 + 1$ when $j = 3$?

problem solving

Choose an appropriate problem-solving strategy to solve this problem. Cassandra likes to write letters to pen pals. She writes 6 letters each month. The envelopes Cassandra uses to send her letters are packaged 45 per box. How many boxes of envelopes must Cassandra purchase to last one year? How many envelopes will she have left over at the end of one year? Explain how you solved the problem.

New Concept

Each place in our decimal number system is assigned a particular value. The value of each place is 10 times greater each time we move one place to the left. So when we multiply a number by 10, the digits all shift one place to the left.

For example, when we multiply 34 by 10, the 3 shifts from the tens place to the hundreds place, and the 4 shifts from the ones place to the tens place. We fill the ones place with a zero.

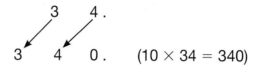

$$3 \quad 4 \quad 0 . \qquad (10 \times 34 = 340)$$

Shifting digits to the left can help us quickly multiply decimal numbers by 10, 100, or 1000. Here we show a decimal number multiplied by 10.

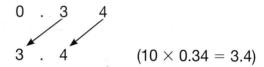

$$3 . 4 \qquad (10 \times 0.34 = 3.4)$$

We see that the digit 3 moved to the other side of the decimal point when it shifted one place to the left. The decimal point holds steady while the digits move. Although it is the digits that change places when the number is multiplied by 10, we can produce the same result by moving the decimal point in the opposite direction.

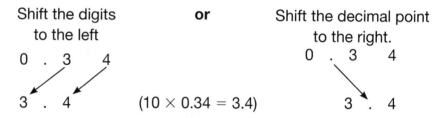

Shift the digits to the left   **or**   Shift the decimal point to the right.

$$(10 \times 0.34 = 3.4)$$

When we multiply by 10, we may simply shift the decimal point one place to the right.

Since 100 is 10 × 10, multiplying by 100 is like multiplying by 10 *twice.* When we multiply by 100, we may shift the decimal point *two* places to the right. Since 1000 is 10 × 10 × 10, we may shift the decimal point *three* places to the right when we multiply by 1000.

The number of places we shift the decimal point is the same as the number of zeros we see in 10 or 100 or 1000.

Example 1

Multiply: 1.234 × 100

To multiply mentally by 100, we may shift the decimal point two places to the right.

$$1.234 \times 100 = 123.4$$

The product is **123.4.**

Generalize Why did we shift the decimal point two places to the right?

When we multiply a decimal by a number that is not 10, 100, or 1000, we use the rule "Multiply, then count."

Example 2

Find the product of 32 and 4.5.

$$\begin{array}{r} 32 \\ \times\ 4.5 \\ \hline 144.0 \end{array}$$

32   0 decimal places
× 4.5   1 decimal place
144.0   1 decimal place

We drop the zero and the decimal point and write **144** as our answer.

Example 3

Find the product of 14.4 and 2.7.

$$\begin{array}{r} 14.4 \\ \times\ 2.7 \\ \hline \mathbf{38.88} \end{array}$$

14.4   1 decimal place
× 2.7   1 decimal places
38.88   2 decimal places

Lesson Practice

Multiply:

a. 1.234 × 10   **b.** 1.234 × 1000   **c.** 0.1234 × 100

d. 0.345 × 10   **e.** 0.345 × 100   **f.** 0.345 × 1000

g. 5.67 × 10   **h.** 5.67 × 1000   **i.** 5.67 × 100

Find each product:

j. 24 × 1.5   **k.** 61 × 2.3   **l.** 12.6 × 9.1

Written Practice *Distributed and Integrated*

*1. Refer to the table to answer parts **a** and **b**.
(74)
   a. What is the median of the recorded temperatures for the day?

   b. What is the mean of the recorded temperatures for the day?

Time	Temperature (°F)
12:00 a.m.	43
3:00 a.m.	46
6:00 a.m.	45
9:00 a.m.	48
12:00 p.m.	58

2. A meter is 100 centimeters, so a centimeter is one hundredth of a
(93) meter (0.01 meter). A meterstick broke into two parts. One part was
0.37 meter long. How long was the other part?

3. Name the total shaded portion of these two squares as a decimal
(58, 80) number and as a reduced mixed number.

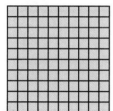 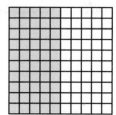

4. **(Estimate)** Write the product of 8.33 and 7.667 by rounding both
(94) decimal numbers to the nearest whole number before multiplying.

*5. Jade earned an A on 7 out of 8 assignments in chemistry class. Find
(97) the percent of her assignment grades that were an A.

6. Three fifths of the 30 students in the class were girls.
(34, 87)

    a. How many girls were in the class?

    b. How many boys were in the class?

    c. What was the ratio of boys to girls in the class?

7. a. The perimeter of the square is how many units?
(59, Inv.
6)
    b. The area of the square is how many square units?

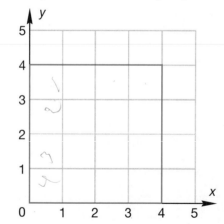

8. Chanisse and her mom purchased three items at a hardware store. The
(50) costs of the items were $8.95, $12.29, and $4.88. Estimate the total
cost of the items by first rounding each cost to the nearest dollar.

*9. There are about 39.37 inches in 1 meter. About how many inches are in
(98) 5 meters?

10. Arrange these numbers in order from least to greatest:
(56)
$$0.96, 0.875, 0.9, 1$$

11. $4\frac{3}{8}$
(71)

$+ 1\frac{3}{8}$

12. $3\frac{7}{10}$
(46)

$+ \frac{3}{10}$

13. 4
(51)

$- 1\frac{3}{10}$

14. $1.23 + 0.4567 + 0.5$
(60)

15. $4 - 1.3$
(51)

16. $8 \times 57 \times 250$
(44)

17. $5 \times \$7.25$
(12)

*18. What is the area of this parallelogram?
(75)

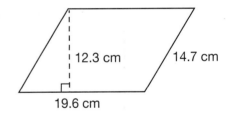

19. $436 \div 21$
(84)

*20. Multiply:
(100)
    a. 3.789×100 **b.** 3.789×1000 **c.** 3.789×10

21. $5 \times \frac{3}{10}$
(78, 81)

22. $5 \div \frac{2}{3}$
(86)

*23. Multiply:
(100)
    a. 0.246×1000 **b.** 0.246×10 **c.** 0.246×100

24. This circle graph shows the fraction of students in a class
(97, Inv. 7) who wear shoes of a certain color. Use this graph to answer
parts **a** and **b**.

Shoe Color of Students

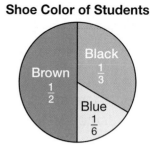

  a. There are 30 students in the class. How many students
  are wearing black shoes? What percent of the students
  are wearing black shoes?

  b. Multiple Choice Which two groups, taken together, total one half
  of the class?

   A black and brown   **B** brown and blue   **C** blue and black

25. a. What is the volume of a cube with the measurements shown?
(Inv. 9)

  b. What is the shape of each surface of the cube?

4 in.

*26. Add: $8 + (-1)$
(89)

27. (**Analyze**) For exercise Diana walked around the park 4 times Monday,
(38, 47) 6 times Tuesday, and 7 times Wednesday. Diana walked around the
park an average of how many times each day? Write your answer as
a mixed number.

28. Multiple Choice Latanya spent most of one day hiking up Giant
(77) Mountain in New York's Adirondack Park. During the hike she
drank about three pints of water. About how many ounces of water
did Latanya drink?

   A 32 oz   **B** 48 oz   **C** 64 oz   **D** 100 oz

29. Find the opposite of each number.
(89)
   a. −5   **b** 4   **c.** 99

30. One morning, three-fifths of the 25 students in class wore a jacket
(34, 37) to school and one-fifth wore a sweater to school. How many of the
students did not wear a sweater or a jacket?

California Mathematics Content Standards

MG 1.0, 1.2 Construct a cube and rectangular box from two-dimensional patterns and use these patterns to compute the surface area for these objects.

MG 1.0, 1.3 Understand the concept of volume and use the appropriate units in common measuring systems (i.e., cubic centimeter [cm³], cubic meter [m³], cubic inch [in³], cubic yard [yd³]) to compute the volume of rectangular solids.

MG 2.0, 2.3 Visualize and draw two-dimensional views of three-dimensional objects made from rectangular solids.

SDAP 1.0, 1.4 Identify ordered pairs of data from a graph and interpret the meaning of the data in terms of the situation depicted by the graph.

Focus on

Cubes

In this investigation we will learn about cubes. As with all other rectangular solids, a cube has 8 vertices, 12 edges, and 6 faces. Each face of a cube is a square. In Investigation 9 we learned to find the volume of an object by finding the number of cubic units of space the object occupies. When we find volume, we label our answer as cubic units.

> **Math Language**
>
> A **cube** is a rectangular solid with 6 congruent faces.

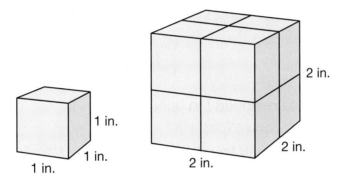

How many 1-inch cubes are needed to build the larger cube?

The larger cube has a length, a width, and a height of 2 inches. We can see that it is built from eight 1-inch cubes. Each 1-inch cube occupies 1 cubic inch of space. So the volume of the larger cube is 8 cubic inches or 8 in³.

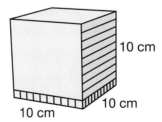

Sometimes we cannot count cubes to determine volume.

For this cube, the area of the base is 10 cm × 10 cm or 100 cm², which means that we would need 100 one-centimeter cubes to form the bottom layer. Altogether, there would be 10 layers of 100 cm³.

We can find the volume of a cube by using the formula $V = lwh$. Since each edge of a cube has the same length, we could also use the formula $V = s^3$ where s = the length of a side.

$$V = lwh$$
$$= 10 \text{ cm} \times 10 \text{ cm} \times 10 \text{ cm}$$
$$= 1000 \text{ cm}^3$$

$$V = s^3$$
$$= (10 \text{ cm})^3$$
$$= 10 \text{ cm} \times 10 \text{ cm} \times 10 \text{ cm}$$
$$= 1000 \text{ cm}^3$$

> **Math Symbols**
>
> s^3 means "use the length of a side as a factor three times."

If we knew the volume of the cube and wanted to find the length of a side, we could find the cube root of the volume. In Lesson 67 we learned about the square root of a number. The cube root of a number is similar.

Find the square root of 100.
Think: What number used as a factor twice equals 100?

$$\sqrt{100} = 10 \text{ since } 10 \times 10 = 100.$$

Find the cube root of 1000.
Think: What number used as a factor three times equals 1000?

$$\sqrt[3]{1000} = 10 \text{ since } 10 \times 10 \times 10 = 1000.$$

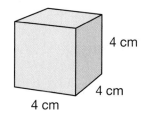

1. How many one-centimeter cubes are needed to build a cube that measures 4 cm on each side?

2. What is the volume of a cube with a side length of 3 yd?

3. **Analyze** What is the volume of a cube if each side of the cube has a measure of 5 m?

We looked at a net for a rectangular solid in Investigation 9. Now we will look at a net for a cube.

If we unfold and flatten a one-inch cube, it can look like the net below.

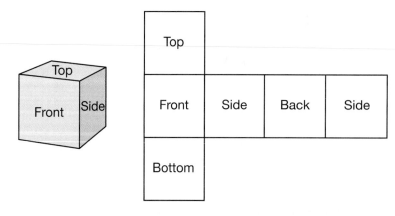

4. Multiple Choice   Here we show three ways to cut apart a box shaped like a cube. We have also shown an arrangement of six squares that does not fold into a cube. Which pattern below does not form a cube?

a.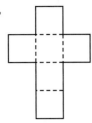

b.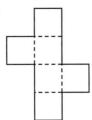

c.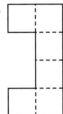

d.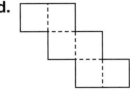

Make a Cube

Materials needed:
- **Lesson Activity 21** Cube Net
- scissors
- ruler
- tape

Use the net from **Lesson Activity 21** to complete to following tasks.

1. (**Model**) Cut out the pattern. Then fold and tape it to form a cube.

2. (**Discuss**) Describe the faces of the cube.

3. Use what you know about area to find the area of each face.

4. (**Conclude**) Estimate the total surface area of the cube. Explain your answer.

5. (**Explain**) Did you label your answer with square units or with cubic units? Explain why.

6. Estimate the volume of the cube.

We can use a function table to represent the volume of a cube.

Side Length (in cm)	1	2	3	4
Volume (in cm³)	1	8	27	64

We can also use a function table to represent the surface area of a cube.

Side Length (in cm)	1	2	3	4
Surface Area (in cm²)	6	24	54	96

7. (**Interpret**) Match each table above with a graph. Explain your reasoning.

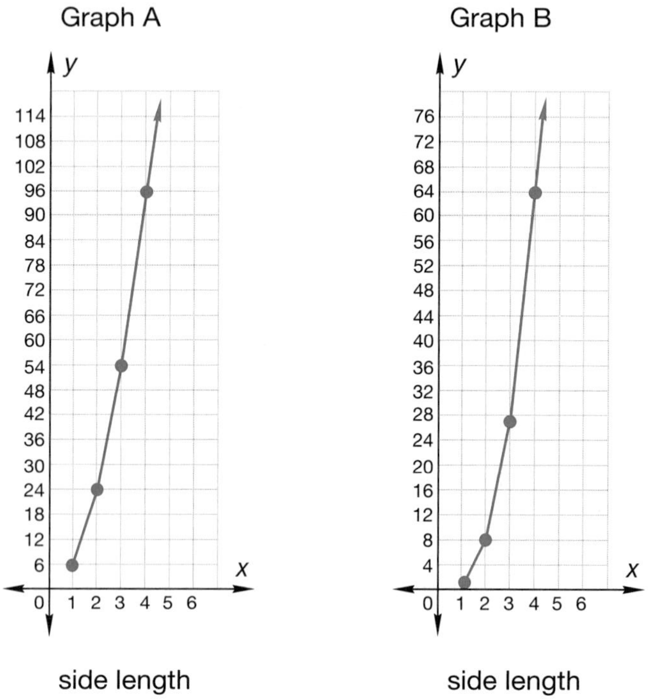

Graph A

side length

Graph B

side length

8. If a cube has a volume of 27 in³, what is the length of one side of the cube?

9. If a cube has a volume of 1 in³, what is the length of one side of the cube?

LESSON
101

• Two-Dimensional Views of Three-Dimensional Figures

✏ *California Mathematics Content Standards*

MG 1.0, 1.2 Construct a cube and rectangular box from two-dimensional patterns and use these patterns to compute the surface area for these objects.

MG 1.0, 1.3 Understand the concept of volume and use the appropriate units in common measuring systems (i.e., cubic centimeter cm³, cubic meter m³, cubic inch in³, cubic yard yd³) to compute the volume of rectangular solids.

MG 2.0, 2.3 Visualize and draw two-dimensional views of three-dimensional objects made from rectangular solids.

facts   Power Up J

mental math

    a. Estimation: Dora estimated that each story of the tall building was 12 feet tall. Dora counted 30 stories in the building. What would be her estimate for the overall height of the building?

    b. Number Sense: Simplify the fractions $\frac{10}{3}$, $\frac{10}{4}$, and $\frac{10}{5}$.

    c. Geometry: The three angles of the equilateral triangle each measure 60°. What is the total measure of the three angles?

    d. Measurement: Lamar jogged a distance of 1 mile and then walked 200 feet. Altogether, how many feet did Lamar jog and walk?

    e. Powers/Roots: $6^2 + 14$

    f. Probability: If the chance of rain is 10%, what is the chance that it will not rain?

    g. Calculation: 50% of 50, + 50, + 2, ÷ 7, + 3, ÷ 7

    h. Evaluate: What is the value of the expression $k^2 - 2$ when $k = 10$?

problem solving

Choose an appropriate problem-solving strategy to solve this problem. The multiples of 7 are 7, 14, 21, 28, 35, and so on. We can use multiples of 7 to help us count days of the week. Seven days after Monday is Monday. Fourteen days after Monday is Monday again. So 15 days after Monday is just 1 day after Monday. What day is 30 days after Monday? 50 days after Saturday? 78 days after Tuesday?

A multiview projection displays three-dimensional objects from three perpendicular viewpoints—top, front, and side (usually the right side).

An isometric view is often included, which is an angled view of the object, as shown in the projection below.

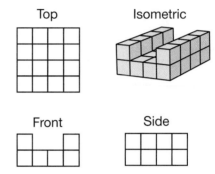

Top   Isometric

Front   Side

Notice that the width of the figure is the same in the top and front views, the height is the same in the front and side views, and the length is the same in the top and side views.

Activity 1

Construct a Three-Dimensional Figure

Materials needed:
- 24 unit cubes
- **Lesson Activity 23**

Use the cubes to complete the following tasks.

1. **Model** Build a figure using 12 unit cubes. Do not make the figure a rectangular solid.

2. **Represent** On the grid paper, draw a front view, top view, and side view (as seen from the right).

3. **Conclude** Exchange your drawing with a partner. Then use the other 12 cubes to build the figure shown in your partner's drawing.

4. Compare the figures with the drawings.

Example 1

Use your cubes to build this three-dimensional figure. Then draw the top, front, and right side views of the figure.

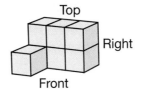

To draw the top view, we look down from above the figure. Then we turn the figure so we can see its front and we draw the front view. Finally, to draw the right side view, we turn the figure so we can see its right side.

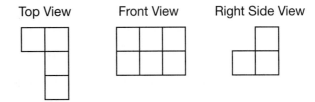

Example 2

Use grid paper to draw the front, top, and side views of this three-dimensional figure.

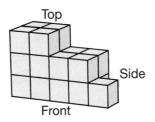

We can see that all of the vertical stacks of cubes are at least two cubes high, except for the cube on the right, which has no cube above or behind it. The top view is one row of 4 cubes and one row of 5 cubes. The front view is one row of 2 cubes, one row of 4 cubes, and one row of 5 cubes. The right side view is three rows of 2 cubes.

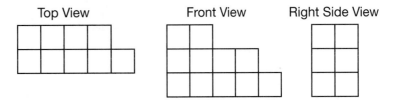

Model Build the figure to verify that the drawings of the different views are correct.

Activity 2

Make a Cube

Materials needed:
- **Lesson Activity 22**
- **Lesson Activity 23**
- ruler
- tape
- scissors

Use the cubes to complete the following tasks.

1. **(Model)** Cut out the three cube patterns. Then fold and tape the patterns to make three 1-inch cubes.

2. **(Model)** Work in a group and combine cubes. Then build a three-dimensional figure.

3. **(Represent)** Use grid paper to draw the front, side (as seen from the right), and top views.

4. **(Conclude)** The measure of each of the edges of the cubes is 1 inch. Estimate the volume of the figure, and then explain why your estimate is reasonable.

5. **(Connect)** What is the surface area of the figure? Explain how you found your answer.

6. **(Explain)** Were your estimates of surface area and volume the same? Explain why or why not.

Lesson Practice

a. Describe each of the following views of this figure as top, right, or front.

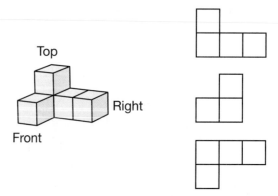

Analyze Use this figure to answer the following questions.

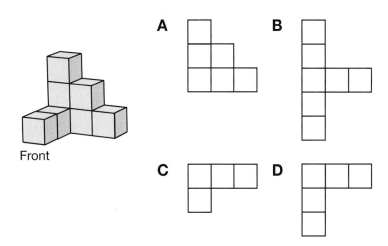

A B C D

Front

b. Which of the following is the top view of the figure?

c. Which of the following is the front view of this figure?

d. **Represent** Draw the top, front, and side views of this three-dimensional figure:

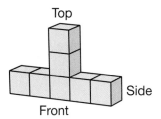

Top

Side

Front

Written Practice
Distributed and Integrated

1. **Analyze** Loretha swam 100 meters in 63.8 seconds. Dericia swam
(90) 100 meters 1 second faster than Loretha. How long did it take Dericia to swim 100 meters?

2. **Estimate** Find the approximate area of this rectangle by
(92) rounding each dimension to the nearest whole number.

$9\frac{7}{8}$ in.

$6\frac{3}{4}$ in.

3. **Explain** The camel could carry 245 kilograms. If each bundle of
(13, 14) straw weighed 15 kilograms, how many full bundles of straw could the camel carry? Explain how you know your answer is correct.

4. ⟨Estimate⟩ Find the total cost of 8 books priced at $6.98 each by rounding the cost per book to the nearest dollar before multiplying.
(94)

*5. If 60 of the 200 students are girls, then what percent of the students are girls?
(97)

6. Simplify each decimal number:
(91)
    a. 09.80   **b.** 09.08   **c.** 09.800

7. Estimate the quotient when 19.8 is divided by 3.875.
(92)

*8. If a bag contains 50 marbles and 10 of them are green, then what percent of the marbles are green?
(97)

9. ⟨Analyze⟩ Write a fraction equal to $\frac{1}{3}$ that has the same denominator as the fraction $\frac{1}{6}$. Then add the fraction to $\frac{1}{6}$. Remember to reduce your answer.
(71)

*10. What is the area of this square?
(98)

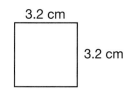

3.2 cm

3.2 cm

*11. Multiply:
(99)
    a. 0.19 × 0.7   **b.** 0.06 × 0.4   **c.** 0.8 × 0.14

12. ⟨Connect⟩ Which arrow could be pointing to 1.3275?
(54)

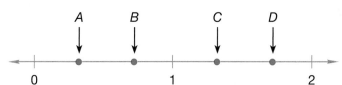

*13. Find the product:
(100)
    a. 32 × 2.7   **b.** 12.3 × 3.8

14. $5 - 3\frac{7}{10}$ **15.** $5 - 3.7$ **16.** 10 × $3.65
(51)   (93)   (18)

17. 468 × 579   **18.** $36.50 ÷ 10
(43)   (42)

*19. Use grid paper to draw the front, top, and side views of this three-dimensional figure.
(101)

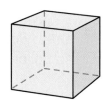

20. $640 \div 32$
(84)

21. $\frac{3}{10} \times \frac{7}{10}$
(63)

22. $4 \div \frac{3}{5}$
(86)

*23. Use grid paper to draw the front, top, and side
(101) views of this three dimensional figure.

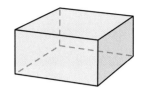

24. Reduce: $\frac{25}{100}$
(80)

25. $10^3 - \sqrt{100}$
(67)

26. **Multiple Choice** Triangle *ABC* is which type of
(24) triangle?

    A acute

    B right

    C obtuse

    D regular

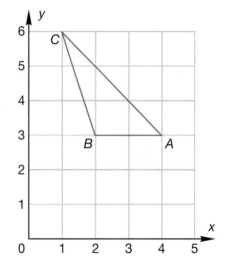

27. Write the coordinates of each vertex of $\triangle ABC$ in problem **26.**
(Inv. 6)

28. (**Estimate**) Find the approximate volume of the box by first
(92) rounding each dimension to the nearest whole number.

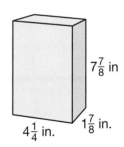

$7\frac{7}{8}$ in

$4\frac{1}{4}$ in.

$1\frac{7}{8}$ in.

29. (**Explain**) To prepare snack mix for a hike, Ephraim mixed $\frac{3}{4}$ of a
(62) pound of raisins with $1\frac{1}{4}$ pounds of peanuts. What was the weight of the peanut and raisin snack mix that Ephraim prepared? Explain why your answer is reasonable.

30. Use this pictograph to answer the questions that follow.
(Inv. 5)

Animal	Typical Life Span (in years)
moose	✹ ✹ ✹ ✹ ✹ ✹
meadow mouse	✹
gray squirrel	✹ ✹
lion	✹ ✹ ✹ ✹ ✹ ✹ ✹ ✹

Key: ✹ = 2 years

a. Write a number of years to represent each life span. Then order the life spans from greatest to least.

b. How does the average life span of a moose compare to the average life span of a gray squirrel?

Real-World Connection

To view a slide of an amoeba, Kymma sets a microscope to enlarge objects to 100 times their actual size.

a. If the actual diameter of the amoeba is 0.095 mm, then what is its diameter as seen through the microscope?

b. If Kymma sets the microscope to enlarge objects to 10 times their actual size and then to 1000 times their actual size, what would the diameter of the amoeba appear to be for those two settings?

✎ *California Mathematics Content Standards*
NS 1.0, 1.2 Interpret percents as a part of a hundred; find decimal and percent equivalents for common fractions and explain why they represent the same value; compute a given percent of a whole number.
NS 2.0, 2.1 Add, subtract, multiply, and divide with decimals; add with negative integers; subtract positive integers from negative integers; and verify the reasonableness of the results.
NS 2.0, 2.5 Compute and perform simple multiplication and division of fractions and apply these procedures to solving problems.
AF 1.0, 1.2 Use a letter to represent an unknown number; write and evaluate simple algebraic expressions in one variable by substitution.

• Finding the Percent of a Number

facts Power Up J

mental math

a. Estimation: Megan purchased $5\frac{4}{5}$ pounds of fruit at the grocery store. She bought $1\frac{7}{8}$ pounds of apples and $1\frac{1}{2}$ pounds of oranges. Using compatible numbers, about how many pounds of fruit did Megan buy that were not apples or oranges?

b. Measurement: One kilogram is about 2 pounds 3 ounces. About how many pounds and ounces is 2 kilograms?

c. Number Sense: Simplify the fractions $\frac{4}{6}$, $\frac{8}{6}$, and $\frac{9}{6}$.

d. Geometry: The three angles of the triangle measure 58°, 62°, and 60°. What is the total measure of the three angles?

e. Powers/Roots: $\sqrt{100} - 3^2$

f. Probability: Kurt labeled the six sides of a cube with the letters *A, B, C, C, C,* and *D.* If Kurt tosses the cube once, what is the probability that it will land with a *C* facing up?

g. Calculation: $\frac{1}{3}$ of 15, × 2, + 2, × 2, ÷ 3, + 1, ÷ 3, ÷ 3

h. Evaluate: What is the value of the expression $3 + l^2$ when $l = 5$?

problem solving

Choose an appropriate problem-solving strategy to solve this problem. If two standard number cubes are rolled, many combinations of pairs are possible. Here are some of the possible combinations:

(1, 1), (1, 2), (1, 3), (1, 4), (1, 5), (1, 6),
(2, 2), (2, 3), (2, 4), (2, 5), (2, 6)

List the rest of the possible combinations. In all, how many combinations are possible?

Math Language

Recall that a **percent** (%) is part of 100. So 20% means 20 out of 100.

We can often use a fraction or a percent to describe part of a group.

One fourth of the students in a class play on the soccer team.

On Monday 20% of the students in a class were wearing white socks.

One way to find a percent of a number is to change the percent to a fraction.

50% means $\frac{50}{100}$, which reduces to $\frac{1}{2}$.

4% means $\frac{4}{100}$, which reduces to $\frac{1}{25}$.

Another way to find a percent of a number is to change the percent to a decimal.

$$65\% = \frac{65}{100} = 0.65 \qquad\qquad 8\% = \frac{8}{100} = 0.08$$

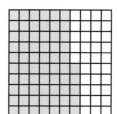 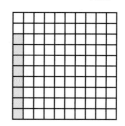

Example 1

What number is 75% of 12?

We can translate this problem into an equation and change the percent to a fraction or to a decimal. In our equation, we will use a letter to represent "what number," an equal sign to represent "is," and a multiplication sign to represent "of."

Change the Percent to a Fraction
What number is 75% of 12?

↓   ↓   ↓   ↓ ↓

$$n = \frac{3}{4} \times 12$$

$$n = \frac{36}{4}$$

$$n = 9$$

Change the Percent to a Decimal
What number is 75% of 12?

↓   ↓   ↓   ↓ ↓

$$n = 0.75 \times 12$$

$$n = 9.00$$

$$n = 9$$

We find that 75% of 12 is **9.**

Example 2

Sixty percent of the 25 students in a class visited the school library on Friday. How many students visited the library that day?

To find a percent of a number, we change the percent to a fraction $(60\% = \frac{60}{100} = \frac{3}{5})$ or to a decimal $(60\% = \frac{60}{100} = 0.6)$. Then we multiply.

Change the Percent to a Fraction

60% of 25

↓ ↓ ↓

$\frac{3}{5}$ × 25

Multiply

$\frac{3}{5} \times \frac{25}{1} = \frac{75}{5}$

$\frac{75}{5} = 15$

Change the Percent to a Decimal

60% of 25

↓ ↓ ↓

0.6 × 25

Multiply

0.6 × 25

$$\begin{array}{r} 0.6 \\ \times\ 25 \\ \hline 15.0 \end{array}$$

We find that **15 students** visited the library on Friday.

Example 3

A sales tax increases the price of something you buy. What is the amount of sales tax for a $15.00 purchase if the sales tax is 6%? What is the total cost of the purchase?

To find 6% of $15.00, we change the percent to a fraction $(6\% = \frac{6}{100} = \frac{3}{50})$ or to a decimal $(6\% = \frac{6}{100} = 0.06)$. Then we multiply. Since it seems easier for us to multiply by 0.06 than to multiply by $\frac{3}{50}$, we will use 0.06.

6% of $15.00 ⟶

$$\begin{array}{r} 0.06 \\ \times\ \$15 \\ \hline 030 \\ +\ 006 \\ \hline \$0.90 \end{array}$$

The product has two decimal places because there are two decimal places in the factors. We find that the amount of sales tax is **$0.90,** and we use addition to find the total cost.

$$\$15.00 + \$0.90 = \$15.90$$

The total cost will be **$15.90.**

A **discount** is an amount that is subtracted from the price of something you buy. For example, a store may advertise a 25% off sale. During such a sale, the price will be 25% less than the regular price.

Example 4

Using the data in the table, write and solve an equation to find the discount in dollars if a jacket is purchased. Then find the sale price of the jacket.

Regular Price (r)	Percent Off (p)	Discount (d)
Belts $10	15%	d
Jackets $50	20%	d
Coats $100	30%	d

To find the discount (d) in dollars, we must find 20% of $50, which is the regular price (r) of the jacket.

$$d = (20\%)(r)$$

To find 20% of $50, we change 20% to a fraction ($\frac{1}{5}$) or to a decimal (0.2). For this example, we choose a decimal.

$d = (20\%)(r)$ Change 20% to 0.2 and substitute $50 for r.

$d = (0.2)(\$50)$ Multiply.

$d = \$10$ The discount will be $10.

Since the discount is **$10,** the sale price of the jacket is $50 − $10 or **$40.**

Verify Why did we multiply to find the discount?

Lesson Practice Find each percent of a number by changing the percent to a decimal:

a. 9% of 200   **b.** 85% of $30   **c.** 4% of 25

Find each percent of a number by changing the percent to a fraction:

d. 25% of $70   **e.** 80% of 50   **f.** 75% of $120

g. Look again at Example 4. Write and solve an equation to find the discount in dollars if a belt is purchased. Then find the sale price of the belt.

Written Practice   *Distributed and Integrated*

1. Simplify: $(-5) - 6 + (-7) - (8) + 4$
(95)

2. **(Analyze)** What is the total cost of 2 items at $1.26 each and 3 items at
(37)   49¢ each, plus a total tax of 24¢?

3. Flora rode her bike 2.5 miles from her house to the library. How far did
(60)   she ride going to the library and back home?

4. If $4y = 20$, then $2y - 1$ equals what number?
(8, 37)

*5. Multiply:
(98)
     a. $\begin{array}{r} 0.16 \\ \times\ 0.2 \\ \hline \end{array}$ **b.** $\begin{array}{r} 0.5 \\ \times\ 7 \\ \hline \end{array}$ **c.** $\begin{array}{r} 0.26 \\ \times\ 0.3 \\ \hline \end{array}$

6. Fifteen of the 25 students in the class are boys.
(87, 97)

     a. What percent of the students are boys?

     b. What is the ratio of boys to girls in the class?

7. **(Estimate)** Find the sum of 12.7 and 8.167 by rounding both numbers
(94)   to the nearest whole number before adding.

8. Write the reduced fraction that equals 80%.
(80, 97)

9. Compare: $50\% \bigcirc \dfrac{1}{2}$ **10.** 45^2
(80, 97)   (67)

11. **(Represent)** Use words to name the number 76.345. Which digit is in
(55)   the tenths place?

12. $\dfrac{1}{2} \div \dfrac{2}{3}$ **13.** $\dfrac{3}{10} \times \dfrac{3}{10}$ **14.** $\dfrac{4}{11} + \dfrac{5}{11}$
(86)   (63)   (28)

15. A blue rectangle is drawn on this grid.
  (59)

    a. The perimeter of the rectangle is how many units?

    b. The area of the rectangle is how many square units?

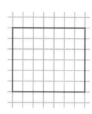

*16. What is the area of the triangle?
  (76, 99)

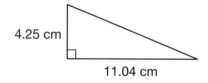

17. 2.386 + 1.2 + 16.25 + 10
  (90)

18. 4.2 − (3 − 0.45)
  (93)

19. (**Analyze**) Write a fraction equal to $\frac{1}{2}$ that has the same denominator
  (69, 71) as $\frac{1}{6}$. Then add the fraction to $\frac{1}{6}$. Remember to reduce your answer.

20. $37.05 ÷ 15
  (84)

*21. Multiply:
  (100)
    a. 4.378 × 10   **b.** 4.378 × 1000   **c.** 4.378 × 100

22. Five sixths of the two dozen juice bars were strawberry. How many of
  (34) the juice bars were strawberry?

*23. Use grid paper to draw the front, top, and side views of this three
  (101) dimensional figure.

24. What is the volume of a closet that is 5 feet wide, 2 feet deep, and
  (Inv. 9) 8 feet high?

25. Two feet is what percent of a yard?
  (61, 97)

26. a. A star has how many lines of symmetry?
  (21)

    b. A star has how many sides? What kind of polygon is a star?

27. This table shows how many students received certain scores out of a possible 20 on the test. Use the table to answer parts **a–d.**

(74, Inv. 7)

Test Results

Score	Number of Students
20	4
19	4
18	5
17	6
16	3
15	2

a. Which score was made by the greatest number of students?

b. If 25 students took the test, how many students got fewer than 15 correct?

c. If the lowest score was 13, what was the range of the scores?

d. If all 25 scores were listed in order like this:

20, 20, 20, 20, 19, 19, …

which score would be in the middle of the list?

*28. Find each percent of a number by changing the percent to a decimal:

(102)

    a. 6% of 400   **b.** 62% of $50

*29. Find each percent of a number by changing the percent to a fraction:

(102)

    a. 20% of $90   **b.** 75% of 160

30. **Estimate** The highest and lowest temperatures ever recorded in the state of Vermont are shown on the thermometers below. When compared to the lowest temperature, how many degrees warmer is the highest temperature?

(9, 96)

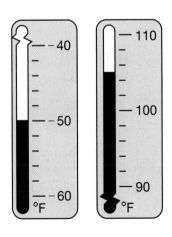

LESSON

103

• Finding the Least Common Multiple of Two Numbers

🖎 *California Mathematics Content Standards*

NS 1.0, 1.3 Understand and compute positive integer powers of nonnegative integers; compute examples as repeated multiplication.

NS 1.0, 1.4 Determine the prime factors of all numbers through 50 and write the numbers as the product of their prime factors by using exponents to show multiples of a factor (e.g., $24 = 2 \times 2 \times 2 \times 3 = 2^3 \times 3$).

MR 2.0, 2.3 Use a variety of methods, such as words, numbers, symbols, charts, graphs, tables, diagrams, and models, to explain mathematical reasoning.

facts   Power Up J

mental math

a. **Number Sense:** Simplify the fractions $\frac{6}{8}$, $\frac{9}{8}$, and $\frac{12}{8}$.

b. **Measurement:** The 1600-meter relay is a race in which 4 runners each run an equal "leg" of the race. How many meters long is each leg?

c. **Measurement:** On November 11, 1911, the temperature in Oklahoma City set a record high for the date at 83°F. By midnight, the temperature had dropped 66 degrees to set a record low for the date. What was the low temperature?

d. **Geometry:** What is the area of a square that is 5 inches on each side?

e. **Estimation:** Choose the more reasonable estimate for the length of your index finger: 6 centimeters or 6 inches.

f. **Powers/Roots:** $10^2 - 100$

g. **Calculation:** $\sqrt{100}$, $\times 5$, $+ 4$, $\div 9$, $\times 7$, $+ 2$, $\div 4$

h. **Evaluate:** What is the value of the expression $24 - m^2$ when $m = 2$?

problem solving

Choose an appropriate problem-solving strategy to solve this problem. Jada wants to use 1-inch cubes to build a cube with edges 2 inches long. How many 1-inch cubes will she need?

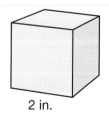

2 in.

New Concept

Here we list the first few multiples of 4 and 6:

Multiples of 4: 4, 8, ⑫, 16, 20, ㉔, 28, 32, ㊱, ...

Multiples of 6: 6, ⑫, 18, ㉔, 30, ㊱, ...

The circled numbers are common multiples of 4 and 6. For any two numbers, there are too many common multiples to count. However, the smallest of those common multiples is a number called the **least common multiple,** or LCM, and the LCM of two numbers is very useful.

(Connect) In the list above, 12, 24, and 36 are the first three common multiples of 4 and 6. Which number is the least common multiple of 4 and 6?

Example 1

Find the least common multiple (LCM) of 7 and 9.

We begin by listing the first few multiples of 7 and 9. Then we circle the multiples they have in common.

Multiples of 7: 7, 14, 21, 28, 35, 42, 49, 56, (63), 70, …

Multiples of 9: 9, 18, 27, 36, 45, 54, (63), 72, 81, 90, …

We find that the least common multiple of 7 and 9 is **63.**

Notice that the product of 7 and 9 is 63, so from Example 1 we learn that the product of two numbers will always be a common multiple of those numbers. We will use the idea that the product of two numbers is a common multiple of those numbers when we find common denominators in Lessons 107 and 108.

Example 2

Find the least common multiple (LCM) of 6 and 8.

We begin by listing the first few multiples of 6 and 8. Then we circle the multiples they have in common.

Multiples of 6: 6, 12, 18, (24), 30, 36, 42, (48), …

Multiples of 8: 8, 16, (24), 32, 40, (48), …

As we see above, the *least* of the common multiples of 6 and 8 is **24.**

(Connect) Is 48 a common multiple of 6 and 8? Explain why or why not.

Notice in Example 2 that the least common multiple of 6 and 8 is greater than either number but less than the product of the numbers, which is 48. We learn that the product of two numbers is not always the least common multiple of those numbers.

Example 3

Find the least common multiple (LCM) of 5 and 15.

We begin by listing the first few multiples of 5 and 15. Then we circle the multiples they have in common.

Multiples of 5: 5, 10, ⑮, 20, 25, . . .

Multiples of 15: ⑮, 30, . . .

We find that the least common multiple of 5 and 15 is **15.**

Connect Why can the LCM of two numbers never be the lesser of those numbers?

We learn in Example 3 that the LCM of two numbers is sometimes the greater of those two numbers.

Activity

Prime Numbers on a Hundreds Chart

Material needed:

- **Lesson Activity 26**

The first prime number is 2 because 2 has two different factors, but 1 has only one factor. Every even number greater than 2 (4, 6, 8, and so on.) is a composite. Since all even numbers are multiples of 2, they have at least 3 factors—the number itself, the number 1, and 2. On a hundred number chart, we can find the prime numbers and cross out the composite numbers, which are all multiples of prime numbers.

1	②	3	4	5	6	7	8	9	10
11	12	13	14	15	16	17	18	19	20
21	22	23	24	25	26	27	28	29	30
31	32	33	34	35	36	37	38	39	40
41	42	43	44	45	46	47	48	49	50
51	52	53	54	55	56	57	58	59	60
61	62	63	64	65	66	67	68	69	70
71	72	73	74	75	76	77	78	79	80
81	82	83	84	85	86	87	88	89	90
91	92	93	94	95	96	97	98	99	100

On this hundreds number chart we circled 2 and began crossing out multiples of 2. On **Lesson Activity 26,** find all the prime numbers. Circle 2 and cross out the multiples of 2. Then circle the next prime number, 3, and cross out the remaining multiples of 3. Then move on to 5, and continue the process until you have found all the prime numbers less than 100.

(**Conclude**) What are the first ten prime numbers?

Prime factors can also be used to find the LCM of two numbers. This method is especially useful when we are asked to find the LCM of larger numbers.

Example 4

Use prime factorization to find the least common multiple (LCM) of 14 and 18.

First we use division by primes or factor trees to find the prime factorization of 14 and of 18. For this example, we choose factor trees.

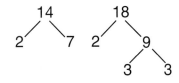

We circle the greatest number of times a prime factor appears in either prime factorization.

$$14 = ② \times ⑦ \qquad 18 = 2 \times ③^2$$

We circle a 2 because the greatest number of times a 2 appears in either factorization is once. We circle 3^2 because the greatest number of times 3 appears is twice. We circle the 7 because the greatest number of times a 7 appears is once. Then we find the product of the circled factors.

$$2 \times 3^2 \times 7 = 126$$

Using prime factorization, we find the LCM of 14 and 18 to be **126.**

(**Lesson Practice**) Find the least common multiple (LCM) of each pair of numbers:

a. 2 and 3   **b.** 5 and 8   **c.** 5 and 10

d. 4 and 6   **e.** 3 and 6   **f.** 6 and 10

g. The denominators of $\frac{5}{8}$ and $\frac{3}{10}$ are 8 and 10. What is the least common multiple of 8 and 10?

h. (Justify) Can the LCM of two numbers ever be greater than the product of those two numbers? Give an example to support your answer.

i. Use prime factorization to find the least common multiple (LCM) of 12 and 14.

Written Practice · *Distributed and Integrated*

1. Multiply:
(99)
    a. 0.16×0.3 **b.** 0.7×0.3

2. Forty of Maggie's 50 answers were correct. What percent of Maggie's
(97) answers were correct?

3. Compare: $\dfrac{1}{10} \times \dfrac{1}{10} \bigcirc 0.1 \times 0.1$
(63, 98)

4. Find each product:
(100)
    a. 16×3.5 **b.** 8.2×6.3

5. (Represent) Use digits to write the decimal number one hundred one
(55) and one hundred one thousandths.

6. (Analyze) Three small blocks of wood are balanced on one
(38) side of a scale with a 100-gram weight and a 500-gram weight on the other side. If each block weighs the same, what is the weight of each block?

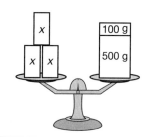

*7. Use grid paper to draw the front, top, and side views of
(101) this three-dimensional figure.

8. (Explain) The total cost of an item Lucie purchased online
(94) was $23.20, which included a shipping charge of $6.95. What is a reasonable estimate of the cost of the item, not including shipping? Explain your answer.

9. A rectangle is drawn on this grid.
(59)
    a. How many units is the perimeter of the rectangle?

    b. How many square units is the area of the rectangle?

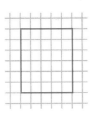

*10. The new dress shop in town is offering 20% off all purchases. Hoshi
(102) found a coat she wanted for $80.00. Find the amount of her discount and the sale price of the coat.

11. $32.3 + 4.96 + 7.5 + 11$
(90)

12. $1 - (1.36 - 0.8)$
(93)

*13. 12×1.2
(98)

*14. 0.15×0.9
(98)

*15. 0.16×10
(100)

16. $13m = 3705$
(17, 84)

*17. Find the least common multiple (LCM) of each pair of numbers:
(103)
    a. 3 and 4   **b.** 6 and 9   **c.** 4 and 8

18. $980 \div 28$
(84)

19. What is the exterior angle measurement of a 43° angle?
(Inv. 3)

20. $4\frac{3}{10}$
(81) $+ 1\frac{2}{10}$

21. $4\frac{3}{10}$
(28) $- 1\frac{2}{10}$

22. (**Analyze**) Write fractions equal to $\frac{2}{3}$ and $\frac{1}{2}$ that have denominators of 6.
(69) Then subtract the smaller fraction from the larger fraction.

23. $\frac{3}{10} \times \frac{1}{3}$
(80)

24. $\frac{3}{4} \div \frac{3}{5}$
(86)

25. $\frac{3}{10} \div 3$
(86)

26. a. The floor of a room that is 12 feet wide and 15 feet long will be
(59)   covered with tiles that are 1 foot square. How many tiles are
         needed?

b. Molding will be nailed around the edge of the ceiling of the room
     described in part **a.** How many feet of molding are needed?

27. What is the volume occupied by a refrigerator with the
(Inv. 9) dimensions shown?

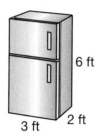

6 ft

3 ft   2 ft

*28. Use prime factorization to find the least common multiple (LCM) of
(103)   12 and 15.

29. A theater is showing a movie twice each evening. The movie is
(10,37) 110 minutes long and the elapsed time between showings is
         40 minutes. If the first showing of the movie begins at 6:45 p.m.,
         when does the last showing begin?

30. The average monthly temperature in Seattle, Washington, during the
(49)   first five months of the year is shown in the table. Display the data in
        a line graph. Then write two questions that can be answered using
        your graph.

**Average Monthly
Temperature Seattle, WA**

Month	Temperature (°F)
January	41
February	44
March	46
April	50
May	56

California Mathematics Content Standards
NS 2.0, 2.4 Understand the concept of multiplication and division of fractions.
NS 2.0, 2.5 Compute and perform simple multiplication and division of fractions and apply these procedures to solving problems.

• Writing Mixed Numbers as Improper Fractions

facts   Power Up J

mental math

a. **Money:** 100¢ ÷ 4

b. **Number Sense:** Simplify the improper fractions $\frac{12}{10}$, $\frac{15}{10}$, and $\frac{25}{10}$.

c. **Percent:** The $30 skirt is on sale for 10% off. What is 10% of $30?

d. **Geometry:** The four angles of a square each measure 90°. What is the total measure of the four angles?

e. **Fractional Parts:** What is $\frac{1}{4}$ of $80?

f. **Time:** How many hours is 3 days?

g. **Calculation:** $\sqrt{36} + \sqrt{9}$

h. **Evaluate:** What is the value of the expression $(39 - n^2) + 1$ when $n = 3$?

problem solving   Choose an appropriate problem-solving strategy to solve this problem. Use your ruler to draw a square that measures 4 inches by 4 inches. What is the area of the rectangle? Now draw a second rectangle that has different dimensions but the same area as the square. What dimensions did you use for the second figure? Which figure has a greater perimeter?

New Concept

The picture below shows $1\frac{1}{2}$ shaded circles. How many half circles are shaded?

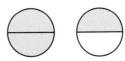

Three halves are shaded. We may name the number of shaded circles as the mixed number $1\frac{1}{2}$ or as the improper fraction $\frac{3}{2}$.

$$1\frac{1}{2} = \frac{3}{2}$$

We have converted improper fractions to mixed numbers by dividing. In this lesson we will practice writing mixed numbers as improper fractions. We will use this skill later when we learn to multiply and divide mixed numbers.

To help us understand changing mixed numbers into fractions, we can draw pictures. Here we show the number $2\frac{1}{4}$ using shaded circles:

To show $2\frac{1}{4}$ as an improper fraction, we divide the whole circles into pieces the same-size as those in the divided circle. In this example we divide each whole circle into fourths.

Now we count the total number of fourths that are shaded. We see that $2\frac{1}{4}$ equals the improper fraction $\frac{9}{4}$.

Example 1

Name the number of shaded circles as an improper fraction and as a mixed number.

To show the improper fraction, we divide the whole circles into pieces the same-size as those in the divided circle (in this case, halves).

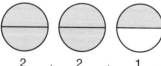

$$\frac{2}{2} \;+\; \frac{2}{2} \;+\; \frac{1}{2} \;=\; \frac{5}{2} \;=\; 2\frac{1}{2}$$

The improper fraction is $\frac{5}{2}$. The mixed number is **$2\frac{1}{2}$.**

Example 2

Change $2\frac{1}{3}$ to an improper fraction.

One way to find an improper fraction equal to $2\frac{1}{3}$ is to draw a picture that illustrates $2\frac{1}{3}$.

We have shaded 2 whole circles and $\frac{1}{3}$ of a circle. Now we divide each whole circle into thirds and count the total number of thirds.

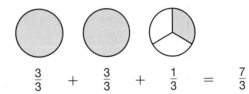

$$\frac{3}{3} \;+\; \frac{3}{3} \;+\; \frac{1}{3} \;=\; \frac{7}{3}$$

We see that seven thirds are shaded. So an improper fraction equal to $2\frac{1}{3}$ is $\frac{7}{3}$.

It is not necessary to draw a picture. We could remember that each whole is $\frac{3}{3}$. So the 2 of $2\frac{1}{3}$ is equal to $\frac{3}{3} + \frac{3}{3}$, which is $\frac{6}{3}$. Then we add $\frac{6}{3}$ to $\frac{1}{3}$ and get $\frac{7}{3}$.

To multiply mixed numbers, we change the mixed numbers to improper fractions before we multiply.

Example 3

Multiply: $1\frac{1}{2} \times 2\frac{3}{4}$

$1\frac{1}{2} \times 2\frac{3}{4}$

$\downarrow \qquad \downarrow$

$\dfrac{3}{2} \times \dfrac{11}{4} = \dfrac{33}{8}$ First we change the mixed numbers to improper fractions. Then we multiply.

$\dfrac{33}{8} = 4\dfrac{1}{8}$ Finally, we change the improper fraction answer to a mixed number by using division.

Example 4

Cleon prepared $2\frac{1}{4}$ cups of liquid plant food for his plants. How much of the mixture should each of 9 plants receive if each plant is to receive the same amount?

Math Language

In a division such as $\frac{9}{4} \div \frac{9}{1}$, $\frac{9}{4}$ represents the dividend and $\frac{9}{1}$ represents the divisor. Recall that the product of any number and its reciprocal is 1, so the reciprocal of $\frac{9}{1}$ (the divisor) is $\frac{1}{9}$ because $\frac{9}{1} \times \frac{1}{9} = \frac{9}{9}$, which is another name for 1.

We must divide $2\frac{1}{4}$ cups into 9 equal parts.

$2\frac{1}{4} \div 9$ Write the division.

$\frac{9}{4} \div \frac{9}{1}$ Change each number to an improper fraction.

$\frac{9}{4} \times \frac{1}{9}$ Multiply by the reciprocal of the divisor.

$\frac{9}{36}$ Reduce.

$\frac{1}{4}$ Each plant should receive $\frac{1}{4}$ **cup.**

Connect Another way to complete the multiplication $\frac{9}{4} \times \frac{1}{9}$ is to cancel factors that are equivalent to 1. Which terms of the fractions in $\frac{9}{4} \times \frac{1}{9}$ are equivalent to 1? Explain your answer.

Lesson Practice

For problems **a–c,** name the number of shaded circles as an improper fraction and as a mixed number.

a.

b.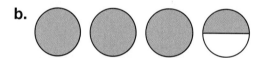

c.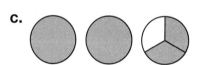

Change each mixed number to an improper fraction:

d. $4\frac{1}{2}$ **e.** $1\frac{2}{3}$ **f.** $2\frac{3}{4}$ **g.** $3\frac{1}{8}$

Multiply. Write each product as a mixed number.

h. $3 \times 3\frac{1}{4}$ **i.** $2\frac{1}{5} \times 2\frac{1}{2}$ **j.** $2\frac{2}{3} \times 6$

Divide. Write each quotient in simplest form.

k. $3\frac{1}{5} \div 2$ **l.** $4 \div 1\frac{1}{2}$ **m.** $2\frac{1}{4} \div 1\frac{1}{8}$

Written Practice   *Distributed and Integrated*

1. **Estimate** Find the product of 5.375 and 3.8 by rounding both
(94)   numbers to the nearest whole number before multiplying.

2. The football team played 10 games and won 5. What percent of the
(97) games did the team win?

3. Multiply:
(100)
    a. 4.732 × 10   **b.** 1.569 × 1000   **c.** 0.817 × 100

4. (Analyze) Two fifths of the 100 passengers stayed in the subway cars
(34, 48) until the last stop. How many of the 100 passengers got off the subway
cars before the last stop?

*5. Dominic bought a new pair of pants for $28.00. The sales-tax rate
(102) was 8%. Find the tax on the $28.00 purchase. Then find the total price
including tax.

6. (Analyze) Write fractions equal to $\frac{5}{6}$ and $\frac{3}{4}$ that have denominators
(62, 69) of 12. Then add the fractions. Remember to convert the sum to a mixed
number.

7. A hexagon is drawn on this grid.
(59)

    a. How many units is the perimeter of this hexagon?

    b. How many square units is the area of the hexagon?

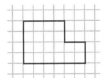

*8. Multiply. Write each product in simplest form.
(104)
    a. $2 \times 2\frac{3}{4}$ **b.** $3\frac{2}{5} \times 1\frac{1}{2}$

*9. Divide. Write each quotient in simplest form.
(104)
    a. $5 \div 1\frac{2}{3}$ **b.** $2\frac{3}{4} \div 3$ **c.** $3\frac{1}{5} \div 1\frac{1}{3}$

*10. 6 − 4.32   **11.** 0.12 × 0.11
(93)   (99)

12. 0.04 × 0.28   **13.** 10 × 0.25
(99)   (18, 100)

14. 19x = 3705   **15.** $\sqrt{400}$ **16.** 30^2
(17, 84)   (67)   (67)

17. $\frac{5}{13} + \frac{10}{13}$ **18.** $\frac{11}{12} - \frac{7}{12}$
(81)   (80)

*19. Find the least common multiple (LCM) of each pair of numbers:
(103)
    a. 5 and 8   **b.** 4 and 9   **c.** 2 and 5

20. $2 \div \dfrac{5}{6}$
(86)

21. $\dfrac{5}{6} \div 2$
(86)

22. (Interpret) This circle graph shows the percent of
(45, 97, Inv. 7) students in the class who made certain grades in math.
Use this graph to answer parts **a–c.**

Math Projects

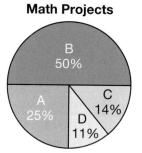

a. Add the percents shown on the graph. What is the total?

b. What grade was made by $\frac{1}{4}$ of the students?

c. If the teacher draws a test from a stack of tests without looking, what is the probability that the test will have a B?

23. (Conclude) Draw the next term of this sequence:
(Inv. 8)

24. The three runners below received medals in the men's 100-meter run
(56, 60) at the 2000 Summer Olympic Games in Sydney, Australia. Refer to this information to answer parts **a** and **b.**

Runner	Country	Time
Ato Bolden	Trinidad and Tobago	9.99 seconds
Maurice Greene	United States	9.87 seconds
Obadele Thompson	Barbados	10.04 seconds

a. Write the last names of the runners in the order of their finish, starting with the first-place runner.

b. The first-place runner ran how many seconds faster than the third-place runner?

25. Add: −1 + 1
(89)

26. How many prime numbers are greater than 20 but less than 25?
(65) How many composite numbers are greater than 20 but less than 25?

27. A recipe for a vegetable medley calls for $\frac{2}{3}$ of a pound of red peppers
(62) and $\frac{2}{3}$ of a pound of green peppers. In simplest form, how many pounds of peppers does the recipe call for?

28. Add: 22 + (−23)
(48)

29. (50) **Explain** Jessie estimated the quotient of 277 ÷ 4 to be about 70. Did Jessie make a reasonable estimate? Explain why or why not.

30. (62, 81) Keiko is making homemade bread for her family reunion. She will make 4 batches. Use the table below to help you find out how much flour she will use.

Batches of bread	1	2	3	4
Cups of flour	$2\frac{1}{4}$	$4\frac{1}{2}$	$6\frac{3}{4}$	

Real-World Connection

Mr. Dunn plans to walk around Century Park every fourth day. He will begin his routine starting January 1. Mr. Nguyen plans to walk around Century Park every seventh day. He will also begin his routine starting January 1.

a. On what day in January will Mr. Dunn and Mr. Nguyen walk around Century Park on the same day, not including January 1?

b. Who will walk around Century Park the greatest number of times in January—Mr. Dunn or Mr. Nguyen?

• Using Formulas

California Mathematics Content Standards

MG 1.0, **1.1** Derive and use the formula for the area of a triangle and of a parallelogram by comparing it with the formula for the area of a rectangle (i.e., two of the same triangles make a parallelogram with twice the area; a parallelogram is compared with a rectangle of the same area by cutting and pasting a right triangle on the parallelogram).

MG 1.0, **1.3** Understand the concept of volume and use the appropriate units in common measuring systems (i.e., cubic centimeter [cm³], cubic meter [m³], cubic inch [in³], cubic yard [yd³]) to compute the volume of rectangular solids.

facts　　Power Up J

mental math

a. Estimation: Estimate the cost of 8 yards of fabric if the price of the fabric is $6.95 per yard.

b. Estimation: Ben's dog weighs 18.2 kg, and his cat weighs 4.9 kg. Round each weight to the nearest kilogram and then add to estimate the total weight of Ben's pets.

c. Fractional Parts: $\frac{1}{5}$ of $20

d. Fractional Parts: $\frac{2}{5}$ of $20

e. Fractional Parts: $\frac{4}{5}$ of $20

f. Measurement: The temperature of the cold glass of water is 2°C. The temperature of the hot soup is 53°C. What is the temperature difference between the two liquids?

g. Calculation: $\sqrt{49}$, × 8, − 1, ÷ 5, − 1, × 4, + 2, ÷ 6

h. Evaluate: What is the value of the expression $\frac{p}{2}$ when $p = 14$?

problem solving

Choose an appropriate problem-solving strategy to solve this problem. Gareth erased the product and one of the factors in a multiplication problem and gave it to Taylor as a problem-solving exercise. He told Taylor that the digits of the product are 1, 2, and 7, though not in that order. Copy Gareth's multiplication problem and find the missing digits for Taylor.

$$\begin{array}{r} \_\,\_\,\_ \\ \times \quad\quad 4 \\ \hline \_\,\_\,\_ \end{array}$$

New Concept

Formulas describe processes for solving certain types of problems. Formulas often use letters and other symbols to show the relationship between various measures. In the examples that follow, we use formulas to solve problems about perimeter, area, and volume.

Example 1

The Jacksons have added a dining room to a corner of their house. Mr. Jackson purchased crown molding that will be installed at the intersection of the walls and the ceiling of his dining room. Crown molding costs $5 per foot to install. What will be Mr. Jackson's cost for having the crown molding installed?

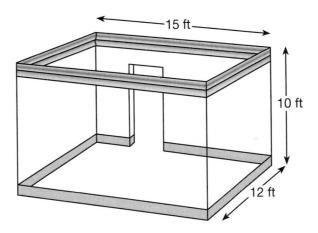

Crown molding is installed at the perimeter of the room. We can use the perimeter formula to determine the total length of crown molding and then multiply that length by $5.

$$P = 2l + 2w$$

$$P = 2(15 \text{ ft}) + 2(12 \text{ ft})$$

$$P = 54 \text{ ft}$$

The perimeter is 54 ft so the cost of the installed molding is $5 × 54 ft, which is **$270.**

Verify Why is the perimeter recorded in feet and not in square feet?

Example 2

Mrs. Jackson wants to buy carpet for the dining room floor. How many square feet of carpet are needed to cover the floor?

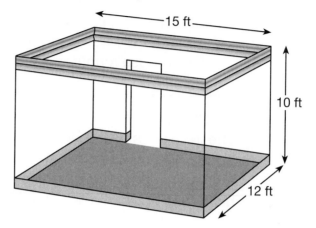

The carpet covers the floor area of the room, so we use the area formula to determine the amount of carpet needed.

$$A = l \times w$$
$$A = 15 \text{ ft} \times 12 \text{ ft}$$
$$A = 180 \text{ sq. ft}$$

Mrs. Jackson will need **180 sq. ft** of carpet to cover the floor.

Analyze The carpet Mrs. Jackson chose costs $5 per square foot. How much will the carpet cost?

Example 3

To heat and cool the new room, the Jacksons need to account for the volume added to their house. How many additional cubic feet of air need to be heated or cooled?

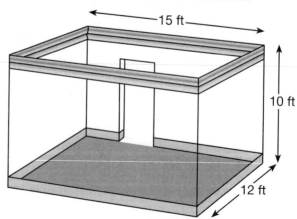

We use the volume formula to determine the amount of cubic feet added to the house.

$$V = l \times w \times h$$
$$V = 15 \text{ ft} \times 12 \text{ ft} \times 10 \text{ ft}$$
$$V = 1800 \text{ cu. ft}$$

The Jacksons have added **1800 cu. ft** of air to heat or cool.

(Verify) Why is the answer recorded in cubic feet and not in square feet?

Example 4

The Jacksons' son, Demont, has a trunk in his room for storing toys.

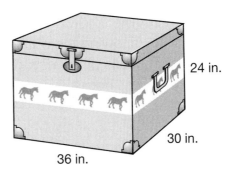

24 in.

30 in.

36 in.

a. **Mrs. Jackson plans to put a liner on the bottom of the trunk. Choose a formula to decide how much area the liner will cover.**

b. **Mrs. Jackson also plans to paste a border of horses around the entire trunk. Choose a formula to determine the minimum length of border she needs to buy.**

a. The shape of the bottom of the trunk is a rectangle. We use the area formula to find the area of the 36 in. by 30 in. rectangle.

$$A = l \times w$$
$$A = 36 \text{ in.} \times 30 \text{ in.}$$
$$A = 1080 \text{ sq. in.}$$

The liner will cover **1080 sq. in.** of the bottom of the trunk.

b. The border is pasted along the perimeter of the trunk, so we find the perimeter of a 36 in. by 30 in. rectangle.

$$P = 2l + 2w$$
$$P = 2(36 \text{ in.}) + 2(30 \text{ in.})$$
$$P = 132 \text{ in.}$$

Mrs. Jackson needs at least **132 in.** of border.

Conclude Mrs. Jackson has decided to paint the trunk before she places a border around it. To help decide how much paint she will need, does Mrs. Jackson need to find the surface area or the volume of the trunk? Explain your reasoning.

Lesson Practice

Refer to the diagrams in the examples of this lesson to help you answer problems **a** and **b**. For each practice problem, show the formula you can use to solve the problem.

a. The Jacksons want to cover one 12-foot-long wall of the dining room with wallpaper. How many square feet must the wallpaper be to cover the wall?

b. Calculate the storage capacity of Demont's toy box in cubic feet. (*Hint:* 30 inches is 2.5 feet.)

c. The following diagram is a top view of the Jackson house showing the outside walls. The dashes show the outside walls of the new dining room. Calculate the perimeter of the house.

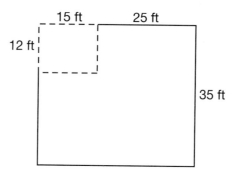

Written Practice *Distributed and Integrated*

1. In three classrooms there were 23 students, 25 students, and 30 students. If the students
(38) in the three classrooms were rearranged so that there were an equal number of students in each room, how many students would there be in each classroom?

2. Poet Julia de Burgos was born in 1914. Poet Sandra Cisneros was born
(5) 40 years later. When was Sandra Cisneros born?

3. a. Write the reduced fraction equal to 25%.
(58, 80)

b. Write the reduced fraction equal to 50%.

4. a. What is the area of each face of the cube?
(Inv. 10)

    b. What is the total surface area of the cube?

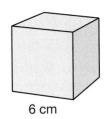

6 cm

5. (**Connect**) Name the shaded portion of this square as a
(58) percent, as a decimal number, and as a reduced fraction.

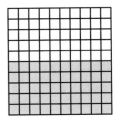

*6. Use grid paper to draw the front, top, and side views of this
(101) three-dimensional figure.

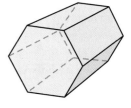

*7. Find each percent of a number by changing the percent to a decimal:
(102)
    a. 7% of 150   **b.** 75% of $48

8. a. How many units long is the perimeter of this shape?
(59)

    b. How many square units is the area of this shape?

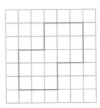

*9. Use prime factorization to find the least common multiple (LCM) of
(103) 15 and 16.

10. 1.23 × 10   **11.** 3.42 × 1000
(18,   *(18,*
100)   *100)*

*12. Name the number of shaded circles as an improper fraction and as a
(104) mixed number:

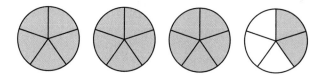

13. 4.3 − 1.21
(93)

14. 0.14 × 0.6
(99)

15. 48 × 0.7
(98)

*16. 0.735 × 10²
(18, 67, 100)

17. (Analyze) Write a fraction equal to $\frac{3}{4}$ that has the same denominator
(62, 69) as $\frac{3}{8}$. Then add the fraction to $\frac{3}{8}$. Remember to convert your answer to
a mixed number.

18. 16)‾4‾0‾0‾0‾
(84)

*19. Layla wants to carpet a room that is 12 feet long and 10 feet wide.
(105) Choose a formula to decide how much carpet is needed. Calculate
the amount.

20. $\frac{7}{11}$
(81) $+ \frac{8}{11}$

21. $3\frac{7}{12}$
(80) $+ \frac{1}{12}$

22. $5\frac{9}{10}$
(71) $- 5\frac{3}{10}$

23. $\frac{7}{2} \times \frac{1}{2}$
(81)

24. $\frac{2}{3} \div \frac{1}{4}$
(86)

25. $3 \div \frac{3}{4}$
(86)

26. Compare: $\sqrt{9} + \sqrt{16} \bigcirc \sqrt{9 + 16}$
(67)

27. The names of two of the 12 months begin with the letter *A*. What
(97) percent of the names of the months begin with the letter *A*?

*28. Hector wants to paint his room a new color. His room is 10 ft square
(105) and his walls are 8 ft high. He plans to paint only the walls, not the
ceiling. Choose a formula and solve to determine how many square
feet the paint will need to cover.

29. Ciante studied this list of flights between Los Angeles and Philadelphia.
(RF29) Refer to this list to answer parts **a–c.**

Los Angeles to Philadelphia

Depart	Arrive
6:15 a.m.	2:34 p.m.
10:10 a.m.	6:33 p.m.
12:56 p.m.	9:15 p.m.
3:10 p.m.	11:19 p.m.

Philadelphia to Los Angeles

Depart	Arrive
7:55 a.m.	10:41 a.m.
10:00 a.m.	12:53 p.m.
1:30 p.m.	4:17 p.m.
5:40 p.m.	8:31 p.m.

a. Ciante wants to arrive in Philadelphia before 8 p.m. However, she does not want to wake up very early to catch a flight. Which departure time is Ciante likely to choose?

b. For her return flight Ciante would like to leave as late as possible and still arrive in Los Angeles by 9:00 p.m. Which departure time is Ciante likely to choose?

c. **Explain** According to the times on the schedule, the 10:10 a.m. flight from Los Angeles to Philadelphia arrives at 6:33 p.m., and the 10:00 a.m. flight from Philadelphia arrives in Los Angeles at 12:53 p.m. What do you suppose accounts for the apparent difference of 5 hours 30 minutes in the durations of the two flights?

30. At Franklin Elementary School, the first recess of the morning lasts for
(63) $\frac{1}{2}$ of $\frac{1}{2}$ of an hour. What fraction of an hour is the length of the first recess? How many minutes long is that recess?

LESSON 106

California Mathematics Content Standards

MG 1.0, 1.1 Derive and use the formula for the area of a triangle and of a parallelogram by comparing it with the formula for the area of a rectangle (i.e., two of the same triangles make a parallelogram with twice the area; a parallelogram is compared with a rectangle of the same area by cutting and pasting a right triangle on the parallelogram).

MG 2.0, 2.3 Visualize and draw two-dimensional views of three-dimensional objects made from rectangular solids.

• Complex Figures

facts   Power Up J

mental math

a. Measurement: One milliliter of water has a mass of 1 gram. What is the mass of 1 liter of water?

b. Measurement: How many pounds is two and a half tons?

c. Fractional Parts: $\frac{1}{3}$ of 100

d. Fractional Parts: $\frac{2}{3}$ of 100

e. Time: Naomi's science class begins at 1:20 p.m. It ends 50 minutes later. At what time does her science class end?

f. Powers/Roots: $2^3 + 3^2$

g. Calculation: $20 \times 30, + 40, \div 10$

h. Evaluate: What is the value of the expression $\frac{12}{q}$ when $q = 4$?

problem solving

Choose an appropriate problem-solving strategy to solve this problem. A roll of nickels contains 40 nickels. A roll of dimes contains 50 dimes. A roll of quarters contains 40 quarters. Using at least one roll of each of these coins, find a combination of these rolls that totals $25.

New Concept

We have practiced finding the area of rectangles and triangles. Sometimes we can find the area of a more complex shape by dividing the shape into basic shapes. We find the area of each shape, and then add the areas of the shapes to find the total area.

Example 1

Nate sketched this floor plan of his bedroom. All angles are right angles. What is the area of the room?

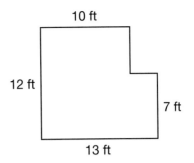

We can solve this problem two different ways.

Method 1

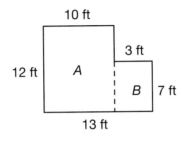

Total area = area A + area B
Area A = 10 ft × 12 ft = 120 ft²
+ Area B = 3 ft × 7 ft = 21 ft²
Total area   = **141 ft²**

Method 2

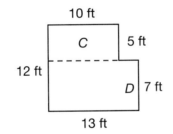

Total area = area C + area D
Area C = 10 ft × 5 ft = 50 ft²
+ Area D = 13 ft × 7 ft = 91 ft²
Total area   = **141 ft²**

Example 2

Find the area of this figure. All angles are right angles.

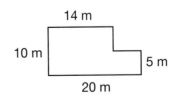

This time we will think of our figure as a large rectangle with a small rectangular piece removed. If we can find the area of the large rectangle and then *subtract* the area of the small rectangle, the answer will be the area of the figure shown above.

Here we show the figure redrawn and the calculations:

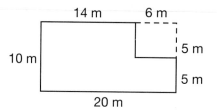

Area of figure = area of large rectangle
  − area of small rectangle

Area of large rectangle = 20 m × 10 m = 200 m²

− Area of small rectangle = 6 m × 5 m = 30 m²

Area of figure = **170 m²**

We did not need to subtract to find the area. We could have added the areas of two smaller rectangles as we did in Example 1.

Discuss Which method do you think is easier? Why?

We have practiced finding the areas of figures that can be divided into two or more rectangles. Now we will begin finding the areas of figures that include triangular regions as well.

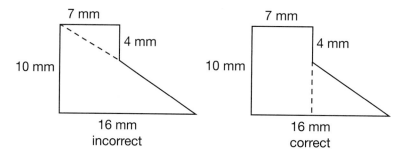

When dividing figures, we must avoid assumptions based on appearances. Although it may appear that the figure above is divided into two triangles, the larger "triangle" is actually a quadrilateral. The slanted "segment" bends where the solid and dashed segments intersect. The assumption that the figure is divided into two triangles leads to an incorrect calculation for the area of the figure.

You may use drawing software to help determine the area of complex shapes. Try designing your own by combining two shapes; for example, combine a triangle and a square, find their areas, and then add to find the total area.

Example 3

Visit www.
SaxonMath.com/
Int5ActivitiesCA for
an online activity.

Find the area of the figure. Corners that look square are square.

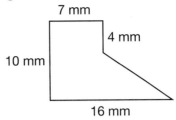

We divide the figure into smaller polygons. In this case we draw dashes that divide the figure into a rectangle and a triangle.

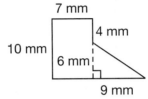

$$
\begin{aligned}
\text{Area of rectangle} \quad &= 7 \times 10 = 70 \text{ mm}^2 \\
+ \text{ Area of triangle} \quad &= \frac{(6 \times 9)}{2} = 27 \text{ mm}^2 \\
\hline
\textbf{Total area} \quad &= \textbf{97 mm}^2
\end{aligned}
$$

Example 4

Find the area of this figure. Corners that look square are square.

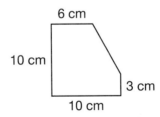

There are many ways to divide this figure.

A 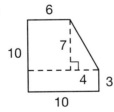   **B** 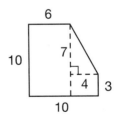   **C**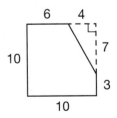

We decided to use **C**. We will find the area of the big rectangle and subtract from it the area of the triangle.

$$
\begin{aligned}
\text{Area of rectangle} \quad &= 10 \times 10 = 100 \text{ cm}^2 \\
- \text{ Area of triangle} \quad &= \frac{(4 \times 7)}{2} = 14 \text{ cm}^2 \\
\hline
\text{Total area of figure} \quad &= \textbf{86 cm}^2
\end{aligned}
$$

Example 5

Find the perimeter and area of quadrilateral *ABCD.* Then find m∠*s.*

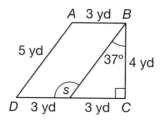

Thinking Skill

Verify

Why do we only use the outside measurements when we find perimeter?

This figure is a parallelogram and a right triangle. To find the perimeter, we will only use the outside measurements.

$$P = 3 \text{ yd} + 5 \text{ yd} + 3 \text{ yd} + 3 \text{ yd} + 4 \text{ yd}$$

$$P = 18 \text{ yd}$$

The perimeter of the figure is **18 yd.**

To find the area, we need to think of the figure as a parallelogram and a triangle. The area of the figure is the area of the parallelogram plus the area of the triangle. We know that the opposite sides of a parallelogram are equal, so the base of the parallelogram is 3 yd. The base of the triangle is 3 yd. The height of the parallelogram will be the same as the height of the triangle, which is 4 yd. Since we know the base and the height of both the parallelogram and the triangle, we can find the area of each.

Area of the Parallelogram	+	Area of the Triangle

$A = bh$

$= 3 \text{ yd} \times 4 \text{ yd}$

$= 12 \text{ yd}^2$

$A = \dfrac{bh}{2}$

$= \dfrac{(3 \text{ yd} \times 4 \text{ yd})}{2}$

$= \dfrac{12 \text{ yd}^2}{2}$

$= 6 \text{ yd}^2$

Thinking Skill

Verify

Why do we subtract from 180° to find the missing angle measure in the triangle?

The area of the figure is 12 yd² + 6 yd², or **18 yd².**

We can find the measure of angle *s* by first finding the measure of the angles in the triangle. We can see that one angle is a right angle and another angle is 37°. Since a right angle is 90°, we can add the sum of these two angles and subtract the sum from 180°.

$$180° - (90° + 37°) = 53°$$

The missing angle measure in the triangle is 53°.

Together, the 53° angle in the triangle and the measure of angle *s* form a straight angle, so we can subtract 53° from the measure of a straight angle to find m∠*s.*

$$\text{Since } 180° - 53° = 127°, \text{ m}\angle s = 127°.$$

Activity

Make a Cube

Material needed:
- **Lesson Activity 23**

Complete the following tasks.

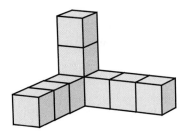

1. **Represent** This figure is made from 2-cm cubes. Draw the top, side, and front views.

2. Find the volume and surface area. Explain your reasoning.

Lesson Practice

a. Find the area of the figure. All angles are right angles.

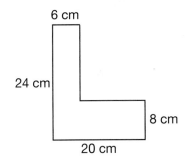

6 cm

24 cm

8 cm

20 cm

b. A 4 in. by 4 in. square was cut from a 10 in. by 12 in. sheet of construction paper. What is the area of the hexagon that remains?

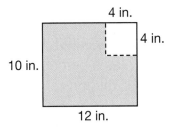

4 in.

4 in.

10 in.

12 in.

c. Find the perimeter and the area of this figure. Then find the m∠x.

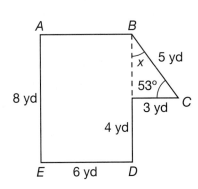

A   *B*

x   5 yd

53°

8 yd

3 yd   *C*

4 yd

E   6 yd   *D*

d. (**Model**) This figure is made from one-centimeter cubes. Draw the top, front, and right side views of the figure. Then find its volume and surface area.

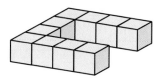

Written Practice — *Distributed and Integrated*

1. (**Estimate**) A small car weighs about one ton. Many large elephants weigh four times that much. About how many pounds would a large elephant weigh?
(64)

2. (**Estimate**) The Arctic Ocean is almost completely covered with the polar ice cap, which averages about 10 feet thick. About how many inches thick is the polar ice cap?
(61)

3. What is the total cost of 10 movie tickets priced at $5.25 each?
(13, 100)

4. Which digit in 375.246 is in the hundredths place?
(55)

5. Use algebraic addition to simplify each expression:
(95)

    a. $(-0.8) - (-0.2)$ **b.** $\left(-\frac{1}{4}\right) + \left(-\frac{2}{4}\right)$

    c. $(1.3) + (-0.4)$ **d.** $\left(\frac{8}{9}\right) - \left(-\frac{2}{9}\right)$

6. Write 12.5 as a mixed number.
(58)

7. (**Connect**) Name the shaded portion of this square as a percent, as a decimal number, and as a reduced fraction.
(58)

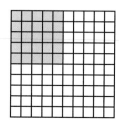

8. Find each percent of a number by changing the percent to a fraction:
(102)
    a. 40% of $60   **b.** 90% of 300

9. What is the perimeter of this equilateral triangle?
(24)

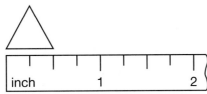

*10. Find the least common multiple (LCM) of 6 and 9.
(103)

*11. **a.** Find the least common multiple of 3 and 7.
(103) **b.** Find the least common multiple of 8 and 10.

12. *WX* is 4.2 cm. *XY* is 3 cm. *WZ* is 9.2 cm. Find *YZ*.
(93)

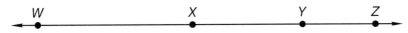

13. 4.38 + 7.525 + 23.7 + 9
(90)

14. 5 − (4.3 − 0.21)   **15.** 3.6 × 40
(93)   (98)

16. 0.15 × 0.5   **17.** 10 × 0.125
(99)   (100)

18. 4w = 300   **19.** 40)‾3000‾   **20.** 25)‾3300‾
(17)   (42)   (84)

21. $3\frac{3}{7} + \left(5 - 1\frac{2}{7}\right)$ **22.** $1\frac{1}{2} - \left(3 \times \frac{1}{2}\right)$
(51, 62)   (28, 78)

*23. Multiply. Write each product in simplest form.
(104)
  a. $3\frac{1}{2} \times 5$ **b.** $3\frac{2}{3} \times 1\frac{1}{5}$

24. Name the coordinates of the vertices of triangle *ABC*.
(21,
Inv. 6)

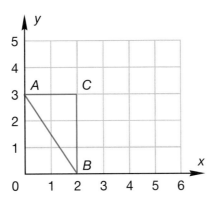

*25. Mrs. Hing needs a storage crate and is deciding between two
(105) different ones. The blue crate is longer but not as tall as the gray
crate. Use the volume formula to determine the storage capacity of
each crate. The blue crate is 36 in. × 32 in. × 20 in. The green crate
is 30 in. × 30 in. × 24 in. Which crate has the greater volume?

26. Find the percent equivalent to $\frac{1}{8}$ by multiplying 100% by $\frac{1}{8}$. Write
(97) the result as a mixed number with the fraction reduced.

*27. Find the area of this figure. All angles are right angles.
(106)

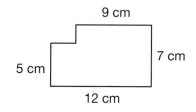

28. Lionel chopped $\frac{3}{4}$ of a cup of celery, but he needed to
(63) use only $\frac{1}{2}$ of that amount in a cream soup recipe. What
amount of chopped celery did the recipe require?

29. The lowest temperature ever recorded in North Dakota was −60°F.
(9) In Montana, the lowest temperature ever recorded was −70°F. Is a
temperature of −60°F warmer or colder than a temperature of −70°F?
How many degrees warmer or colder?

*30. Find the area of this figure. Corners that look square
(106) are square.

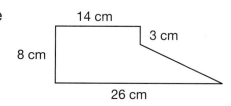

LESSON
107

California Mathematics Content Standards
NS 2.0, **2.3** Solve simple problems, including ones arising in concrete situations, involving the addition and subtraction of fractions and mixed numbers (like and unlike denominators of 20 or less), and express answers in the simplest form.
MR 2.0, 2.3 Use a variety of methods, such as words, numbers, symbols, charts, graphs, tables, diagrams, and models, to explain mathematical reasoning.

• Finding Common Denominators

facts   Power Up J

mental math

a. Estimation: Use compatible numbers to estimate the cost of 9.8 gallons of gas at 2.49\frac{9}{10}$ per gallon.

b. Estimation: Choose the more reasonable estimate for the weight of a sheet of $8\frac{1}{2}$" by 11" notebook paper: 2 g or 2 kg.

c. Percent: What is 50% of $40? 25% of $40? 10% of $40?

d. Measurement: Sierra needs one quart of water to mix with the frozen juice concentrate. How many times must she fill a pint container to measure out one quart?

e. Measurement: Antonia needs a gallon of water to mix with detergent. How many times must she fill a quart container to measure out one gallon?

f. Geometry: Two angles of the parallelogram each measure 75°. The other two angles each measure 105°. What is the total measure of the four angles?

g. Calculation: $\sqrt{49} \times \sqrt{49}$

h. Evaluate: What is the value of the expression $10 + \frac{r}{5}$ when $r = 15$?

problem solving

Choose an appropriate problem-solving strategy to solve this problem. If a coin is flipped, there are two possible outcomes: heads (H) or tails (T). If a coin is flipped twice, there are four possible outcomes: heads then heads (H, H), heads then tails (H, T), tails then heads (T, H), or tails then tails (T, T). How many outcomes are possible for a coin that is flipped three times? List all the possible outcomes, starting with heads then heads then heads (H, H, H).

Fractions that do not have the same denominators may be difficult to compare. For example, which is larger, $\frac{5}{8}$ or $\frac{2}{3}$? If we model $\frac{5}{8}$ and $\frac{2}{3}$ using our fraction pieces, it is still difficult to decide.

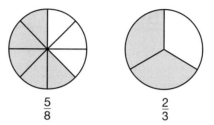

$$\frac{5}{8} \qquad\qquad \frac{2}{3}$$

It is much easier to compare fractions when they have *common* denominators. One way to rewrite two fractions so that they have common denominators is to multiply each fraction by a name for 1 that uses the denominator of the other fraction. We can rewrite $\frac{5}{8}$ and $\frac{2}{3}$ with common denominators by multiplying $\frac{5}{8}$ by $\frac{3}{3}$ and $\frac{2}{3}$ by $\frac{8}{8}$.

$$\frac{5}{8} \times \frac{3}{3} = \frac{15}{24} \qquad\qquad \frac{2}{3} \times \frac{8}{8} = \frac{16}{24}$$

When fractions have common denominators, we compare the fractions by comparing the numerators. For the fractions $\frac{5}{8}$ and $\frac{2}{3}$, we find that $\frac{5}{8} < \frac{2}{3}$ because $\frac{15}{24} < \frac{16}{24}$.

Notice that the numerator 15 was formed by multiplying 5 by 3, and that the numerator 16 was formed by multiplying 2 by 8. Another way to represent these factors and products is shown below. The numbers 15 and 16 are often called **cross products**. The cross products are the numerators of the fractions $\frac{5}{8}$ and $\frac{2}{3}$ after the denominators have been changed to common denominators.

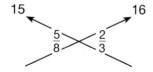

We can use cross products to compare two fractions. If the cross products of two fractions are equal, the fractions are equal. The cross products below are equal and show that $\frac{1}{2}$ is equal to $\frac{4}{8}$.

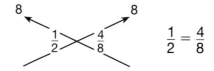

If the cross products of two fractions are not equal, the greater cross product is above the greater fraction. The cross products below tell us that $\frac{3}{4}$ is greater than $\frac{7}{10}$ because $30 > 28$.

$$30 \diagdown\diagup 28$$
$$\frac{3}{4} \bowtie \frac{7}{10} \qquad \frac{3}{4} > \frac{7}{10}$$

To compare fractions, we can use common denominators or cross products.

Example 1

Use common denominators to compare $\frac{2}{3}$ and $\frac{3}{5}$.

To change different denominators to common denominators, we multiply each fraction by a name for 1 that uses the denominator of the other fraction.

$$\frac{2}{3} \times \frac{5}{5} = \frac{10}{15} \qquad \frac{3}{5} \times \frac{3}{3} = \frac{9}{15}$$

Since $\frac{10}{15} > \frac{9}{15}$, we find that $\frac{2}{3} > \frac{3}{5}$.

Example 2

Use cross products to compare $\frac{5}{6}$ and $\frac{7}{8}$.

To find cross products, we multiply the denominator of the first fraction by the numerator of the second fraction, and we multiply the denominator of the second fraction by the numerator of the first fraction.

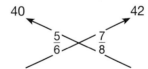

Since $40 < 42$, we find that $\frac{5}{6} < \frac{7}{8}$.

Example 3

Use cross products to compare $\frac{3}{12}$ and $\frac{1}{4}$.

To find cross products, we multiply the denominator of the first fraction by the numerator of the second fraction, and we multiply the denominator of the second fraction by the numerator of the first fraction.

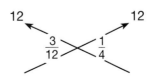

Since the cross products are equal, we find that $\frac{3}{12} = \frac{1}{4}$.

We use common denominators to add or subtract fractions with different denominators.

Example 4

Add: $\frac{1}{3} + \frac{1}{6}$

We rewrite the fractions by multiplying each fraction by a name for 1 that uses the denominator of the other fraction. We rewrite $\frac{1}{3}$ and $\frac{1}{6}$ with common denominators by multiplying $\frac{1}{3}$ by $\frac{6}{6}$ and $\frac{1}{6}$ by $\frac{3}{3}$.

$$\frac{1}{3} \times \frac{6}{6} = \frac{6}{18}$$
$$+ \frac{1}{6} \times \frac{3}{3} = \frac{3}{18}$$
$$\frac{9}{18}$$

We reduce a fraction by dividing both terms of the fraction by the GCF of the terms.

$$\frac{9 \div 9}{18 \div 9} = \frac{1}{2}$$

The GCF of 9 and 18 is 9, and we find that $\frac{1}{3} + \frac{1}{6} = \frac{1}{2}$.

Example 5

Subtract: $\frac{7}{10} - \frac{2}{3}$

We rewrite $\frac{7}{10}$ and $\frac{2}{3}$ with common denominators by multiplying $\frac{7}{10}$ by $\frac{3}{3}$ and $\frac{2}{3}$ by $\frac{10}{10}$.

$$\frac{7}{10} \times \frac{3}{3} = \frac{21}{30}$$
$$- \frac{2}{3} \times \frac{10}{10} = \frac{20}{30}$$
$$\frac{1}{30}$$

The difference is in simplest form, and we find that $\frac{7}{10} - \frac{2}{3} = \frac{1}{30}$.

Lesson Practice

Write the cross products of each comparison. Then write >, <, or = to complete the comparison.

a. $\frac{1}{3} \bigcirc \frac{2}{5}$

b. $\frac{3}{4} \bigcirc \frac{4}{5}$

c. $\frac{2}{3} \bigcirc \frac{6}{9}$

d. $\frac{5}{6} \bigcirc \frac{2}{3}$

e. $\frac{6}{8} \bigcirc \frac{3}{4}$

f. $\frac{2}{5} \bigcirc \frac{3}{8}$

Rewrite each pair of fractions so that the denominators are the same. Then write $>$, $<$, or $=$ to complete the comparison.

g. $\frac{2}{3} \bigcirc \frac{1}{4}$
h. $\frac{3}{5} \bigcirc \frac{3}{4}$

i. $\frac{1}{5} \bigcirc \frac{1}{2}$

Rewrite each pair of fractions so that the denominators are the same. Then add or subtract, and write your answer in simplest form.

j.
$$\begin{array}{r} \frac{3}{4} \\ -\frac{1}{3} \\ \hline \end{array}$$

k.
$$\begin{array}{r} \frac{4}{5} \\ +\frac{3}{4} \\ \hline \end{array}$$

l.
$$\begin{array}{r} \frac{1}{2} \\ +\frac{1}{3} \\ \hline \end{array}$$

m. $\frac{2}{5} - \frac{1}{6}$

n. $\frac{7}{8} + \frac{2}{3}$

o. $\frac{3}{5} - \frac{1}{2}$

Written Practice   *Distributed and Integrated*

1. Use grid paper to draw the front, top, and side views of this
(101) three-dimensional figure.

2. **Estimate** Estimate the product of 634 and 186 by rounding both
(50) numbers to the nearest hundred before multiplying.

3. a. $\frac{1}{10} = \frac{\square}{100}$
(58, 69)

   b. What percent equals the fraction $\frac{1}{10}$?

4. The weight of an object on the moon is about $\frac{1}{6}$ of the weight of the
(34) same object on Earth. A person on Earth who weighs 108 pounds
would weigh about how many pounds on the moon?

*5. **Connect** Name the total number of shaded circles as an
(104) improper fraction and as a mixed number.

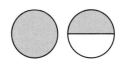

6. a. An inch is about 2.5 cm. What is the perimeter of this square in inches? In centimeters?
(59)

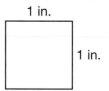

1 in.

1 in.

b. What is the area of this square in square inches? In square centimeters?

7. What fraction of a year is 3 months? What percent of a year is 3 months?
(10, 21, 97)

*8. Alexandra wants to put wallpaper border all around her bedroom at the top of each wall. Her rectangular bedroom is 10 ft by 12 ft. Use a formula to find the number of feet of border Alexandra will need.
(105)

9. The denominators of $\frac{1}{6}$ and $\frac{1}{4}$ are 6 and 4. What is the least common multiple (LCM) of the denominators?
(103)

10. (Connect) To what mixed number is the arrow pointing?
(25, 71)

5   6

11. 4.239 + 25 + 6.79 + 12.5
(90)

12. 6.875 − (4 − 3.75)
(7, 93)

13.   3.7
(98)   × 0.8

14.   0.125
(100)   ×   100

15.   0.32
(99)   × 0.04

16. $\frac{408}{17}$
(84)

17. 27)‾705
(84)

*18. Use cross products to write >, <, or = to complete each comparison.
(107)

a. $\frac{3}{4}$ ◯ $\frac{2}{3}$ **b.** $\frac{1}{3}$ ◯ $\frac{2}{6}$ **c.** $\frac{3}{5}$ ◯ $\frac{3}{6}$

*19. Rewrite each pair of fractions so that the denominators are the same. Then write >, <, or = to complete the comparison.
(107)

a. $\frac{1}{3}$ ◯ $\frac{2}{5}$ **b.** $\frac{3}{8}$ ◯ $\frac{3}{4}$ **c.** $\frac{2}{3}$ ◯ $\frac{6}{9}$

20. $5\dfrac{5}{8}$
(71)
$+\ \dfrac{1}{8}$
___

21. $\quad 7$
(51)
$-\ 4\dfrac{3}{10}$
___

22. $\dfrac{5}{6}$ of 4
(78)

23. Find the area of this figure. Corners that look square
(106) are square.

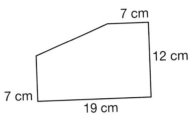

7 cm

12 cm

7 cm

19 cm

24. $\dfrac{3}{8} \div \dfrac{1}{2}$
(86)

25. Josette spent $\dfrac{1}{6}$ of an hour walking to school and $\dfrac{1}{4}$ of an hour walking
(69) home from school. How many minutes did Josette spend walking to and from school? What fraction of an hour did Josette spend walking to and from school? (*Hint*: Write fractions equal to $\dfrac{1}{6}$ and $\dfrac{1}{4}$ that have denominators of 12. Then add the fractions.)

26. (**Interpret**) Lillian is planning a trip from San Diego to San Luis Obispo.
(13) The schedules for the trains she plans to take are printed below. Use this information to answer parts **a–c.**

Station		#29		#48
San Diego	Dp	9:30 a.m.	Ar	7:50 p.m.
Anaheim		11:26 a.m.		5:51 p.m.
Los Angeles		12:30 p.m.		4:55 p.m.
Ventura		2:21 p.m.		2:39 p.m.
Santa Barbara		3:10 p.m.		1:40 p.m.
Solvang		4:05 p.m.		12:45 p.m.
San Luis Obispo		5:30 p.m.		11:10 a.m.
Paso Robles	Ar	6:20 p.m.	Dp	10:00 a.m.

Key
Dp = Departure
Ar = Arrival

a. The trip from San Diego to San Luis Obispo takes how long?

b. Train #48 stops in Santa Barbara for 15 minutes before continuing. At what time does the train depart from Santa Barbara?

c. **Multiple Choice** The distance between San Diego and San Luis Obispo is about 320 miles. From departure to arrival, the train travels about how many miles each hour?

    A 30 miles   **B** 40 miles   **C** 50 miles   **D** 60 miles

27. **a.** What is the volume of a chest of drawers with the dimensions shown?
(Inv. 9)

b. What is the area of the top of the chest?

c. What is the perimeter of the top of the chest?

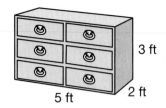

3 ft

2 ft

5 ft

28. The girls softball team held a fundraiser by selling shirts. Shaquana
(37) sold twice as many shirts as Mackenzie, and Cherise sold four more shirts than Shaquana. Mackenzie sold ten shirts. How many shirts did Cherise sell?

29. (Explain) Dawson mailed two packages at the post office. One
(30) package weighed $2\frac{1}{4}$ pounds, and the other weighed $3\frac{3}{4}$ pounds. The clerk told Dawson that the total weight of the packages was exactly 6 pounds. Was the clerk correct? Explain your answer.

30. (Interpret) Use the table to answer the questions that follow.
(74)

**Number of School Days per Year
(by country)**

Country	Number of School Days
Japan	243
China	230
Korea	220
United States	180

a. Find the mean of the data.

b. Find the range of the data.

Real-World Connection

A standard sheet of paper in America, called *letter size*, measures $8\frac{1}{2}$ by 11 inches. It has an area of 93.5 square inches. There are other sizes of paper and many have interesting names. Refer to the table below.

Paper Name	Paper Dimensions (inches)
atlas	26 × 34
elephant	23 × 28
double elephant	27 × 40
emperor	48 × 72
foolscap	$12\frac{1}{2}$ × 17

a. Which has a greater area, 2 sheets of foolscap paper or 1 sheet of atlas paper?

b. Does a sheet of double elephant have twice the area of a sheet of elephant?

LESSON

108

• Using the Least Common Denominator (LCD)

🖊 **California Mathematics Content Standards**

NS 2.0, ➋➌ Solve simple problems, including ones arising in concrete situations, involving the addition and subtraction of fractions and mixed numbers (like and unlike denominators of 20 or less), and express answers in the simplest form.
MR 2.0, 2.3 Use a variety of methods, such as words, numbers, symbols, charts, graphs, tables, diagrams, and models, to explain mathematical reasoning.
MR 3.0, 3.3 Develop generalizations of the results obtained and apply them in other circumstances.

Power Up

facts   Power Up J

mental math

a. Estimation: Estimate the cost of 10.17 gallons of gas at $2.69 $\frac{9}{10}$ per gallon.

b. Time: How many years is half a century?

c. Fractional Parts: $\frac{1}{4}$ of $80

d. Fractional Parts: $\frac{3}{4}$ of $80

e. Percent: 50% of $\frac{1}{2}$

f. Measurement: The high temperature was 37°C. The nighttime low was 23°C. What was the difference between the high and low temperatures?

g. Calculation: $\sqrt{64} \times \sqrt{64}$

h. Evaluate: What is the value of the expression $18 - \frac{18}{s}$ when $s = 9$?

problem solving

Choose an appropriate problem-solving strategy to solve this problem. Bianca wants to use 1-inch cubes to build a larger cube with edges 3 inches long. How many 1-inch cubes will she need?

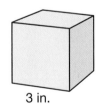

3 in.

New Concept

In the previous lesson, we learned that we can compare two fractions that have different denominators by using the product of the denominators as the common denominator. Another way to compare two fractions is to use the least common multiple (LCM) of the denominators. The LCM of the denominators is called the **least common denominator.**

Example 1

Use the least common denominator to compare: $\frac{5}{8} \bigcirc \frac{3}{4}$

We begin by listing the first few multiples of 8 and 4. Then we circle the least number that is common to both lists.

Multiples of 8: ⑧, 16, 24, 32, …
Multiples of 4: 4, ⑧, 12, 16, …

We find that the least common denominator of 8 and 4 is 8. Since the denominator of $\frac{5}{8}$ is the least common denominator, we need only to change $\frac{3}{4}$ to eighths.

$$\frac{3}{4} \times \frac{2}{2} = \frac{6}{8}$$

Now we compare. Since $\frac{5}{8} < \frac{6}{8}$, we find that $\frac{5}{8} < \frac{3}{4}$.

Thinking Skill

Does multiplying $\frac{3}{4}$ by $\frac{2}{2}$ change the value of $\frac{3}{4}$? Explain why or why not.

In the previous lesson, we also learned that we can add or subtract two fractions that have different denominators by using the product of the denominators as the common denominator. Another way to add or subtract two fractions is to use the least common denominator of the fractions.

Example 2

Use the least common denominator to add: $\frac{1}{8} + \frac{5}{6}$

We begin by listing the first few multiples of 8 and 6. Then we circle the least number that is common to both lists.

Multiples of 8: 8, 16, ㉔, 32, 40, 48, 56, 64, …

Multiples of 6: 6, 12, 18, ㉔, 30, 36, 42, 48, …

We find that the least common denominator of 8 and 6 is 24. We then rewrite the fractions by multiplying each fraction by a name for 1 that results in a common denominator of 24.

$$\frac{1}{8} \times \frac{3}{3} = \frac{3}{24} \qquad \frac{5}{6} \times \frac{4}{4} = \frac{20}{24}$$

Now we add.

$$\begin{array}{r} \frac{3}{24} \\ + \frac{20}{24} \\ \hline \frac{23}{24} \end{array}$$

Since the sum of $\frac{3}{24}$ and $\frac{20}{24}$ is $\frac{23}{24}$, we find that $\frac{1}{8} + \frac{5}{6} = \frac{23}{24}$.

Example 3

Use the least common denominator to subtract: $\frac{3}{4} - \frac{1}{6}$

We begin by listing the first few multiples of 4 and 6. Then we circle the least number that is common to both lists.

Multiples of 4: 4, 8, ⑫, 16, …

Multiples of 6: 6, ⑫, 18, …

We find that the least common denominator of 4 and 6 is 12. We then rewrite the fractions by multiplying each fraction by a name for 1 that results in a common denominator of 12.

$$\frac{3}{4} \times \frac{3}{3} = \frac{9}{12} \qquad \frac{1}{6} \times \frac{2}{2} = \frac{2}{12}$$

Now we subtract.

$$\begin{array}{r} \frac{9}{12} \\ - \frac{2}{12} \\ \hline \frac{7}{12} \end{array}$$

Since the difference of $\frac{9}{12} - \frac{2}{12}$ is $\frac{7}{12}$, we find that $\frac{3}{4} - \frac{1}{6} = \frac{7}{12}$.

Lesson Practice

Rewrite each fraction using the least common denominator. Then write >, <, or = to complete the comparison.

a. $\frac{1}{2} \bigcirc \frac{5}{6}$　　　　**b.** $\frac{7}{8} \bigcirc \frac{3}{4}$　　　　**c.** $\frac{2}{5} \bigcirc \frac{2}{3}$

For problems **d–i**, follow these steps to find each sum or difference:

* Find the least common denominator.
* Rename one or both fractions.
* Add or subtract the fractions.
* Reduce the answer when possible.

d. $\begin{array}{r} \frac{3}{8} \\ + \frac{1}{2} \\ \hline \end{array}$　　　　**e.** $\begin{array}{r} \frac{1}{3} \\ - \frac{1}{6} \\ \hline \end{array}$　　　　**f.** $\begin{array}{r} \frac{5}{8} \\ + \frac{1}{4} \\ \hline \end{array}$

g. $\frac{8}{9} - \frac{1}{3}$　　　　**h.** $\frac{1}{6} + \frac{7}{12}$　　　　**i.** $\frac{2}{3} - \frac{5}{12}$

j. **Verify** Is the first multiple of a number greater than that number? Explain why or why not, and give an example to support your explanation.

k. **Connect** How does the least common denominator of two fractions compare to the least common multiple of the denominators?

1. **Represent** Draw a circle and shade all but $\frac{1}{3}$ of it. What percent of the
(Inv. 2, 58) circle is shaded?

2. **Multiple Choice** Which of these units of length would probably be
(61) used to measure the length of a room?

   A inches   **B** feet

   C miles   **D** light years

3. Simplify each decimal number:
(91)
   a. 8.020   **b.** 0.400   **c.** 10.010

*4. Raven wants to put tile on her kitchen floor. Her kitchen is 12 ft by
(105) 14 ft, and the tiles are 12-inch squares. Use a formula to determine how
many tile squares it will take to cover Hana's kitchen floor.

*5. Write $1\frac{3}{4}$ as an improper fraction.
(104)

6. **Explain** Is it possible for one friend to eat $\frac{1}{3}$ of a pizza and for
(46, 69) another friend to eat $\frac{5}{6}$ of the same pizza? Explain why or why not.

*7. The denominators of $\frac{3}{8}$ and $\frac{5}{6}$ are 8 and 6. What is the least common
(103) multiple (LCM) of the denominators?

8. Refer to this spinner to answer parts **a** and **b.**
(45)

   a. What fraction names the probability that with one spin
   the spinner will stop on sector A?

   b. What is the probability that with one spin the spinner
   will stop on sector B?

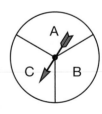

*9. Rewrite each pair of fractions so that the denominators are the same.
(107) Then add or subtract, and write your answer in simplest form.

   a. $\frac{3}{5} - \frac{1}{3} =$ ___   **b.** $\frac{2}{3} + \frac{1}{6} =$ ___   **c.** $\frac{1}{2} + \frac{2}{8} =$ ___

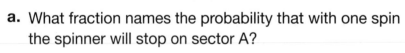

10. $45 + 16.7 + 8.29 + 4.325$
(90)

11. $4.2 - (3.2 - 1)$ **12.** 0.75×0.05
(7, 90)   *(99)*

13. 0.6 × 38
(98)

14. 100 × 7.5
(100)

15. $24.36 ÷ 12
(82)

16. 4600 ÷ 25
(84)

*17. Rewrite each fraction using the least common denominator. Then write
(108) >, <, or = to complete the comparison.

a. $\frac{2}{3} \bigcirc \frac{3}{4}$ **b.** $\frac{2}{5} \bigcirc \frac{2}{4}$ **c.** $\frac{7}{9} \bigcirc \frac{4}{6}$

18. $5\frac{4}{9} + 3\frac{5}{9}$
(62)

19. $4 ÷ \frac{1}{8}$
(86)

20. $4 × \frac{1}{8}$
(78, 80)

21. At the Little League baseball game there were 18 players and
(87) 30 spectators. What was the ratio of players to spectators at
the game?

22. a. (Connect) What percent of the rectangle is shaded?
(97)

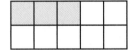

b. What percent of the rectangle is not shaded?

23. a. Write the reduced fraction equal to 60%.
(58, 80)

b. Write the reduced fraction equal to 70%.

24. a. (Analyze) A loop of string can be arranged to form a
(59) rectangle that is 12 inches long and 6 inches wide. If the
same loop of string is arranged to form a square, what
would be the length of each side of the square?

12 in.

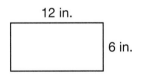

6 in.

b. What is the area of the rectangle pictured in part **a?**

c. What is the area of the square described in part **a?**

25. Find the percent equivalent to $\frac{1}{6}$ by multiplying 100% by $\frac{1}{6}$ and writing
(97) the answer as a mixed number with the fraction reduced.

26. (Explain) What is the result of doubling $7\frac{1}{2}$ and dividing the product
(37) by 3? Explain why your answer is reasonable.

*27. Find each sum or difference using the least common denominator:
(108)

a. $\dfrac{7}{8}$
$-\dfrac{1}{4}$

b. $\dfrac{4}{5}$
$-\dfrac{1}{3}$

c. $\dfrac{2}{3}$
$+\dfrac{1}{9}$

*28. Add: 3 + (−10)
(89)

29. **Explain** The baseball spikes Orin purchased online arrived in a
(94) shoe box. The box measured $11\frac{3}{8}$ in. by $8\frac{3}{4}$ in. by 4 in. Estimate the
volume of the box, and explain why your estimate is reasonable.

*30. Two squares form this hexagon. Refer to this figure to answer
(59, parts **a** and **b.**
106)

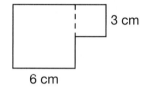
3 cm

6 cm

a. What is the area of each square?

b. Combine the areas of the two squares to find the area of
the hexagon.

LESSON 109

California Mathematics Content Standards

NS 2.0, 2.1 Add, subtract, multiply, and divide with decimals; add with negative integers; subtract positive integers from negative integers; and verify the reasonableness of the results.

NS 2.0, 2.2 Demonstrate proficiency with division, including division with positive decimals and long division with multidigit divisors.

MR 2.0, 2.1 Use estimation to verify the reasonableness of calculated results.

MR 2.0, 2.4 Express the solution clearly and logically by using the appropriate mathematical notation and terms and clear language; support solutions with evidence in both verbal and symbolic work.

MR 3.0, 3.3 Develop generalizations of the results obtained and apply them in other circumstances.

• Dividing a Decimal Number by a Whole Number

Power Up

facts   Power Up J

mental math

    a. Estimation: Choose the more reasonable estimate for the weight of a pencil: 8 grams or 8 kilograms.

    b. Fractional Parts: $\frac{1}{8}$ of 80

    c. Fractional Parts: $\frac{3}{8}$ of 80

    d. Percent: 25% of 80

    e. Money: Haley bought a juice for $1.89 and a snack bar for $0.97. What was the total cost of the two items?

    f. Probability: What is the probability that with one spin, the spinner will land on 2?

    g. Calculation: $\sqrt{81}$, $\times\,10$, $-\,2$, $\div\,2$, $+\,1$, $\div\,5$

    h. Evaluate: What is the value of the expression $3 + (t \cdot 2)$ when $t = 5$?

problem solving

Choose an appropriate problem-solving strategy to solve this problem. Austin wonders about how many seconds each day he is awake and about how many seconds he is asleep. He figures that he sleeps 9 hours each night. About how many seconds is Austin awake each day? About how many seconds is he asleep each day? Altogether, how many seconds are in one day? Explain your reasoning.

New Concept

Dividing a decimal number by a whole number is like dividing money by a whole number. The decimal point in the quotient is directly above the decimal point inside the division box.

In the chart below "÷ by whole (*W*)" means "division by a whole number." The memory cue "up" reminds us where to place the decimal in the quotient. (We will later learn a different rule for dividing by a decimal number.)

Thinking Skill

Generalize

How is dividing a money amount by a whole number the same as dividing two whole numbers? How is it different?

Decimals Chart

Operation	+ or −	×	÷ by whole (*W*)
Memory cue	line up $\pm\ .$	×; then count $\times\ .\_$	up $W)\overline{\ .}$

You may need to ...
- Place a decimal point on the end of whole numbers.
- Fill each empty place with a zero.

We sometimes need to use one or more zeros as placeholders when dividing decimal numbers. Here we show this using money.

Suppose $0.12 is shared equally by 3 people. The division will look like this:

$$\begin{array}{r} \$\ .\ 4 \\ 3)\overline{\$0.12} \\ \underline{12} \\ 0 \end{array} \longrightarrow \begin{array}{r} \$0.04 \\ 3)\overline{\$0.12} \\ \underline{12} \\ 0 \end{array} \begin{array}{l} \text{decimal} \\ \text{point "up"} \end{array}$$

Notice that the decimal point in the quotient is directly above the decimal point in the dividend. We fill each empty place with a zero and see that each person will receive $0.04.

Example 1

For an art project, Corbin must cut a length of ribbon in half. The ribbon is 4.8 meters long. If he cuts the ribbon correctly, how long will each length of ribbon be?

We are dividing 4.8 meters by 2, which is a whole number. We remember the memory cue "up" and place the decimal point in the answer directly above the decimal point inside the division box. Then we divide. Each length of cut ribbon will be **2.4 meters.**

$$\begin{array}{r} 2.4 \\ 2)\overline{4.8} \\ \underline{4} \\ 0\ 8 \\ \underline{8} \\ 0 \end{array}$$

Example 2 ··

Divide: $3\overline{)0.42}$

We place the decimal point in the answer "straight up." Then we divide.

$$
\begin{array}{r}
0.14 \\
3\overline{)0.42} \\
\underline{3} \\
12 \\
\underline{12} \\
0
\end{array}
$$

Example 3 ··

Divide: 0.15 ÷ 3

We rewrite the problem using a division box. The decimal point in the answer is "straight up." We divide and remember to fill empty places with zeros.

$$
\begin{array}{r}
0.05 \\
3\overline{)0.15} \\
\underline{15} \\
0
\end{array}
$$

(**Generalize**) How is dividing a decimal by a whole number similar to dividing a money amount by a whole number? How is it different?

Example 4 ··

Divide: 0.0024 ÷ 3

We rewrite the problem using a division box. The decimal point in the answer is "straight up." We divide and remember to fill empty places with zeros.

$$
\begin{array}{r}
0.0008 \\
3\overline{)0.0024}
\end{array}
$$

Example 5 ··

Divide: 24.55 ÷ 5

We rewrite the problem using a division box. Since the divisor is a whole number, we place a decimal point in the quotient and then begin the division.

We note in this example that we must bring down the 5 in the hundredths place of the quotient to complete the division.

$$
\begin{array}{r}
4.91 \\
5\overline{)24.55} \\
\underline{20} \\
4\,5 \\
\underline{4\,5} \\
05 \\
\underline{5} \\
0
\end{array}
$$

(**Connect**) Before completing the division, would it be possible to know if the quotient was going to be greater than 1? Explain why or why not.

Lesson Practice Divide:

    a. $4\overline{)0.52}$ **b.** $6\overline{)3.6}$ **c.** $0.85 \div 5$

    d. $5\overline{)7.5}$ **e.** $5\overline{)0.65}$ **f.** $2.1 \div 3$

    g. $4\overline{)0.16}$ **h.** $0.35 \div 7$ **i.** $5\overline{)0.0025}$

    j. $0.08 \div 4$ **k.** $6\overline{)0.24}$ **l.** $0.0144 \div 3$

    m. (**Estimate**) A gallon is about 3.78 liters. About how many liters is half a gallon?

    n. (**Estimate**) Round the dividend to find the quotient of $11.76 \div 3$, and then complete the division to find the exact quotient.

Written Practice
Distributed and Integrated

*1. The price of the recliner chair was $450 and the sales tax rate was
(102) 7%. How much is the tax? What is the total price of the recliner plus tax?

2. (**Connect**) Name the total number of shaded circles below as an
(104) improper fraction and as a mixed number.

3. a. What fraction names the probability that with one spin
(45) the spinner will stop on sector A?

    b. What is the probability that with one spin the spinner will stop on sector B?

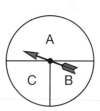

*4. Rewrite each pair of fractions so the denominators are the same. Then
(107) add or subtract, and write your answer in simplest form.

    a. $\dfrac{4}{5} - \dfrac{2}{3}$ **b.** $\dfrac{5}{6} + \dfrac{1}{3}$ **c.** $\dfrac{3}{4} - \dfrac{1}{8}$

5. Lawrencia's first class of the afternoon begins $1\frac{1}{2}$ hours after 11:40 a.m.
(10) What time of the day does her first class of the afternoon begin?

*6. Moesha studied for her spelling test for $\frac{9}{10}$ of an hour. Sun studied for
(108)   the test for $\frac{2}{3}$ of an hour. Find a common denominator and compare to
        see who studied longer.

7. The denominators of $\frac{2}{5}$ and $\frac{2}{3}$ are 5 and 3. Find the least common
(103)   multiple (LCM) of the denominators.

8. a. Estimate the perimeter of this rectangle.
(94)
   b. Estimate the area of this rectangle.

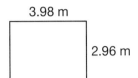

3.98 m

2.96 m

9. 42.98 + 50 + 23.5 + 0.025
(90)

10. (**Represent**) How much greater than 5.18 is 6? Use words to write your
(55, 60)   answer.

11.   0.375
(100) $\times$ 10

12.   0.14
(99) $\times$ 0.06

13.   7.8
(98) $\times$ 19

14. 2340 ÷ 30
(82)

15. $18\overline{)2340}$
(84)

*16. An inch is 2.54 centimeters. How many centimeters is half
(109)   an inch?

17. $\frac{1}{2} + \frac{3}{10}$
(107, 108)

18. $\frac{11}{12} - \frac{2}{3}$
(107, 108)

19. $\frac{4}{5} \times \frac{2}{3}$
(63)

20. $\frac{4}{5} \div \frac{2}{3}$
(86)

21. $\frac{2}{5} = \frac{\square}{15}$
(69)

22. $\frac{2}{3} = \frac{\square}{15}$
(69)

23. In problems **21** and **22** you made fractions equal to $\frac{2}{5}$ and $\frac{2}{3}$ with
(81)   denominators of 15. Add the fractions you made. Remember to convert
        the answer to a mixed number.

*24. Divide:
(109)
   a. $2\overline{)0.162}$ **b.** $4\overline{)3.52}$ **c.** 0.65 ÷ 5

*25. a. What is the area of this hexagon?
(106)

    b. What is the perimeter of the hexagon?

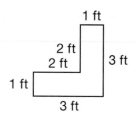

26. What fraction of a square mile is a field that is $\frac{1}{2}$ mile
(63) long and $\frac{1}{4}$ mile wide?

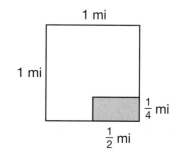

27. **Explain** Sasha says that multiplying $4\frac{1}{8}$ by 3 and then subtracting
(37) 1 gives an answer of $11\frac{3}{8}$. Explain how rounding can be used to help
decide if Sasha's answer is reasonable.

28. Add: $-24 + 7$
(49)

29. a. Does this prism have parallel lines?
(101)

    b. Does this prism have perpendicular lines?

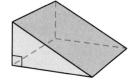

*30. Two squares form this hexagon. If the squares were
(106) separated, their perimeters would be 12 cm and 24 cm,
respectively. However, the perimeter of the hexagon is
not the sum of the perimeters of the squares because
one side of the small square and part of one side of the
large square are not part of the perimeter of the hexagon.
Copy the hexagon on your paper, and show the length
of each of the six sides. What is the perimeter of the
hexagon?

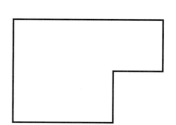

• More on Dividing Decimal Numbers

California Mathematics Content Standards
NS 2.0, 2.1 Add, subtract, multiply, and divide with decimals; add with negative integers; subtract positive integers from negative integers; and verify the reasonableness of the results.
NS 2.0, 2.2 Demonstrate proficiency with division, including division with positive decimals and long division with multidigit divisors.
MR 2.0, 2.4 Express the solution clearly and logically by using the appropriate mathematical notation and terms and clear language; support solutions with evidence in both verbal and symbolic work.
MR 2.0, 2.6 Make precise calculations and check the validity of the results from the context of the problem.

facts   Power Up J

mental math

a. Estimation: Estimate the product of $8\frac{3}{4}$ and $5\frac{1}{4}$ by rounding each mixed number to the nearest whole number and then multiplying.

b. Measurement: How many centimeters are in $5\frac{1}{2}$ meters?

c. Number Sense: Simplify the fractions $\frac{6}{9}$, $\frac{12}{9}$, and $\frac{24}{9}$.

d. Number Sense: $1 - \frac{5}{8}$

e. Time: How many minutes are in $\frac{1}{4}$ of an hour?

f. Geometry: If the perimeter of a square is 36 cm, what is the length of each side?

g. Calculation: $\frac{1}{6}$ of 30, $\times$ 5, + 2, $\div$ 3, $\times$ 4, $\div$ 6

h. Evaluate: What is the value of the expression $20 - (u \div 2)$ when $u = 8$?

problem solving

Choose an appropriate problem-solving strategy to solve this problem. Ricardo scored 84 and 92 on the first two tests. What is his average score for the two tests? What does Ricardo need to score on the next test to have a three-test average of 90? Explain how you arrived at your answer.

New Concept

We usually do not write remainders with decimal division problems. The procedure we will follow for now is to continue dividing until the "remainder" is zero. In order to continue the division, we may need to attach extra zeros to the decimal number that is being divided.

Remember, attaching extra zeros to the back of a decimal number does not change the value of the number.

Example 1

Divide: 0.6 ÷ 5

The first number goes inside the division box. The decimal point is straight up. As we divide, we attach a zero and continue dividing.

Justify Why is 60 hundredths equal to 6 tenths?

$$\begin{array}{r} 0.12 \\ 5\overline{)0.60} \\ \underline{5} \\ 10 \\ \underline{10} \\ 0 \end{array}$$

Example 2

Divide: 0.3 ÷ 4

As we divide, we attach zeros and continue dividing. We fill each empty place in the quotient with a zero.

$$\begin{array}{r} 0.075 \\ 4\overline{)0.300} \\ \underline{28} \\ 20 \\ \underline{20} \\ 0 \end{array}$$

Verify Demonstrate how to check the answer.

Example 3

Divide: 3.4 ÷ 10

As we divide, we attach a zero to 3.4 and continue dividing. Notice that the same digits appear in the quotient and dividend but they are in different places.

$$\begin{array}{r} 0.34 \\ 10\overline{)3.40} \\ \underline{3\,0} \\ 40 \\ \underline{40} \\ 0 \end{array}$$

When we divide a number by 10, we find that the answer has the same digits but that the digits have shifted one place to the right.

$$10\overline{)340.} \to 34. \qquad 10\overline{)3.40} \to .34$$

We can use this pattern to find the answer to a decimal division problem when the divisor is 10. The shortcut is very similar to the method we use when multiplying a decimal number by 10.

In both cases it is the digits that are shifting places, but, we can make the digits appear to shift places by shifting the decimal point instead. To divide by 10, we shift the decimal point one place to the left.

$$3.4 \div 10 = .34$$

Dividing by 100 is like dividing by 10 twice. When we divide by 100, we shift the decimal point two places to the left. When we divide by 1000, we shift the decimal point three places to the left. We shift the decimal point the same number of places as there are zeros in the number we are dividing by (10, 100, 1000, and so on).

We can remember which way to shift the decimal point if we keep in mind that dividing a number into more parts produces *smaller* numbers. As a decimal point moves to the left, the value of the number becomes smaller and smaller.

Example 4

Mentally divide 3.5 by 100.

When we divide by 10, 100, or 1000, we can find the answer mentally without performing the division algorithm. To divide by 100, we shift the decimal point two places. We know that the answer will be less than 3.5, so we remember to shift the decimal point to the left. We fill the empty place with a zero.

$$3.5 \div 100 = \mathbf{0.035}$$

(Connect) Explain how to mentally divide 3.5 by 1000.

Example 5

Two situations are described below. For which situation would you write the quotient as a decimal, and for which situation would you write the quotient as a mixed number? Explain your reasons.

  a. **Four friends earned $9.20 for recycling aluminum cans. If the money is to be divided equally, what amount will each friend receive?**

  b. **How many lengths of fabric, each $3\frac{2}{3}$ yards long, can be cut from a piece of fabric that is $12\frac{5}{6}$ yards long?**

  a. Quotients representing amounts of money are usually written as **decimal numbers.** If we complete the division, we find that each friend should receive $9 \div 4$, or $2.30. It would not be sensible for us to say that each friend should receive $2\frac{3}{10}$ dollars.

b. Quotients are usually written as **mixed numbers** when dividends and divisors are mixed numbers. If we complete the division, we find that $3\frac{1}{2}$ lengths of fabric, each $3\frac{2}{3}$ yards long, could be cut from the piece of fabric that is $12\frac{5}{6}$ yards long.

Lesson Practice

Divide:

a. $0.6 \div 4$ **b.** $0.12 \div 5$ **c.** $0.1 \div 4$

d. $0.1 \div 2$ **e.** $0.4 \div 5$ **f.** $1.4 \div 8$

g. $0.5 \div 4$ **h.** $0.6 \div 8$ **i.** $0.3 \div 4$

Mentally perform the following divisions:

j. $2.5 \div 10$ **k.** $32.4 \div 10$ **l.** $2.5 \div 100$

m. $32.4 \div 100$ **n.** $2.5 \div 1000$ **o.** $32.4 \div 1000$

p. $12 \div 10$ **q.** $12 \div 100$ **r.** $12 \div 1000$

Two situations are described below. For which situation would you write the quotient as a decimal, and for which situation would you write the quotient as a mixed number? Explain your reasons.

s. A length of ribbon is $90\frac{9}{16}$ inches long. How many shorter lengths of ribbon, each $8\frac{5}{8}$ inches long, can be cut from the longer length?

t. A brother and a sister earn a monthly allowance. The allowance is $15 and is shared equally. What amount of money does each person earn as a monthly allowance?

Written Practice   *Distributed and Integrated*

1. **Represent** Draw a circle. Shade all but $\frac{1}{6}$ of it. What percent of the
(58, 97)   circle is shaded?

2. Isabella Baumfree was born in 1797, changed her name to Sojourner
(5)   Truth in 1843, and died in 1883. For how many years did she keep her original name?

3. a. What is the chance of the spinner stopping on 4 with one
(45)   spin?

   b. What is the probability that with one spin the spinner will
   stop on a number less than 4?

4. At basketball practice Narciso made 70% of his free throws. If he shot
(102)   the ball 110 times, how many free throws did he make?

*5. Compare these fractions. First write the fractions with common
(107)   denominators.

$$\frac{2}{3} \bigcirc \frac{5}{6}$$

6. (Connect) Name the total number of shaded circles as an improper
(104)   fraction and as a mixed number.

7. Alberto counted 100 cars and 60 trucks driving by the school. What
(87)   was the ratio of trucks to cars that Alberto counted driving by the
   school?

*8. a. What is the perimeter of this square?
(98)

0.5 cm

   b. What is the area of the square?

*9. The Bartlett family keeps their winter clothes in a trunk in the attic. The
(105)   trunk measures 45 inches by 22 inches by 15 inches. Use a formula to
   find the cubic inches of space inside the trunk.

*10. $\frac{1}{4} + \frac{1}{8}$ ***11.** $\frac{3}{4} - \frac{1}{2}$ ***12.** $\frac{7}{8} - \frac{3}{4}$
(107)   (107)   (107)

*13. Find each sum or difference. Reduce the answer when possible.
(108)
   a. $\frac{5}{6} - \frac{1}{3}$ **b.** $\frac{7}{8} - \frac{1}{2}$ **c.** $\frac{11}{12} - \frac{1}{4}$

*14. Brayden is 1.8 meters tall. His 2-year-old son is exactly half as tall as his dad.
(109)   How tall is Brayden's son?

*15. Divide:
(110)

      a. 0.08 ÷ 5   **b.** 0.3 ÷ 6   **c.** 0.6 ÷ 5

16. $\frac{3}{5} \times 3$ **17.** $3 \div \frac{3}{5}$
(78, 81)   (86)

18. 6.5 × 100   **19.** 4.6 × 80   **20.** 0.18 × 0.4
(100)   (98)   (99)

21.   **a.** 1.2 ÷ 10   **b.** 1.2 ÷ 100
(109,
110)

22.   **a.** 0.24 ÷ 4   **b.** 0.24 ÷ 5
(109,
110)

23.   **a.** 1.4 ÷ 7   **b.** 1.4 ÷ 8
(109,
110)

24. Which angle in quadrilateral *ABCD* is an obtuse angle?
(20, 21)

*25. Add these fractions. First rename the fractions so that they have a
(107) common denominator of 12.

$$\frac{1}{4} + \frac{2}{3}$$

*26. What is the area of this figure?
(106)

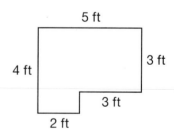

27. **Explain** Is it possible to arrange exactly 85 chairs in 12 rows and
(82) have the same number of chairs in each row? Explain why or why not.

28. **Explain** The capacity of the fuel tank on Kendis's car is 12.3
(39, 50) gallons, and Kendis can travel an average of 29 miles for every gallon
of fuel his car uses. What is a reasonable estimate of the distance
Kendis can travel with one full tank of fuel? Explain why your estimate
is reasonable.

*29. **Explain** These fractions do not add to the same sum.
(107)

$$\frac{2}{3} + \frac{3}{4} \qquad \frac{3}{8} + \frac{2}{5}$$

Which sum is greater? Explain how you can compare each addend to $\frac{1}{2}$ to find the answer.

*30 Mentally perform each division:
(110)
    a. $61.7 \div 100$ **b.** $61.7 \div 10$ **c.** $61.7 \div 1000$

Early Finishers

Real-World Connection

Mount Vesuvius is an active volcano located to the east of Naples, Italy. To reach the top of the volcano, visitors must climb to an elevation of 4202.76 feet. A group of hikers start their climbing from sea level (elevation 0) and want to climb Mount Vesuvius in three days. If they want to gain the same amount of elevation each day, how many feet would this be? If they climb down the mountain in two days, how many feet of elevation did they lose per day?

INVESTIGATION 11

California Mathematics Content Standards

AF 1.0, 1.1 Use information taken from a graph or equation to answer questions about a problem situation.

AF 1.0, 1.4 Identify and graph ordered pairs in the four quadrants of the coordinate plane.

AF 1.0, 1.5 Solve problems involving linear functions with integer values; write the equation; and graph the resulting ordered pairs of integers on a grid.

SDAP 1.0, 1.4 Identify ordered pairs of data from a graph and interpret the meaning of the data in terms of the situation depicted by the graph.

SDAP 1.0, 1.5 Know how to write ordered pairs correctly; for example, (x, y).

Focus on

Analyzing Relationships

As we have seen, functions can be displayed as graphs on a coordinate plane. Let's review what we have learned. To graph a function, we use each pair of numbers (x, y) as coordinates of a point on the plane.

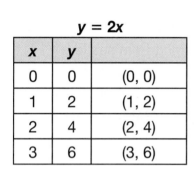

$y = 2x$

x	y	
0	0	(0, 0)
1	2	(1, 2)
2	4	(2, 4)
3	6	(3, 6)

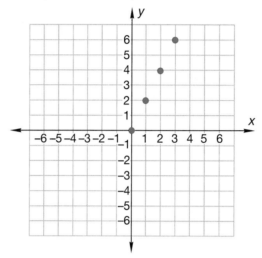

On the coordinate plane above, we graphed four pairs of numbers that satisfy the equation of the function. Although the table lists only four pairs of numbers for the function, the graph of the function includes many other pairs of numbers that satisfy the equation.

By extending a line through and beyond the graphed points, we graph all possible pairs of numbers that satisfy the equation. Each point on the following graphed line represents a pair of numbers that satisfies the equation of the function $y = 2x$.

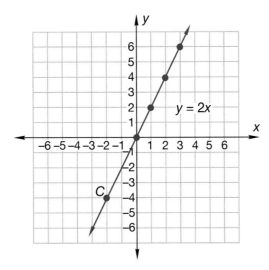

1. (**Verify**) Name the coordinates for point *C*.

This is a graph of the line $y = x + 2$.

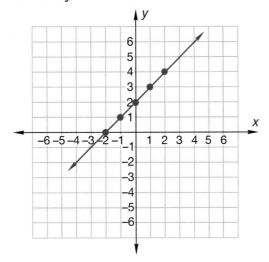

2. Write five (x, y) pairs to represent the five points on the line.

3. Write an ordered (x, y) pair to name another point on the line.

4. (**Explain**) Does (5, 5) represent a point on the line? Why or why not?

Look at the graph of this line.

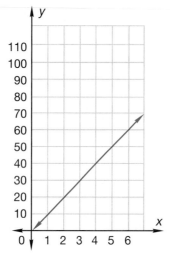

5. **Interpret** Write five (x, y) pairs that represent five points on the line.

6. Explain how the x- and y-values of the pairs in the table are related.

7. **Generalize** Write the equation of the line.

8. **Connect** Name a real-world situation that could be represented by the equation and its graph.

To help support the school's soccer team, Jenna's class is selling friendship bracelets. The class goal is to sell 220 bracelets by the end of the school year. The graph below shows how many bracelets had been sold by the end of each month.

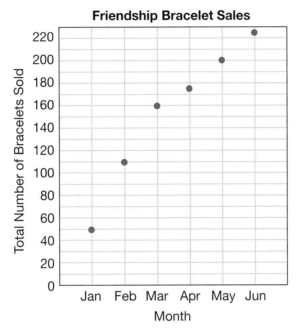

Friendship Bracelet Sales

Interpret Use the graph to answer problems **9–12.**

9. **Interpret** What is the interval of the vertical axis?

10. What is the graph about?

11. How many bracelets were sold during January?

12. The class goal was to sell 220 bracelets. During which month did the total number of bracelets sold reach one half of the class goal?

Devon walks for exercise at an average of 4 miles per hour.

13. **Generalize** Write an equation that can be used to find the number of miles Devon walks for any number of hours he walks. Use x to represent hours and y to represent miles.

14. Make a table of (x, y) pairs to represent five points on the graph of the equation.

15. Use (x, y) pairs from the table to graph the equation.

Investigate Further

Look at this pattern of squares:

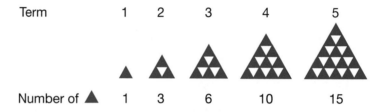

Term	1	2	3	4	5
Number of Squares	1	4	9	16	25

a. **Conclude** How many squares will be in the sixth term of the pattern? The seventh term? Explain how you know.

b. **Predict** Write an equation that can be used to find the number of squares for any term of the pattern. (Such an equation is called a general rule and such a term is called the *n*th term.) Use *s* to represent the number of squares and *n* to represent the term of the pattern.

Look at this pattern of triangles:

Term	1	2	3	4	5
Number of ▲	1	3	6	10	15

c. **Conclude** How many blue triangles are in the sixth term? The seventh term? Explain how you know.

d. **Discuss** Explain why the equation $b = \frac{n(n+1)}{2}$ (where b = the number of blue triangles and n = the term of the sequence) can be used to predict the number of blue triangles for the *n*th term of the pattern.

California Mathematics Content Standards
NS 2.0, 2.3 Solve simple problems, including ones arising in concrete situations, involving the addition and subtraction of fractions and mixed numbers (like and unlike denominators of 20 or less), and express answers in the simplest form.
MR 2.0, 2.3 Use a variety of methods, such as words, numbers, symbols, charts, graphs, tables, diagrams, and models, to explain mathematical reasoning.

• Adding and Subtracting Mixed Numbers

facts	Power Up K
mental math	**a. Estimation:** Estimate $7\frac{4}{5} \div 3\frac{3}{4}$ by rounding each mixed number to the nearest whole number and then dividing.
	b. Estimation: Choose the more reasonable estimate for the temperature on a cold winter day: 31°F or 31°C
	c. Measurement: How many meters are in one kilometer? In one tenth of a kilometer?
	d. Percent: What is 50% of $10? 25% of $10? 10% of $10?
	e. Percent: The calculator is on sale for 25% off the regular price of $10. What is the sale price?
	f. Number Sense: Write these numbers in order from least to greatest: 0.02, 0.20, 0.19.
	g. Calculation: $\frac{1}{3}$ of 60, × 2, + 2, ÷ 6, × 4, + 2, ÷ 2
	h. Evaluate: What is the value of the expression $4 + v \times 4$ when $v = 1$?
problem solving	Choose an appropriate problem-solving strategy to solve this problem. Baseboard is a material that can be placed where the floor meets a wall. The outer edges of this scale drawing indicate walls. The open spaces in the wall represent doors where baseboard is not used. Use your ruler to determine how many meters of baseboard are needed for the room represented by the scale drawing.

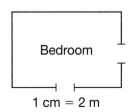

Bedroom

1 cm = 2 m

Recall that a mixed number is made up of a whole number and a fraction. To add and subtract mixed numbers, we first add or subtract the fractions. Then we add or subtract the whole numbers.

Example 1

A group of campers hiked $7\frac{3}{10}$ miles in the morning. After stopping for lunch and to rest, the group hiked $5\frac{4}{10}$ miles in the afternoon. How many miles altogether did the group hike that day?

We add mixed numbers to solve the problem. The fractions have common denominators, so we add the fractions and then add the whole numbers.

$$\begin{array}{r} \frac{3}{10} \\ + \frac{4}{10} \\ \hline \frac{7}{10} \end{array} \qquad \begin{array}{r} 7 \\ + 5 \\ \hline 12 \end{array} \qquad 12 + \frac{7}{10} = 12\frac{7}{10}$$

We find that the grouped hiked $12\frac{7}{10}$ **miles** that day.

Example 2

Rory lives $2\frac{3}{4}$ miles from school. How far does Rory ride if he rides from home to school, and then back home?

We add mixed numbers to solve the problem. The fractions have common denominators, so we add the fractions and then add the whole numbers.

$$\begin{array}{r} 2\frac{3}{4} \\ + 2\frac{3}{4} \\ \hline 4\frac{6}{4} \end{array}$$

The fraction part of the answer can be reduced.

$$\frac{6}{4} = \frac{4}{4} + \frac{2}{4}$$
$$\frac{6}{4} = 1 + \frac{2}{4}$$
$$\frac{6}{4} = 1 + \frac{1}{2}$$
$$\frac{6}{4} = 1\frac{1}{2}$$

Since $4 + 1\frac{1}{2} = 5\frac{1}{2}$, we find that Rory rides $5\frac{1}{2}$ **miles.**

Example 3

An old computer took $2\frac{5}{6}$ hours to perform a complex calculation. A new computer performed the same calculation in $1\frac{1}{6}$ hours. How many fewer hours did the new computer require?

We subtract mixed numbers to solve the problem. We subtract the fractions and then subtract the whole numbers.

$$\begin{array}{cc} \frac{5}{6} & 2 \\ -\frac{1}{6} & -1 \\ \hline \frac{4}{6} & 1 \end{array}$$

The fraction part of the answer can be reduced: $\frac{4}{6} = \frac{4 \div 2}{6 \div 2} = \frac{2}{3}$

We find that the new computer required **$1\frac{2}{3}$ fewer hours.**

Example 4

Subtract: $7\frac{1}{3} - 4\frac{2}{3}$

To subtract mixed numbers, we subtract the fractions first. We cannot subtract $\frac{2}{3}$ from $\frac{1}{3}$, so we rename $7\frac{1}{3}$. We change one of the seven wholes into $\frac{3}{3}$. Then we combine 6 and $\frac{3}{3} + \frac{1}{3}$ to get $6\frac{4}{3}$. Now we can subtract.

$$\begin{array}{c} 7\frac{1}{3} \\ -4\frac{2}{3} \end{array} \xrightarrow{6 + \frac{3}{3} + \frac{1}{3}} \begin{array}{c} 6\frac{4}{3} \\ -4\frac{2}{3} \\ \hline 2\frac{2}{3} \end{array}$$

Lesson Practice

Add or subtract. Write your answer in simplest form.

a.
$$\begin{array}{r} 1\frac{1}{4} \\ + 1\frac{3}{4} \\ \hline \end{array}$$

b.
$$\begin{array}{r} 4\frac{2}{3} \\ - 1\frac{1}{3} \\ \hline \end{array}$$

c.
$$\begin{array}{r} 2\frac{5}{6} \\ + 2\frac{5}{6} \\ \hline \end{array}$$

d. $6\frac{7}{8} - 2\frac{3}{8}$

e. $9\frac{7}{10} + 5\frac{3}{10}$

f. $8\frac{1}{4} - 6\frac{3}{4}$

g. (**Model**) Select one problem from **a–f** and draw a picture to check your answer.

h. (**Formulate**) Select another problem from **a–f** and write a word problem to represent the exercise.

i. $1\frac{1}{3} + 1\frac{1}{3} + 1\frac{1}{3}$

j. $3\frac{7}{8} + 2\frac{4}{8}$

k. $12\frac{5}{9} - 3\frac{2}{9}$ **l.** $7\frac{1}{8} - 1\frac{7}{8}$

Written Practice

Distributed and Integrated

*1. (107) **(Represent)** Write the following sentence using digits and symbols:
The sum of one sixth and one third is one half.

2. (37) **(Analyze)** Gilbert scored half of his team's points. Juan scored 8 fewer points than Gilbert. The team scored 36 points. How many points did Juan score?

*3. (108) Terrel practiced the piano for $\frac{5}{6}$ of an hour. Caleb practiced for $\frac{4}{5}$ of an hour. Who practiced longer?

$$\frac{5}{6} \bigcirc \frac{4}{5}$$

4. (45, 47) **a.** What are all the possible outcomes when the spinner is spun?

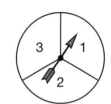

b. What is the probability that with one spin the spinner will stop on a number greater than one?

c. What is the chance of landing on 3 with one spin?

5. (58) **(Connect)** Name the shaded portion of this rectangle as a fraction, as a decimal, and as a percent.

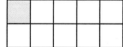

6. (21, 111) If each side of an octagon is $7\frac{1}{2}$ inches long, then the perimeter of the octagon is how many feet? What formula could you use?

7. (104) **(Represent)** Name the total number of shaded circles as an improper fraction and as a mixed number.

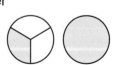

*8. (110) Mentally perform these divisions:

a. $0.6 \div 10$ **b.** $0.6 \div 100$ **c.** $0.6 \div 1000$

9. In rectangle *ABCD* at right, *AB* is 3 cm and *BC* is 4 cm.
(20, 59)

    a. Which segment is parallel to $\overline{AB}$?

    b. What is the perimeter of the rectangle?

    c. What is the area of the rectangle?

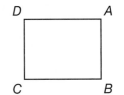

10. Anan's hallway locker measures 12 inches wide by 12 inches deep by
(Inv. 9) 5 feet tall. What is the volume of the locker in cubic feet?

11. Add or subtract. Write your answer in simplest form.
(111)

    a. $\quad 7\frac{3}{8}$ **b.** $\quad 6\frac{5}{6}$ **c.** $\quad 8\frac{1}{3}$

    $\quad\underline{+\ 2\frac{5}{8}}$ $\quad\underline{-\ 2\frac{2}{6}}$ $\quad\underline{-\ 5\frac{2}{3}}$

* 12. $(3.6 + 4) \div 5$
(90, 110)

* 13. **a.** How much greater is 2.5 than 2.125?
(90, 111)

    b. How much greater is $2\frac{4}{8}$ than $2\frac{1}{8}$?

14. 4.3×100 **15.** 6.4×3.7
(100)   (98)

16. 0.36×0.04 *** 17.** $3.4 \div 8$
(99)   (110)

* 18. $7\overline{)0.0049}$ **19.** 1.35×90
(109)   (98)

* 20. $\quad 2\frac{3}{8}$ *** 21.** $\quad \frac{1}{3}$ *** 22.** $\quad \frac{7}{10}$ *** 23.** $\quad 3\frac{9}{10}$
(108)   (108)   (108)   (108)

   $\underline{+\ 1\frac{7}{8}}$ $\underline{+\ \frac{1}{6}}$ $\underline{-\ \frac{1}{2}}$ $\underline{-\ 1\frac{3}{10}}$

24. $4 \times \frac{3}{2}$ **25.** $\frac{3}{4} \div \frac{1}{4}$ **26.** Reduce: $\frac{18}{144}$
(78, 81)   (86)   (80)

* 27. Find the sum of $3\frac{1}{5}$ and $2\frac{1}{2}$ by first rewriting the fractions with 10 as the
(107)   common denominator.

28. To finish covering the floor of a room, Abby needed
a rectangular piece of floor tile 6 inches long and
3 inches wide.

(59, 63, 107, 111)

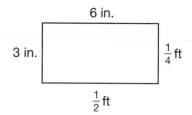

a. What is the area of this rectangle in square inches?

b. What is the area of the rectangle in square feet?

29. A 2-inch by 2-inch square is joined with a 5-inch by
5-inch square to form a hexagon. Refer to the figure
to answer parts **a** and **b**.

(106)

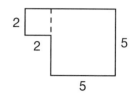

a. What is the area of the hexagon?

b. Copy the hexagon and show the lengths of all six sides.
Then find the perimeter of the hexagon.

*30. Mahdi is a jewelry designer. She has three irregular 10-karat gold
nuggets. The weights of the nuggets are $28\frac{1}{3}$ grams, $56\frac{2}{3}$ grams,
and 85 grams. What is the total weight in grams of the nuggets?

(111)

Early Finishers

Real-World Connection

Taydren needs to purchase some blank discs for his computer. He
researched some companies on the Internet to find the best deal.
He wrote down his findings in a table.

Company	Quantity Price
Disc Palace	4 for $1.28
Compu-Disc	8 for $2.48
Disc Domain	6 for $2.10

a. If Taydren buys 4 discs from *Disc Palace,* how much will he pay per
disc?

b. Which company sells discs for the lowest unit price?

c. Even though *Disc Domain* offers the highest unit price, list some reasons
why Taydren may still choose to buy from that store.

California Mathematics Content Standards
NS 2.0, 2.3 Solve simple problems, including ones arising in concrete situations, involving the addition and subtraction of fractions and mixed numbers (like and unlike denominators of 20 or less), and express answers in the simplest form.
MR 2.0, 2.3 Use a variety of methods, such as words, numbers, symbols, charts, graphs, tables, diagrams, and models, to explain mathematical reasoning.
MR 2.0, 2.6 Make precise calculations and check the validity of the results from the context of the problem.

• Subtracting Mixed Numbers with Regrouping

facts	Power Up K
mental math	**a. Estimation:** Estimate the cost of 98 tickets priced at $2.50 each.
	b. Measurement: Lucy was feeling ill. Her fever was 100.7°F. How many degrees was Lucy's fever above her normal temperature of 98.6°F?
	c. Measurement: The liquid medicine dropper can hold 1 milliliter of liquid. How many full droppers equal half a liter?
	d. Fractional Parts: What is $\frac{1}{10}$ of 30? $\frac{3}{10}$ of 30? $\frac{9}{10}$ of 30?
	e. Probability: The box contains equal amounts of three flavors of dog treats: peanut butter, vegetable, and chicken. If Grey pulls one dog treat from the box without looking, what is the probability it will *NOT* be chicken?
	f. Geometry: If the area of a square is 9 cm², what is the length of each side?
	g. Calculation: $\sqrt{100}$, ÷ 2, × 7, + 1, ÷ 6, × 4, ÷ 2
	h. Evaluate: What is the value of the expression $6 + w \div 2$ when $w = 10$?

problem solving

Choose an appropriate problem-solving strategy to solve this problem. Victor dropped a rubber ball and found that each bounce was half as high as the previous bounce. He dropped the ball from 8 feet, measured the height of each bounce, and recorded the results in a table. Copy this table and complete it through the fifth bounce.

Heights of Bounces

First	4 ft
Second	
Third	
Fourth	
Fifth	

New Concept

Thinking Skill

How many sixths equal one whole?

When we subtract whole numbers and fractions, we sometimes need to rename to complete the subtraction.

This is also true when we subtract mixed numbers, and we can illustrate this fact with circles.

A restaurant employee arranged $3\frac{1}{6}$ pizzas on a table.

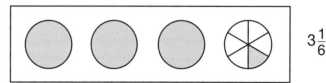

$3\frac{1}{6}$

After the employee divided one whole pizza into sixths, there were $2\frac{7}{6}$ pizzas, which is the same as $3\frac{1}{6}$ pizzas.

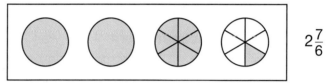

$2\frac{7}{6}$

Customers took away $1\frac{2}{6}$ pizzas.

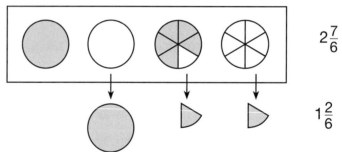

$2\frac{7}{6}$

$1\frac{2}{6}$

So $1\frac{5}{6}$ pizzas remained.

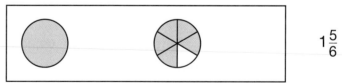

$1\frac{5}{6}$

Thinking Skill

Verify

How can you check the answer to the subtraction problem?

Now we show the arithmetic for subtracting $1\frac{2}{6}$ from $3\frac{1}{6}$.

$$3\frac{1}{6} \text{ pizzas}$$
$$-1\frac{2}{6} \text{ pizzas}$$

We cannot subtract $\frac{2}{6}$ from $\frac{1}{6}$, so we rename $3\frac{1}{6}$. Just as the server sliced one of the pies into sixths, we change one of the three wholes into $\frac{6}{6}$. This makes two whole pizzas plus $\frac{6}{6}$ plus $\frac{1}{6}$, which is $2\frac{7}{6}$. Now we can subtract.

$$3\frac{1}{6}$$ $$\xrightarrow{\;2 + \frac{6}{6} + \frac{1}{6}\;}$$ $$2\frac{7}{6} \text{ pizza}$$

$$-1\frac{2}{6}$$ $$-1\frac{2}{6} \text{ pizza}$$

$$1\frac{5}{6} \text{ pizza}$$

Example 1

Subtract: $5\frac{1}{3} - 2\frac{2}{3}$

We cannot subtract $\frac{2}{3}$ from $\frac{1}{3}$, so we rename $5\frac{1}{3}$. We change one of the five wholes into $\frac{3}{3}$. Then we combine 4 and $\frac{3}{3} + \frac{1}{3}$ to get $4\frac{4}{3}$. Now we can subtract.

$$5\frac{1}{3} \xrightarrow{\;4 + \frac{3}{3} + \frac{1}{3}\;} 4\frac{4}{3}$$

$$-2\frac{2}{3}$$ $$-2\frac{2}{3}$$

$$2\frac{2}{3}$$

Example 2

Subtract: $7 - 1\frac{3}{4}$

We cannot subtract $\frac{3}{4}$ from 7 because there are no fourths to subtract from. So we change 7 to $6 + \frac{4}{4}$ and then subtract.

$$7 \xrightarrow{\;6 + \frac{4}{4}\;} 6\frac{4}{4}$$

$$-1\frac{3}{4}$$ $$-1\frac{3}{4}$$

$$5\frac{1}{4}$$

Why is $\frac{4}{4}$ another name for 1?

Lesson Practice   Subtract

a. $4\frac{1}{3}$

$-1\frac{2}{3}$

b.   9

$-4\frac{1}{2}$

c. $5\frac{3}{8}$

$-2\frac{5}{8}$

d. $9 - 1\frac{1}{5}$

e. $3\frac{1}{6} - 2\frac{5}{6}$

f. $6\frac{1}{4}$

$-2\frac{3}{4}$

g. (**Model**) Select one of the problems **a–f** to model with a drawing.

h. (**Formulate**) Select another problem and write a word problem that is solved by the subtraction.

1. Use prime factorization to find the least common multiple (LCM) of
(103) 16 and 18.

2. Nasha estimated the product of $6\frac{1}{10}$ and $4\frac{7}{8}$ by first rounding each
(92) factor to the nearest whole number. What estimate did Nasha make for the product?

3. Mrs. Benitez wants to wallpaper all four walls of her dining room.
(105) The room is 10 ft by 12 ft and has walls 8 ft high. Choose a formula and determine how many square feet of wallpaper are needed to cover the walls.

* 4. It took Jovany and Mia $4\frac{3}{4}$ hours to paint their bedroom. It only took
(111) them $1\frac{1}{4}$ hours to paint their bathroom. How many more hours did it take tthem to paint their bedroom than their bathroom?

5. The first roll knocked down 3 of the 10 bowling pins. What percent of
(97) the pins were still standing?

6. a. Write the fraction equal to 4%.
(58, 80)

    b. Write the fraction equal to 5%.

7. a. (**Represent**) Name the total number of shaded circles
(104) as an improper fraction and as a mixed number.

    b. If $1\frac{3}{4}$ of the shaded circles in part **a** are removed, how many shaded circles will remain?

8. Alba has been asked to divide $1\frac{3}{8}$ cups of wheat flour into two
(63, 104) equal amounts. She knows that the improper fraction $\frac{11}{8}$ can be used to represent $1\frac{3}{8}$, and she knows that dividing by 2 is the same as multiplying by $\frac{1}{2}$. How many cups of flour will each of the equal amounts represent?

9. Subtract:
(112)

    a. $8\frac{3}{5}$ $\quad -5\frac{4}{5}$

    b. $6\frac{1}{4}$ $\quad -2\frac{3}{4}$

    c. $3\frac{1}{6}$ $\quad -1\frac{5}{6}$

*10. Arrange these numbers in order from least to greatest:
(108)

$$\frac{5}{3}, \frac{5}{6}, \frac{5}{5}$$

*11. The perimeter of this square is 1.2 meters.
(99, 109)

    a. How long is each side of this square?

    b. What is the area of this square?

*12. $(4.0 + 8) \div 8$
(90, 109)

13. (**Represent**) Subtract 1.234 from 2. Use words to write the answer.
(55, 93)

*14. $0.0125 \div 5$
(109)

15. 4.2×100
(100)

16. 0.5×0.17
(99)

*17. $0.6 \div 4$
(110)

*18. $0.6 \div 10$
(110)

*19. $4\overline{)1.8}$
(110)

*20. $\frac{1}{9}$ $\quad +\frac{1}{3}$
(108)

*21. $\frac{1}{3}$ $\quad +\frac{5}{6}$
(108)

*22. $\frac{7}{8}$ $\quad -\frac{1}{4}$
(108)

*23. $4\frac{7}{10}$ $\quad +1\frac{9}{10}$
(111)

*24. Subtract:
(112)

    a. 7 $\quad -3\frac{3}{5}$

    b. 6 $\quad -1\frac{2}{3}$

    c. 4 $\quad -1\frac{1}{4}$

25. a. $6 \times \frac{2}{3}$ $\qquad\qquad\qquad$ **b.** $6 \div \frac{2}{3}$
(78, 86)

*26. Neil worked at a task for $1\frac{1}{4}$ hours before taking a break. The task takes
(108) $2\frac{3}{4}$ hours to complete. After Neil begins working again, how long will it take him to complete the task?

*27. Divide mentally:
(110)

    a. $3.5 \div 100$ $\qquad\qquad\qquad$ **b.** $87.5 \div 10$

28. Compare: $\sqrt{81} + \sqrt{100}$ ◯ $9^2 + 10^2$
(67)

29. A 2 cm by 3 cm rectangle is joined to a 4 cm by 6 cm
(106) rectangle to form this hexagon. Refer to the figure to
answer parts **a** and **b**.

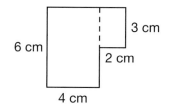

6 cm

3 cm

2 cm

4 cm

    a. What is the area of the hexagon?

    b. Copy the hexagon and show the lengths of all six sides.
    Then find the perimeter of the hexagon.

30. **Explain** On his way home from work, Poiiu purchased
(37) 3 gallons of milk for $2.19 per gallon and 2 loaves of bread
for $1.69 per loaf. What is a reasonable estimate of Poiiu's
total cost? Explain why your estimate is reasonable.

Early Finishers

Real-World Connection

Mr. Chandler has 7 new candles. Each candle is identical in size. His plan is to light one candle a day and burn it down to $\frac{1}{4}$ of its original size. When he has enough burned candles saved, he will melt them down and recycle them into another candle. He will do this as many times as possible until he is no longer able to make another whole candle.

    a. If Mr. Chandler burns one candle each day and carries out his recycling plan, how many days will the 7 new candles last?

    b. If Mr. Chandler begins with 10 new candles, how many days will they last?

LESSON
113

California Mathematics Content Standards
NS 2.0, **2.3** Solve simple problems, including ones
arising in concrete situations, involving the addition
and subtraction of fractions and mixed numbers
(like and unlike denominators of 20 or less), and
express answers in the simplest form.
MR 3.0, 3.3 Develop generalizations of the results
obtained and apply them in other circumstances.

• Adding and Subtracting Mixed Numbers with Unlike Denominators

facts	Power Up K
mental math	**a. Measurement:** The swimming pool holds a maximum of 12,000 gallons of water. Cole has already put about 5500 gallons into the pool. About how many more gallons of water are needed to fill the pool?
	b. Number Sense: Simplify the fractions $\frac{8}{12}$, $\frac{9}{12}$, and $\frac{15}{12}$.
	c. Percent: 25% of 12
	d. Percent: 50% of 19
	e. Percent: 75% of 12
	f. Geometry: A hectare is an area of land equivalent to a square that is 100 meters on each side. How many hectares is a field that is 200 meters on each side?
	g. Calculation: $\frac{1}{6}$ of 24, × 5, + 1, ÷ 3, × 8, − 2, ÷ 9
	h. Evaluate: What is the value of the expression $16 - y \cdot 3$ when $y = 5$?
problem solving	Choose an appropriate problem-solving strategy to solve this problem. Blake is saving money for a new telescope. In January Blake saved $10. In the months February through May, he saved $35 each month. By the end of August, Blake will have doubled the total amount of money he had at the end of May. At that time, will Blake have enough money to purchase a telescope that costs $280? Explain your reasoning.

If the fraction parts of mixed numbers do not have common denominators, we must rename the fractions before we add or subtract.

Example 1

Add: $1\frac{3}{4} + 2\frac{1}{8}$

The denominators of the fractions are 4 and 8. If we listed the multiples of 4 and of 8, we would find that the least common denominator of the fractions is 8. So we multiply $\frac{3}{4}$ by a name for 1 that results in a denominator of 8.

$$\frac{3}{4} \times \frac{2}{2} = \frac{6}{8}$$

We rewrite $1\frac{3}{4}$ and then add.

$$\begin{array}{ccc} 1\frac{3}{4} & \longrightarrow & 1\frac{6}{8} \\ +\,2\frac{1}{8} & & +\,2\frac{1}{8} \\ \hline & & 3\frac{7}{8} \end{array}$$

We find that the sum of $1\frac{3}{4} + 2\frac{1}{8}$ is $\mathbf{3\frac{7}{8}}$.

Example 2

Subtract: $4\frac{1}{2} - 1\frac{1}{3}$

The least common denominator of 2 and 3 is the product of 2×3, so we multiply each fraction by a name for 1 that results in a denominator of 6.

$$\frac{1}{2} \times \frac{3}{3} = \frac{3}{6} \qquad \frac{1}{3} \times \frac{2}{2} = \frac{2}{6}$$

Now we rewrite $4\frac{1}{2}$ and $1\frac{1}{3}$, then subtract.

$$\begin{array}{ccc} 4\frac{1}{2} & \longrightarrow & 4\frac{3}{6} \\ -\,1\frac{1}{3} & \longrightarrow & -\,1\frac{2}{6} \\ \hline & & 3\frac{1}{6} \end{array}$$

We find that the difference of $4\frac{1}{2} - 1\frac{1}{3}$ is $\mathbf{3\frac{1}{6}}$.

The sum or difference of mixed numbers is not always in simplest form.

Example 3

Subtract: $6\frac{5}{6} - 2\frac{1}{2}$

The least common denominator of 6 and 2 is 6, so we multiply $\frac{1}{2}$ by a name for 1 that results in a denominator of 6.

$$\frac{1}{2} \times \frac{3}{3} = \frac{3}{6}$$

Now we rewrite $2\frac{1}{2}$, subtract, and write the answer in simplest form.

$$
\begin{array}{ccc}
6\frac{5}{6} & \rightarrow & 6\frac{5}{6} \\
-2\frac{1}{2} & \rightarrow & -2\frac{3}{6} \\
\hline
& & 4\frac{2}{6} = 4\frac{1}{3}
\end{array}
$$

We find that the difference of $6\frac{5}{6} - 2\frac{1}{2}$ is **$4\frac{1}{3}$**.

Sometimes when we subtract mixed numbers, we must find common denominators and rename.

Example 4

Subtract: $5\frac{1}{3} - 2\frac{3}{4}$

The least common denominator of 3 and 4 is 12, so we multiply each fraction by a name for 1 that results in a denominator of 12.

$$\frac{1}{3} \times \frac{4}{4} = \frac{4}{12} \qquad\qquad \frac{3}{4} \times \frac{3}{3} = \frac{9}{12}$$

We rewrite $5\frac{1}{3}$ and $2\frac{3}{4}$.

$$
\begin{array}{ccc}
5\frac{1}{3} & \rightarrow & 5\frac{4}{12} \\
-2\frac{3}{4} & \rightarrow & -2\frac{9}{12}
\end{array}
$$

We cannot subtract $\frac{9}{12}$ from $\frac{4}{12}$, so we rename $5\frac{4}{12}$.

$$
\begin{array}{ccc}
& 4 + \frac{12}{12} + \frac{4}{12} & \\
5\frac{4}{12} & \xrightarrow{\hspace{2cm}} & 4\frac{16}{12} \\
-2\frac{9}{12} & & -2\frac{9}{12}
\end{array}
$$

Now we subtract.

$$4 + \frac{12}{12} + \frac{4}{12}$$

$$5\frac{4}{12} \xrightarrow{} 4\frac{16}{12}$$

$$-2\frac{9}{12} \qquad -2\frac{9}{12}$$

$$\overline{} \qquad \overline{2\frac{7}{12}}$$

Note that in Example 4, we first changed the fraction parts of the mixed numbers from different denominators to common denominators. Next we renamed the whole number part of a mixed number. Then we completed the subtraction.

Lesson Practice Find each sum or difference:

a. $6\frac{2}{3}$
$-4\frac{1}{6}$

b. $1\frac{1}{2}$
$+3\frac{1}{3}$

c. $6\frac{1}{4}$
$-2\frac{3}{8}$

d. $2\frac{3}{5} + 2\frac{1}{2}$

e. $8\frac{1}{2} - 7\frac{1}{4}$

f. $5\frac{3}{4} + 4\frac{5}{6}$

g. $12\frac{1}{2} - 2\frac{1}{6}$

h. $6\frac{5}{6} + 1\frac{2}{3}$

i. $5\frac{1}{3} - 4\frac{1}{2}$

j. On June 10 the corn stalk was $28\frac{1}{8}$ inches high. On June 17 the stalk was $32\frac{1}{2}$ inches high. How many inches taller did the stalk grow during the week?

k. The rectangular picture frame was $12\frac{1}{2}$ inches long and $8\frac{3}{4}$ inches wide. What was the perimeter of the frame?

Written Practice *Distributed and Integrated*

1. The music store was having a 20%-off sale. Xavier chose four CDs he
(102) wanted for a total of $40. What will the CDs cost after the 20% has been subtracted?

2. The ages of five neighborhood friends are 9, 8, 7, 6, and 5 years. What
(38) is the average age of the friends?

*3. Add or subtract. Write your answer in simplest form.
(111)
a. $5\frac{3}{4}$
$+2\frac{3}{4}$

b. $4\frac{4}{10}$
$-1\frac{7}{10}$

c. $8\frac{1}{5}$
$-3\frac{3}{5}$

4. What is the volume of a cube with a side of length 4 mm?
(Inv. 10)

5. Subtract:
(112)

a. 8
$$-3\frac{2}{5}$$

b. 7
$$-2\frac{1}{4}$$

c. $9\frac{1}{3}$
$$-4\frac{2}{3}$$

6. Write the mixed number $3\frac{1}{3}$ as an improper fraction. Then multiply the
(63, 81, 104) improper fraction by $\frac{3}{4}$. Remember to simplify your answer.

7. ⟨ **Conclude** ⟩ Refer to quadrilateral *ABCD* to answer parts **a** and **b.**
(21, 33)
  a. Which angle appears to be an obtuse angle?

  b. What type of quadrilateral is quadrilateral *ABCD*?

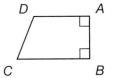

*8. $3\frac{1}{2}$
(113)
$$+1\frac{1}{3}$$

*9. $2\frac{1}{6}$
(113)
$$+1\frac{1}{2}$$

*10. $5\frac{5}{6}$
(113)
$$-1\frac{1}{2}$$

*11. $4\frac{2}{3}$
(113)
$$-1\frac{1}{4}$$

*12. $6\overline{)0.0144}$
(109)

*13. $5\overline{)1.2}$
(110)

14. $12\overline{)1800}$
(23, 82)

15. Add or subtract. Write answers in simplest form.
(113)

a. $2\frac{2}{3}$
$$+4\frac{3}{4}$$

b. $1\frac{1}{5}$
$$+3\frac{2}{3}$$

c. $6\frac{1}{3}$
$$-2\frac{7}{9}$$

16. $50\overline{)1000}$
(23, 42)

*17. Subtract. Write answers in simplest form.
(113)

a. $4\frac{3}{4}$
$$-1\frac{7}{8}$$

b. $3\frac{1}{2}$
$$-2\frac{7}{10}$$

c. $6\frac{2}{5}$
$$-3\frac{2}{3}$$

*18. Divide mentally:
(110)
  a. $0.5 \div 10$

  b. $0.5 \div 100$

19. $(3 - 1.6) - 0.16$
(7, 93)

20.
(99)
$$\begin{array}{r} 0.12 \\ \times\ 0.30 \\ \hline \end{array}$$

21.
(100)
$$\begin{array}{r} 0.12 \\ \times\ \ \ 10 \\ \hline \end{array}$$

22.
(39)
$$\begin{array}{r} 75 \\ \times\ 48 \\ \hline \end{array}$$

23. a. $4 \times \dfrac{3}{8}$
(78)

b. $4 \div \dfrac{3}{8}$

* **24. a.** $0.27 \div 3$
(109,
110)

b. $0.27 \div 5$

* **25. a.** What is the perimeter of this rectangle?
(108)

b. What is the area of this rectangle?

$\frac{1}{2}$ ft

$\frac{1}{3}$ ft

26. What is the volume of a room that is 10 feet wide, 12 feet long, and
(Inv. 9) 8 feet high?

* **27.** Two squares are joined to form the hexagon at right.
(106) **a.** What is the area of the hexagon

b. Copy the hexagon and show the lengths of the six sides.
Then find the perimeter of the hexagon.

10 ft

5 ft

28. Jess took a poll of fifth graders to find out how many items
(Inv. 5) they put in a backpack. The data below shows the results
of his poll.

3, 2, 5, 5, 8, 4, 3, 4, 7, 2, 4, 8, 5, 10, 5

a. (**Represent**) Display the data in a line plot.

b. Find the median of the data.

c. Find the mode or modes of the data.

d. Find the range of the data.

* **29. a.** What is the volume of a cube with a side of length 10 ft?
(29, Inv.
10)
b. What is the volume of a cube with a side of length 20 ft?

c. How many 10-foot cubes could fit inside a cube with a length of 20 ft?

30. **(Estimate)** The number of students enrolled at five different elementary
(22, 38) schools is shown below.

341   307   462   289   420

a. Estimate the number of students altogether who attend the schools.

b. Use your estimated total to find the average number of students in each
school.

*Real-World
Connection*

A community center is planning to build a tennis court. A regulation
tennis court has a length of 78 ft and a width of 36 ft. In addition, a
clearance of 12 ft on each side of the court and a clearance of 21 ft
on each end of the court is needed. Find the area of the entire ground
space needed for the tennis court.

California Mathematics Content Standards

NS 2.0, **2.1** Add, subtract, multiply, and divide with decimals; add with negative integers; subtract positive integers from negative integers; and verify the reasonableness of the results.
NS 2.0, **2.2** Demonstrate proficiency with division, including division with positive decimals and long division with multidigit divisors.
MR 2.0, 2.6 Make precise calculations and check the validity of the results from the context of the problem.

• Dividing by a Decimal Number

facts   Power Up K

mental math

a. Number Sense: Hassan spent $2\frac{1}{2}$ hours doing homework on Monday, $1\frac{1}{2}$ hours on Tuesday, and 2 hours on Wednesday. What was the average amount of time he spent per day on homework?

b. Measurement: It took the turtle one minute to travel $2\frac{1}{4}$ feet. How many inches is $2\frac{1}{4}$ feet?

c. Fractional Parts: $\frac{1}{8}$ of 24

d. Fractional Parts: $\frac{3}{8}$ of 24

e. Fractional Parts: $\frac{5}{8}$ of 24

f. Powers/Roots: 4^3

g. Calculation: 25% of 40, $+\ 2$, $\times\ 2$, $+\ 1$, $\div\ 5$, $\times\ 3$, $+\ 1$, $\div\ 8$, $-\ 2$

h. Evaluate: What is the value of the expression $25 - z \div 5$ when $z = 20$?

problem solving

Choose an appropriate problem-solving strategy to solve this problem. Tamara had 24 square tiles on her desk. She arranged them into a rectangle made up of one row of 24 tiles. Then she arranged them into a new rectangle made up of two rows of 12 tiles.

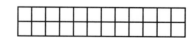

Draw two more rectangles Tamara could make using all 24 tiles.

We have practiced dividing decimal numbers by whole numbers. In this lesson we will practice dividing decimal numbers by decimal numbers.

Look at these two problems. They are different in an important way.

$$3\overline{)0.12} \qquad 0.3\overline{)0.12}$$

The problem on the left is division *by a whole number.* The problem on the right is division *by a decimal number.*

When dividing by a decimal number with pencil and paper, we take an extra step. Before dividing, we shift the decimal points so that we are dividing by a whole number instead of by a decimal number.

$$0.3\overline{)0.12}$$

We move the decimal point of the divisor so that it becomes a whole number. Then we move the decimal point of the dividend the same number of places. The decimal point in the quotient will be straight up from the new location of the dividend's decimal point.

To remember how to divide by a decimal number, we may think, "Over, over, and up."

$$\overset{\text{up}}{0.3\overline{)0.12}}$$
over over

To help us understand why this procedure works, we will write "0.12 divided by 0.3" with a division bar.

$$\frac{0.12}{0.3}$$

Notice that we can change the divisor, 0.3, into a whole number by multiplying by 10. So we multiply by $\frac{10}{10}$ to make an equivalent division problem.

$$\frac{0.12}{0.3} \times \frac{10}{10} = \frac{1.2}{3}$$

Multiplying by $\frac{10}{10}$ moves both decimal points "over." Now the divisor is a whole number and we can divide.

$$3\overline{)1.2} \quad \text{with quotient } 0.4$$

Thinking Skill

How is dividing a decimal by a whole number the same as dividing a decimal by a decimal? How is it different?

We will add this memory cue to the decimals chart. In the last column, "÷ by decimal (D)" means "division by a decimal number."

Decimals Chart

Operation	+ or −	×	÷ by whole (W)	÷ by decimal (D)
Memory cue	line up $\cdot$ $\pm\ \cdot$ $\cdot$	×; then count $\cdot\ \_$ $\times\ \cdot\ \_$ $\cdot\ \_\ \_$	up $W)\overline{\ \cdot}$	over, over, up $D)\overline{\ \cdot}$

You may need to ...
- Place a decimal point on the end of whole numbers.
- Fill each empty place with a zero.

Example 1

Divide: $0.6)\overline{2.34}$

We are dividing by the decimal number 0.6. We change 0.6 into a whole number by moving its decimal point "over." We also move the decimal point in the dividend "over." The decimal point in the quotient will be "straight up" from the new location of the decimal point in the division box.

$$
\begin{array}{r}
3.9 \\
0.6)\overline{2.3\ 4} \\
1\ 8 \\
\hline
5\ 4 \\
5\ 4 \\
\hline
0
\end{array}
$$

Verify Demonstrate how to check the answer.

Example 2

Divide: $3.2)\overline{8.192}$

Since the divisor 3.2 is not a whole number, we must move its decimal point one place to the right. We also move the decimal point in the dividend 8.192 one place to the right. Then we divide.

$$
\begin{array}{r}
2.56 \\
3.2.)\overline{8.1.9\,2} \\
6\ 4 \\
\hline
1\ 7\ 9 \\
1\ 6\ 0 \\
\hline
1\ 9\ 2 \\
1\ 9\ 2 \\
\hline
0
\end{array}
$$

Lesson Practice

Divide:

a. $0.3)\overline{1.2}$ **b.** $0.3)\overline{0.42}$ **c.** $1.2)\overline{0.24}$

d. $0.4)\overline{0.24}$ **e.** $0.4)\overline{5.6}$ **f.** $1.2)\overline{3.6}$

g. $0.6)\overline{2.4}$ **h.** $0.5)\overline{0.125}$ **i.** $1.2)\overline{2.28}$

j. $0.3)\overline{0.6}$ **k.** $0.6)\overline{0.3}$ **l.** $0.6)\overline{1.5}$

m. $0.2)\overline{0.8}$ **n.** $0.8)\overline{0.2}$ **o.** $0.8)\overline{1.5}$

* 1. Rewrite each pair of fractions so that the denominators are the same.
(107) Then write >, <, or = to complete the comparison.

a. $\frac{2}{3} \bigcirc \frac{3}{5}$ **b.** $\frac{3}{4} \bigcirc \frac{7}{8}$ **c.** $\frac{1}{2} \bigcirc \frac{2}{5}$

2. Divide:
(109, 110)
a. $0.72 \div 4$ **b.** $1.4 \div 8$ **c.** $0.3 \div 5$

* 3. Add or subtract. Write your answer in simplest form.
(111)

a. $3\frac{2}{5}$ **b.** $4\frac{3}{8}$ **c.** $8\frac{5}{7}$

$+\ 6\frac{3}{5}$ $+\ 5\frac{7}{8}$ $-\ 3\frac{3}{7}$

4. Multiple Choice Which of these is not equal to $\frac{1}{2}$?
(58, 91)
A 0.5   **B** 50%   **C** 0.50   **D** 0.05

5. **Explain** Nina cares for a cat and a kitten. The cat weighs $7\frac{3}{4}$
(50, 51) pounds. What is a reasonable estimate of the kitten's weight if the cat and the kitten together weigh about 11 pounds? Explain why your estimate is reasonable.

6. In rectangle *ABCD*, $\overline{BC}$ is twice the length of $\overline{AB}$. Segment
(20, 59) *AB* is 3 inches long.

a. What is the perimeter of the rectangle?

b. What is the area of the rectangle?

c. Name two pairs of parallel sides.

d. Name two pairs of perpendicular sides.

7. Shantell can input 4 pages in 1 hour. At that rate, how long will it take
(37) her to input 100 pages?

8. Emilio is about to roll a standard number cube.
(45, 65, 97)
a. What is the probability that he will get a prime number in one roll?

b. What is the chance that he will not get a prime number in one roll?

* 9. Subtract:
(112)

    a. $7\frac{3}{10}$ **b.** $9\frac{3}{8}$ **c.** $6\frac{2}{5}$

        $-2\frac{7}{10}$ $-6\frac{7}{8}$ $-2\frac{4}{5}$

10. What is the average of 2, 4, 6, and 8?
(38)

11. Subtract:
(113)

    a. $8\frac{1}{4}$ **b.** $12\frac{1}{3}$ **c.** $9\frac{2}{3}$

        $-2\frac{7}{8}$ $-3\frac{4}{5}$ $-6\frac{3}{4}$

12. 38.248 + 7.5 + 37.23 + 15
(90)

13. $6 − ($1.49 − 75¢)   *** 14.** 2.4 × 100
(7, 57)   (100)

15. 0.24 × 0.12   **16.** 25 × 50
(99)   (18, 39)

* 17. 8$\overline{)0.1000}$ *** 18.** 0.5$\overline{)4.35}$ **19.** 12$\overline{)1440}$
(109)   (114)   (82)

20. $3\frac{1}{3}$ **21.** $\frac{3}{7}$ **22.** $6\frac{14}{15}$ **23.** $\frac{4}{5}$
(113)   (108)   (113)   (108)

    $+7\frac{3}{4}$ $+\frac{1}{2}$ $-1\frac{1}{5}$ $-\frac{1}{3}$

* 24. Divide:
(114)

    a. 0.2$\overline{)2.6}$ **b.** 0.4$\overline{)0.36}$ **c.** 0.3$\overline{)4.8}$

* 25. Divide:
(114)

    a. 1.2$\overline{)4.8}$ **b.** 1.3$\overline{)0.39}$ **c.** 1.2$\overline{)1.44}$

26. **a.** What is the area of a bedroom that is 3 meters wide and
(98)   4.5 meters long?

    b. What is the perimeter?

27. What is the volume of a drawer that is 2 ft by 1.5 ft by 0.5 ft?
(Inv. 9, 98)

0.5 ft

1.5 ft

2 ft

* 28. Refer to the figure to answer parts **a–c.**
(97, Inv. 8)

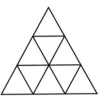

a. (**Analyze**) The perimeter of each small equilateral triangle is 6 inches. What is the perimeter of the large equilateral triangle?

b. The area of one small triangle is what percent of the area of the large triangle?

c. (**Conclude**) Shown below is a sequence of triangle patterns. Draw the next triangle in the pattern. How many small triangles form the large triangle in your drawing?

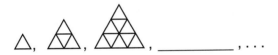

29. Four-hour admission to an outdoor water park costs $12.50 per person.
(37) Latoya and three friends plan to visit the park and use a discount coupon for $2 off per person. What is the total cost of the tickets?

30. (**Explain**) Xavier estimated the quotient of 189 ÷ 5 to be about 40.
(50) Did Xavier make a reasonable estimate? Explain why or why not.

Real-World Connection

Mr. Lambourne's sink has a leak. He knows that his water faucet fills the sink at a rate of 3.5 gallons each minute. He also knows that water leaks out of the sink at a rate of 1 gallon each minute. If the capacity of the sink is 20 gallons, how many minutes will it take to fill the sink to the top?

California Mathematics Content Standards

NS 2.0, **2.1** Add, subtract, multiply, and divide with decimals; add with negative integers; subtract positive integers from negative integers; and verify the reasonableness of the results.

AF 1.0, **1.2** Use a letter to represent an unknown number; write and evaluate simple algebraic expressions in one variable by substitution.

• How to Solve Equations by Finding Unknown Factors

How do we solve an equation like $4x = 8$? The unknown value x is an unknown factor. To find the unknown factor, this multiplication equation can be written as a division equation; $4x = 8$ is the same as $x = 8 \div 4$. We find that the unknown factor x is equal to 2.

Any multiplication equation with an unknown factor can be written as a division equation in order to find the value of the unknown factor.

Example 1

Solve the equation $3x = 19$ for x.

$3x = 19$ can be written as $x = 19 \div 3$. So to find the unknown factor, we divide the product 19 by 3.

$$\begin{array}{r} 6\ \text{R}\ 1 \\ 3\overline{)19} \\ -18 \\ \hline 1 \end{array}$$

So $x = 6\frac{1}{3}$.

We can use this method with any kind of number: whole numbers, decimals, fractions, and percents.

Example 2

Solve the equation $0.2x = 14$ for x.

$0.2x = 14$ can be written as $x = 14 \div 0.2$.

$$0.2\overline{)14} \rightarrow \begin{array}{r} 70 \\ 2\overline{)140} \\ -14 \\ \hline 00 \end{array}$$

Dividing tells us that $x = \mathbf{70}$.

The following rule can be used to solve any unknown factor problem:

For any numbers a, b, and x, $ax = b$ is the same as $x = \frac{b}{a}$.

Verify Show that the process works for the following percent and fraction problems.

a. 36% of $x = 180$ **b.** $\frac{2}{3}x = 5$

A

acute angle
(20)

An angle whose measure is more than 0° and less than 90°.

right angle   obtuse angle

acute angle   not **acute angles**

*An **acute angle** is smaller than both a right angle and an obtuse angle.*

ángulo agudo

Ángulo que mide más de 0° y menos de 90°.

*Un **ángulo agudo** es menor que un ángulo recto y que un ángulo obtuso.*

---

acute triangle
(24)

A triangle with three acute angles.

right triangle   obtuse triangle

acute triangle   not **acute triangles**

triángulo acutángulo

Triángulo con tres ángulos agudos.

---

addend
(3)

Any one of the numbers added in an addition problem.

$7 + 3 = 10$ The **addends** in this problem are 7 and 3.

sumando

Cualquiera de los números que se suman en un problema de suma.

$7 + 3 = 10$ Los **sumandos** en este problema son el 7 y el 3.

---

adjacent sides
(33)

Sides that intersect.

*In triangle ABC above, sides AB and BC, sides BC and AC, and sides AC and AB are pairs of **adjacent sides.***

lados adyacentes

Lados que se intersecan.

*En el triángulo ABC de arriba, los lados AB y BC, los lados BC y AC, y los lados AC y AB son pares de **lados adyacentes.***

---

algorithm
(17)

A process for solving a mathematical problem.

*In the addition **algorithm** we add the ones first, then the tens, and then the hundreds.*

algoritmo

Un proceso para resolver un problema matemático.

*En el **algoritmo** de la suma, primero sumamos las unidades, después las decenas y al final las centenas.*

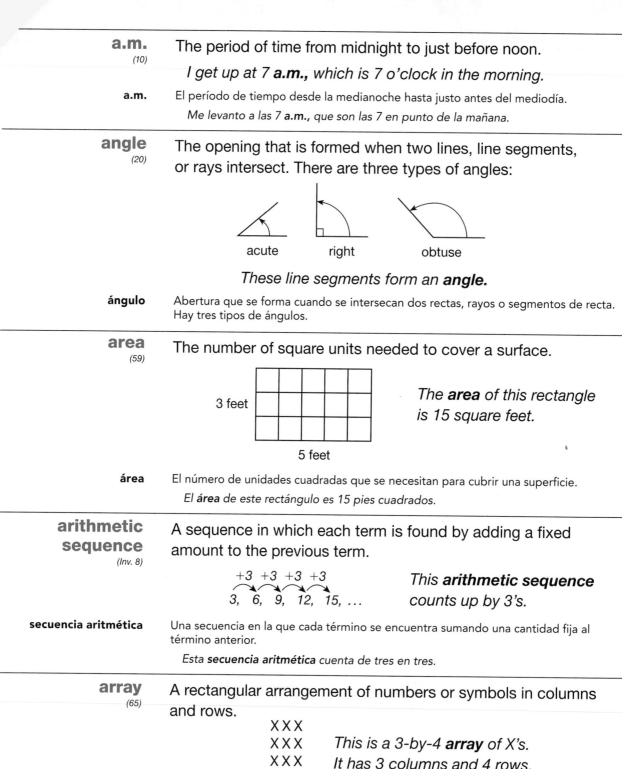

a.m.
(10)

The period of time from midnight to just before noon.

*I get up at 7 **a.m.**, which is 7 o'clock in the morning.*

a.m.

El período de tiempo desde la medianoche hasta justo antes del mediodía.

*Me levanto a las 7 **a.m.**, que son las 7 en punto de la mañana.*

angle
(20)

The opening that is formed when two lines, line segments, or rays intersect. There are three types of angles:

acute   right   obtuse

*These line segments form an **angle.***

ángulo

Abertura que se forma cuando se intersecan dos rectas, rayos o segmentos de recta. Hay tres tipos de ángulos.

area
(59)

The number of square units needed to cover a surface.

3 feet

5 feet

*The **area** of this rectangle is 15 square feet.*

área

El número de unidades cuadradas que se necesitan para cubrir una superficie.

*El **área** de este rectángulo es 15 pies cuadrados.*

arithmetic sequence
(Inv. 8)

A sequence in which each term is found by adding a fixed amount to the previous term.

+3 +3 +3 +3
3, 6, 9, 12, 15, ...

*This **arithmetic sequence** counts up by 3's.*

secuencia aritmética

Una secuencia en la que cada término se encuentra sumando una cantidad fija al término anterior.

*Esta **secuencia aritmética** cuenta de tres en tres.*

array
(65)

A rectangular arrangement of numbers or symbols in columns and rows.

X X X
X X X
X X X
X X X

*This is a 3-by-4 **array** of X's. It has 3 columns and 4 rows.*

matriz

Un arreglo rectangular de números o símbolos en columnas y filas.

*Esta es una **matriz** de X de 3-por-4. Tiene 3 columnas y 4 filas.*

Associative Property of Addition
(7)

The grouping of addends does not affect their sum. In symbolic form, $a + (b + c) = (a + b) + c$. Unlike addition, subtraction is not associative.

$(8 + 4) + 2 = 8 + (4 + 2)$
*Addition is **associative.***

$(8 - 4) - 2 \neq 8 - (4 - 2)$
*Subtraction is not **associative.***

propiedad asociativa de la suma	La agrupación de los sumandos no altera la suma. En forma simbólica, $a + (b + c) = (a + b) + c$. A diferencia de la suma, la resta no es asociativa.

$(8 + 4) + 2 = 8 + (4 + 2)$
*La suma es **asociativa**.*

$(8 - 4) - 2 \neq 8 - (4 - 2)$
*La resta no es **asociativa**.*

Associative Property of Multiplication
(7)

The grouping of factors does not affect their product. In symbolic form, $a \times (b \times c) = (a \times b) \times c$. Unlike multiplication, division is not associative.

$(8 \times 4) \times 2 = 8 \times (4 \times 2)$
*Multiplication is **associative**.*

$(8 \div 4) \div 2 \neq 8 \div (4 \div 2)$
*Division is not **associative**.*

propiedad asociativa de la multiplicación

La agrupación de los factores no altera el producto. En forma simbólica, $a \times (b \times c) = (a \times b) \times c$. A diferencia de la multiplicación, la división no es asociativa.

$(8 \times 4) \times 2 = 8 \times (4 \times 2)$
*La multiplicación es **asociativa**.*

$(8 \div 4) \div 2 \neq 8 \div (4 \div 2)$
*La división no es **asociativa**.*

---

average
(38)

The number found when the sum of two or more numbers is divided by the number of addends in the sum; also called *mean*.

*To find the **average** of the numbers 5, 6, and 10, add.*

$$5 + 6 + 10 = 21$$

Then, since there were three addends, divide the sum by 3.

$$21 \div 3 = 7$$

*The **average** of 5, 6, and 10 is 7.*

promedio

Número que se obtiene al dividir la suma de un conjunto de números por la cantidad de sumandos; también se le llama media.

*Para calcular el **promedio** de los números 5, 6 y 10, primero se suman.*

Como hay tres sumandos, se divide la suma entre 3.

*El **promedio** de 5, 6 y 10 es 7.*

B

---

bar graph
(Inv. 7)

A graph that uses rectangles (bars) to show numbers or measurements.

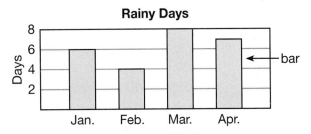

*This **bar graph** shows how many rainy days there were in each of these four months.*

gráfica de barras

Una gráfica que usa rectángulos (barras) para mostrar números o medidas.

*Esta **gráfica de barras** muestra cuántos días lluviosos hubo en cada uno de estos cuatro meses.*

base
(31, 67)

1. The lower number in an exponential expression.

base ⟶ 5^3 ⟵ exponent

5^3 means $5 \times 5 \times 5$, and its value is 125.

2. A designated side or face of a geometric figure, usually drawn on the bottom.

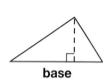 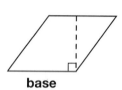

base   base   base

base

1. El número inferior en una expresión exponencial.

5^3 significa $5 \times 5 \times 5$ y su valor es 125.

2. Un lado o cara designada de una figura geométrica, comúnmente dibujada en la parte de abajo.

---

base-ten system
(11)

A place-value system in which each place value is 10 times larger than the place value to its right.

*The decimal system is a **base-ten system.** For example, 0.1 is 10 times larger than 0.01, 0.01 is 10 times larger than 0.001, and so on.*

sistema base diez

Un sistema de valor posicional en el que el valor de la posición es 10 veces mayor que el valor de la posición a su derecha.

*El sistema decimal es un **sistema de base diez.** Por ejemplo, 0.1 es 10 veces más grande que 0.01, 0.01 es 10 veces más grande que 0.001, etc.*

C

---

capacity
(77)

The amount of liquid a container can hold.

*Cups, gallons, and liters are units of **capacity.***

capacidad

Cantidad de líquido que puede contener un recipiente.

*Tazas, galones y litros son medidas de **capacidad.***

---

categories
(Inv. 7)

A set of people or things sharing a particular quality.

*The letters of the alphabet come in two **categories:** consonants and vowels.*

categorías

Un conjunto de personas o cosas que comparten una cualidad particular.

*Las letras del alfabeto pertenecen a dos **categorías:** consonantes y vocales.*

Celsius
(9)

A scale used on some thermometers to measure temperature.

*On the **Celsius** scale, water freezes at 0°C and boils at 100°C.*

Celsius

Escala que se usa en algunos termómetros para medir la temperatura.

*En la escala **Celsius,** el agua se congela a 0°C y hierve a 100°C.*

center
(RF23)

The point inside a circle from which all points on the circle are equally distant. Circles are usually named by their centers.

*The **center** of circle A is 2 inches from every point on the circle.*

centro

Punto interior de un círculo o esfera, que equidista de cualquier punto del círculo o de la esfera. Los círculos comúnmente reciben el nombre de sus centros.

*El **centro** del círculo A está a 2 pulgadas de cualquier punto del círculo.*

centigrade
(9)

A metric system temperature scale with one hundred gradations, or degrees, between the freezing and boiling points of water.

*The Celsius scale is a **centigrade** scale.*

centígrado

Una escala de temperatura del sistema métrico con cien gradaciones o grados, entre el punto de ebullición y el de congelación del agua.

*La escala Celsius es una escala de **centígrados**.*

centimeter
(32)

One hundredth of a meter.

*The width of your little finger is about one **centimeter**.*

centímetro

Una centésima de un metro.

*El ancho de tu dedo meñique mide aproximadamente un **centímetro**.*

century
(10)

A period of one hundred years.

*The years 2001–2100 make up one **century**.*

siglo

Un período de tiempo de cien años.

*Los años del 2001 al 2100 forman un **siglo**.*

certain
(45)

An event is certain when the event's probability is 1. This means the event will definitely occur.

seguro

Un evento es seguro cuando la probabilidad de que el evento ocurra es 1. Esto significa que el evento definitivamente ocurrirá.

chance
(maintained)

A way of expressing the likelihood of an event; the probability of an event expressed as a percentage.

*The **chance** of rain is 20%. It is not likely to rain.*

*There is a 90% **chance** of snow. It is likely to snow.*

posibilidad

Modo de expresar la probabilidad de ocurrencia de un suceso; la probabilidad de un suceso expresada como porcentaje.

*La **posibilidad** de lluvia es del 20%. Es poco probable que llueva.*

*Hay un 90% de **posibilidad** de nieve. Es muy probable que nieve.*

GLOSSARY

circle (RF23)	A closed, curved shape in which all points on the shape are the same distance from its center.

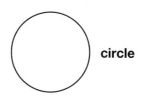

circle

círculo	Una figura cerrada y curva en la cual todos los puntos en la figura están a la misma distancia de su centro.

---

circle graph (Inv. 7)	A graph made of a circle divided into sectors. Also called *pie chart* or *pie graph*.

Shoe Colors of Students

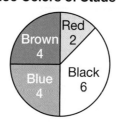

*This **circle graph** displays data on students' shoe color.*

gráfica circular	Una gráfica circular está formada por un círculo dividido en sectores. También llamada diagrama circular.

*Esta **gráfica circular** representa los datos del color de zapatos de los estudiantes.*

---

circumference (RF23)	The distance around a circle; the perimeter of a circle.

*If the distance from point A around to point A is 3 inches, then the **circumference** of the circle is 3 inches.*

circunferencia	La distancia alrededor de un círculo. Perímetro de un círculo.

*Si la distancia desde el punto A alrededor hasta el punto A es 3 pulgadas, entonces la **circunferencia** del círculo es 3 pulgadas*

---

class (Inv. 7)	See **categories**.

clase	Ver **categorías**.

classify
(24)

To sort according to a particular quality.

*The teacher **classified** the students by the state in which they were born, and displayed the data in this chart:*

Student Origins Chart	
Nevada	ⅠⅠⅠⅠⅠ Ⅰ
Oregon	ⅠⅠⅠ
Arizona	ⅠⅠⅠⅠ
California	ⅠⅠⅠⅠⅠ ⅠⅠⅠⅠⅠ ⅠⅠⅠ

clasificar

Separar de acuerdo a una cualidad en particular.

*La maestra **clasificó** a los estudiantes según el estado donde nacieron y mostró los datos en la tabla de arriba.*

---

cluster
(Inv. 5)

A group of data points that are very close together.

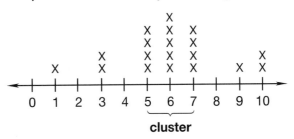

cúmulo

Un grupo de puntos de datos que están muy cerca uno de los otros.

---

common denominators
(28)

denominadores comunes

Denominators that are the same.

*The fractions $\frac{2}{5}$ and $\frac{3}{5}$ have **common denominators.***

Denominadores que son iguales.

*Las fracciones $\frac{2}{5}$ y $\frac{3}{5}$ tienen **denominadores comunes.***

---

common fraction
(53)

A fraction with whole-number terms.

$$\frac{1}{2} \quad \frac{5}{7} \quad \frac{3}{4} \qquad \frac{1.2}{2.4} \quad \frac{3}{4.5}$$

common fractions   not **common fractions**

fracción común

Una fracción con términos que son números enteros.

---

common year
(10)

A year with 365 days; not a leap year.

*The year 2000 is a leap year, but 2001 is a **common year.***

*In a **common year** February has 28 days. In a leap year February has 29 days.*

año común

Un año con 365 días; no un año bisiesto.

*El año 2000 es un año bisiesto, pero el año 2001 es un **año común.***

*En un **año común** febrero tiene 28 días. En un año bisiesto febrero tiene 29 días.*

Commutative Property of Addition *(7)*	Changing the order of addends does not change their sum. In symbolic form, $a + b = b + a$. Unlike addition, subtraction is not commutative.
	$$8 + 2 = 2 + 8 \qquad\qquad 8 - 2 \neq 2 - 8$$
	*Addition is **commutative**.* *Subtraction is not **commutative**.*
propiedad conmutativa de la suma	El orden de los sumandos no altera la suma. En forma simbólica, $a + b = b + a$. A diferencia de la suma, la resta no es conmutativa.
	*La suma es **conmutativa**.* *La resta no es **conmutativa**.*

Communicative Property of Multiplication *(7)*	Changing the order of factors does not change their product. In symbolic form, $a \times b = b \times a$. Unlike multiplication, division is not commutative.
	$$8 \times 2 = 2 \times 8 \qquad\qquad 8 \div 2 \neq 2 \div 8$$
	*Multiplication is **commutative**.* *Division is not **commutative**.*
propiedad conmutativa de la multiplicación	El orden de los factores no altera el producto. En forma simbólica, $a \times b = b \times a$. A diferencia de la multiplicación, la división no es conmutativa.
	*La multiplicación es **conmutativa**.* *La división no es **conmutativa**.*

comparative bar graph *(83)*	A method of displaying data, usually used to compare two or more related sets of data.

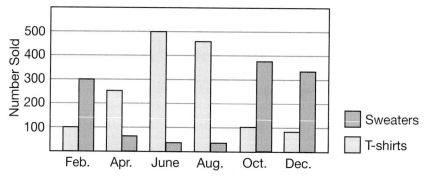

*This **comparative bar graph** compares the number of sweaters sold with the number of T-shirts sold in each of these six months.*

gráfica comparativa de datos	Un método para mostrar datos, usualmente usado para comparar dos o más conjuntos de datos relacionados.
	*Esta **barra comparativa de datos** compara el número de suéteres vendidos con el número de camisetas vendidas en cada uno de estos seis meses.*

comparison symbol *(2)*	A mathematical symbol used to compare numbers.
	***Comparison symbols** include the equal sign (=) and the "greater than/less than" symbols (> or <).*
signo de comparación	Un símbolo matemático que se usa para comparar números.
	*El **signo de comparación** incluye el signo de igual (=) y los signos "mayor que/ menor que" (> ó <).*

compatible numbers (22)	Numbers that are close in value to the actual numbers and are easy to add, subtract, multiply, or divide mentally.
	$163 \div 42$
	*To estimate the answer to this problem, we use **compatible numbers** to estimate the answer to be 160 ÷ 40 = 4.*
números compatibles	Números que están cerca en valor a los números actuales y que son fáciles de sumar, restar, multiplicar o dividir mentalmente.
	*Para estimar la respuesta a este problema, utilizamos **números compatibles** para estimar la respuesta como 160 ÷ 40 = 4.*
composite number (65)	A counting number greater than 1 that is divisible by a number other than itself and 1. Every composite number has three or more factors. Every composite number can be expressed as a product of two or more prime numbers.
	*9 is divisible by 1, 3, and 9. It is **composite.***
	*11 is divisible by 1 and 11. It is not **composite.***
número compuesto	Número de conteo mayor que 1, divisible entre algún otro número distinto de sí mismo y de 1. Cada número compuesto tiene tres o más divisores. Cada número compuesto puede ser expresado como el producto de dos o más números primos.
	*9 es divisible entre 1, 3 y 9. Es **compuesto.***
	*11 es divisible entre 1 y 11. No es **compuesto.***
cone (RF27)	A three-dimensional solid with a circular base and one curved surface. The pointed end of a cone is its apex.
	 cone
cono	Un sólido tridimensional con una base circular y una superficie curva. El extremo puntiagudo de un cono es su ápice.
congruent (21)	Having the same size and shape.
	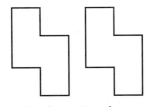 *These polygons are **congruent.** They have the same size and shape.*
congruentes	Que tienen igual tamaño y forma.
	*Estos polígonos son **congruentes.** Tienen igual tamaño y forma.*
continuous data (49)	Data that can be measured on a scale, such as length, elapsed time, temperature, and cost.
	*Line graphs often display **continuous data.***
datos continuos	Datos que se pueden medir en una escala, tal como longitud, tiempo transcurrido, temperatura y precio.
	*Las gráficas lineales frecuentemente muestran **datos continuos.***

coordinate(s) *(Inv. 6)*	**1.** A number used to locate a point on a number line.

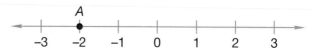

The coordinate of point A is −2.

2. A pair of numbers used to locate a point on a coordinate plane.

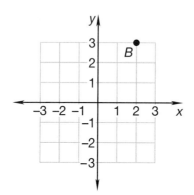

The **coordinates** of point B are (2, 3). The x-coordinate is listed first and the y-coordinate is listed second.

coordenada(s)	**1.** Número que se utiliza para ubicar un punto sobre una recta numérica.

*La **coordenada** del punto A es −2.*

2. Par ordenado de números que se utiliza para ubicar un punto sobre un plano coordenado.

*Las **coordenadas** del punto B son (2, 3). La coordenada x se escribe primero, seguida de la coordenada y.*

---

coordinate plane *(Inv. 6)*	A grid on which any point can be identified by its distances from the x- and y-axes.

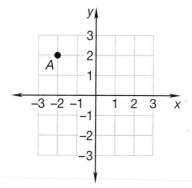

Point A is located at (−2, 2) on this **coordinate plane.**

plano coordenado	Cuadrícula en la cual cualquier punto se puede identificar por sus distancias a los ejes x e y.

*El punto A está ubicado en la posición (−2, 2) sobre este **plano coordenado.***

---

counting numbers *(1)*	The numbers used to count; the numbers in this sequence: 1, 2, 3, 4, 5, 6, 7, 8, 9, ...

The numbers 12 and 37 are **counting numbers,** but 0.98, −1, and $\frac{1}{2}$ are not.

números de conteo	Números que se utilizan para contar; los números en esta secuencia: 1, 2, 3, 4, 5, 6, 7, 8, 9, ...

*Los números 12 y 37 son **números de conteo** pero 0.98, −1 y $\frac{1}{2}$ no lo son.*

cross product
(107)

The product of the numerator of one fraction and the denominator of another fraction.

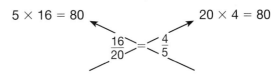

*To compare the fractions $\frac{16}{20}$ and $\frac{4}{5}$, find the **cross products** $5 \times 16 = 80$ and $20 \times 4 = 80$. Since both **cross products** are equal, $\frac{16}{20} = \frac{4}{5}$.*

producto cruzado

El producto del numerador de una fracción y del denominador de otra fracción.

*Para comparar las fracciones $\frac{16}{20}$ y $\frac{4}{5}$, encuentra los **productos cruzados** $5 \times 16 = 80$ y $20 \times 4 = 80$. Ya que los **productos cruzados** son iguales, $\frac{16}{20} = \frac{4}{5}$.*

cube
(Inv. 9)

A three-dimensional solid with six square faces. Adjacent faces are perpendicular and opposite faces are parallel.

cube

cubo

Sólido tridimensional con seis caras cuadradas. Las caras adyacentes son perpendiculares y las caras opuestas son paralelas.

cubic unit
(Inv. 9)

A cube with edges of designated length. Cubic units are used to measure volume.

*The shaded part is 1 **cubic unit.** The volume of the large cube is 8 **cubic units.***

unidad cúbica

Un cubo con aristas de una longitud designada. Las unidades cúbicas se usan para medir volumen.

*La parte sombreada tiene 1 **unidad cúbica.** El volumen del cubo mayor es de 8 **unidades cúbicas.***

cylinder
(RF27)

A three-dimensional solid with two circular bases that are opposite and parallel to each other.

cylinder

cilindro

Un sólido tridimensional con dos bases circulares que son opuestas y paralelas una a la otra.

D

data *(49)*	(Singular: *datum*) Information gathered from observations or calculations. *82, 76, 95, 98, 97, 93, 96* *These **data** are the average daily temperatures for one week in Utah.*
datos	Información reunida de observaciones o cálculos. *Estos **datos** son el promedio diario de las temperaturas de una semana en Utah.*
decade *(10)*	A period of ten years. *The years 2001–2010 make up one **decade**.*
década	Un periodo de diez años. *Los años 2001–2010 forman una **década**.*
decimal number *(maintained)*	A numeral that contains a decimal point. *23.94 is a **decimal number** because it contains a decimal point.*
número decimal	Número que contiene un punto decimal. *23.94 es un **número decimal**, porque tiene punto decimal.*
decimal place(s) *(52)*	Places to the right of the decimal point. *5.47 has two **decimal places**.* *6.3 has one **decimal place**.* *8 has no **decimal places**.*
cifra(s) decimal(es)	Números ubicados a la derecha del punto decimal. *5.47 tiene dos **cifras decimales**.* *6.3 tiene una **cifra decimal**.* *8 no tiene **cifras decimales**.*
decimal point *(maintained)*	A symbol used to separate the ones place from the tenths place in decimal numbers (or dollars from cents in money). *34.15* ↑ **decimal point**
punto decimal	Símbolo que se usa en números decimales para separar el lugar de las unidades del lugar de las décimas (o en dinero, para separar dólares de centavos).
decimeter *(RF25)*	A metric unit of measurement equal to one tenth of a meter.
decímetro	Una unidad de medida métrica igual a una décima de un metro.

degree (°)
(9, Inv. 3)

1. A unit for measuring angles.

*There are 90 **degrees** (90°) in a right angle.*

*There are 360 **degrees** (360°) in a circle.*

2. A unit for measuring temperature.

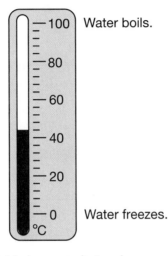

Water boils.

Water freezes.

*There are 100 **degrees** (100°) between the freezing and boiling points of water on the Celsius scale.*

grado (°)

1. Unidad para medir ángulos.
2. Unidad para medir temperaturas.

*Hay 90 **grados** (90°) en un ángulo recto.*

*Hay 360 **grados** (360°) en un círculo.*

*Hay 100 **grados** de diferencia entre los puntos de ebullición y congelación del agua en la escala Celsius, o escala centígrada.*

denominator
(7)

The bottom number of a fraction; the number that tells how many parts are in a whole.

$\frac{1}{4}$

*The **denominator** of the fraction is 4. There are 4 parts in the whole circle.*

denominador

El número inferior de una fracción; el número que indica cuántas partes hay en un todo.

*El **denominador** de la fracción es 4. Hay 4 partes en el círculo completo.*

diagonal
(31)

A line segment in a polygon connecting two opposite vertices.

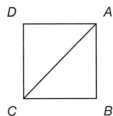

*Segment AC is a **diagonal** of rectangle ABCD.*

diagonal

Un segmento de recta en un polígono que conecta a dos vértices opuestos.

*El segmento AC es una **diagonal** del rectángulo ABCD.*

diameter (RF23)	The distance across a circle through its center.
	*The **diameter** of this circle is 3 inches.*
diámetro	Distancia entre dos puntos opuestos de un círculo a través de su centro. *El **diámetro** de este círculo mide 3 pulgadas.*
difference (3)	The result of subtraction. $12 - 8 = 4$ *The **difference** in this problem is 4.*
diferencia	Resultado de una resta. *La **diferencia** en este problema es 4.*
digit (maintained)	Any of the symbols used to write numbers: 0, 1, 2, 3, 4, 5, 6, 7, 8, 9. *The last **digit** in the number 7862 is 2.*
dígito	Cualquiera de los símbolos que se utilizan para escribir números: 0, 1, 2, 3, 4, 5, 6, 7, 8, 9. *El último **dígito** en el número 7862 es 2.*
dimension (maintained)	The perpendicular measures of a figure. *Length and width are **dimensions** of a rectangle. Length, width, and height are **dimensions** of a rectangular prism.*
dimensión	Las medidas perpendiculares de una figura. *Largo y ancho son **dimensiones** de un rectángulo. Largo, ancho y altura son **dimensiones** de un prisma rectangular.*
Distributive Property (39)	A number times the sum of two addends is equal to the sum of that same number times each individual addend: $$a \times (b + c) = (a \times b) + (a \times c)$$ $$8 \times (2 + 3) = (8 \times 2) + (8 \times 3)$$ *Multiplication is **distributive** over addition.*
propiedad distributiva	Un número multiplicado por la suma de dos sumandos es igual a la suma de los productos de ese número por cada uno de los sumandos. *La multiplicación es **distributiva** con respecto a la suma.*
dividend (6)	A number that is divided by another number. $12 \div 3 = 4$ $3\overline{)12}^{\,4}$ $\dfrac{12}{3} = 4$ *The **dividend** is 12 in each of these problems.*
dividendo	Número que se divide entre otro número. *El **dividendo** es 12 en cada una de estas operaciones.*
divisibility (29)	The ability for a number to be divided by another number without a remainder. *See **divisible**.*
divisibilidad	La característica de un número de ser dividido entre otro número sin dar residuo. *Ver **divisible**.*

divisible
(29)

Able to be divided by a whole number without a remainder.

$$\begin{array}{r} 5 \\ 4\overline{)20} \end{array}$$

*The number 20 is **divisible** by 4, since 20 ÷ 4 has no remainder.*

$$\begin{array}{r} 6\ R\ 2 \\ 3\overline{)20} \end{array}$$

*The number 20 is not **divisible** by 3, since 20 ÷ 3 has a remainder.*

divisible

Número que se puede dividir sin residuo entre un entero.

*El número 20 es **divisible** entre 4, ya que 20 ÷ 4 no tiene residuo.*

*El número 20 no es **divisible** entre 3, ya que 20 ÷ 3 tiene residuo.*

---

division
(RF20)

An operation that separates a number into a given number of equal parts or into a number of parts of a given size.

$21 \div 3 = 7$ *We use **division** to separate 21 into 3 groups of 7.*

división

Una operación que separa un número en un número dado de partes iguales o en un número de partes de una medida dada.

*Usamos la **división** para separar 21 en 3 grupos de 7.*

---

division algorithm
(17)

A series of steps that can be used to divide one number (the dividend) by another (the divisor) to obtain a result (the quotient).

$$\begin{array}{r} 462 \\ 18\overline{)8316} \\ -72 \\ \hline 111 \\ -108 \\ \hline 36 \\ -36 \\ \hline 0 \end{array}$$

*In the **division algorithm** we divide and write a number, then multiply and write a number, then subtract and write a number, then bring down the next digit, and repeat until there are no digits left to bring down.*

algoritmo de división

Una serie de pasos que pueden ser usados para dividir un número (el dividendo) entre otro (el divisor) para obtener un resultado (el cociente).

*En el **algoritmo de la división** dividimos y escribimos un número y después multiplicamos y escribimos un número, después restamos y escribimos un número, después bajamos el siguiente dígito, y repetimos esto hasta que ya no hayan dígitos que bajar.*

---

division by primes
(66)

A method for prime factorization in which a number is divided repeatedly by the smallest prime factor of the quotient.

$$\begin{array}{r} 1 \\ 3\overline{)3} \\ 3\overline{)9} \\ 2\overline{)18} \end{array}$$

*To find the prime factorization of 18 using **division by primes,** we first divide 18 by 2, its smallest prime factor, then divide 9 (the quotient of 18 ÷ 2) by 3.*

división entre primos

Un método para la factorización prima en el cual un número se divide repetidamente entre el factor primo más pequeño del cociente.

Para encontrar la factorización prima de 18, primero dividimos 18 entre 2, su factor primo más pequeño, después dividimos 9 (el cociente de 18 ÷ 2) entre 3.

divisor *(6)*	A number by which another number is divided. $$12 \div 3 = 4 \quad 3\overline{)12}^{\,4} \quad \frac{12}{3} = 4$$ *The **divisor** is 3 in each of these problems.*
divisor	Número que divide a otro en una división. *El **divisor** es 3 en cada una de estas operaciones.*
dodecagon *(21)*	A polygon with twelve sides. regular dodecagon irregular dodecagon
dodecágono	Un polígono de doce lados.
double-line graph *(maintained)*	A method of displaying a set of data, often used to compare two performances over time. 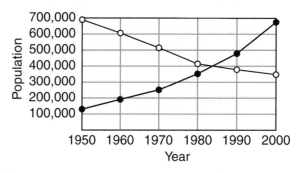
gráfica de doble línea	Un método para mostrar un conjunto de datos, comúnmente usado para comparar dos comportamientos al paso del tiempo.

E

edge *(RF27)*	A line segment formed where two faces of a solid intersect. 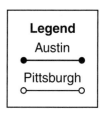 *The arrow is pointing to one **edge** of this cube. A cube has 12 **edges.***
arista	Segmento de recta formado por la intersección de dos caras de un sólido. *La flecha apunta hacia una **arista** de este cubo. Un cubo tiene 12 **aristas.***
elapsed time *(5)*	The difference between a starting time and an ending time, or the length of time between two events. *The race started at 6:30 p.m. and finished at 9:12 p.m. The **elapsed time** of the race was 2 hours 42 minutes.*
tiempo transcurrido	La diferencia entre el tiempo de comienzo y tiempo final, o el tiempo entre dos sucesos. *La carrera comenzó a las 6:30 p.m. y terminó a las 9:12 p.m . El **tiempo transcurrido** de la carrera fue de 2 horas 42 minutos.*

endpoint(s) *(RF13)*	The points at which a line segment ends. 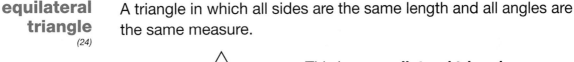 *Points A and B are the **endpoints** of line segment AB.*
punto(s) extremo(s)	Puntos donde termina un segmento de recta. *Los puntos A y B son los **puntos extremos** del segmento AB.*
equation *(3)*	A number sentence that uses the equal sign (=) to show that two quantities are equal. $3 + 7 = 10$ $x = 3$ $4 + 1$ $x < 7$ **equations** not **equations**
ecuación	Enunciado de números que usa el símbolo de igualdad (=) para indicar que dos cantidades son iguales.
equilateral triangle *(24)*	A triangle in which all sides are the same length and all angles are the same measure. *This is an **equilateral triangle.** All of its sides are the same length. All of its angles are the same measure.*
triángulo equilátero	Triángulo que tiene todos sus lados de la misma longitud y todos sus ángulos de la misma medida. *Éste es un **triángulo equilátero.** Todos sus lados tienen la misma longitud. Todos sus ángulos tienen la misma medida.*
equivalent fractions *(54)*	Different fractions that name the same amount. 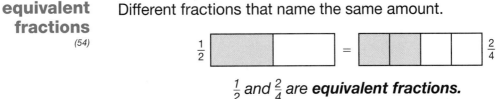 $\frac{1}{2}$ and $\frac{2}{4}$ are **equivalent fractions.**
fracciones equivalentes	Fracciones diferentes que representan la misma cantidad. $\frac{1}{2}$ y $\frac{2}{4}$ son **fracciones equivalentes.**
estimate *(22)*	To find an approximate value. *I **estimate** that the sum of 199 and 205 is about 400.*
estimar	Encontrar un valor aproximado. *Puedo **estimar** que la suma de 199 más 205 es aproximadamente 400.*
evaluate *(8)*	To find the value of an expression. *To **evaluate** a + b for a = 7 and b = 13, we replace "a" with 7 and "b" with 13:* $7 + 13 = 20$
evaluar	Calcular el valor de una expresión. *Para **evaluar** a + b, con a = 7 y b = 13, se reemplaza "a" por 7 y "b" por 13.*

even numbers *(RF2)*	Numbers that can be divided by 2 without a remainder; the numbers in this sequence: 0, 2, 4, 6, 8, 10, …. ***Even numbers*** *have 0, 2, 4, 6, or 8 in the ones place.*
números pares	Números que se pueden dividir entre 2 sin residuo; los números en esta secuencia: 0, 2, 4, 6, 8, 10 …. *Los **números pares** tienen 0, 2, 4, 6 u 8 en el lugar de las unidades.*
event *(45)*	An outcome or group of outcomes in an experiment involving probability. *The **event** of rolling a 4 with one roll of a standard number cube has a probability of $\frac{1}{6}$.*
suceso	El resultado o grupo de resultados en un experimento que involucra probabilidad. *El **suceso** de obtener un 4 al lanzar una vez un cubo de números tiene una probabilidad de $\frac{1}{6}$.*
expanded form *(RF3)*	*See **expanded notation***.
forma desarrollada	*Ver **notación desarrollada**.*
expanded notation *(36)*	A way of writing a number that shows the value of each digit. *Two ways to write 234 in **expanded notation** are* $$200 + 300 + 4$$ *and* $$(2 \times 100) + (3 \times 10) + (4 \times 1)$$
notación desarrollada	Manera de escribir un número como la suma de los productos de cada uno de sus dígitos por su valor de posición. *Dos maneras de escribir 234 en **notación desarrollada** son* $$200 + 300 + 4$$ *y* $$(2 \times 100) + (3 \times 10) + (4 \times 1)$$
experiment *(45)*	A test to find or illustrate a rule. *Flipping a coin and selecting an object from a collection of objects are two **experiments** that involve probability.*
experimento	Una prueba para encontrar o ilustrar una regla. *Lanzar una moneda y seleccionar un objeto de una colección de objetos son dos **experimentos** que involucran probabilidad.*
exponent *(67)*	The upper number in an exponential expression; it shows how many times the base is to be used as a factor. base $\longrightarrow 5^3 \longleftarrow$ **exponent** 5^3 *means* $5 \times 5 \times 5$*, and its value is 125.*
exponente	El número superior en una expresión exponencial; muestra cuántas veces debe usarse la base como factor. *5^3 significa $5 \times 5 \times 5$ y su valor es 125.*

exponential expression *(67)*	An expression that indicates that the base is to be used as a factor the number of times shown by the exponent.
	$$4^3 = 4 \times 4 \times 4 = 64$$
	*The **exponential expression** 4^3 uses 4 as a factor 3 times. Its value is 64.*
expresión exponencial	Expresión que indica que la base debe usarse como factor el número de veces que indica el exponente.
	*La **expresión exponencial** 4^3 utiliza 4 como factor tres veces. Su valor es 64.*
expression *(7)*	A number, a letter, or a combination of both. Expressions do not include comparison symbols, such as an equal sign.
	*3n is an **expression** that can also be written as 3 × n.*
expresión	Un número, una letra o una combinación de los dos. Las expresiones no incluyen símbolos de comparación, como el símbolo de igualdad.
	*3n es una **expresión** que también puede ser escrita como 3 × n.*

F

face *(RF27)*	A flat surface of a geometric solid.
	*The arrow is pointing to one **face** of the cube. A cube has six **faces.***
cara	Superficie plana de un sólido geométrico.
	*La flecha apunta a una **cara** del cubo. Un cubo tiene seis **caras.***
fact family *(RF8)*	A group of three numbers related by addition and subtraction or by multiplication and division.
	*The numbers 3, 4, and 7 are a **fact family.** They make these four facts:*
	$$3 + 4 = 7 \qquad 4 + 3 = 7 \qquad 7 - 3 = 4 \qquad 7 - 4 = 3$$
familia de operaciones	Grupo de tres números relacionados por sumas y restas o por multiplicaciones y divisiones.
	*Los números 3, 4 y 7 forman una **familia de operaciones.** Con ellos se pueden formar estas cuatro operaciones:*
	$$3 + 4 = 7 \qquad 4 + 3 = 7 \qquad 7 - 3 = 4 \qquad 7 - 4 = 3$$

factor *(6)*	**1.** Noun: Any one of the numbers multiplied in a multiplication problem. $2 \times 3 = 6$ *The **factors** in this problem are 2 and 3.* **2.** Noun: A whole number that divides another whole number without a remainder. *The numbers 2 and 3 are **factors** of 6.* **3.** Verb: To write as a product of **factors.** *We can **factor** the number 6 by writing it as 2 × 3.*
factor (n); factorizar (v)	**1.** Nombre o sustantivo: Cualquiera de los números multiplicados en un problema de multiplicación. $2 \times 3 = 6$ *Los **factores** en esta operación son el 2 y el 3.* **2.** Nombre o sustantivo: Número entero que divide a otro número entero sin residuo. *Los números 2 y 3 son **factores** de 6.* **3.** Verbo: Escribir como producto de **factores.** *Se puede **factorizar** el número 6 escribiéndolo como 2 × 3.*
factor tree *(66)*	A way to diagram the prime factorization of a number. *This **factor tree** shows the prime factorization of 210.*
árbol de factores	Una manera de hacer un diagrama de la factorización prima de un número. *Este **árbol de factores** muestra la factorización prima de 210.*
Fahrenheit scale *(9)*	A scale used on some thermometers to measure temperature. *On the **Fahrenheit scale**, water freezes at 32°F and boils at 212°F.*
escala Fahrenheit	Escala que se usa en algunos termómetros para medir temperatura. *En la **escala Fahrenheit**, el agua se congela a 32°F y hierve a 212°F.*
Fibonacci sequence *(Inv. 8)*	A famous sequence in mathematics, which follows an addition pattern. *1, 1, 2, 3, 5, 8, …* *Each term equals the sum of the two terms before it.* *1 + 1 = 2, 1 + 2 = 3, 2 + 3 = 5 …*
secuencia de Fibonacci	Una famosa secuencia matemática que sigue un patrón de suma. *1, 1, 2, 3, 5, 8 …* *Cada término es igual a la suma de los dos términos anteriores.* *1 + 1 = 2, 1 + 2 = 3, 2 + 3 = 5 …*
fluid ounce *(77)*	A unit of liquid measurement in the customary system equal to one sixteenth of a pint.

onza líquida (oz. liq.)	Una unidad de medida para líquidos en el sistema usual que es igual a un dieciseisavo de pinta.

formula *(4)*	An expression or equation that describes a method for solving a certain type of problem. We often write formulas with letters that stand for complete words. *A **formula** for the perimeter of a rectangle is P = 2l + 2w, where P stands for "perimeter," l stands for "length," and w stands for "width."*
fórmula	Una expresión o ecuación que describe un método para resolver cierto tipo de problemas. Frecuentemente escribimos fórmulas con letras que representan palabras completas. *Una **fórmula** para el perímetro de un rectángulo es P = 2l + 2w, donde P representa "perímetro", l representa "longitud" y w representa "ancho".*

fraction *(7)*	A number that names part of a whole.

$\frac{1}{4}$ of the circle is shaded.

$\frac{1}{4}$ is a **fraction.**

fracción	Número que representa una parte de un entero. $\frac{1}{4}$ del círculo está sombreado. $\frac{1}{4}$ es una **fracción.**

frequency *(Inv. 5)*	The number of times an event or outcome occurs.

Purchased Lunch

Lunch Food	Tally	Frequency
Salad	||	2
Baked potato	|	1
Sandwich	||||	4
Soup	|||	3

*This table shows the **frequency** of lunches that students purchased.*

frecuencia	El número de veces que un suceso o resultado ocurre. *Esta tabla muestra la **frecuencia** de almuerzos que los estudiantes compraron.*

frequency table
(Inv. 5)

A table that is used to tally and display the number of times an event or outcome occurs.

Race Results

Laps Completed	Tally	Frequency
0		0
1	I	1
2	IIII	4
3	Ж II	7
4	Ж Ж	10
5	III	3

*This **frequency table** summarizes the class's performace in a fitness test.*

tabla de frecuencias

Una tabla que se utiliza para tabular y mostrar el número de veces que un suceso o resultado ocurre.

*Esta **tabla de frecuencias** resume el desempeño de la clase en una prueba de rendimiento.*

---

function
(RF18)

A rule for changing an "in" number to an "out" number.

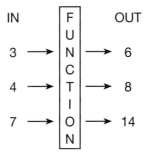

In	Out
3	6
4	8
7	14

*This **function** uses the rule "multiply the 'in' number by two."*

función

Regla para convertir un número de "entrada" a un número de "salida".

*Esta **función** utiliza la regla "multiplicar el número 'in' por dos".*

G

---

geometric sequence
(Inv. 8)

A sequence in which each term is found by multiplying the previous term by a fixed amount.

$$\overset{\times 3 \; \times 3 \; \times 3 \; \times 3}{1, \quad 3, \quad 9, \quad 27, \quad 81, \ldots}$$

*We multiply a term by 3 to find the term that follows it in this **geometric sequence.***

progresión geométrica

Una secuencia en la que cada término se encuentra multiplicando el término anterior por una cantidad fija.

$$\overset{\times 3 \; \times 3 \; \times 3 \; \times 3}{1, \quad 3, \quad 9, \quad 27, \quad 81, \ldots}$$

*Multiplicamos un término por 3 para encontrar el término que sigue en esta **progresión geométrica.***

geometric solid
(RF27)

A shape that takes up space.

geometric solids   not **geometric solids**

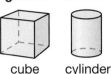   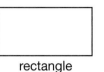

cube cylinder   circle   rectangle   hexagon

sólido geométrico Figura que ocupa un espacio.

geometry
(RF13)

A major branch of mathematics that deals with shapes, sizes, and other properties of figures.

*Some of the figures we study in **geometry** are angles, circles, and polygons.*

geometría Una rama principal de matemáticas que trata de las formas, tamaños y otras propiedades de figuras.

*Algunas de las figuras que se estudian en **geometría** son los ángulos, círculos y polígonos.*

graph
(Inv. 5)

1. Noun: A diagram that shows data in an organized way. *See also* **bar graph, circle graph, histogram, line graph,** *and* **pictograph.**

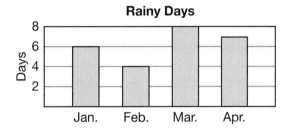 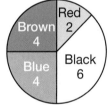

bar **graph**   circle **graph**

2. Verb: To draw a diagram or a point, line, or curve on a coordinate plane.

gráfica (n); graficar (v)

1. Nombre: Un diagrama que muestra datos de una forma organizada. *Ver también* **gráfica de barras, gráfica circular, histograma, gráfica lineal** y **pictograma.**

2. Verbo: Dibujar un diagrama o un punto, línea o curva en un plano coordenado.

greatest common factor (GCF)
(73)

The largest whole number that is a factor of two or more given numbers.

The factors of 20 are 1, 2, 4, 5, 10, and 20.

The factors of 30 are 1, 2, 3, 5, 6, 10, 15, and 30.

The common factors of 20 and 30 are 1, 2, 5, and 10.

*The **greatest common factor** of 20 and 30 is 10.*

máximo común divisor (MCD) Es el mayor número entero que es factor de dos o más números.

Los factores de 20 son 1, 2, 4, 5, 10 y 20.

Los factores de 30 son 1, 2, 3, 5, 6, 10, 15 y 30.

*El **máximo común divisor** de 20 y 30 es 10.*

H

half
(RF2)

One of two equal parts that together equal a whole.

mitad

Una de dos partes que juntas forman un todo.

height
(75)

The height of a polygon is the perpendicular distance from its base to the point farthest from its base.

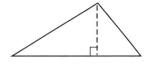 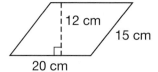 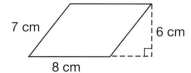

*The dotted lines represent the **heights** of these polygons.*

altura

La altura de un polígono es la distancia perpendicular desde su base hasta el punto más alejado de la base.

*Las líneas punteadas representan las **alturas** de estos polígonos.*

hexagon
(21)

A six-sided polygon.

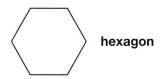

hexágono

Un polígono de seis lados.

histogram
(Inv. 7)

A method of displaying a range of data. A histogram is a special type of bar graph that displays data in intervals of equal size with no space between bars.

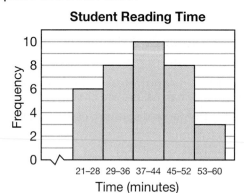

This is a **histogram.**

histograma

Método para representar un conjunto de datos. Un histograma es un tipo especial de gráfica de barras que muestra los datos a intervalos de igual tamaño y de manera continua sin espacios entre las barras.

| **horizontal** (9) | Side to side; perpendicular to vertical. |

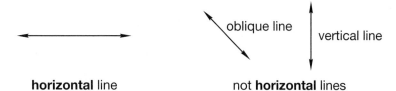

horizontal line   not **horizontal** lines

| **horizontal** | Lado a lado; perpendicular a una vertical. |

| **horizontal axis** (maintained) | The scale of a graph that runs from left to right. |

| **eje horizontal** | La escala de una gráfica que va de izquierda a derecha. |

I

| **icon** (Inv. 7) | A symbol used in a pictograph to represent data. |

Consumed by Matt in One Day	
Water	🥛 🥛 🥛 🥛 🥛 🥛
Soda	🥛
Milk	🥛 🥛 🥛 🥛
Juice	🥛 🥛 🥛

Key: 🥛 = 1 cup = 8 ounces

*Each **icon** in the pictograph represents 1 cup of liquid that was consumed.*

| **icono** | Un símbolo que se usa en un pictograma para representar datos. |

*Cada **icono** en el pictograma representa 1 taza de líquido consumida.*

| **Identity Property of Addition** (RF6) | The sum of any number and 0 is equal to the initial number. In symbolic form, $a + 0 = a$. The number 0 is referred to as the *additive identity*. |

*The **Identity Property of Addition** is shown by this statement:*

$$13 + 0 = 13$$

| **propiedad de identidad de la suma** | La suma de cualquier número más 0 es igual al número inicial. En forma simbólica, $a + 0 = a$. El 0 se conoce como *identidad aditiva*. |

*La **propiedad de identidad de la suma** se muestra en el siguiente enunciado:*

$$13 + 0 = 13$$

GLOSSARY

Identity Property of Multiplication *(69)*	The product of any number and 1 is equal to the initial number. In symbolic form, $a \times 1 = a$. The number 1 is referred to as the *multiplicative identity*.
	The ***Identity Property of Multiplication*** *is shown by this statement:*
	$$94 \times 1 = 94$$
propiedad de identidad de la multiplicación	El producto de cualquier número por 1 es igual al número inicial. En forma simbólica, $a \times 1 = a$. El número 1 se conoce como *identidad multiplicativa*.
	La **propiedad de identidad de la multiplicación** *se muestra en el siguiente enunciado:*
	$$94 \times 1 = 94$$
impossible *(45)*	An event is impossible when the event's probability is 0. This means the event will definitely not occur.
	*It is **impossible** to roll more than a 12 on two number cubes.*
imposible	Un suceso es imposible cuando la probabilidad de que el suceso ocurra es 0. Esto significa que el suceso definitivamente no ocurrirá.
	*Es **imposible** obtener más de 12 al lanzar dos cubos de números.*
improper fraction *(62)*	A fraction with a numerator greater than or equal to the denominator.
	$\dfrac{4}{3}$ $\dfrac{2}{2}$ *These fractions are **improper fractions.***
fracción impropia	Fracción con el numerador igual o mayor que el denominador.
	$\dfrac{3}{4}$ $\dfrac{2}{2}$ *Estas fracciones son **fracciones impropias**.*
integers *(2)*	The set of counting numbers, their opposites, and zero; the members of the set $\{\ldots, -2, -1, 0, 1, 2, \ldots\}$.
	*-57 and 4 are **integers**. $\frac{15}{8}$ and -0.98 are not **integers**.*
enteros positivos, negativos y el cero	Conjunto de números de conteo, sus opuestos y el cero; los elementos del conjunto $\{\ldots, -2, -1, 0, 1, 2, \ldots\}$.
	*-57 y 4 son **enteros**. $\frac{15}{8}$ y -0.98 no son **enteros**.*
International System of Units *(32)*	*See **metric system**.*
Sistema internacional de unidades	*Ver **sistema métrico**.*
intersect *(20)*	To share a common point or points.
	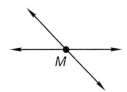 *These two lines **intersect**. They share the common point M.*

intersecar	Tener uno o más puntos en común.
	*Estas dos rectas se **intersecan**. También se dice que son rectas secantes. Tienen el punto común M.*

---

intersecting lines
(20)

Lines that cross.

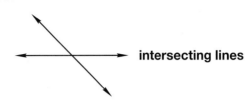

intersecting lines

líneas que se intersecan

Líneas que se cruzan.

---

inverse operation(s)
(3)

An operation that undoes another.

$$a + b - b = a$$
$$a - b + b = a$$

*Addition is the **inverse operation** of subtraction.*

$$a \times b \div b = a \quad (b \neq 0)$$
$$a \div b \times b = a \quad (b \neq 0)$$

*Multiplication and division are **inverse operations.***

$$\sqrt{a^2} = a \quad (a \geq 0)$$
$$(\sqrt{a})^2 = a \quad (a \geq 0)$$

*Squaring and finding square roots are **inverse operations.***

operación inversa

Una operación que cancela a otra.

$$a + b - b = a$$
$$a - b + b = a$$
$$a \times b \div b = a \quad (b \neq 0)$$
$$a \div b \times b = a \quad (b \neq 0)$$
$$\sqrt{a^2} = a \quad (a \geq 0)$$
$$(\sqrt{a})^2 = a \quad (a \geq 0)$$

*La suma es la **operación inversa** de la resta.*
*La multiplicación y la división son **operaciones inversas.***
*Elevar a una potencia y calcular la raíz cuadrada son **operaciones inversas.***

---

invert
(85)

To switch the numerator and denominator of a fraction to form its reciprocal.

*If we **invert** the fraction $\frac{3}{4}$, we get $\frac{4}{3}$.*

invertir

Intercambiar el numerador y el denominador en una fracción para formar su recíproco.

*Si **invertimos** la fracción $\frac{3}{4}$, obtenemos $\frac{4}{3}$.*

---

isosceles triangle
(24)

A triangle with at least two sides of equal length and two angles of equal measure.

*Two of the sides of this **isosceles triangle** have equal lengths. Two of the angles have equal measures.*

triángulo isósceles

Triángulo que tiene por lo menos dos lados de igual longitud y dos ángulos de igual medida.

*Dos de los lados de este **triángulo isósceles** tienen igual longitud. Dos de los ángulos tienen igual medida.*

K

kilometer
(61)

A metric unit of length equal to 1000 meters.

*One **kilometer** is approximately 0.62 mile.*

kilómetro

Una unidad métrica de longitud igual a 1000 metros.

*Un **kilómetro** es aproximadamente 0.62 milla.*

L

leap year
(10)

A year with 366 days; not a common year.

*A **leap year** occurs every year that is divisible by 4, except for century years that are not divisible by 400. Thus, the years 1700, 1800, and 1900 are not leap years because they are not divisible by 400, but 2000 is a leap year.*

año bisiesto

Un año con 366 días; no es un año común.

*Un **año bisiesto** ocurre cada año que es divisible entre 4, a excepción de siglos que no son divisibles entre 400. Por lo tanto, los años 1700, 1800 y 1900 no fueron años bisiestos porque no son divisibles entre 400 pero el 200 fue un año bisiesto.*

least common denominator (LCD)
(108)

The smallest whole number that is a multiple of the denominators of two fractions. The LCD is useful when comparing, adding, or subtracting fractions with unlike denominators.

*To add $\frac{1}{8}$ and $\frac{5}{6}$, we find their **least common denominator**. The least common multiple (LCM) of the denominators 8 and 6 is 24, so we rewrite the fraction $\frac{1}{8}$ as $\frac{3}{24}$, and we rewrite the fraction $\frac{5}{6}$ as $\frac{20}{24}$. We can now easily add $\frac{3}{24}$ to $\frac{20}{24}$ to obtain the sum $\frac{23}{24}$.*

mínimo común denominador (mcd)

El número entero más pequeño que es múltiplo de los denominadores de dos fracciones. El mcd es útil para comparar, sumar, o restar fracciones con distintos denominadores.

*Para sumar $\frac{1}{8}$ y $\frac{5}{6}$, encontramos su **mínimo común denominador**. El mínimo común múltiplo (mcm) de los denominadores 8 y 6 es 24, así que reescribimos la fracción $\frac{1}{8}$ como $\frac{3}{24}$ y reescribimos la fracción $\frac{5}{6}$ como $\frac{20}{24}$. Ahora fácilmente podemos sumar $\frac{3}{24}$ y $\frac{20}{24}$ para obtener la suma total $\frac{23}{24}$.*

least common multiple (LCM)
(103)

The smallest whole number that is a multiple of two or more given numbers.

The multiples of 4 are 4, 8, 12, 16, 20, 24, ….

The multiples of 6 are 6, 12, 18, 24, 30, 36, ….

*The **least common multiple** of 4 and 6 is 12.*

mínimo común múltiplo (mcm)

El menor número entero que es múltiplo común de dos o más números dados.

Los múltiplos de 4 son 6, 8, 12, 16, 20, ….

Los múltiplos de 6 son 6, 12, 18, 24, 30, ….

*El **mínimo común múltiplo** de 4 y 6 es 12.*

legend	A notation on a map, graph, or diagram that describes the
(Inv. 7)	meaning of the symbols and/or the scale used.

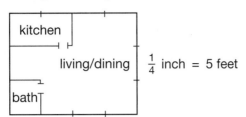

The **legend** of this scale drawing shows that $\frac{1}{4}$ inch represents 5 feet.

rótulo — Nota en un mapa, gráfica o diagrama, que describe el significado de los símbolos o escala usados.

El **rótulo** de este dibujo a escala muestra que $\frac{1}{4}$ pulg representa 5 pies.

---

length
(32)

A measure of the distance between any two points.

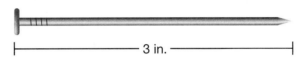

*The **length** of this nail is 3 inches.*

longitud — Una medida de la distancia entre dos puntos.

*La **longitud** de este clavo es 3 pulgadas.*

---

line
(RF13)

A straight collection of points extending in opposite directions without end.

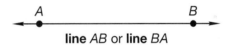

recta — Sucesión de puntos que se extiende indefinidamente en ambas direcciones.

---

line graph
(49)

A graph that connects points to show how information changes over time.

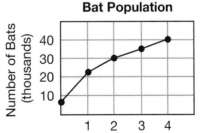

*This is a **line graph.***

gráfica lineal — Una gráfica que conecta puntos que muestran como cambia la información con el tiempo.

*Esta es una **gráfica lineal.***

line of symmetry *(RF28)*	A line that divides a figure into two halves that are mirror images of each other. *See also* **symmetry.**

lines of symmetry   not **lines of symmetry**

eje de simetría   Recta que divide una figura en dos mitades, en la cual una mitad es la imagen especular de la otra. *Ver también* **simetría.**

---

line plot
 (Inv. 5)

A method of plotting a set of numbers by placing a mark above a number on a number line each time it occurs in the set.

*This is a **line plot** of the numbers 5, 8, 8, 10, 10, 11, 12, 12, 12, 12, 13, 13, 14, 16, 17, 17, 18, and 19.*

diagrama de puntos   Método para representar un conjunto de números, que consiste en colocar una marca sobre un número de una recta numérica cada vez que dicho número ocurre en el conjunto.

*Éste es un **diagrama de puntos** de los números 5, 8, 8, 10, 10, 11, 12, 12, 12, 12, 13, 13, 14, 16, 17, 17, 18, y 19.*

---

line segment
 (2)

A part of a line with two distinct endpoints.

*$\overline{AB}$ is a **line segment.***

segmento de recta   Parte de una recta con dos extremos distintos.

*$\overline{AB}$ es un **segmento de recta.***

---

liter
 (77)

A metric unit of capacity or volume.

*A **liter** is a little more than a quart.*

litro   Una unidad métrica de capacidad o volumen.

*Un **litro** es un poco más que un cuarto.*

---

lowest terms
 (80)

A fraction is in lowest terms if it cannot be reduced.

*In **lowest terms,** the fraction $\frac{8}{20}$ is $\frac{2}{5}$.*

mínima expresión   Una fracción está en su mínima expresión si no puede ser reducida.

*Cuando se escribe en su **mínima expresión,** la fracción $\frac{8}{20}$ se convierte en $\frac{2}{5}$.*

M

mass
 (64)

The amount of matter an object contains. A kilogram is a metric unit of mass.

*The **mass** of a bowling ball would be the same on the moon as on Earth, even though the weight of the bowling ball would be different.*

masa	Cantidad de materia contenida en un objeto. Un kilogramo es una unidad métrica de masa.
	*La **masa** de una bola de boliche es la misma en la Luna que en la Tierra, aunque el peso de la bola de boliche es diferente.*

mean *(74)*	*See* **average.**
media	*Ver* **promedio.**

measure of central tendency *(74)*	A value that describes a property of a list of data, such as the middle number of an ordered list or the number that appears in a list most often. *See also* **mean, median,** *and* **mode.**
	1, 3, 5, 6, 8, 9, 13
	*The median of this set is 6. The median of a set is one **measure of central tendency.***
medida de tendencia central	Un valor que describe la propiedad de una lista de datos, tal como el número de en medio de la lista o el número que aparece en la lista con mayor frecuencia. *Ver también* **media, mediana** *y* **moda**
	1, 3, 5, 6, 8, 9, 13
	*La mediana en este conjunto es 6. La mediana de un conjunto es una **medida de tendencia central.***

median *(Inv. 5)*	The middle number (or the average of the two central numbers) of a list of data when the numbers are arranged in order from the least to the greatest.
	1, 1, 2, 4, 5, 7, 9, 15, 24, 36, 44
	*In this list of data, 7 is the **median.***
mediana	Número de en medio (o el promedio de los dos números centrales) en una lista de datos, cuando los números se ordenan de menor a mayor.
	1, 1, 2, 4, 5, 7, 9, 15, 24, 36, 44
	*En esta lista de datos, 7 es la **mediana.***

meter *(RF25)*	The basic unit of length in the metric system.
	*Many classrooms are about 10 **meters** long and 10 **meters** wide.*
metro	La unidad básica de longitud en el sistema métrico.
	*Muchos salones de clase miden aproximadamente 10 **metros** de largo por 10 **metros** de ancho.*

metric system *(32)*	An international system of measurement in which units are related by a power of ten. Also called the *International System.*
	*Centimeters and kilograms are units in the **metric system.***
sistema métrico	Un sistema internacional de medición en el cual las unidades de medida se relacionan por potencias de diez. También se le llama el *Sistema internacional.*
	*Centímetros y kilogramos son unidades del **sistema métrico.***

millennium *(10)* **milenio**	A period of one thousand years. *The years 2001–3000 make up one **millennium.*** Un período de mil años. *Los años 2001–3000 forman un **milenio.***
millimeter *(32)* **milímetro**	A metric unit of length equal to one thousandth of a meter. *There are 1000 **millimeters** in 1 meter and 10 **millimeters** in one centimeter.* Una unidad métrica de longitud que es igual a una milésima de un metro. *Hay 1000 **milímetros** en 1 metro y 10 **milímetros** en un centímetro.*
minuend *(3)* **minuendo**	A number from which another number is subtracted. $$12 - 8 = 4$$ *The **minuend** in this problem is 12.* Un número del cual otro se resta. $$12 - 8 = 4$$ *El **minuendo** en este problema es 12.*
mixed number *(25)* **número mixto**	A number expressed as a whole number plus a fraction. *The **mixed number** $2\frac{1}{3}$ means "two and one third."* Número expresado como un número entero más una fracción. *El **número mixto** $2\frac{1}{3}$ significa "dos y un tercio".*
mode *(Inv. 5)* **moda**	The number or numbers that appear most often in a list of data. *5, 12, 32, 5, 16, 5, 7, 12* *In this list of data, the number 5 is the **mode.*** Número o números que aparecen con más frecuencia en una lista de datos. *5, 12, 32, 5, 16, 5, 7, 12* *En esta lista de datos, el número 5 es la **moda.***
multiple *(18)*	A multiple of a number is any product of that number and a counting number. Any multiple of a number can be divided by the number without a remainder. *Multiples of 6 are 6, 12, 18, 24, ...* *Fourteen is a **multiple** of seven because 14 ÷ 7 does not have a remainder.*

| múltiplo | Un múltiplo de un número es cualquier producto de ese número y de un número de conteo. Cualquier múltiplo de un número puede ser dividido entre el número sin dejar residuo. |

Múltiplos de 6 son 6, 12, 18, 24, …

*Catorce es un **múltiplo** de siete porque14 ÷ 7 no tiene residuo.*

multiplication table
(RF16)

A table used to find the product of two numbers. The product of two numbers is found at the intersection of the row and the column for the two numbers.

Multiplication Table

	0	1	2	3	4	5	6	7	8	9	10	11	12
0	0	0	0	0	0	0	0	0	0	0	0	0	0
1	0	1	2	3	4	5	6	7	8	9	10	11	12
2	0	2	4	6	8	10	12	14	16	18	20	22	24
3	0	3	6	9	12	15	18	21	24	27	30	33	36
4	0	4	8	12	16	20	24	28	32	36	40	44	48
5	0	5	10	15	20	25	30	35	40	45	50	55	60
6	0	6	12	18	24	30	36	42	48	54	60	66	72
7	0	7	14	21	28	35	42	49	56	63	70	77	84
8	0	8	16	24	32	40	48	56	64	72	80	88	96
9	0	9	18	27	36	45	54	63	72	81	90	99	108
10	0	10	20	30	40	50	60	70	80	90	100	110	120
11	0	11	22	33	44	55	66	77	88	99	110	121	132
12	0	12	24	36	48	60	72	84	96	108	120	132	144

tabla de multiplicación

Una tabla que se utiliza para encontrar el producto de dos números. El producto de dos números se encuentra en la intersección de la fila y la columna para los dos números.

mutually exclusive
(Maintained)

Categories are mutually exclusive if each data point can be placed in one, and only one, of the categories.

*When flipping one coin, the categories are "landing heads-up" and "landing tails-up." One coin cannot land both heads-up and tails-up on the same toss. Thus, the categories "landing heads-up" and "landing tails-up" are **mutually exclusive.***

mutuamente excluyentes

Dos categorías son mutuamente excluyentes si cada dato puntual puede ser colocado en una, y solo una, de las categorías.

*Cuando se lanza una moneda las categorías son "que caiga cara arriba" y "que caiga cara abajo", una moneda no puede caer cara arriba y cara abajo en el mismo lanzamiento. Por lo tanto, las categorías "que caiga cara arriba" y "que caiga cara abajo" son **mutuamente excluyentes.***

N

negative numbers
(2)

Numbers less than zero.

*−15 and −2.86 are **negative numbers.***

19 and 0.74 are not **negative numbers.**

números negativos   Los números menores que cero.

−15 y −2.86 son **números negativos.**

19 y 0.74 no son **números negativos.**

---

number line
(2)

A line for representing and graphing numbers. Each point on the line corresponds to a number.

recta numérica   Recta para representar y graficar números. Cada punto de la recta corresponde a un número.

---

numeral
(maintained)

A symbol or group of symbols that represents a number.

4, 72, and $\frac{1}{2}$ are examples of **numerals.**

"Four," "seventy-two," and "one half" are words that name numbers but are not **numerals.**

numeral   Símbolo, o grupo de símbolos numéricos, que representa un número.

4, 72 y $\frac{1}{2}$ son ejemplos de **numerales.**

"Cuatro", "setenta y dos" y "un medio" son palabras que identifican números, pero no son **numerales.**

---

numerator
(7)

The top number of a fraction; the number that tells how many parts of a whole are counted.

$\frac{1}{4}$

The **numerator** of the fraction is 1.
One part of the whole circle is shaded.

numerador   El término superior de una fracción. El número que nos dice cuántas partes de un entero se cuentan.

El **numerador** de la fracción es 1. Una parte del círculo está sombreada.

O

---

oblique line
(20)

1. Slanted or sloping; not horizontal or vertical.

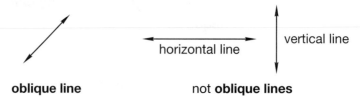

oblique line   not **oblique lines**

2. Lines in the same plane that are neither parallel nor perpendicular.

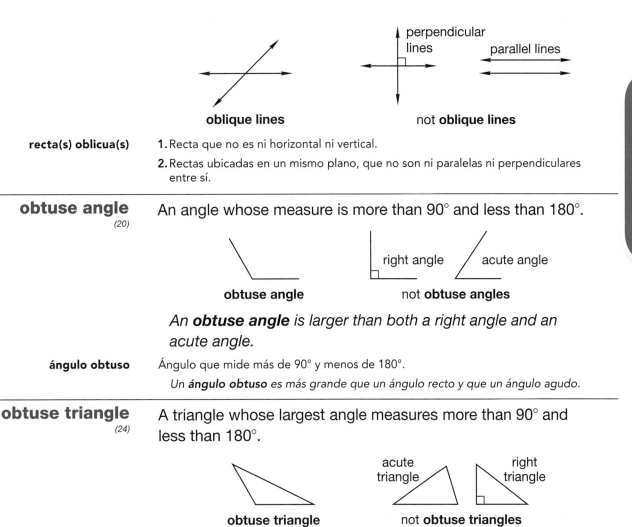

oblique lines   not **oblique lines**

recta(s) oblicua(s)   1. Recta que no es ni horizontal ni vertical.

2. Rectas ubicadas en un mismo plano, que no son ni paralelas ni perpendiculares entre sí.

---

obtuse angle
(20)

An angle whose measure is more than 90° and less than 180°.

right angle   acute angle

obtuse angle   not **obtuse angles**

*An **obtuse angle** is larger than both a right angle and an acute angle.*

ángulo obtuso   Ángulo que mide más de 90° y menos de 180°.

*Un **ángulo obtuso** es más grande que un ángulo recto y que un ángulo agudo.*

---

obtuse triangle
(24)

A triangle whose largest angle measures more than 90° and less than 180°.

acute triangle   right triangle

obtuse triangle   not **obtuse triangles**

triángulo obtusángulo   Triángulo cuyo ángulo mayor mide más que 90° y menos que 180°.

---

octagon
(21)

A polygon with eight sides.

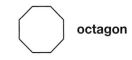
octagon

octágono   Un polígono con ocho lados.

---

odd numbers
(RF2)

Numbers that have a remainder of 1 when divided by 2; the numbers in this sequence: 1, 3, 5, 7, 9, 11, ...

***Odd numbers** have 1, 3, 5, 7, or 9 in the ones place.*

números impares   Números que cuando se dividen entre 2 tienen residuo 1; los números en la secuencia: 1, 3, 5, 7, 9, 11, ...

*Los **números impares** tienen 1, 3, 5, 7 ó 9 en el lugar de las unidades.*

operation (7) **operación**	*See* **operations of arithmetic.** *Ver* **operaciones aritméticas**
operations of arithmetic (RF6) **operaciones aritméticas**	The four basic mathematical operations: addition, subtraction, multiplication, and division. $$1 + 9 \qquad 21 - 8 \qquad 6 \times 22 \qquad 3 \div 1$$ the **operations of arithmetic** Las cuatro operaciones matemáticas básicas: suma, resta, multiplicación y división.
opposite numbers (89) **números opuestos**	Two numbers are opposite numbers if they are the same distance from zero, but in opposite directions. The sum of two opposite numbers is zero. *Negative six and positive six are* **opposite numbers** *because* $-6 + (+6) = 0.$ Dos números son opuestos si siempre están a la misma distancia del cero, pero en direcciones opuestas. La suma de dos números opuestos es cero. *El seis negativo y el seis positivo son* **númerso opuestos** *porque* $-6 + (+6) = 0.$
opposite sides (33) **lados opuestos**	Sides that are across from each other. opposite sides Lados que están uno enfrente del otro.
ordered pair (Inv. 6)	Points on a coordinate plane are given by an ordered pair of numbers. The *x*-coordinate is listed first, followed by the *y*-coordinate.

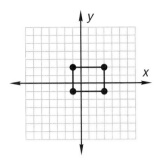

*In the coordinate plane above, the coordinates of the corners of the rectangle are given by the **ordered pairs** (−1,−1), (−1, 2), (3, 2), and (3, −1).*

par ordenado   Puntos sobre un plano coordenado dados por un par ordenado de números. La coordenada x se enlista primero, seguida por la coordenada y.

*En el plano coordenado de arriba, las coordenadas de las esquinas del rectángulo están dadas por los **pares ordenados** (−1, −1), (−1, 2), (3, 2), y (3, −1).*

order of operations
(7)

A set of rules to determine the correct order in which to evaluate expressions, used whenever two or more operations are present in a problem. The order of operations is:

• Complete operations inside parentheses first.

• Simplify any exponents and roots.

• Multiply and divide from left to right.

• Add and subtract from left to right.

*To simplify an expression such as $(8 \div 2)^2 + 1$, we follow the **order of operations**. First we complete the operations inside the parentheses.*

$$(8 \div 2)^2 + 1 = (4)^2 + 1$$

Then we simplify the exponent.

$$(4)^2 + 1 = 16 + 1$$

Then we add.

$$16 + 1 = 17$$

orden de las operaciones   Un conjunto de reglas para determinar el orden correcto para evaluar expresiones. Se utiliza cuando dos o más operaciones se presentan en un problema. El orden de las operaciones es:

• Completar las operaciones dentro de paréntesis primero.

• Simplificar exponentes y raíces.

• Multiplicar y dividir, de izquierda a derecha.

• Sumar y restar, de izquierda a derecha.

Para simplificar una expresión como $(8 \div 2)^2 + 1$, primero completamos las operaciones dentro del paréntesis:

$$(8 \div 2)^2 + 1 = (4)^2 + 1$$

Después simplificamos el exponente:

$$(4)^2 \times 1 = 16 \times 1$$

Después sumamos:

$$16 + 1 = 17$$

---

ordinal numbers
(RF7)

Numbers that describe position or order.

*"First," "second," and "third" are **ordinal numbers.***

números ordinales

Números que describen orden o posición.

*"Primer," "segundo" y "tercero" son **números ordinales.***

---

origin
(Inv. 6)

1. The location of the number 0 on a number line.

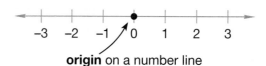

origin on a number line

2. The point (0,0) on a coordinate plane.

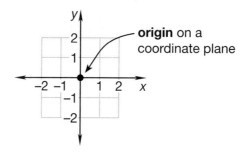

origin on a coordinate plane

origen

1. Posición del número 0 en una recta numérica.

2. El punto (0, 0) en un plano coordenado.

---

ounce
(35)

A unit of weight in the customary system equal to $\frac{1}{16}$ lb. *See* **fluid ounce.**

*Sixteen **ounces** equals a pound. Sixteen **ounces** equals a pint.*

onza

Una unidad de peso en el sistema usual es igual a $\frac{1}{16}$ lb. *Ver* **onza líquida.**

*Dieciséis **onzas** es igual a una libra. Dieciséis **onzas** es igual a una pinta.*

---

outcome
(45)

Any possible result of an experiment.

*When rolling a number cube, the possible **outcomes** are 1, 2, 3, 4, 5, and 6.*

resultado

Cualquier resultado posible de un experimento.

*Cuando se lanza un cubo de números los **resultados** posibles son 1, 2, 3, 4, 5 y 6.*

---

outlier
(Inv. 5)

A number that is distant from most of the other numbers in a list of data.

1, 5, 4, 3, 6, 28, 7, 2

*In the data above, the number 28 is an **outlier** because it is* *distant from the other numbers in the list.*

valor extremo

Número en una lista de datos, que es mucho mayor o mucho menor que los demás números de la lista.

*En los datos de arriba, el número 28 es un **valor extremo**, porque su valor es mayor que el de los demás números de la lista.*

P

parallel lines
(20)

Lines that stay the same distance apart; lines that do not cross.

parallel lines

rectas paralelas

Rectas ubicadas en un mismo plano y que nunca se intersecan.

parallelogram
(33)

A quadrilateral that has two pairs of parallel sides.

parallelograms   not a
                    parallelogram

paralelogramo

Cuadrilátero que tiene dos pares de lados paralelos.

parentheses
(7)

A pair of symbols used to separate parts of an expression so that those parts may be evaluated first: ( ).

$$15 - (12 - 4)$$

*In the expression 15 − (12 − 4), the **parentheses** indicate that 12 − 4 should be calculated before subtracting the result from 15.*

paréntesis

Un par de símbolos que se utilizan para separar partes de una expresión para que esas partes puedan ser evaluadas primero: ().

*En la expresión 15 − (12 − 4) los **paréntesis** indican que 12 − 4 debe ser calculado antes de restar el resultado de 15.*

partial product
(39)

When multiplying using pencil and paper, a product resulting from multiplying one factor by one digit of the other factor. The final product is the sum of the partial products.

$$
\begin{array}{r}
53 \\
\times\ 26 \\
\hline
318 \\
106 \\
\hline
1378
\end{array}
$$

← → **partial products**

producto parcial

Cuando se multiplica usando lápiz y papel, el producto resulta de multiplicar un factor por un dígito del otro factor. El producto final es la suma de los productos parciales.

percent *(19)*	A fraction whose denominator of 100 is expressed as a percent sign (%). One percent is one one hundredth of a whole. $$\frac{99}{100} = 99\% = 99 \textbf{ percent}$$
porcentaje	Fracción cuyo denominador de 100 se expresa con un signo (%), que se lee *por ciento*. Uno por ciento es un centésimo de un todo.
perfect square *(67)*	The product when a whole number is multiplied by itself. *The number 9 is a **perfect square** because 3 × 3 = 9.*
cuadrado perfecto	Producto cuando un número entero se multiplica por sí mismo. *El número 9 es un **cuadrado perfecto**, porque 3 × 3 = 9.*
perimeter *(8)*	The distance around a closed, flat shape. 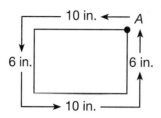 *The **perimeter** of this rectangle (from point A around to point A) is 32 inches.*
perímetro	Distancia alrededor de una figura cerrada y plana. *El **perímetro** de este rectángulo (desde el punto A alrededor del rectángulo hasta el punto A) es 32 pulgadas.*
period *(Inv. 8)*	The period of a repeating pattern or sequence is the number of terms in a repeating unit. *M, B, H, M, B, H, ... This pattern has **period** 3.* *2, 5, 6, 7, 2, 5, 6, 7, ... This pattern has **period** 4.*
período	El período de un patrón que se repite o secuencia es el número de términos en la unidad que se repite. *M, B, H, M, B, H, ... Este patrón tiene un **período** de 3.* *2, 5, 6, 7, 2, 5, 6, 7, ... Este patrón tiene un **período** de 4.*
permutation *(maintained)*	One possible arrangement of a set of objects. *2 4 3 1* *The arrangement above is one possible **permutation** of the numbers 1, 2, 3, and 4.*
permutación	Un arreglo posible de un conjunto de objetos. *El arreglo anterior es una **permutación** posible de los números 1, 2, 3 y 4.*
perpendicular lines *(20)*	Two lines that intersect at right angles. 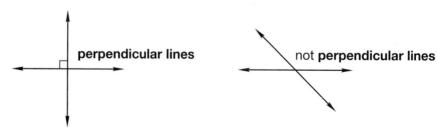

rectas perpendiculares   Dos rectas que se intersecan formando ángulos rectos.

pictograph
(Inv. 7)

A graph that uses symbols to represent data.

Stars We Saw	
Tom	☆ ☆ ☆ ☆ ☆
Bob	☆ ☆
Sue	☆ ☆ ☆ ☆
Ming	☆ ☆ ☆ ☆ ☆
Juan	☆ ☆ ☆ ☆ ☆ ☆

*This is a **pictograph**. It shows how many stars each person saw.*

pictograma   Gráfica que utiliza símbolos para representar datos.

*Éste es un **pictograma**. Muestra el número de estrellas que vio cada persona.*

pie graph
(Inv. 7)

*See **circle graph**.*

gráfica circular   *Vea **diagrama circular***

place value
(maintained)

The value of a digit based on its position within a number.

$$\begin{array}{r} 341 \\ 23 \\ + \quad 7 \\ \hline 371 \end{array}$$

*__Place value__ tells us that 4 in 341 is worth "4 tens." In addition problems, we align digits with the same **place value**.*

valor posicional   Valor de un dígito de acuerdo al lugar que ocupa en el número.

*El **valor posicional** indica que el 4 en 341 vale "cuatro decenas". En los problemas de suma y resta, se alinean los dígitos que tienen el mismo **valor posicional**.*

plane
(21)

A flat surface that has no boundaries.

*The flat surface of a desk is part of a **plane**.*

plano   Superficie plana ilimitada.

*La superficie plana de un escritorio es parte de un **plano**.*

plane figure
(RF27)

A flat shape.

plane figures   not a **plane figure**

figura plana   Una figura plana.

p.m.
(10)

The period of time from noon to just before midnight.

*I go to bed at 9 **p.m.**, which is 9 o'clock at night.*

p.m.   Período de tiempo desde el mediodía hasta justo la medianoche.

*Me voy a dormir a las 9 **p.m.**, lo cual es las 9 en punto de la noche.*

point
(RF13)

An exact position.

$\bullet A$ *This dot represents **point** A.*

punto   Una posición exacta.

*Esta marca representa el **punto** A.*

---

polygon
(21)

A closed, flat shape with straight sides.

polygons   not **polygons**

polígono   Figura cerrada y plana que tiene lados rectos.

---

positive numbers
(RF2)

Numbers greater than zero.

*0.25 and 157 are **positive numbers.***

*−40 and 0 are not **positive numbers.***

números positivos   Números mayores que cero.

*0.25 y 157 son **números positivos.***

*−40 y 0 no son **números positivos.***

---

power
(67)

1. The value of an exponential expression.

*16 is the fourth **power** of 2 because $2^4 = 16$.*

2. An exponent.

*The expression 2^4 is read "two to the fourth **power.**"*

potencia   1. El valor de una expresión exponencial.

*16 es la cuarta **potencia** de 2, porque $2^4 = 16$.*

2. Un exponente.

*La expresión 2^4 se lee "dos a la cuarta **potencia**".*

---

prime factorization
(66)

The writing of a composite number as a product of its prime factors.

*The **prime factorization** of 24 is $2^3 \times 3$.*

factorización prima   Escribir un número compuesto como el producto de sus factores primos.

*La **factorización prima** de 24 es $2^3 \times 3$.*

---

prime number
(16)

A counting number greater than 1 whose only two factors are the number 1 and itself.

*7 is a **prime number.** Its only factors are 1 and 7.*

*10 is not a **prime number.** Its factors are 1, 2, 5, and 10.*

número primo   Número de conteo mayor que 1, cuyos dos únicos factores son el 1 y el propio número.

*7 es un **número primo.** Sus únicos factores son 1 y 7.*

*10 no es un **número primo.** Sus factores son 1, 2, 5 y 10.*

---

prism
(maintained)

A three-dimensional solid with two congruent bases.

prisma	Un sólido tridimensional con dos bases congruentes.

probability
(45)

A way of describing the likelihood of an event; the ratio of favorable outcomes to all possible outcomes.

*The **probability** of rolling a 3 with a standard number cube is $\frac{1}{6}$.*

probabilidad

Manera de describir la ocurrencia de un suceso; la razón de resultados favorables a todos los resultados posibles.

*La **probabilidad** de obtener 3 al lanzar un cubo estándar de números es $\frac{1}{6}$.*

product
(6)

The result of multiplication.

$5 \times 3 = 15$ The **product** of 5 and 3 is 15.

producto

Resultado de una multiplicación.

$5 \times 3 = 15$ El **producto** de 5 por 3 es 15.

proper fraction
(62)

A fraction whose denominator is greater than its numerator.

$\frac{3}{4}$ *is a **proper fraction.***

$\frac{4}{3}$ *is not a **proper fraction.***

fracción propia

Una fracción cuyo denominador es mayor que su numerador.

$\frac{3}{4}$ *es una fracción **propia.***

$\frac{4}{3}$ *no es una fracción **propia.***

protractor
(Inv. 3)

A tool used to measure and draw angles.

This is a **protractor.**

transportador

Instrumento que sirve para medir y trazar ángulos.

pyramid
(RF27)

A three-dimensional solid with a polygon as its base and triangular faces that meet at a vertex.

pyramid

pirámide

Un sólido tridimensional con un polígono en su base y caras triangulares que se encuentran en un vértice.

Q

quadrant
(Inv. 6)

One of four parts of the coordinate plane divided by the *x*-axis and the *y*-axis.

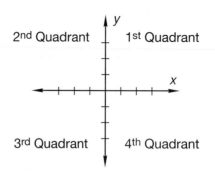

| cuadrante | Una de cuatro partes de un plano coordenado dividido por el eje X y por el eje Y. |

quadrilateral
(21)

Any four-sided polygon.

Each of these polygons has 4 sides. They are all **quadrilaterals.**

cuadrilátero

Polígono de cuatro lados.

*Cada uno de estos polígonos tiene 4 lados. Todos son **cuadriláteros.***

quotient
(6)

The result of division.

$$12 \div 3 = 4 \qquad 3\overline{)12} \quad \overset{4}{} \qquad \frac{12}{3} = 4$$

*The **quotient** is 4 in each of these problems.*

cociente

Resultado de una división.

*El **cociente** es 4 en cada una de estas operaciones.*

R

radius
(RF23)

(Plural: *radii*) The distance from the center of a circle to a point on the circle.

2 in.

*The **radius** of this circle is 2 inches.*

radio

Distancia desde el centro de un círculo hasta un punto del círculo.

*El **radio** de este círculo es 2 pulgadas.*

range
(Inv. 5)

The difference between the largest number and the smallest number in a list.

6, 17, 12, 34, 29, 13

*To calculate the **range** of this list, we subtract the smallest number from the largest number. The **range** of this list is 28.*

intervalo

Diferencia entre el número mayor y el número menor de una lista.

*Para calcular el **intervalo** de esta lista, se resta el número menor del número* *mayor. El **intervalo** de esta lista es 89.*

ratio
(87)

A comparison of two numbers by division.

*There are 3 triangles and 5 stars. The **ratio** of triangles to stars is "three to five," or $\frac{3}{5}$.*

razón

Comparación de dos números por división.

*Hay 3 triángulos y 5 estrellas. La **razón** de triángulos a estrellas es "tres a cinco" ó $\frac{3}{5}$.*

---

ray
(5)

A part of a line that begins at a point and continues without end in one direction.

ray AB $(\overrightarrow{AB})$

rayo

Parte de una recta que empieza en un punto y continúa indefinidamente en una dirección.

---

reciprocals
(85)

Two numbers whose product is 1.

$$\frac{3}{4} \times \frac{4}{3} = \frac{12}{12} = 1$$

*Thus, the fractions $\frac{3}{4}$ and $\frac{4}{3}$ are **reciprocals.** The **reciprocal** of $\frac{3}{4}$ is $\frac{4}{3}$.*

recíprocos

Dos números cuyo producto es igual a 1.

*Las fracciones $\frac{3}{4}$ y $\frac{4}{3}$ son **recíprocas.** El **recíproco** de $\frac{3}{4}$ es $\frac{4}{3}$.*

---

rectangle
(33)

A quadrilateral that has four right angles.

 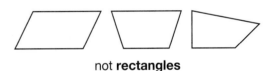

rectangles   not **rectangles**

rectángulo

Cuadrilátero que tiene cuatro ángulos rectos.

---

rectangular solid
(RF27)

A three-dimensional solid having six rectangular faces. Adjacent faces are perpendicular and opposite faces are parallel.

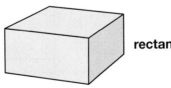

rectangular solid

sólido rectangular

Un sólido tridimensional que tiene 6 caras rectangulares. Las caras adyacentes son perpendiculares y las caras opuestas son paralelas.

---

reduce
(71)

To rewrite a fraction in lowest terms.

*If we **reduce** the fraction $\frac{9}{12}$, we get $\frac{3}{4}$.*

reducir

Reescribir o escribir una fracción en su mínima expresión.

*Al **reducir** la fracción $\frac{9}{12}$, se obtiene $\frac{3}{4}$.*

reflection *(maintained)*	Flipping a figure to produce a mirror image. 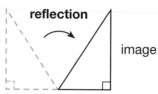
reflexión	Inversión de una figura para lograr una imagen especular; imagen reflejada en un espejo.

---

reflective symmetry *(RF28)*	A figure has ***reflective symmetry*** if it can be divided into two halves that are mirror images of each other. *See also* **line of symmetry.** These figures have **reflective symmetry.** These figures do not have **reflective symmetry.**
simetría de reflexión	Una figura tiene *simetría de reflexión* si puede dividirse en dos mitades especulares. *Ver también **eje de simetría.***

---

regular polygon *(RF23)*	A polygon in which all sides have equal lengths and all angles have equal measures. **regular polygons** not **regular polygons**
polígono regular	Polígono en el cual todos los lados tienen la misma longitud y todos los ángulos tienen la misma medida.

---

relative frequency table *(maintained)*	A frequency table in which the frequencies for all categories are displayed as the numerator of a fraction with the total number of outcomes as the denominator.

Outcome	Tally	Relative Frequency
1	IIII IIII IIII II	$\frac{17}{50}$
2	IIII IIII IIII IIII IIII III	$\frac{28}{50}$
3	IIII	$\frac{5}{50}$

*This **relative frequency table** shows data obtained by spinning the spinner at left 50 times.*

tabla de frecuencias relativas	Una tabla de frecuencias en donde las frecuencias para todas las categorías se muestran como el numerador de una fracción con el número total de resultados como el denominador. *Esta **tabla de frecuencias relativas** muestra datos obtenidos al girar la rueda de arriba 50 veces.*

remainder
(14)

An amount left after division.

$$2\overline{)15}^{\ 7\,R\,1}$$
$$\underline{14}$$
$$1$$

When 15 is divided by 2, there is a **remainder** of 1.

residuo

Cantidad que queda después de dividir.

*Cuando se divide 15 entre 2, queda **residuo** 1.*

---

rhombus
(33)

A parallelogram with all four sides of equal length.

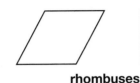 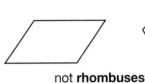

rhombuses　　　　　　　　　　　not **rhombuses**

rombo

Paralelogramo con sus cuatro lados de igual longitud.

---

right angle
(20)

An angle that forms a square corner and measures 90°. It is often marked with a small square.

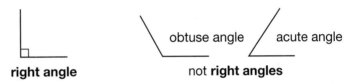

right angle　　　　　not **right angles**

*A **right angle** is larger than an acute angle and smaller than an obtuse angle.*

ángulo recto

Ángulo que forma una esquina cuadrada y mide 90°. Frecuentemente se indica con un pequeño cuadrado.

*Un **ángulo recto** es mayor que un ángulo agudo y menor que un ángulo obtuso.*

---

right triangle
(24)

A triangle whose largest angle measures 90°.

right triangle　　　　　not **right triangles**

triángulo rectángulo

Triángulo cuyo ángulo mayor mide 90°.

Roman numerals
(maintained)

Symbols used by the ancient Romans to write numbers.

*The **Roman numeral** for 3 is III.*

*The **Roman numeral** for 13 is XIII.*

números romanos

Símbolos empleados por los antiguos romanos para escribir números.

*El **número romano** para 3 es III.*

*El **número romano** para 13 es XIII.*

rotation *(maintained)*	Turning a figure about a specified point called the *center of rotation*.

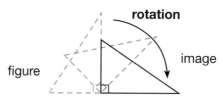

rotación	Giro de una figura alrededor de un punto específico llamado *centro de rotación*.

rotational symmetry *(RF28)*	A figure has rotational symmetry if it can be rotated less than a full turn and appear in its original orientation.

These figures have **rotational symmetry.**   These figures do not have **rotational symmetry.**

simetría rotacional	Una figura tiene simetría rotacional cuando no requiere de una rotación completa para que la figura aparezca en la misma posición en que comenzó la rotación.

round *(22)*	Selecting a close but less precise number than a given number. **Rounding** a number can help us estimate.
redondear	Seleccionar un número que esté cerca pero menos preciso que un número dado. **Redondear** un número nos ayuda a estimar.

S

scale *(9)*	**1.** A type of number line used for measuring.

The distance between each mark on this ruler's **scale** *is 1 centimeter.*

2. A ratio that shows the relationship between a scale model and the actual object.

If a model airplane is $\frac{1}{24}$ the size of the actual airplane, the **scale** *of the model is 1 to 24.*

escala	1. Un tipo de recta numérica que se utiliza para hacer mediciones. *La distancia entre cada marca en la* **escala** *de esta regla es 1 centímetro.* 2. Una razón que nos muestra la relación entre un modelo a escala y el objeto actual. *Si el modelo de un avión es $\frac{1}{24}$ del tamaño real del avión, la* **escala** *del modelo es 1 a 24.*

scale drawing *(maintained)*	A two-dimensional representation of a larger or smaller object.

dibujo a escala	*Blueprints and maps are examples of **scale drawings.***
	Representación bidimensional de un objeto más grande o más pequeño.
	*Los planos y los mapas son ejemplos de **dibujos a escala.***
scale model *(maintained)*	A three-dimensional rendering of a larger or smaller object.
	*Globes and model airplanes are examples of **scale models.***
modelo a escala	Una representación tridimensional de un objeto más pequeño o más grande.
	*Los globos terrestres y aviones de juguete son ejemplos de **modelos a escala.***
scalene triangle *(24)*	A triangle with three sides of different lengths.

*All three sides of this **scalene triangle** have different lengths.*

triángulo escaleno	Triángulo con todos sus lados de diferente longitud.
	*Los tres lados de este **triángulo escaleno** tienen diferente longitud.*
sector *(45)*	A region bordered by part of a circle and two radii.

*This circle is divided into 3 **sectors.** One **sector** of the circle is shaded.*

sector	Región de un círculo limitada por un arco y dos radios.
	*Este círculo esta dividido en 3 **sectores.** Un **sector** está sombreado.*
segment *(2)*	*See **line segment.***
segmento	*Ver **segmento de recta***
sequence *(1)*	A list of numbers arranged according to a certain rule.
	*The numbers 2, 4, 6, 8, ... form a **sequence.** The rule is "count up by twos."*
secuencia	Lista de números ordenados de acuerdo a una regla.
	*Los números 2, 4, 6, 8, ... forman una **secuencia.** La regla es "contar de dos en dos".*
short division *(29)*	A form of division that differs from long division. In **short division** we keep track of some numbers in our head.
división corta	Una forma de división que difiere de una división larga. En la división corta llevamos la cuenta de algunos números mentalmente.

side (21)	A line segment that is part of a polygon.

*The arrow is pointing to one **side.***
*This pentagon has 5 **sides.***

lado	Segmento de recta que forma parte de un polígono.

*La flecha apunta hacia uno de los **lados.** Este pentágono tiene 5 **lados.***

similar (21)	Having the same shape but not necessarily the same size. Dimensions of similar figures are proportional.

$\triangle ABC$ and $\triangle DEF$ are **similar.** They have the same shape, but not the same size.

semejante	Que tiene la misma forma, pero no necesariamente el mismo tamaño. Las dimensiones de figuras semejantes son proporcionales.

$\triangle ABC$ y $\triangle DEF$ son **semejantes.** Tienen la misma forma, pero diferente tamaño.

simplest form (71)	The form of a fraction when it is reduced to lowest terms.
forma reducida	La forma de una fracción cuando se escribe en su mínima expresión.

solid (RF27)	*See* **geometric solid.**
sólido	Ver **sólido geométrico.**

sphere (RF27)	A round geometric solid having every point on its surface at an equal distance from its center.

sphere

esfera	Superficie geométrica cuyos puntos están todos a la misma distancia de su centro.

spread (74)	A value that describes how the data in a set are distributed. *See also* **range.**

5, 12, 3, 20, 15

The range of this set is 17. Range, which is the difference *between the greatest and least numbers, is one measure of the **spread** of data.*

extensión Un valor que describe como los datos en un conjunto son distribuidos. *Ver también* **intervalo**.

5, 12, 3, 20, 15

*El intervalo de este conjunto es 17. El intervalo, que es la diferencia entre el mayor y el menor número, es una medida de la **extensión** de los datos.*

---

square
(33)

1. A rectangle with all four sides of equal length.

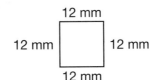

*All four sides of this **square** are 12 mm long.*

2. The product of a number and itself.

*The **square** of 4 is 16.*

cuadrado
1. Paralelogramo que tiene cuatro lados de igual longitud.

   *Los cuatro lados de este **cuadrado** miden 2 pulgadas de longitud.*

2. El producto de un número por sí mismo.

   *El **cuadrado** de 4 es 16.*

---

square centimeter
(59)

A measure of area equal to that of a square with 1-centimeter sides.

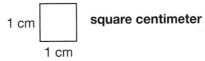

centímetro cuadrado Medida de un área igual a la de un cuadrado con lados de 1 centímetro.

---

square inch
(59)

A measure of area equal to that of a square with 1-inch sides.

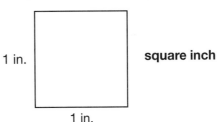

pulgada cuadrada Medida de un área igual a la de un cuadrado con lados de 1 pulgada.

---

square root
(67)

One of two equal factors of a number. The symbol for the principal, or positive, **square root** of a number is $\sqrt{}$.

*A **square root** of 49 is 7 because $7 \times 7 = 49$.*

$$\sqrt{49} = 7$$

raíz cuadrada Uno de dos factores iguales de un número. El símbolo de la **raíz cuadrada** principal, o positiva, de un número es $\sqrt{}$.

*La **raíz cuadrada** de 49 es 7, porque $7 \times 7 = 49$.*

---

standard form
(36)

The usual way of writing numbers, using place to indicate a digit's value.

To write three hundred forty-two in **standard form,** write "342."

forma estándar

La manera común de escribir números, utilizando la posición para indicar el valor del dígito.

*Para escribir trescientos cuarenta y dos en **forma estándar,** escribe "342".*

---

statistics
(Inv. 5)

A branch of mathematics that deals with the collection, analysis, organization, and display of numerical data.

*Some activities performed in **statistics** are taking surveys and organizing data.*

estadística

Una rama de las matemáticas que trata con la recolección, el análisis, la organización y la exhibición de los datos numéricos.

*Algunas actividades que se llevan a cabo en **estadística** son hacer encuestas y organizar datos.*

---

stem-and-leaf plot
(Inv. 7)

A method of graphing a collection of numbers by placing the "stem" digits (or initial digits) in one column and the "leaf" digits (or remaining digits) out to the right.

Stem	Leaf
2	1 3 5 6 6 8
3	0 0 2 2 4 5 6 6 8 9
4	0 0 1 1 1 2 3 3 5 7 7 8
5	0 1 1 2 3 5 8

*In this **stem-and-leaf plot,** 3|2 represents 32.*

diagrama de tallo y hojas

Un método para graficar una colección de números colocando los dígitos del "tallo" (o dígitos iniciales) en una columna y los dígitos de las "hoja" (o dígitos restantes) hacia la derecha.

*En este **diagrama de tallo y hojas,** 3|2 representa 32.*

---

straight angle
(20)

An angle that measures 180°, forming a straight line.

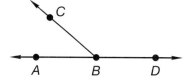

*Angle ABD is a **straight angle.** Angles ABC and CBD are not **straight angles.***

ángulo llano

Un ángulo que mide 180° y por lo tanto forma una línea recta.

*El ángulo ABD es un **ángulo llano.** Los ángulos ABC y CBD no son **ángulos llanos.***

---

subtrahend
(3)

A number that is subtracted.

$12 - 8 = 4$ The **subtrahend** in this problem is 8.

sustraendo

Un número que se sustrae de otro.

*$12 - 8 = 4$ El **sustraendo** en este problema es 8.*

---

sum
(3)

The result of addition.

$7 + 6 = 13$ The **sum** of 7 and 6 is 13.

total de suma

El resultado de la suma.

*$7 + 6 = 13$ La **suma** de 7 y 6 es 13.*

T

---

tally mark
(maintained)

A small mark used to help keep track of a count.

*I used **tally marks** to count cars.*
I counted seven cars.

marca de conteo   Una pequeña marca que se usa para llevar la cuenta.

*Usé **marcas de conteo** para contar carros. Yo conté siete carros.*

term
(1, 71)

1. A number that serves as a numerator or denominator of a fraction.

$$\frac{5}{6} \Big\rangle \text{ terms}$$

2. A number in a sequence.

1, 3, 5, 7, 9, 11, …

*Each number in this sequence is a **term.***

término

1. Número que se usa como numerador o denominador en una fracción.
2. Un número de una secuencia.

1, 3, 5, 7, 9, 11, …

*Cada número de esta secuencia es un **término.***

tessellation
(maintained)

The repeated use of shapes to fill a flat surface without gaps or overlaps.

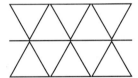 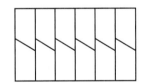 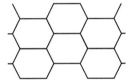

tessellations

mosaico   El uso repetido de figuras para llenar una superficie plana sin dejar huecos ni superposiciones.

transformation
(maintained)

Changing a figure's position through rotation, reflection, or translation.

Transformations

Movement	Name
Flip	Reflection
Slide	Translation
Turn	Rotation

transformación   Cambio en la posición de una figura por medio de una rotación, reflexión o traslación.

translation
(maintained)

Sliding a figure from one position to another without turning or flipping the figure.

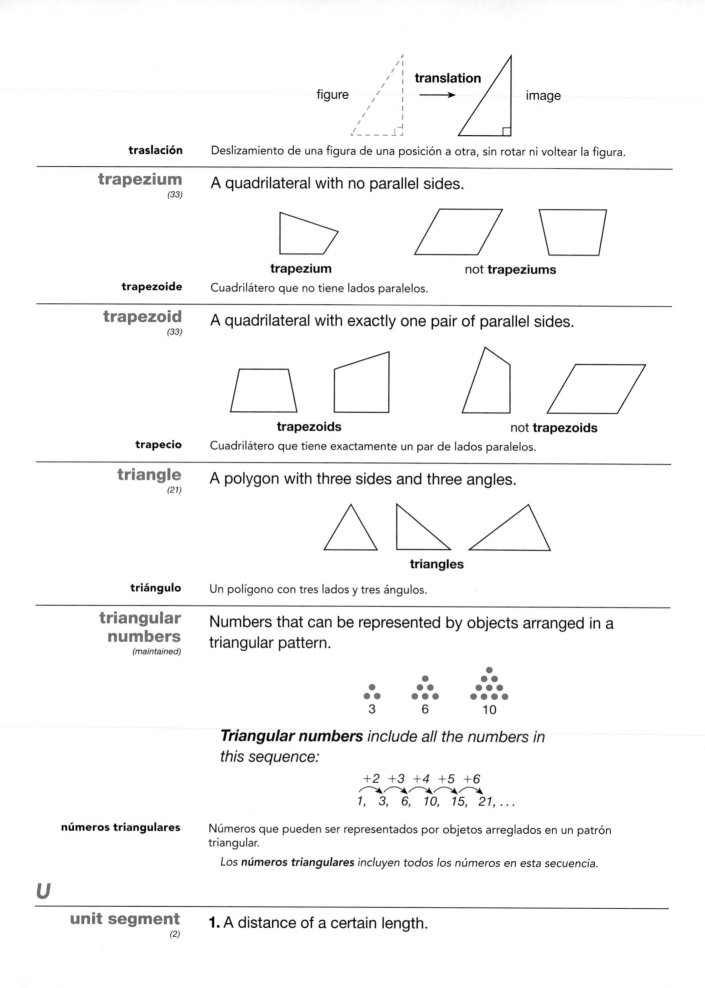

figure **translation** image

traslación — Deslizamiento de una figura de una posición a otra, sin rotar ni voltear la figura.

trapezium
(33)

A quadrilateral with no parallel sides.

trapezium   **not trapeziums**

trapezoide — Cuadrilátero que no tiene lados paralelos.

trapezoid
(33)

A quadrilateral with exactly one pair of parallel sides.

trapezoids   **not trapezoids**

trapecio — Cuadrilátero que tiene exactamente un par de lados paralelos.

triangle
(21)

A polygon with three sides and three angles.

triangles

triángulo — Un polígono con tres lados y tres ángulos.

triangular numbers
(maintained)

Numbers that can be represented by objects arranged in a triangular pattern.

3   6   10

Triangular numbers include all the numbers in this sequence:

+2 +3 +4 +5 +6
1, 3, 6, 10, 15, 21, ...

números triangulares — Números que pueden ser representados por objetos arreglados en un patrón triangular.

Los números triangulares incluyen todos los números en esta secuencia.

U

unit segment
(2)

1. A distance of a certain length.

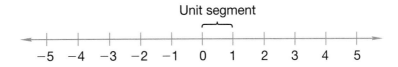

Unit segment

2. The length of one unit.

segmento unitario 1. Una distancia de cierta longitud.

2. La longitud de una unidad.

---

unknown
(3)

A value that is not given. A letter is frequently used to stand for an unknown number.

*In the equation 34 ÷ k = 17, k is an **unknown**.*

incógnita Un valor no dado. Frecuentemente se utiliza una letra para representar a un número desconocido.

*En la ecuación 34 ÷ k = 17, k es una **incógnita**.*

U.S. Customary System
(32)

A system of measurement used almost exclusively in the United States.

*Pounds, quarts, and feet are units in the **U.S. Customary System**.*

Sistema usual de EE.UU. Sistema de medición que se usa casi exclusivamente en EE.UU.

*Libras, cuartos y pies son unidades del **Sistema usual de EE.UU.***

V

variable
(3)

A quantity that can change or assume different values. Also, a letter used to represent an unknown in an expression or equation.

*In the statement x + 7 = y, the letters x and y are **variables**.*

variable Una cantidad que puede cambiar o tomar valores diferentes. También, una letra que se usa para representar a una incógnita en una expresión o ecuación.

*En el enunciado x + 7 = y, las letras x e y son **variables**.*

Venn diagram
(maintained)

A diagram made of circles used to display data.

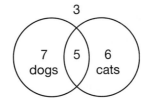

*This **Venn diagram** shows data on students' pets. Three students do not have a cat or a dog. Seven students have a dog but not a cat. Six students have a cat but not a dog. Five students have both a dog and a cat.*

diagrama de Venn Un diagrama que utiliza círculos para mostrar datos.

*Este **diagrama de Venn** muestra los datos de las mascotas de estudiantes. Tres estudiantes no tienen gato ni perro. Siete estudiantes tienen perro pero no gato. Seis estudiantes tienen gato pero no perro. Cinco estudiantes tienen tanto gato como perro.*

---

vertex
(21)

(Plural: *vertices*) A point of an angle, polygon, or solid where two or more lines, rays, or line segments meet.

*The arrow is pointing to one **vertex** of this cube. A cube has eight **vertices.***

vértice   Punto de un ángulo, polígono o poliedro, donde se unen dos o más rectas, rayos o segmentos de recta.

*La flecha apunta hacia un **vértice** de este cubo está coloreado. Un cubo tiene ocho **vértices.***

---

vertical
(9)

Upright; perpendicular to horizontal.

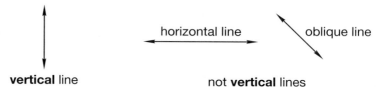

vertical line   not **vertical** lines

vertical   Perpendicular a la horizontal.

---

vertical axis
(maintained)
eje vertical

The scale of a graph that runs from top to bottom.

La escala de una gráfica que corre de arriba hacia abajo.

---

volume
(Inv. 9)

The amount of space a geometric solid occupies. Volume is measured in cubic units.

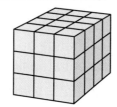

*This rectangular solid is 3 units wide, 3 units high, and 4 units deep. Its **volume** is 3 · 3 · 4 = 36 cubic units.*

volumen   Cantidad de espacio ocupado por un sólido geométrico. El volumen se mide en unidades cúbicas.

*Este sólido rectangular tiene 3 unidades de ancho, 3 unidades de altura y 4 unidades de profundidad. Su **volumen** es 3 · 3 · 4 = 36 unidades cúbicas.*

W

---

weight
(64)

The measure of the force of gravity on an object. Units of weight in the U.S. Customary System include ounces, pounds, and tons.

*The **weight** of a bowling ball is less on the moon than on Earth because the force of gravity is weaker on the moon.*

peso   La medida de la fuerza de gravedad sobre un objeto. Las unidades de peso en el sistema usual de EE.UU. incluyen onzas, libras y toneladas.

*El **peso** de una bola de boliche es menor en la Luna que en la Tierra porque la fuerza de gravedad es menor en la Luna.*

whole numbers (2)	All the numbers in this sequence: 0, 1, 2, 3, 4, 5, 6, 7, 8, 9, …. *0, 25, and 134 are **whole numbers.*** *−3, 0.56, and 103$\frac{1}{2}$ are not **whole numbers.***
números enteros	Todos los números en esta secuencia: 0, 1, 2, 3, 4, 5, 6, 7, 8, 9 …. *0, 25 y 134 son **números enteros.*** *−3, 0.56 y 103$\frac{1}{2}$ no son **números enteros.***

X

x-axis *(maintained)*	The horizontal number line of a coordinate plane. 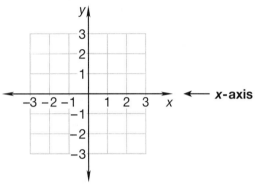
eje de las x	Recta numérica horizontal en un plano coordenado.

Y

y-axis *(maintained)*	The vertical number line of a coordinate plane. 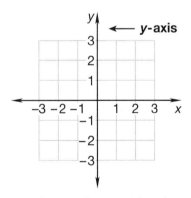
eje de las y	La recta numérica vertical en un plano coordenado.

Z

Zero Property of Multiplication (RF16)	Zero times any number is zero. In symbolic form, $0 \times a = 0$. *The **Zero Property of Multiplication** tells us that* *$89 \times 0 = 0$.*
propiedad del cero en la multiplicación	Cero multiplicado por cualquier número es cero. En forma simbólica, $0 \times a = 0$. *La **propiedad del cero en la multiplicación** dice que $89 \times 0 = 0$.*

Symbols

Symbol	Meaning	Example
$\triangle$	Triangle	$\triangle ABC$
$\angle$	Angle	$\angle ABC$
$\longrightarrow$	Ray	$\overrightarrow{AB}$
$\longleftrightarrow$	Line	$\overleftrightarrow{AB}$
$\overline{}$	Line segment	$\overline{AB}$
$\perp$	Perpendicular to	$\overline{AB} \perp \overline{BC}$
$\parallel$	Parallel to	$\overline{AB} \parallel \overline{BC}$
$<$	Less than	$2 < 3$
$>$	Greater than	$3 > 2$
$=$	Equal to	$2 = 2$
°F	Degrees Fahrenheit	$100°F$
°C	Degrees Celsius	$32°C$
$\llcorner$	Right angle (90° angle)	
…	And so on	1, 2, 3, …
$\times$	Multiply	9×3
$\cdot$	Multiply	$3 \cdot 3 = 9$
$\div$	Divide	$9 \div 3$
$+$	Add	$9 + 3$
$-$	Subtract	$9 - 3$
$\overline{)}$	Divided into	$3\overline{)9}$
R	Remainder	3 R 2
%	Percent	50%
x^2	"x" squared (times itself)	$3^2 = 3 \times 3 = 9$
x^3	"x" cubed	$3^3 = 3 \times 3 \times 3 = 27$
$\sqrt{}$	Square root	$\sqrt{9} = 3$ because $3 \times 3 = 9$.

Abbreviations

Abbreviation	Meaning
ft	foot
in.	inch
yd	yard
mi	mile
m	meter
cm	centimeter
mm	millimeter
km	kilometer
L	liter
ml or mL	milliliter
lb	pound
oz	ounce
kg	kilogram
g	gram
mg	milligram
pt	pint
qt	quart
c	cup
gal	gallon

Formulas

Purpose	Formula
Perimeter of rectangle	$P = 2l + 2w$
Area of a square	$A = s^2$
Area of a rectangle	$A = l \cdot w$
Volume of a cube	$V = s^3$
Volume of a rectangular solid	$V = l \cdot w \cdot h$

Símbolos/Signos

Símbolo/Signo	Significa	Ejemplo
$\triangle$	Triángulo	$\triangle ABC$
$\angle$	Ángulo	$\angle ABC$
$\rightarrow$	Rayo	$\overrightarrow{AB}$
$\leftrightarrow$	Recta	$\overleftrightarrow{AB}$
$-$	Segmento de recta	$\overline{AB}$
$\perp$	Perpendicular a	$\overline{AB} \perp \overline{BC}$
$\parallel$	Paralelo a	$\overline{AB} \parallel \overline{BC}$
$<$	Menor que	$2 < 3$
$>$	Mayor que	$3 > 2$
$=$	Igual a	$2 = 2$
°F	Grados Fahrenheit	100°F
°C	Grados Celsius	32°C
⌐	Ángulo recto (ángulo de 90°)	
…	Y más, etcétera	1, 2, 3, …
$\times$	Multiplica	9×3
$\cdot$	Multiplica	$3 \cdot 3 = 9$
$\div$	Divide	$9 \div 3$
$+$	Suma	$9 + 3$
$-$	Resta	$9 - 3$
$\overline{)\,}$	Dividido entre	$3\overline{)9}$
R	Residuo	3 R 2
%	Por ciento, porcentaje	50%
x^2	"x" al cuadrado (por sí mismo)	$3^2 = 3 \times 3 = 9$
x^3	"x" al cubo	$3^3 = 3 \times 3 \times 3 = 27$
$\sqrt{}$	Raíz cuadrada	$\sqrt{9} = 3$ por que $3 \times 3 = 9$.

Abreviaturas

Abreviatura	Significa
pie	pie
pulg	pulgada
yd	yarda
mi	milla
m	metro
cm	centímetro
mm	milímetro
km	kilómetro
L	litro
mL	mililitro
lb	libra
oz	onza
kg	kilogramo
g	gramo
mg	miligramo
ct	cuarto
pt	pinta
tz	taza
gal	galón

Fórmulas

Propósito	Fórmula
Perímetro de un rectángulo	$P = 2L + 2a$
Área de un cuadrado	$A = l^2$
Área de un rectángulo	$A = L \cdot a$
Volumen de un cubo	$V = l^3$
Volumen de un sólido rectangular	$V = L \cdot a \cdot h$

INDEX

number lines, 169–174
quotients, 185–190
reducing answers, 830–831
regrouping, 835–840
rounding, 684–689
subtracting, 204–210, 367–372, 829–834, 835–840
writing, 185–188, 334–335, 459–460

Mode, 362, 447, 544–550

Models, 544–550. *See also* **Representation**

Money
decimal places in, 376–377
division algorithms, 113
multiplication of, 82
rounding with, 354

Months, 64

Multi-digit multiplication, decimals, 741–746

Multiple-step word problems, 265–270

Multiples. *See also* **Least common multiple** (LCM)
dividing by, 301–306
multiplying by, 119–124

Multiplication. *See also* **Exponents**
Associative Property of, 48, 718
Commutative Property of, 48, 574, 718
cross product, 797–804
of decimals, 315, 727–734, 735–740, 741–746
Distributive Property of, 279–280, 284–290, 500
division as inverse of, 39–44
fractions, 461–467, 573–579, 644, 797–804
Identity Property of, 505
missing numbers, 39–44
of mixed numbers, 204–210
of money, 82
one-digit numbers, 81-83
order of operations, 46–47
three-digit numbers, 307–312, 313–318
two-digit numbers, 277–283
whole numbers by fractions, 574–576

N _____

Naming. *See also* **Renaming**
complex shapes, 788–796
decimal numbers, 396–402
parts of groups, 719–726
percents, 719–726
polygons, 140–148

Negative numbers
integers as, 651–658
on number lines, 13–18

Nets, 675

Nonprime numbers. *See* **Composite numbers**

Notation. *See* **Expanded notation; Standard notation**

Number lines. *See also* **Graphs**
comparing using, 15
counting numbers on, 14–17
decimals on, 389–395
fractions on, 169–171, 389–392, 535

horizontal, 57
integers on, 14, 703–704, 710–711
mixed numbers on, 169–174
negative numbers on, 13–18
origin of, 13–18
percents on, 535
tick marks on, 13–14
vertical, 57, 659–660
whole numbers on, 13–14

Number sentences. *See* **Equations**

Number systems
commas in, 74–75
place value in, 375–376

Numbers. *See also* **Digits; Integers**
composite, 475–481
counting. *See* **Counting numbers**
decimal. *See* **Decimals**
letters used to represent, 40
missing. *See* **Unknown numbers**
mixed. *See* **Mixed numbers**
negative. *See* **Negative numbers**
nonprime. *See* **Composite numbers**
percents of. *See* **Percents**
positive. *See* **Positive numbers**
prime. *See* **Prime numbers**
whole. *See* **Whole numbers**
writing. *See* **Expanded notation; Standard notation**

Numerators. *See also* **Fractions**
changing mixed numbers to improper fractions, 452–458, 603–609, 773–779
as term of a fraction, 69

O _____

Oblique lines, 132–133

Obtuse angles, 133–134, 163, 211

Obtuse triangles, 164–165

Octagons, 142–143

Odd number sequences, 10–11

One, as multiplicative identity, 505

One-digit numbers, multiplication, 79–85

Operations. *See* **Inverse operations; Order of Operations**

Opposite numbers, 661

Order of Operations
division, 46–47
evaluating expressions and equations, 52–53
with exponents, 497–503
parentheses in, 46–47
rules for, 46–47
subtraction, 46–47

Ordered pairs, 56, 439, 598–601

Ordering
decimals, 403–409
prime factors, 484

Ounce (oz), 274, 567–572

INDEX

R

Range, 362–364, 447, 544–550

Ratios, 645–650

Reading
graphs, 518–524, 618–621
large numbers, 74–75
powers, 489–496

Reading math. *See also* **Developing Academic Language.** 8, 26, 28, 34, 40, 41, 65, 74, 88, 192, 227, 248, 260, 266, 278, 297, 301, 462, 463, 574, 625, 678, 720, 729, 736

Real-World Connection, 44, 55, 62, 68, 78, 85, 92, 118, 136, 156, 182, 210, 253, 264, 283, 300, 560, 616, 634, 643, 658, 664, 758, 779, 804, 823, 834, 840, 847, 853

Reciprocals, 629, 637–643

Rectangles
area of, 425–432
characteristics of, 425–432
constructing, 243–246
on coordinate plane, 441–442
drawing, 243–246, 425–432
as parallelograms, 234–242, 551–560
perimeter of, 425
as quadrilaterals, 234–242
similar, 144
as squares, 234–242
sum of angle measures, 217–224

Rectangular solids, 672–676

Reducing fractions
common factors in, 525–532
manipulatives for, 71
prime factorization for, 589
rules for, 525–532

Regrouping in subtraction of mixed numbers, 835–840

Relationships. *See also* **Inverse operations**
analyzing, 824–828
remainders and divisors, 93–99

Remainders
checking in division, 114
in decimal division, 115
defined, 187
divisors and, 93–99
as mixed numbers, 185–190
writing, 93–99, 459–460
of zero, 96

Renaming. *See also* **Naming**
fractions, multiplying by one, 504–510

Representation
model, 71, 82, 138, 139, 165-166, 176, 191, 192, 293, 419, 420-421, 427, 429, 462, 526, 527, 528, 535, 576, 581, 582, 630, 676, 749, 752, 754, 831, 837
represent, 9-10, 15-16, 23, 30, 48, 53, 59-60, 62, 66, 68, 75, 77, 90, 97-98, 100, 117, 124, 130, 133, 145-147, 155, 165-166, 173, 179, 181, 190,

201, 203, 207, 210, 215, 221-222, 231-232, 239-241, 249-250, 252-253, 256, 258, 261, 268, 275, 280-282, 288, 298-299, 303-304, 309-310, 315-316, 324-325, 330-332, 336-337, 342-343, 350, 352, 355-356, 363, 370, 378, 380, 385-386, 398-399, 413-414, 429, 438, 448, 455-456, 458, 464, 467, 471-472, 480, 485, 487, 492-494, 496, 501-502, 518-520, 523, 541, 570, 579, 583, 590, 609, 621, 632, 640, 655, 694, 702, 713-714, 731, 752, 754-755, 763, 770, 793, 808, 815, 820, 832, 838-839, 846

Rhombuses, 237–238

Right angles, 133–134, 163, 211

Right triangles, 164–165

Roots. *See* **Square roots**

Rounding. *See also* **Estimation**
decimals, 696–702
estimating by, 149–155, 354–355
mixed numbers, 684–689
money, 354

Rounding up, 696–702

Rulers, 245, 291–294

Rules. *See also* **Order of Operations**
for decimal division, 115–118, 817–823, 848–853
of functions, 824–828
for reducing fractions, 525–532
of sequences, 7–11

S

Scalene triangles, 164–165

Scales, reading, 57–62

Seconds (time), 63, 404

Segments. *See also* **Lines**
in creating complex shapes, 790
length of, 230–231
number lines, 14

Sequences. *See also* **Patterns**
arithmetic, 594
dots, 8
even number, 8–10
geometric, 594
odd number, 10–11
period, 595
repetition, 595
terms, 7–12,
types of, 7–11, 594–595

Shapes, complex. *See* **Complex shapes**

Short-division method, 198–203

Sides
of parallelograms, 235–237
of quadrilaterals, 235–239
of regular polygons, 140–148
of squares, 238

Signs. *See* **Symbols and signs**

Similar figures, 144

U

Unit multipliers. *See* **Conversion**

Units of measure. *See also* **Measurement**
    capacity, 567–572
    of length, 227–231, 445–448
    mass and weight, 468–474
    metric system, 567–572
    U.S. Customary System, 567–572
    for volume, 672

Unknown numbers
    addition, 19–24
    in division and multiplication, 39–42
    letter representation, 40
    missing products, 39–44
    subtraction, 19–24
    in word problems, 25–29, 33–36

Unlike denominators, 225, 841–847

U.S. Customary System, 567–572. *See also* **Units of measure**

Use Logical Reasoning (Problem-Solving Strategy), 19, 39, 86, 93, 105, 131, 149, 163, 169, 198, 217, 271, 319, 327, 367, 389, 396, 403, 410, 433, 452, 468, 482, 497, 525, 539, 561, 587, 703, 751

V

Vertex (vertices)
    angles, 211–216
    polygons, 140–148

Vocabulary. *See* **Developing Academic Language,** *See also* the Glossary in this book.

Volume
    cubes, 747–750
    defined, 672
    estimation, 699
    rectangular solids, 672–674
    units of measure, 672

W

Week, 64

Weight *versus* **mass,** 468–474

Whole numbers
    decimals, 433–438, 665–671, 691–695, 696–702, 811–816
    in expanded notation, 259–264
    factors and, 105–110
    finding the whole, 339–342, 759–763
    fraction is known, 339–345
    fractions, 225–226, 339–345, 367–372, 573–579
    mixed numbers from, 204–210
    multiplying, 79–83, 573–576
    naming, 73–78
    number lines, 13-15
    percent is known, 759–765
    place value in, 373–377
    rounding, decimals, 696–702
    subtracting, 367–372, 665–671
    writing as fractions, 339–345

Word problems
    addition and subtraction, 25–32
    comparing, 33–38
    fraction of a group, 247–253
    multiple-step, 265–268

Work Backwards (Problem-Solving Strategy), 86, 93, 105, 131, 149, 163, 177, 185, 191, 271, 333, 425, 525, 544, 573, 587, 691, 727, 780, 817

Write a Number Sentence or Equation (Problem-Solving Strategy), 111, 191, 227, 265, 295, 319, 327, 333, 353, 396, 410, 417, 425, 445, 461, 475, 504, 544, 567, 580, 617, 629, 637, 645, 651, 703, 727, 741, 766, 773, 788, 805, 811, 829, 841

Writing. *See also* **Communication**
    decimals. *See* **Decimals**
    exponents, 489–493, 497–503
    hundred thousands, 73–78
    hundredths, 381–388, 396–402
    large numbers, 73–78
    numbers. *See* **Expanded notation; Proportions; Standard notation**
    percents. *See* **Percents**
    quotients with mixed numbers, 185–190, 333–338
    ratios, 645–647
    remainders, 93–99
    tenths, 381–388, 396–402, 727–734
    thousandths, 396–402

X

x-axis, 439, 599

Y

y-axis, 439, 599

Years, 64. *See also* **Age**, calculating; **Elapsed-time**

Z

Zero
    decimals, 691–695
    division, 157–159, 635–636
    expanded notation, 259–264, 297
    multiplication, 313–318
    placeholder, 308, 314, 735–740
    properties of, 652
    remainders of, 96
    sign of, 652
    simplifying, 677–680
    subtraction, 691–695

Zero Property of Multiplication, 635